T0366615

LOEB CLASSICAL LIBRARY

FOUNDED BY JAMES LOEB 1911

EDITED BY

JEFFREY HENDERSON

CICERO

XXVI

LCL 216

CICERO

LETTERS TO FRIENDS

VOLUME II

EDITED AND TRANSLATED BY

D. R. SHACKLETON BAILEY

HARVARD UNIVERSITY PRESS

CAMBRIDGE, MASSACHUSETTS

LONDON, ENGLAND

2001

Copyright © 2001 by the President and Fellows
of Harvard College
All rights reserved

First published 2001

LOEB CLASSICAL LIBRARY® is a registered trademark
of the President and Fellows of Harvard College

Library of Congress Control Number 00-047259
CIP data available from the Library of Congress

ISBN 978-0-674-99589-5

*Composed in ZephGreek and ZephText by
Technologies 'N Typography, Merrimac, Massachusetts.
Printed on acid-free paper and bound by
The Maple-Vail Book Manufacturing Group*

CONTENTS

CICERO'S

LETTERS TO FRIENDS

114 (IX.25)

Scr. Laodiceae fort. med. m. Mart. an. 50

CICERO IMP. PAETO

1   Summum me ducem litterae tuae reddiderunt. plane
nesciebam te tam peritum esse rei militaris; Pyrrhi te libros et Cineae video lectitasse. itaque obtemperare cogito
praeceptis tuis; hoc amplius, navicularum habere aliquid
in ora maritima. contra equitem Parthum negant ullam
armaturam meliorem inveniri posse. sed quid ludimus?
nescis quo cum imperatore tibi negotium sit. Παιδείαν
Κύρου, quam contrieram legendo, totam in hoc imperio
2   explicavi. sed iocabimur alias coram, ut spero, brevi tempore.

Nunc ades ad imperandum, vel ad parendum potius; sic
enim antiqui loquebantur. cum M. Fabio, quod scire te arbitror, mihi summus usus est valdeque eum diligo cum
propter summam probitatem eius ac singularem modes-
tiam tum quod in iis controversiis quas habeo cum tuis
3   combibonibus Epicuri‹i›s optima opera eius uti soleo. is,
cum ad me Laodiceam venisset mecumque ego eum esse
vellem, repente percussus est atrocissimis litteris, in qui-

---

[1] King Pyrrhus of Epirus wrote a treatise on tactics, and his
minister Cineas epitomized a work on strategy by one Aelian.

[2] Xenophon's work on the Ideal Ruler (cf. *Letters to Atticus* 23
(II.3).2), much of which is concerned with the Ruler as General.

114 (IX.25)
CICERO TO PAPIRIUS PAETUS

Laodicea, mid March (?) 50

From Cicero, Imperator, to Paetus.

Your letter has made a first-rate general out of me. I had no idea you were such a military expert—evidently you have thumbed the treatises of Pyrrhus and Cineas.[1] So I intend to follow your precepts, with one addition—I mean to keep a few boats handy on the coast. They say there's no better weapon against Parthian cavalry! But why this frivolity? You don't know what sort of Commander-in-Chief you have to deal with. In my command here I have put into practice the whole *Education of Cyrus,*[2] a work which I read so often that I wore out the book. But we'll joke another time when we meet, as soon I hope we shall.

Now stand by for orders (or rather to obey them), to use the ancient expression. I have a great deal to do with M. Fabius, as I think you know, and a great regard for him as a man of the highest integrity and unusual modesty, also because he helps me very effectively in my controversies[3] with your Epicurean boozing partners. After he joined me at Laodicea and I asked him to stay with me, he received a quite appalling letter, a bolt from the blue, informing him

---

[3] Perhaps with reference to the *De Republica.* M. Fabius Gallus was an Epicurean and a *littérateur.*

bus scriptum erat fundum Herculanensem a Q. Fabio fratre proscriptum esse, qui fundus cum eo communis esset. id M. Fabius pergraviter tulit existimavitque fratrem suum, hominem non sapientem, impulsu inimicorum suorum eo progressum esse.

Nunc, si me amas, mi Paete, negotium totum suscipe, molestia Fabium libera. auctoritate tua nobis opus est et consilio et etiam gratia. noli pati litigare fratres et iudiciis turpibus conflictari. Matonem et Pollionem inimicos habet Fabius. quid multa? non mehercule tam[1] perscribere possum quam mihi gratum feceris si otiosum Fabium reddideris. id ille in te positum esse putat mihique persuadet.

115 (II.18)

Scr. Laodiceae in. m. Mai. an. 50

M. CICERO IMP. S. D. Q. THERMO PRO PR.

1   Officium meum erga Rhodonem ceteraque mea studia quae tibi ac tuis praestiti tibi, homini gratissimo, grata esse vehementer gaudeo, mihique scito in dies maiori curae esse dignitatem tuam; quae quidem a te ipso integritate et clementia tua sic amplificata est ut nihil addi posse videa-

2   tur. sed mihi magis magisque cottidie de rationibus tuis cogitanti placet illud meum consilium quod initio Aristoni

---

[1] tantum *coni.* SB

---

[4] Unknowns, unless Pollio is the famous Asinius Pollio.

that a farm near Herculaneum, which he owns jointly with his brother, Q. Fabius, had been put up for sale by the latter. M. Fabius has taken this very much to heart. He believed that his brother, who is not remarkable for good sense, had been instigated by his (Marcus') enemies to take this extraordinary step.

Now, my dear Paetus, be a friend and take the whole affair upon yourself, and relieve Fabius of the worry. We need your name and sound judgement, and your personal influence too. Don't let the brothers get into litigation and become embroiled in discreditable lawsuits. Mato and Pollio[4] are Fabius' enemies. Briefly, I assure you that I cannot write down in full how much you will oblige me if you put Fabius' mind at ease. He thinks, and persuades me, that it all depends on you.

115 (II.18)
CICERO TO Q. THERMUS

Laodicea, early May 50

From M. Cicero, Imperator, to Q. Thermus, Propraetor, greetings.

I am very happy to find you appreciative of the service I rendered Rhodo and of my other acts of good will towards you and yours—gratitude is a great point with you. Please rest assured that my solicitude for your credit increases every day, though your own integrity and clemency have so enhanced it that any addition seems impossible. But constantly thinking of your interests as I do, I grow more and more convinced of the soundness of the view I originally intimated to our friend Aristo when he came to see me,

5

nostro, ut ad me venit, ostendi, gravis te suscepturum inimicitias si adulescens potens et nobilis a te ignominia adfectus esset. et hercule sine dubio erit ignominia. habes
enim neminem honoris gradu superiorem; ille autem, ut
omittam nobilitatem, hoc ipso vincit viros optimos homi-
nesque innocentissimos legatos tuos, quod et quaestor est
et quaestor tuus. nocere tibi iratum neminem posse perspicio, sed tamen tris fratres summo loco natos, promptos,
non indisertos, te nolo habere iratos, iure praesertim; quos
3 video deinceps tribunos pl. per triennium fore. tempora
autem rei publicae qualia futura sint quis scit? mihi quidem turbulenta videntur fore. cur ego te velim incidere in
terrores tribunicios, praesertim cum sine cuiusquam re-
prehensione quaestori⟨i⟩s legatis quaestorem possis anteferre? qui si ⟨se⟩[1] dignum maioribus suis praebuerit, ut
spero et opto, tua laus ex aliqua parte fuerit; sin quid offenderit, sibi totum, nihil tibi offenderit.

Quae mihi veniebant in mentem quae ad te pertinere
arbitrabar, quod in Ciliciam proficiscebar, existimavi me
ad te oportere scribere. tu quod egeris, id velim di appro-
bent. sed si me audies, vitabis inimicitias et posteritatis
otio consules.

[1] *(Graevius)*

---

[1] L. Antonius, Thermus' Quaestor. Cicero advises that he be
left in charge of the province of Asia after Thermus' departure.

that you would make formidable enemies if you put a slight upon a powerful young nobleman.[1] And it will be a slight, make no mistake. You have nobody of superior official rank available, and the young man in question has a better claim than your excellent and irreproachable Legates from the very fact (to say nothing of family) that he is Quaestor and *your* Quaestor. I am well aware that nobody's grudge can hurt you, but I should none the less be sorry to see you an object of resentment to three brothers of the highest birth and no mean qualities of enterprise and eloquence, especially if their resentment was justified. It is apparent that they will become Tribunes of the Plebs in three successive years.[2] Who can tell what sort of political conditions lie ahead? To me they seem likely to be disturbed. So why should I want you to fall in the way of tribunician menaces, especially when you can give a Quaestor preference to quaestorian Legates without a word of criticism from anybody? If he proves himself worthy of his forbears, as I expect and hope he will, some part of the credit will go to you. If he stumbles, the damage will be entirely his, not yours at all.

I feel it right to let you know such thoughts as cross my mind and seem to concern you, because I am leaving for Cilicia. Whatever you do, the Gods be with it! But if you listen to me, you will keep clear of feuds and take thought for a quiet future.

[2] Apparently an inference from the fact (not otherwise established) that L. Antonius' two elder brothers, Marcus (Mark Antony) and Gaius, had been Quaestors in 52 and 51 (or, more probably, both in 51). Marcus stood successfully for the Tribunate in 50.

116 (II.19)

Scr. in castris ad Pyramum c. IX *Kal. Quint. an. 50*

M. TULLIUS M. F. ‹M. N.›[1] CICERO IMP. S. D. C. COELIO
L. F. C. N. CALDO Q.

1   Cum optatissimum nuntium accepissem te mihi quaestorem obtigisse, eo iucundiorem mihi eam sortem sperabam fore quo diutius in provincia mecum fuisses. magni enim videbatur interesse ad eam necessitudinem quam nobis fors[2] tribuisset consuetudinem quoque accedere. postea, cum mihi nihil neque a te ipso neque ab ullo alio de adventu tuo scriberetur, verebar ne ita caderet, quod etiam nunc vereor, ne,[3] ante quam tu in provinciam venisses, ego de provincia decederem. accepi autem a te missas litteras in Cilicia, cum essem in castris, a. d. x Kal. Quint., scriptas humanissime, quibus facile et officium et ingenium tuum perspici posset; sed neque unde nec quo die datae essent aut quo tempore te exspectarem significabant, nec is qui attulerat a te acceperat, ut ex eo scirem quo ex loco aut quo tempore essent datae.

2   Quae cum essent incerta, existimavi tamen faciendum esse ut ad te statores meos et lictores cum litteris mitterem. quas si satis opportuno tempore accepisti, gratissimum mihi feceris si ad me in Ciliciam quam primum veneris. nam quod ad me Curi‹u›s, consobrinus tuus, mihi, ut scis, maxime necessarius, quod item C. Vergilius, propin-

---

[1] *(Or.)*
[2] sors R
[3] ut *coni. SB*

116 (II.19)
CICERO TO COELIUS CALDUS

Camp on the Pyramus, ca. 22 June 50

From M. Tullius, son of Marcus, grandson of Marcus, Imperator, to C. Coelius Caldus, son of Lucius, grandson of Gaius, Quaestor, greetings.

After I received the most welcome news of your appointment by lot as my Quaestor, it was my expectation that the more time you spent with me in the province the more pleasure I should derive from that event. I felt it very important that the close tie which chance had established between us should be supplemented by personal intercourse. But time passed, and no word of your arrival reached me either from yourself or any other person; so I began to fear, as I still do, lest it might turn out that I left the province before you entered it. I have received a letter from you while in camp in Cilicia on 21 June. It is most kindly expressed, clear evidence of a conscientious and talented writer; but it contains no indication of the place and date of dispatch or of when I may expect you; neither could the bearer, who did not receive it from your own hand, enlighten me as to where and when you sent it.

Despite my uncertainty on these points, I judge it proper to send you orderlies and lictors of mine with a letter. If you receive it in good enough time, you will greatly oblige me by joining me in Cilicia as soon as possible. Your cousin Curius,[1] who, as you know, is a close friend of mine, and your relative C. Vergilius, also one of my nearest inti-

---

[1] Usually but not very plausibly identified with M'. Curius of Patrae.

quus tuus, familiarissimus noster, de te accuratissime scripsit, valet id quidem apud me multum, sicuti debet hominum amicissimorum diligens commendatio, sed tuae litterae de tua praesertim dignitate et de nostra coniunctione maximi sunt apud me ponderis. mihi quaestor optatior obtingere nemo potuit. quam ob rem quaecumque a me ornamenta ad te ⟨proficisci poterunt⟩[4] proficiscentur, ut omnes intellegant a me habitam esse rationem tuae maiorumque tuorum dignitatis. sed id facilius consequar si ad me in Ciliciam veneris. quod ego et mea et rei publicae et maxime tua interesse arbitror.

117 (II.17)

Scr. Tarsi c. XV *Kal. Sext. an.* 50

M. CICERO IMP. S. D. †CANINI SAL⟨L⟩USTIO†[1] PRO Q.

1   Litteras a te mihi ⟨binas⟩[2] stator tuus reddidit Tarsi a. d. XVI Kal. Sext. his ego ordine, ut videris velle, respondebo.

De successore meo nihil audivi ne⟨que⟩ quemquam fore arbitror. quin ad diem decedam nulla causa est, praesertim sublato metu Parthico. commoraturum me nusquam sane arbitror. Rhodum Ciceronum causa puerorum

[4] (*Madvig*: ita *post* poterunt *add. Watt, duce Purser*)
[1] CN. SALLUSTIO *Quartier*: C. ANNIO *(Huschke)* LUSCO *Earl*
[2] *(Lamb.)*

[2] In fact Coelius' nobility was of recent vintage, starting with his grandfather, Consul in 94.

mates, have written to me at length about you. Their words carry great weight with me, as a particular recommendation from such friends ought to do; but most of all I am impressed by your letter, especially by what you say of your own standing and our association. No Quaestor more welcome could have fallen to me. Therefore whatever I can do by way of compliment to you shall be done, and my sense of your personal and family status[2] shall be made plain to all. But this will be easier for me if you join me in Cilicia, which I believe will be in my and the public interest and most of all in your own.

117 (II.17)
CICERO TO CN. (?) SALLUSTIUS

Tarsus, ca. 18 July 50

From M. Cicero, Imperator, to Cn. (?) Sallustius,[1] Pro-quaestor,[2] greetings.

Your orderly delivered your two letters to me at Tarsus on 17 July. I shall reply point by point, as that seems to be what you wish.

I have heard nothing about my successor, and I am not expecting any appointment. There is no reason why I should not leave on the day fixed, especially now the Parthian danger is out of the way. I hardly expect to make any considerable halts. I think I shall touch at Rhodes for the

[1] Almost certainly not Cicero's friend of that name nor yet the historian C. Sallustius Crispus. The manuscripts have CANINI SALUSTIO.

[2] In Syria.

accessurum puto, neque id tamen certum. ad urbem volo
quam primum venire; sed tamen iter meum rei publicae et
rerum urbanarum ratio gubernabit. successor tuus non
potest ita maturare ullo modo ut tu me in Asia possis convenire.

2   De rationibus referendis, non erat incommodum te
nullas[3] referre, quam tibi scribis a Bibulo fieri potestatem;
sed id vix mihi videris per legem Iuliam facere posse, quam
Bibulus certa quadam ratione non servat, tibi magno opere
servandam censeo.

3   Quod scribis Apamea praesidium deduci non opor-
tuisse, videbam item ceteros existimare molesteque ferebam de ea re minus commodos sermones malevolorum
fuisse. ⟨sed⟩[4] Parthi transierint necne praeter te video
dubitare neminem. itaque omnia praesidia, quae magna et
firma paraveram, commotus hominum non dubio sermone
dimisi.

4   Rationes mei quaestoris nec verum fuit me tibi mittere
nec tamen erant confectae. eas nos Apameae[5] deponere
cogitabamus. de praeda mea praeter quaestores urbanos,
id est populum Romanum, terruncium nec attigit nec tac-
turus est quisquam. Laodiceae me praedes accepturum
arbitror omnis pecuniae publicae, ut et mihi et populo
cautum sit sine vecturae periculo. quod scribis ad me de
drach⟨m⟩um[6] CCCIↃↃ, nihil est quod in isto genere cui-

---

3 nullam *(Ursinus)*   4 *(SB)*
5 Apameae ⟨et Laodiceae⟩ *T.–P.*   6 *(Wes.)*

---

3 Bibulus denied the validity of Caesar's legislation as Consul,
since it had been passed in defiance of his own religious block.
    4 Not the Phrygian city mentioned in the next paragraph, nor,

sake of our two boys, but that is not certain. I want to get back to Rome as soon as possible. However, the ordering of my journey will depend upon the political situation and the state of affairs in the capital. Your successor cannot possibly make such good time as to enable you to meet me in Asia.

As regards the rendering of accounts, there would have been some convenience in making no return, for which you say you have Bibulus' licence. But I hardly think you can take that course in view of the lex Julia. Bibulus has his own reasons for not observing that law,[3] but I think you should be very careful to observe it.

You say that the garrison ought not to have been withdrawn from Apamea.[4] I find that your opinion is generally shared, and I am sorry that this step has caused some untoward talk among the ill-disposed. But nobody except yourself seems to be in any doubt as to whether or not the Parthians have crossed the river. Accordingly, under the impression of the general, unambiguous report, I have dismissed all the defensive forces which I had prepared in great strength.

It would not have been correct for me to send you my Quaestor's accounts, and in any case they are not ready. I intend to deposit them at Apamea. Not a penny of my booty has been or will be touched by any person except the City Quaestors, which is to say the Roman People. I propose to take sureties at Laodicea for all public moneys, so that both the state and I myself may be insured against transport risks. As for the 100,000 drachmae you mention,

as usually supposed, Apamea on the Orontes, but another place of the same name on the east side of the Euphrates.

quam possim commodare. omnis enim pecunia ita tracta-
tur ut praeda a praefectis, quae autem mihi attributa est a
quaestore curetur.

5   Quod quaeris quid existimem de legionibus quae de-
cretae sunt in Syriam, antea dubitabam venturaene essent;
nunc mihi non est dubium quin, si antea auditum erit
otium esse in Syria, venturae non sint. Marium quidem
successorem tarde video esse venturum, propterea quod
senatus ita decrevit ut cum legionibus iret.

6   Uni epistulae respondi; venio ad alteram. petis a me ut
Bibulo te quam diligentissime commendem. in quo mihi
voluntas non deest, sed locus esse videtur tecum expostu-
landi. solus enim tu ex omnibus qui cum Bibulo sunt certiorem me numquam fecisti quam valde Bibuli voluntas a
me sine causa abhorreret. permulti enim ad me detule-
runt, cum magnus Antiocheae metus esset et magna spes
in me atque in exercitu meo, solitum dicere quidvis se
perpeti malle quam videri eguisse auxilio meo. quod ego
officio quaestorio te adductum reticere de praetore tuo
non moleste ferebam, quamquam quem ad modum tracta-
rere audiebam. ille autem, cum ad Thermum de Parthico
bello scriberet, ad me litteram numquam misit, ad quem
intellegebat eius belli periculum pertinere. tantum de au-
guratu fili sui scripsit ad me; in quo ego misericordia
commotus, et quod semper amicissimus Bibulo fui, dedi

7   operam ut ei quam humanissime scriberem. ille si ⟨in⟩
omnis est malevolus, quod numquam existimavi, minus
offendor in me; sin autem a me est alienior, nihil tibi meae

---

5 Bibulus had just lost two sons, murdered in Egypt.

I am unable to oblige anyone in such a matter. All moneys are handled by the Prefects or the Quaestor; booty by the former, funds assigned to me by the latter.

You ask my opinion about the legions which have been decreed for Syria. I was previously doubtful whether they would be coming. Now I have no doubt that they will *not* be coming, if the news that all is quiet in Syria arrives beforehand. I suppose your successor Marius will be delayed because the Senate instructed him to accompany the legions.

Having replied to one letter, I come to the other. You request me to recommend you to Bibulus as warmly as possible. The will on my side is not lacking, but I think I have a bone to pick with you in this connection. Of all Bibulus' entourage you are the only one who had never told me how causelessly unfriendly his disposition towards me is. Any number of people have let me know that, when Antioch was in great danger and great hope rested on me and my army, he used to say that he would sooner anything than appear to have stood in need of help from me. I was not annoyed with you for keeping silent from a sense of your duty as Quaestor towards your official superior, although I heard of the treatment to which you were subjected. As for Bibulus, although he wrote to Thermus about the Parthian war, he never sent a line to me, whom he knew to be directly involved in the danger of that war. He only wrote to *me* about an Augurate for his son. Out of pity,[5] and because I was always very friendly to him, I was at pains to write to him in the kindest possible way. If he has a spite against the whole world, which I never supposed to be the case, I do not so much resent his behaviour to me. But if he is unfriendly to me in particular, a letter of

15

litterae proderunt. nam[7] ad senatum quas Bibulus litteras misit, in iis, quod mihi cum illo erat commune sibi soli attribuit; se ait curasse ut cum quaestu populi pecunia permutaretur. quod autem meum erat proprium, ut alariis Transpadanis uti negarem, id etiam populo se remisisse scribit. quod vero illius erat solius id mecum communicat: 'equitibus auxiliariis' inquit 'cum amplius frumenti postularemus.' illud vero pusilli animi et ‹in›[8] ipsa malevolentia ieiuni atque inanis, quod Ariobarzanem, quia senatus per me regem appellavit mihique commendavit, iste in litteris non regem sed regis Ariobarzanis filium appellat. hoc animo qui sunt deteriores fiunt rogati. sed tibi morem gessi, litteras ad eum scripsi. quas cum acceperis, facies quod voles.

118 (XV.11)

Scr. Tarsi post. parte m. Quint. an. 50

M. CICERO IMP. S. D. C. MARCELLO COS.

1   Quantae curae tibi meus honos fuerit et quam idem exstiteris consul in me ornando et amplificando qui fueras semper cum parentibus tuis et cum tota domo, etsi res ipsa

[7] iam *coni. SB*
[8] *(Schütz)*

---

[1] The Supplication.

mine will not do you any good. I may add that in the dispatch which Bibulus sent to the Senate (a) he took sole credit for a thing we did jointly—he says that *he* took steps to see that moneys were exchanged at a profit to the state; (b) with reference to an action entirely mine, my declining to make use of Transpadane auxiliaries, he writes that *he* has relieved the state of that obligation also; (c) on the other hand he makes me share in something for which he was solely responsible: 'When we asked for an additional issue of grain for the auxiliary cavalry,' says he. His pettiness of spirit, the paltry, piddling character of his very malice, comes out when he calls Ariobarzanes in his dispatch not 'King' but 'son of King Ariobarzanes,' because the Senate had granted him the royal title through me and had recommended him to my care. Persons of this mentality are not improved by being asked favours. However, I have complied with your wish and written a letter addressed to him. When you get it, you will do what you please.

118 (XV.11)

CICERO TO C. MARCELLUS

Tarsus, late July 50

From M. Cicero, Imperator, to C. Marcellus, Consul, greetings.

All my friends have told me in their letters (though the facts speak loudly enough for themselves) of the interest you have taken in the honour[1] conferred upon me. As Consul you have shown the same concern for my distinction and advancement in dignity as you always showed in the

17

loquebatur, cognovi tamen ex meorum omnium litteris.
itaque nihil est tantum quod ego non tua causa debeam
2 facturusque sim [cum][1] studiose ac libenter. nam magni
interest cui debeas, debere autem nemini malui quam tibi,
cui me cum studia communia, beneficia paterna tuaque
iam ante coniunxerant, tum accedit mea quidem sententia
maximum vinculum, quod ita rem publicam geris atque
gessisti, qua mihi carius nihil est, ut, quantum tibi omnes
boni debeant, quo minus tantundem ego unus debeam
non recusem. quam ob rem tibi velim ii sint exitus quos
mereris et quos fore confido.

Ego, si me navigatio non morabitur, quae incurrebat in
ipsos etesias, propediem te, ut spero, videbo.

119 (XIV.5)

Scr. Athenis XVII *Kal. Nov. an. 50*

TULLIUS S. D. TERENTIAE SUAE

1   Si tu et Tullia, lux nostra, valetis, ego et suavissimus
Cicero valemus.

Prid. Id. Oct. Athenas venimus, cum sane adversis ventis usi essemus tardeque et incommode navigassemus. de
nave exeuntibus nobis Acastus cum litteris praesto fuit uno
et vicesimo die sane strenue. accepi tuas litteras, quibus

[1] *(Or.)*

past, together with your parents and your whole family circle. Accordingly no service on my part can exceed your deserts, and there is none which I shall not zealously and gladly render. When one owes a favour, personalities make a great difference, and there is no man in respect to whom I have been more content to be in that position. Our common pursuits and the kindnesses I have received from your father and yourself had already attached me to you, but to this has now to be added what is in my eyes the greatest bond of all—your past and present administration of the commonwealth, which is as precious to me as anything in the world. I have no reluctance to owe you in my single person just as much as the whole body of honest citizens. Accordingly let me wish you such outcomes as you deserve and as I believe will be yours.

As for me, I look forward to seeing you shortly, if I am not delayed on the voyage, which is just coinciding with the Etesians.

119 (XIV.5)
CICERO TO TERENTIA

Athens, 16 October 50

From Tullius to his dear Terentia greetings.

If you and our beloved Tullia are well, darling Marcus and I are well too.

We arrived in Athens on 14 October, having experienced pretty unfavourable weather at sea—it has been a slow, disagreeable voyage. Acastus met us with letters as we came ashore. He had been three weeks on the way, which is pretty good going. I got your letter, in which you

intellexi te vereri ne superiores mihi redditae non essent.
omnes sunt redditae diligentissimeque a te perscripta sunt
omnia, idque mihi gratissimum fuit. neque sum admiratus
hanc epistulam quam Acastus attulit brevem fuisse. iam
enim me ipsum exspectas, sive nos ipsos, qui quidem quam
primum ad vos venire cupimus, etsi in quam rem publicam
veni<a>mus[1] intellego. cognovi enim ex multorum amicorum litteris, quas attulit Acastus, ad arma rem spectare, ut
mihi, cum venero, dissimulare non liceat quid sentiam. sed
quoniam subeunda fortuna est, eo citius dabimus operam
ut veniamus, quo facilius de tota re deliberemus. tu velim,
quod commodo valetudinis tuae fiat, quam longissime
poteris obviam nobis prodeas.

2   De hereditate Preciana, quae quidem mihi magno
dolori est (valde enim illum amavi)—sed hoc velim cures,
si auctio ante meum adventum fiet, ut Pomponius aut, si
is minus poterit, Camillus nostrum negotium curet; nos,
cum salvi venerimus, reliqua per nos agemus. sin tu iam
Roma profecta eris, tamen curabis ut hoc ita fiat. nos, si di
adiuvabunt, circiter Id. Nov. in Italia speramus fore. vos,
mea suavissima et optatissima Terentia, si nos amatis,
curate ut valeatis.

Vale.

Athenis a. d. xv<ii>[2] Kal. Nov.

[1] *(Lamb.)*
[2] *(Gruber)*

appear to be afraid that your earlier letters have not been delivered. All of them were in fact delivered. You covered all items most carefully, and I was most grateful. Nor was I surprised at the shortness of the letter which Acastus brought. After all, you are now expecting me in person, or rather *us* in person, and very impatient we are to see you both—though I well see what sort of situation we are coming home to. Letters brought by Acastus from many friends tell me that war is on the horizon, so that, once I arrive, I shall not be able to disguise my sentiments. But we must take what Fortune sends, and I shall try to come all the faster so that we can consult together about the whole position. I shall be glad if you will come to meet us as far as you can without detriment to your health.

About the Precius[1] bequest (I am really sorry to get it—I was very fond of him), would you please see that, if the auction takes place before my arrival, Pomponius or, if he can't manage it, Camillus looks after my interest? When I am safely back I shall see to the rest myself. If you have already left Rome, please arrange this all the same. If the Gods are kind, we hope to be in Italy about the Ides of November. Now my darling and most longed-for Terentia, if you both love us, take care of yourselves. Good-bye.

Athens, 16 October.

[1] Cf. *Letters to Atticus* 123 (VI.9).2.

120 (XVI.1)

Scr. in itinere a Patris Alyziam III *Non. Nov. an.* 50

TULLIUS TIRONI SUO S. P. D. ⟨ET⟩[1] CICERO MEUS ET
FRATER ET FRATRIS F.

1   Paulo facilius putavi posse me ferre desiderium tui, sed
plane non fero et, quamquam magni ad honorem nostrum
interest quam primum ad urbem me venire, tamen pec-
casse mihi videor qui a te discesserim. sed quia tua voluntas ea videbatur esse ut prorsus nisi confirmato corpore
nolles navigare, approbavi tuum consilium neque nunc
muto, si tu in eadem es sententia; sin autem, postea quam
cibum cepisti, videris tibi posse me consequi, tuum consilium est. Marionem ad te eo misi ut aut tecum ad me quam
primum veniret aut, si tu morarere, statim ad me rediret.

2   Tu autem hoc tibi persuade, si commodo valetudinis
tuae fieri possit, nihil me malle quam te esse mecum; si
autem intelleges opus esse te Patris convalescendi causa
paulum commorari, nihil me malle quam te valere. si statim navigas, nos Leucade consequere; sin te confirmare
vis, et comites et tempestates et navem idoneam ut habeas
diligenter videbis. unum illud, mi Tiro, videto, si me amas,
ne te Marionis adventus et hae litterae moveant. quod
valetudini tuae maxime conducet si feceris, maxime ob-
3 temperaris voluntati meae. haec pro tuo ingenio conside-
ra. nos ita te desideramus ut amemus. amor ut valentem

---

[1] *(Calderius)*

---

[1] Tiro had been left behind sick at Patrae.

120 (XVI.1)
CICERO TO TIRO

Between Patrae and Alyzia, 3 November 50

From Tullius to his dear Tiro best greetings, also from my son Marcus, and my brother and nephew.

I thought I could bear the want of you not too hard,[1] but frankly I find it unendurable; and though in view of the honour I have in prospect it is important for me to get back to Rome as soon as possible, I feel I did wrong to leave you. However, since it seemed to be your definite inclination not to sail until your health was recovered, I approved your plan; nor am I changing now, if you are still of the same mind. But if, after you are able to take nourishment, you think you can overtake me, the decision is in your hands. I am sending Mario to you with the intention that he should either join me in your company as soon as possible or return to me at once, if you stay on.

Now do understand that, provided it can be managed without detriment to your health, there is nothing I want more than to have you with me; but that if you find you need to stay a little longer at Patrae to convalesce, there is nothing I want more than for you to be well again. If you take ship straight away, you will catch us up at Leucas. If you want to get back your strength, however, you must take good care that you have suitable companions, good weather, and the right sort of boat. Only, if you love me, my dear Tiro, do be sure not to let Mario's arrival and this letter affect your judgement. If you do what is best for your health, you will best comply with my wishes. So think it over in that clever head of yours. I miss you, but I love you. Loving you, I want to see you fit and well; missing you, I

videamus hortatur, desiderium ut quam primum. illud igitur potius. cura ergo potissimum ut valeas. de tuis innumerabilibus in me officiis erit hoc gratissimum.

III Non. Nov.

121 (XVI.2)

Scr. Alyziae Non. Nov. an. 50

TULLIUS TIRONI SUO S.

Non queo ad te nec libet scribere quo animo sim adfectus. tantum scribo, et tibi et mihi maximae voluptati fore si te firmum quam primum videro. tertio die abs te ad Alyziam accesseramus. is locus est citra Leucadem stadia CXX. Leucade aut te ipsum aut tuas litteras a Marione putabam me accepturum. quantum me diligis tantum fac ut valeas, vel quantum te a me scis diligi.

Non. Nov. Alyzia.

122 (XVI.3)

Scr. Alyziae VIII Id. Nov. an. 50

TULLIUS ET CICERO TIRONI SUO S. D. ET Q. PATER ET FILIUS

1   Nos apud Alyziam, ex quo loco tibi litteras ante dederamus, unum diem commorati sumus, quod Quintus nos consecutus non erat. is dies fuit Non. Nov. inde ante lucem

---

1 About fourteen English miles.

want to see you as soon as possible. The former, therefore, must come first. So make it your chief concern to get well. Of your countless services to me this will be the one I shall most appreciate.

3 November.

121 (XVI.2)
CICERO TO TIRO

Alyzia, 5 November 50

From Tullius to his dear Tiro greetings.

I can't and don't want to write to you how I feel. I will only say that it will be to our very great pleasure, both yours and mine, if I see you in good health as soon as possible. Two days after leaving you we put in at Alyzia, within 120 stades[1] distance of Leucas. At Leucas I expect I shall see you in person or get a letter from you by Mario. As you care for me, so be sure to look after your health—or as you know I care for you.

Nones of November, from Alyzia.

122 (XVI.3)
CICERO TO TIRO

Alyzia, 6 November 50

From Tullius and Marcus to their dear Tiro greetings, also from Quintus senior and junior.

We stayed at Alyzia (from where I sent you a letter yesterday) for one day, because Quintus had not come up with us. That was the Nones of November. From there I

proficiscentes a. d. VIII Id. Nov. has litteras dedimus.

2 Tu si nos omnis amas et praecipue me, magistrum tuum, confirma te. ego valde suspenso animo exspecto primum te scilicet, deinde Marionem cum tuis litteris. omnes cupimus, ego in primis, quam primum te videre, sed, mi Tiro, valentem. qua re nihil properaris. satis cito te[1] videro si valebis. utilitatibus tuis possum carere; te valere tua causa primum volo, tum mea.

Mi Tiro, vale.

123 (XVI.4)

Scr. Leucade VII *Id. Nov. an.* 50

TULLIUS TIRONI SUO S. P. D. ET CICERO ET Q. FRATER ET Q. F.

1 Varie sum adfectus tuis litteris, valde priore pagina perturbatus, paulum altera recreatus. qua re nunc quidem non dubito quin, quo⟨a⟩d plane valeas, te neque navigationi neque viae committas. satis te mature videro si plane confirmatum videro.

De medico et tu bene existimari scribis et ego sic audio, sed plane curationes eius non probo. ius enim dandum tibi non fuit cum κακοστόμαχος esses. sed tamen et ad illum

2 scripsi accurate et ad Lysonem. ad Curium vero, suavissimum hominem et summi offici summaeque humanitatis,

---

[1] cotidie (*Ern.*)

---

[1] Or 'gravy' or 'sauce.'
[2] Cicero's host at Patrae in whose house Tiro was staying.

am dispatching this letter as we leave before daybreak on the 6th.

If you love us all, and especially me, your schoolmaster, get back your strength. I am looking forward in great suspense, first of course to seeing you, but, if not that, to seeing Mario with a letter from you. We all, and I especially, are anxious to see you as soon as possible, but fit and well, my dear Tiro. So no hurry. I shall see you soon enough if you are in good health. I can do without your manifold usefulness, but I want you to be well again, first for your sake and then for my own.

My dear Tiro, good-bye.

123 (XVI.4)
CICERO TO TIRO

Leucas, 7 November 50

From Tullius to his dear Tiro best greetings, also from Marcus and my brother Quintus and Quintus junior.

I read your letter with varying feelings. The first page upset me badly, the second brought me round a little. So now, if not before, I am clear that until your health is quite restored you should not venture upon travel by either land or water. I shall see you soon enough if I see you thoroughly strong again.

You say the doctor has a good reputation, and so I hear myself; but frankly, I don't think much of his treatments. You ought not to have been given soup[1] with a weak stomach. However, I have written to him at some length, and also to Lyso.[2] To Curius, who is a most agreeable fellow, very obliging and good-natured, I have written a great

multa scripsi, in his etiam ut, si tibi videretur, te ad se
traferret. Lyso enim noster vereor ne neglegentior sit, primum quia omnes Graeci, deinde quod, cum a me litteras
accepisset, mihi nullas remisit. sed eum tu laudas; tu igitur
quid faciendum sit iudicabis. illud, mi Tiro, te rogo, sump-
tu ne parcas ulla in re, quod ad valetudinem opus sit. scripsi ad Curium quod dixisses daret. medico ipsi puto aliquid
dandum esse quo sit studiosior.

3   Innumerabilia tua sunt in me officia, domestica, foren-
sia, urbana, provincialia, in re privata, in publica, in studiis,
in litteris nostris: omnia viceris si, ut spero, te validum videro. ego puto te bellissime, si recte erit, cum quaestore
Mescinio decursurum. non inhumanus est teque, ut mihi
visus est, diligit. sed[1] cum valetudini tuae diligentissime
consulueris, tum, mi Tiro, consulito navigationi. nulla in re
iam te festinare volo. nihil laboro nisi ut salvus sis.

4   Sic habeto, mi Tiro, neminem esse qui me amet quin
idem te amet; et cum tua et mea maxime interest te valere,
tum multis est curae. adhuc, dum mihi nullo loco deesse
vis, numquam te confirmare potuisti; nunc te nihil impedit. omnia depone, corpori servi. quantam diligentiam in
valetudinem tuam contuleris, tanti me fieri a te iudicabo.

Vale, mi Tiro, vale, vale et salve. Lepta tibi salutem dicit
et omnes. vale.

VII Id. Nov. Leucade.

[1] et (*Ern.*)

---

3 Apparently the doctor (whose name was Asclapo; cf. Letter
286) was not charging a special fee. He may have looked after
Lyso's household for a regular payment.

deal, including the suggestion that, if you agree, he should move you over to his house. I am afraid our friend Lyso is a little casual. All Greeks are; also, he has not replied to a letter he received from me. However, you commend him; so you must judge for yourself what is best. One thing, my dear Tiro, I do beg of you: don't consider money at all where the needs of your health are concerned. I have told Curius to advance whatever you say. I imagine the doctor ought to be given something to make him more interested in your case.[3]

Your services to me are beyond count—in my home and out of it, in Rome and abroad, in private affairs and public, in my studies and literary work. You will cap them all if I see you your own man again, as I hope I shall. I think it would be very nice, if all goes well, for you to sail home with Quaestor Mescinius. He is not uncivilized, and he seemed to me to have a regard for you. But when you have given every possible attention to your health, *then* my dear Tiro, attend to sailing arrangements. I don't now want you to hurry in any way. My only concern is for you to get well.

Take my word for it, dear Tiro, that nobody cares for me who does not care for you. Your recovery is most important to you and me, but many others are concerned about it. In the past you have never been able to recruit yourself properly, because you wanted to give me of your best at every turn. Now there is nothing to stand in your way. Put everything else aside, think only of your bodily well-being. I shall believe you care for me in proportion to the care you devote to your health.

Good-bye, my dear Tiro, good-bye and fondest good wishes. Lepta sends you his, so do we all. Good-bye.

7 November, from Leucas.

124 (XVI.5)

Scr. Leucade eodem die

TULLIUS ET CICERO ET QQ. TIRONI HUMANISSIMO ET
OPTIMO S. P. D.

1   Vide quanta sit in te suavitas. duas horas Thyrrei fuimus: Xenomenes hospes tam te diligit quasi vixerit tecum.
is omnia pollicitus est quae tibi essent opus; facturum
puto. mihi placebat, si firmior esses, ut te Leucadem de-
portaret, ut ibi te plane confirmares. videbis quid Curio,
quid Lysoni, quid medico placeat. volebam ad te Marionem remittere quem, cum meliuscule tibi esset, ad me
mitteres; sed cogitavi unas litteras Marionem adferre
2   posse, me autem crebras exspectare. ⟨quod⟩[1] poteris igitur; et facies, si me diligis, ut cottidie sit Acastus in portu.
multi erunt quibus recte litteras dare possis qui ad me
libenter perferant. equidem Patras euntem neminem
praetermittam.

Ego omnem spem tui diligenter curandi in Curio habeo. nihil potest illo fieri humanius, nihil nostri amantius.
ei te totum trade. malo te paulo post valentem quam statim
imbecillum videre. cura igitur nihil aliud nisi ut valeas; cetera ego curabo.

Etiam atque etiam vale.

Leucade proficiscens VII Id. Nov.

[1] (*SB*: quot *Watt*)

124 (XVI.5)
CICERO TO TIRO

Leucas, same day

From Tullius and Marcus and the Quinti to their nicest and best of Tiros best greetings.

Look what a charmer you are! We spent two hours at Thyrreum,[1] and our host Xenomenes is as fond of you as though he had been your bosom companion. He has promised you everything you need, and I believe he will be as good as his word. I think it would be a good plan for him to take you to Leucas when you are stronger, to finish your convalescence there. You must see what Curius and Lyso and the doctor think. I wanted to send Mario back to you for you to send him to me with a letter when you were a little better, but I reflected that Mario could bring me only one letter, and I expect them one after another. So do what you can, and, if you care for me, see that Acastus goes down to the harbour every day. There will be plenty of folk to whom you can safely give a letter and who will be glad to carry it to me. For my part I shall take advantage of every traveller to Patrae.

I pin all my hope of your getting proper treatment and attention on Curius. He has the kindest of hearts and the truest affection for me. Put yourself entirely in his hands. I had rather see you fit and well a little later on than weak straight away. So attend to nothing except getting well—I shall attend to the rest.

Good-bye once again.

Leaving Leucas, 7 November.

[1] On the *outward* journey in 51.

125 (XVI.6)

Scr. Actii eodem die

TULLIUS ET CICERO ET QQ. TIRONI S. P. D.

1   Tertiam ad te hanc epistulam scripsi eodem die magis
instituti mei tenendi causa, quia nactus eram cui darem,
quam quo haberem quid scriberem. igitur illa: quantum
me diligis tantum adhibe in te diligentiae; ad tua innumerabilia in me officia adde hoc, quod mihi erit gratissimum
omnium. cum valetudinis rationem, ut spero, habueris, ha-
2   beto etiam navigationis. in Italiam euntibus omnibus ad
me litteras dabis, ut ego euntem Patras neminem praeter-
mitto. cura, cura te, mi Tiro. quoniam non contigit ut simul
navigares, nihil est quod festines nec quicquam cures nisi
ut valeas.

Etiam atque etiam vale.

VII Id. Nov. Actio vesperi.

126 (XVI.7)

Scr. Corcyrae XV *Kal. Dec. an. 50*

TULLIUS ET CICERO S. D. TIRONI SUO

Septimum iam diem Corcyrae tenebamur, Quintus
autem pater et filius Buthroti. solliciti eramus de tua valetudine mirum in modum nec mirabamur nihil a te litterarum. iis enim ventis istim navigatur qui si essent nos

125 (XVI.6)
CICERO TO TIRO

Actium, 7 November 50 (evening)

From Tullius and Marcus and the Quinti to Tiro best greetings.

This is my third letter to you in one day. I am writing it more to keep up my established practice, having happened on a bearer, than because I have anything to say. Well then, yet again: as you care for me, so take care of yourself. Add this to your countless services to me; it will be the most agreeable to me of them all. When you have done (I hope) thinking about your health, think about arrangements for sailing too. Please give all travellers to Italy letters to me, just as I never fail to take advantage of anyone going to Patrae. Look after yourself, my dear Tiro, do. Seeing that bad luck has prevented you sailing with me, you have no reason to hurry or to bother about anything except getting well.

Good-bye once more.

7 November; from Actium, in the evening.

126 (XVI.7)
CICERO AND HIS SON TO TIRO

Corcyra, 16 November 50

From Tullius and Marcus to their dear Tiro greetings.

We have been held up at Corcyra for a week. Quintus senior and junior are at Buthrotum. We are dreadfully anxious about your health, but not surprised that there has been no letter from you; for the sailing winds from your

33

Corcyrae non sederemus. cura igitur te et confirma et, cum commode et per valetudinem et per anni tempus navigare poteris, ad nos amantissimos tui veni. nemo nos amat qui te non diligat. carus omnibus exspectatusque venies. cura ut valeas.

Etiam atque etiam, Tiro noster, vale.

xv Kal. Dec.[1] Corcyra.

127 (XVI.9)

Scr. Brundisii iv *Kal. Dec. an. 50*

TULLIUS ET CICERO TIRONI SUO S.P. D.

1   Nos a te, ut scis, discessimus a. d. iiii Non. Nov. Leucadem venimus a. d. viii Id. Nov., a. d. vii Act⟨i⟩um. ibi propter tempestatem a. d. vi Id. morati sumus. inde a. d. v Id. Corcyram bellissime navigavimus. Corcyrae fuimus usque ad a. d. xvi Kal. Dec., tempestatibus retenti. a. d. xv Kal. in portum Corcyraeorum ad Cassiopen stadia cxx processimus. ibi retenti ventis sumus usque ad a. d. viiii Kal. interea qui cupide profecti sunt multi naufragia fece-

2 runt. nos eo die cenati solvimus. inde austro lenissimo caelo sereno nocte illa et die postero in Italiam ad Hydruntem ludibundi pervenimus eodemque vento postridie (id erat a. d. vii Kal. Dec.) hora iiii Brundisium venimus, eodemque tempore simul nobiscum in oppidum introiit Terentia, quae te facit plurimi.

A. d. v Kal. Dec. servus Cn. Planci Brundisi tandem ali-

---

[1] nov. *(Corr.)*

present whereabouts are the same winds but for the want of which *we* should not be stuck at Corcyra. So look after yourself and get strong, and when your health and the time of year enable you to make the voyage conveniently, rejoin us who love you dearly. Nobody loves us who is not fond of you. Everybody will be glad to see you and looking forward to your return. Take care of your health.

Good-bye again, dear Tiro.

16 November, from Corcyra.

127 (XVI.9)
CICERO AND HIS SON TO TIRO

Brundisium, 27 November 50

From Tullius and Marcus to their dear Tiro best greetings.

As you know, we left you on 2 November. We reached Leucas on 6 November and Actium on the 7th, where we stayed over the 8th on account of the weather. Thence on the 9th we had a beautiful voyage to Corcyra. At Corcyra we stayed until the 15th, held up by weather. On the 16th we moved on 120 stades to Corcyra Harbour near Cassiope. Contrary winds held us there until the 22nd. Meanwhile many travellers who were too impatient to wait were shipwrecked. That day we weighed anchor after dinner. A gentle southerly breeze was blowing, the skies were clear. Sailing at our ease through the night and the next day, we reached Italy at Hydrus, and on the day following (24 November) under the same wind arrived at Brundisium at 10 a.m. Terentia, who thinks a great deal of you, entered the town at the same time as ourselves.

At Brundisium on 26 November a slave of Cn. Plancius

quando mihi a te exspectatissimas litteras reddidit datas
Id. Nov., quae me molestia valde levarunt. utinam omnino
liberassent! sed tamen Asclapo medicus plane confirmat
propediem te valentem fore.

3   Nunc quid ego te horter ut omnem diligentiam adhibeas ad convalescendum? tuam prudentiam, temperan-
tiam, amorem erga me novi. scio te omnia facturum ut
nobiscum quam primum sis, sed tamen ita velim ut ne quid
properes. symphoniam Lysonis vellem vitasses ne in quar-
tam hebdomada incideres. sed quoniam pudori tuo ma-
luisti obsequi quam valetudini, reliqua cura. Curio misi ut
medico honos haberetur et tibi daret quod opus esset; me
cui iussisset curaturum. equum et mulum Brundisi tibi
reliqui. Romae vereor ne ex Kal. Ian. magni tumultus sint.
nos agemus omnia modice.

4   Reliquum est ut te hoc rogem et a te petam ne temere
naviges (solent nautae festinare quaestus sui causa), cautus
sis, mi Tiro; mare magnum et difficile tibi restat. si poteris,
cum Mescinio (caute is solet navigare), si minus, cum
honesto aliquo homine, cuius auctoritate navicularius mo-
veatur. in hoc omnem diligentiam si adhibueris teque
nobis incolumem stiteris, omnia a te habebo.

     Etiam atque etiam, noster Tiro, vale. medico, Curio,
Lysoni de te scripsi diligentissime. vale, salve.

---

[1] Illnesses were supposed to reach a crisis every seventh day.

gave me at long last the letter from you that I had been waiting for so impatiently, dispatched on the Ides of November. It greatly relieved my anxiety—if only the relief had been total! However, Doctor Asclapo definitely assures us that you will soon be well.

Now I do not think I need urge you to apply all possible care to the business of convalescing. I know your good sense, your temperate habits, and your affection for me. I know you will do everything in your power to be with us at the earliest possible moment. But at the same time I should not want you to be in any sort of hurry. I wish you had stayed away from Lyso's concert—you might have had a fourth weekly crisis.[1] However, since you chose to put good manners before your health, be careful in future. I am sending word to Curius to do something for the doctor and advance you what you need, with a promise that I shall repay to anyone he designates. I am leaving a horse and mule for you at Brundisium. I am afraid there will be great alarms and excursions in Rome after the Kalends of January. I shall take a moderate line in all things.

The only other thing is to ask and beg you not to take ship without proper care. Sailors with their money to make are apt to be in a hurry. Take no chances, my dear Tiro. You have a long, difficult voyage ahead. If possible, go with Mescinius—he is not one to take chances with the sea. If not, then with some man of position whom the skipper will respect. If you take every care about this and render yourself up to me safe and sound, I shall have all I ever want of you.

Again, dear Tiro, good-bye. I have written to the doctor, to Curius, and to Lyso most particularly about you. Goodbye and good wishes.

128 (V.20)

Scr. ad urbem c. Non. Ian. an. 49

CICERO RUFO

1   Quo⟨quo⟩[1] modo potuissem te convenissem si eo quo constitueras venire voluisses. qua re, etsi mei commodi causa commovere me noluisti, tamen ita existimes velim, me antelaturum fuisse, si ad me misisses, voluntatem tuam commodo meo.

    Ad ea quae scripsisti commodius equidem possem de singulis ad te rebus scribere si M. Tullius, scriba meus, adesset. a quo mihi exploratum est in rationibus dumtaxat referendis (de ceteris rebus adfirmare non possum) nihil eum fecisse scientem quod esset contra aut rem aut existi-mationem tuam; dein, si[2] rationum referendarum ius vetus et mos antiquus maneret, me relaturum rationes nisi te-cum pro coniunctione nostrae necessitudinis contulissem 2 confecissemque non fuisse. quod igitur fecissem ad urbem si consuetudo pristina maneret, id, quoniam lege Iulia relinquere rationes in provincia necesse erat easdemque totidem verbis referre ad aerarium, feci in provincia; ne-que ita feci ut te ad meum arbitrium adducerem, sed tribui tibi tantum quantum me tribuisse numquam me paenite-bit. totum enim scribam meum, quem tibi video nunc esse suspectum, tibi tradidi. tu ei M. Mindium, fratrem tuum, adiunxisti. rationes confectae me absente sunt tecum; ad

---

[1] *(Man.)*   [2] ⟨scito,⟩ si *Wes.*: ⟨sic habeto,⟩ si *coni. SB*

---

[1] See Glossary.

LETTER 128 (V.20)

128 (V.20)
CICERO TO MESCINIUS RUFUS

Outside Rome, ca. 5 January 49

From Cicero to Rufus.

One way or another I should have met you if you had chosen to go to the place arranged. Regardful of my convenience, you did not want to put me about; but I should like you to believe that, if you had sent me word, I should have set your wish above my convenience.

It would be easier for me to reply to your letter in detail if my Secretary,[1] M. Tullius, were here. As to him, I am fully assured that so far as the rendering of accounts goes (on other matters I cannot speak for certain) he has not intentionally done anything contrary to your financial interest or reputation. Further, I can assure you that, if the old law and ancient custom were still in force, I should not have rendered my accounts without previously comparing and making them up with you, suitably to the intimate connection between us. Now that the lex Julia makes it necessary to leave accounts in the province and present an identical copy to the Treasury, I did in the province what I should have done at Rome if the previous practice had still held good. Nor did I do it in such a way as to oblige you to conform to my pattern, but on the contrary gave you a latitude which I shall never regret having given. I put my Secretary, of whom I see you now entertain suspicions, entirely in your hands. You associated with him your brother,[2] M. Mindius. The accounts were made up in my absence

[2] I.e. brother (or cousin) adopted into another family or half-brother (accounting for the different *gentilicia*).

quas ego nihil adhibui praeter lectionem. ita accepi librum
a meo [servo][3] scriba ut eundem acceperim a fratre tuo. si
honos is fuit, maiorem tibi habere non potui; si fides, maiorem tibi habui quam paene ipsi mihi; si providendum fuit
ne quid aliter ac tibi et honestum et utile esset referretur,
non habui cui potius id negoti darem quam ⟨cui⟩[4] dedi.
illud quidem certe factum est quod lex iubebat, ut apud
duas civitates, Laodicensem et Apamensem, quae nobis
maxime videbantur, quoniam ita necesse erat, rationes
confectas collatas deponeremus. itaque huic loco primum
respondeo me, quamquam iustis de causis rationes referre[5] properarim, tamen te exspectaturum fuisse nisi in provincia relictas rationes pro ⟨re⟩latis[6] haberem. quam ob
rem * * *

3   De Volusio quod scribis, non est id rationum. docue-
runt enim me periti homines, in his cum omnium peritis-
simus tum mihi amicissimus, C. Camillus, ad Volusium
traferri nomen a Valerio non potuisse; praedes Valerianos
teneri (neque id erat HS ⌈XXX⌉, ut scribis, sed HS ⌈XX⌉[7]);
erat enim curata nobis pecunia Valeri mancipis nomine, ex
4   qua reliquum quod erat in rationibus rettuli. sed sic me et

---

³ *(Man.)*   ⁴ *(Graevius)*   ⁵ deferre *(Gron.)*
⁶ *(Rut.)*   ⁷ xix *(SB)*

---

³ He seems to have acted as Cicero's agent-in-charge *(procu-
rator)* in Rome during the Proconsulate.

⁴ Probably the P. Valerius mentioned in *Letters* to *Atticus* 114
(V.21).14 as a penniless dependent of King Deiotarus. He seems
to have acted as an agent of Q. Volusius, one of Cicero's following
(cf. ibid. 6), in a speculation on a public (revenue?) contract and to

with your cooperation. All I did was to read them, and I regarded the book I received from my Secretary as coming from your brother also. If this was a compliment, I could not have made you a greater; if an act of trust, I placed almost more trust in you than in myself; if the object was to ensure that nothing should be presented other than to your credit and advantage, I had nobody more proper to the business than the person to whom I gave it. At any rate what the law required was done; I deposited accounts, made up and compared, with the two communes which appeared to me most suitable, since it had to be done in this way, namely Laodicea and Apamea. So on this point my first answer is that, although for good reasons I was in a hurry to present my accounts, I should have waited for you if I had not looked upon the accounts left behind in the province as already rendered. Therefore * * *.

As for what you write about Volusius, this does not concern the accounts. I was advised by experts, including the greatest expert of them all and my very good friend C. Camillus,[3] that the debt could not be transferred from Valerius[4] to Volusius, and that Valerius' sureties were liable (the amount was not HS3,000,000, as stated in your letter, but HS2,000,000). For the money was paid to me in the name of Valerius as purchaser. That part of it which was arrears I entered in the accounts. But writing as you

have given as sureties certain of the principal members of Cicero's staff. When Valerius failed to pay the Treasury, the sureties became liable. The maneuvre by which Cicero extricated them is not clearly stated. According to an interpretation first advanced in 1961, he reckoned money paid by Valerius in respect of an earlier contract as discharging the debt.

liberalitatis fructu privas et diligentiae et, quod minime
tamen laboro, mediocris etiam prudentiae: liberalitatis,
quod mavis scribae mei beneficio quam meo legatum
meum ⟨M. Anneium⟩[8] praefectumque Q. Leptam maxima calamitate levatos, cum praesertim non deberent esse
obligati; diligentiae, quod existimas de tanto officio meo,
tanto etiam periculo,[9] nec scisse me quicquam nec cogita-
visse, scribam quicquid voluisset, cum id mihi ne recita-
visset quidem, rettulisse; prudentiae, cum rem a me non
insipienter excogitatam ⟨ne cogitatam⟩[10] quidem putas.
nam et Volusi liberandi meum fuit consilium et ut multa
tam gravis Valerianis praedibus ipsique T. Mario depelle-
retur a me inita ratio est. quam quidem omnes non solum
probant sed etiam laudant, et, si verum scire vis, hoc uni
5   scribae meo intellexi non nimium placere. sed ego putavi
esse viri boni, cum populus suum servaret, consulere fortunis tot vel amicorum vel civium.

   Nam de Lucceio[11] est ita actum ut auctore Cn. Pompeio ista pecunia in fano poneretur. id ego agnovi meo
iussu esse factum. qua pecunia Pompeius est usus, ut ea[12]
quam tu deposueras Sestius. sed haec ad te nihil intellego
pertinere. illud me non animadvertisse moleste ferrem ut
adscriberem te in fano pecuniam iussu meo deposuisse,
nisi ista pecunia gravissimis esset certissimisque monu-

---

[8] *(Wes.)*   [9] periculo ⟨meorum⟩ *T.–P.*   [10] *(Vict.)*
[11] logeo *Lamb.*: λογείᾳ *coni. SB*   [12] tua *(Ern.)*

---

   [5] Unknown; perhaps one of the Marii of Arpinum, with whom
the Ciceros had a family connection.   [6] We know no details
about these two deposits. P. Sestius was appointed governor of
Cilicia in the second week of January, but was still in Italy.

do, you rob me of the satisfaction of liberality, conscientiousness, and a measure of business sense (though I set little enough store by *that*). (a) Liberality: you prefer to suppose that it was thanks to my Secretary, and not to me, that my Legate, M. Anneius, and my Prefect, Q. Lepta, were relieved of a very heavy liability, which moreover they should not in fairness have incurred. (b) Conscientiousness: you suppose that I neither knew nor thought about a matter so gravely involving my duty, and with such dangerous potentialities, but presented whatever my Secretary thought fit without even having him read it over to me. (c) Business sense: you imagine that the procedure which I rather intelligently thought out was not so much as thought about. Actually the plan of freeing Volusius was mine, and it was I who devised the expedient whereby Valerius' sureties and T. Marius[5] himself escaped so severe a penalty. That expedient has been universally approved, applauded in fact; and, if you want the truth, my Secretary was the only one who, as I could see, was not too happy about it. But I took the view that an honourable man should have regard to the financial welfare of so many friends or fellow countrymen, seeing that the public kept its due.

As regards Lucceius (?), what happened was that the money was deposited in a temple at the instance of Cn. Pompeius. I acknowledged that this was done on my instructions. Pompey has used the money, just as Sestius[6] has used the sum you deposited. But so far as I can see, all this has nothing to do with you. I should be very sorry, however, that I inadvertently omitted to add that you deposited the money in the temple on my instructions, were it not that there is the most weighty and unimpeachable documen-

mentis testata, cui data, quo senatus consulto, quibus tuis,
quibus meis litteris P. Sestio tradita esset. quae cum viderem tot vestigiis impressa ut in iis errari non posset, non
adscripsi id quod tua nihil referebat. ego tamen adscrip-
6   sisse mallem, quoniam id te video desiderare. sicut scribis
tibi id esse referendum, idem ipse sentio, neque in eo
quicquam a meis rationibus discrepabunt tuae; addes
enim tu, meo iussu; quod ego, qui non addidi, nec causa est
cur negem nec, si causa esset et tu nolles, negarem.

Nam de sestertiis nongentis milibus, certe ita relatum
est ut tu sive frater tuus referri voluit. sed si quid est, quoniam de λογείᾳ[13] parum †gravisum†[14] est, quod ego in
rationibus referendis etiam nunc corrigere possim, de eo
mihi, quoniam senatus consulto non sum usus, quid per
leges liceat considerandum est. te certe in pecuniae exac-
tae[15] i‹s›ta referre[16] ex meis rationibus relatis non oportuit, nisi quid me fallit; sunt enim alii peritiores. illud cave
dubites quin ego omnia faciam quae interesse tua aut
etiam velle te existimem si ullo modo facere possim.

7   Quod scribis de beneficiis, scito a me et tribunos militaris et praefectos et contubernalis dumtaxat meos delatos
esse. in quo quidem me ratio fefellit; liberum enim mihi
tempus ad eos deferendos existimabam dari; postea certior
sum factus triginta diebus deferri necesse esse quibus ra-

---

[13] logaeo *(SB)*   [14] gra‹phice› visum *tempt. SB*
[15] ia -ta ⌐   [16] ita efferre (Crat.)

---

7 Gratuities or other benefits given or promised to military and
other personnel by a governor during his term of office. A list had
to be presented to the Treasury. Apparently this could be done
either by the Governor himself or by his Quaestor.

tary evidence showing to whom that money was given as well as the senatorial decrees and the written authorities, yours and mine, on which it was handed over to P. Sestius. Seeing that all this was unmistakably attested in a number of places, I did not put in a supplement which would have been of no advantage to you. But I wish I had, since you evidently regard it as an omission. You say that *you* had better enter it so, and I quite agree; there will not be the least discrepancy on this point between your accounts and mine. You will add that it was on my instructions; and I, though I did not so add, have no reason to deny it; nor, if I *had* such a reason, should I deny it against your wish.

The entry concerning the HS900,000 was certainly made in the form in which you, or your brother, wanted it made. However, if there is any point which even at this stage I might be able to correct in presenting the accounts, since you thought the entry about the contribution rather maladroit(?), I shall have to consider what is legally permissible, as I have not taken advantage of the senatorial decree. At all events I don't think you should have entered these items from my rendered accounts under the heading of 'money levied,' unless I am in error—I am not the world's greatest expert. One thing you must never doubt, that I will do anything I think your interests or even your wishes require, if I possibly can.

With reference to what you say about bounties,[7] I must tell you that I have given in the names of the Military Tribunes, Prefects, and my personal staff only. Here I was under a misapprehension. I thought I had time at my disposal in which to present the list. But I was later informed that it had to be sent in within thirty days after I rendered

tiones rettulissem. sane moleste tuli non illa beneficia tuae
potius ambitioni reservata esse quam meae, qui ambitione
nihil uterer. de centurionibus tamen et de tribunorum
militarium contubernalibus res est in integro. genus enim
horum beneficiorum definitum lege non erat.

8   Reliquum est de sestertiis centum milibus, de quibus
memini mihi a te Myrina litteras esse adlatas, non mei er-
rati sed tui; in quo peccatum videbatur esse, si modo erat,
fratris tui et Tulli. sed cum id corrigi non posset, quod iam
depositis rationibus ex provincia decessimus, credo me
quidem tibi pro animi mei voluntate proque ea spe faculta-
tum quam tum habebamus quam humanissime potuerim
rescripsisse. sed neque tum me humanitate litterarum
mearum obligatum puto neque me tuam hodie epistulam
de HS $\overline{c}$ sic accepisse ut ii accipiunt quibus epistulae per
9 haec tempora molestae sunt. simul illud cogitare debes,
me omnem pecuniam quae ad me salvis legibus pervenis-
set Ephesi apud publicanos deposuisse; id fuisse HS $\overline{\lceil\text{XXII}\rceil}$:
eam omnem pecuniam Pompeium abstulisse. quod ego
sive aequo animo sive iniquo fero, tu de HS $\overline{c}$ aequo animo
ferre debes et existimare eo minus ad te vel de tuis cibariis
vel de mea liberalitate pervenisse. quod si mihi expensa
ista HS $\overline{c}$ tulisses, tamen, quae tua est suavitas quique in
me amor, nolles a me hoc tempore aestimationem acci-
pere; nam numeratum si cuperem, non erat. sed haec ioca-

---

8 This sum would seem to have been entered in the accounts
by error as due from Mescinius to the Treasury.

9 Debtors. With war about to break out creditors were trying
to call in their loans.

10 This was not so. A year later the money was still in Ephesus;
Letters to Atticus 211 (XI.1).2. Shortly afterwards Cicero with-

the accounts. I was extremely sorry that those bounties should not have stood to your credit rather than mine, having myself no axe to grind. However, on the Centurions and the staffs of the Military Tribunes we are still uncommitted, bounties in this category not being specified in the statute.

That leaves the matter of the HS100,000.[8] I remember getting a letter from you on this point written from Myrina, and the mistake was not mine but yours. The persons to blame, if blame there was, appeared to be your brother and Tullius. Correction being impossible, because I deposited my accounts before leaving the province, I believe I did reply in as accommodating a fashion as I could, in accordance with my personal feelings and my financial expectations at that time. But I do not consider myself as bound by the accommodating terms of my letter then, nor today, having received your letter about the HS100,000, do I feel myself in the position of persons to whom letters these days spell trouble![9] You should also bear in mind that I deposited the whole of the sum which had legally accrued to me with the tax farmers at Ephesus, that it amounted to HS2,200,000, and that Pompey has taken the lot.[10] Whether I like that or I lump it, you ought to take a matter of HS100,000 coolly enough. You should set it off against your allowances or my liberality. Suppose you had made me a loan of that HS100,000, you have too amiable a disposition and too much affection for me to wish to take my property at valuation at this time—as for cash, I couldn't raise it if I wanted. But don't think I mean all this

drew half of it and lent it to Pompey. But he may have told Pompey that it was at his disposal.

tum me putato, ut ego te existimo. ego tamen, cum Tullius
rure redierit, mittam eum ad te, si quid ad rem putabis
pertinere.

Hanc epistulam cur conscindi[17] velim causa nulla est.

129 (XIII.55)

Scr. fort. Tarsi ex. an. 51 vel in. an. 50

CICERO THERMO PRO PR. S.

1   Etsi mihi videor intellexisse, cum tecum Ephesi de re
M. Annei, legati mei, locutus sum, te ipsius causa vehementer omnia velle, tamen et M. Anneium tanti facio ut
mihi nihil putem praetermittendum quod illius intersit et
me a te tanti fieri puto ut non dubitem quin ad tuam voluntatem magnus cumulus accedat commendationis meae.[1]
nam cum iam diu diligerem M. Anneium deque eo sic exis-
timarem ut res declarat, qui[2] ultro ei detulerim legationem
cum multis petentibus denegassem, tum vero, postea
quam mecum in bello atque in re militari fuit, tantam in eo
virtutem, prudentiam, fidem tantamque erga me benevolentiam cognovi ut hominem neminem pluris faciam.

Eum cum Sardianis habere controversiam scis. causam
tibi exposuimus Ephesi; quam tu tamen coram facilius me-
2   liusque cognosces. de reliquo, mihi mehercule diu dubium
fuit quid ad te potissimum scriberem. ius enim quem ad
modum dicas clarum et magna cum tua laude notum est.

---

[17] non scindi *(Hirschfeld)*
[1] -datione mea *Schneider*
[2] qu(a)e *(Wes.)*

seriously; no more do I suppose you were serious either. All the same, if you think it would be of any use, I'll send Tullius over to you, when he gets back from the country.

There is no reason why I should want this letter torn up.

129 (XIII.55)
CICERO TO MINUCIUS THERMUS

Tarsus (?), 51 (end) or 50 (early)

From Cicero to Thermus, Propraetor, greetings.

When I spoke to you in Ephesus about the affair of my Legate, M. Anneius, I formed the impression that you were very anxious to oblige him for his own sake. But I think so much of him that I feel I must leave nothing undone which might be to his benefit, and I have sufficient confidence in your regard for me to feel sure that my recommendation will serve to enhance your friendly sentiments towards him in no small measure. I have long had a regard for M. Anneius. My opinion of him is evident from the fact that I offered him his present post of my own accord after refusing many applications for it. And now that he has been with me on active service in the recent operations, I have so highly approved his courage, skill, loyalty, and personal good will towards me that nobody stands higher in my esteem.

You know that he has a dispute with the people of Sardis. I explained the case to you in Ephesus, but you will acquaint yourself more easily and accurately face to face. For the rest, I give you my word that for some time I could not make up my mind just what to write to you. Your manner of administering justice is well-known, and redounds

49

nobis autem in hac causa nihil aliud opus est nisi te ius
instituto tuo dicere. sed tamen, cum me non fugiat quanta
sit in praetore auctoritas, praesertim ista integritate, gravitate, clementia qua te esse inter omnis constat, peto abs
te pro nostra coniunctissima necessitudine plurimisque
officiis paribus ac mutuis ut voluntate, auctoritate, studio
tuo perficias ut M. Anneius intellegat te et sibi amicum
esse (quod non dubitat; saepe enim mecum locutus est) et
multo amiciorem his meis litteris esse factum. in tuo toto
imperio atque provincia nihil est quod mihi gratius facere
possis. nam apud ipsum, gratissimum hominem atque
optimum virum, quam bene positurus sis studium tuum
atque officium dubitare te non existimo.

130 (XIII.53)

Scr. in Cilicia an. 51 vel 50

CICERO THERMO PRO PR. S.

1   L. Genucilio Curvo iam pridem utor familiarissime,
optimo viro et homine gratissimo. eum tibi penitus commendo atque trado, primum ut omnibus in rebus ei [te][1]
commodes, quoad fides tua dignitasque patietur; patietur
autem in omnibus; nihil enim abs te umquam quod sit alie-
2   num tuis aut etiam suis moribus postulabit. praecipue
autem tibi commendo negotia eius quae sunt in Helles-
ponto: primum ut obtineat id iuris in agris quod ei Pariana

    [1] (Man.)

to your great credit; and in this case all we need is for you to follow your usual judicial practice. However, I am not unaware of the weight of a governor's influence, especially of one so upright, responsible, and merciful as you are universally acknowledged to be. May I therefore request you in virtue of the very close connection between us and our many equal and mutual good offices to exert your benevolent influence on M. Anneius' behalf, so as to make it clear to him that you are his friend (which he does not doubt—he has often talked to me) and have become much more so as a result of this letter of mine. In the whole sphere of your authority you could do nothing to oblige me more. As for Anneius himself, he is an excellent fellow and does not forget a kindness. I imagine you make no doubt that your friendly efforts will be well placed.

130 (XIII.53)
CICERO TO MINUCIUS THERMUS

Province of Cilicia, 51 or 50

From Cicero to Thermus, Propraetor, greetings.

I have long been on very familiar terms with L. Genucilius Curvus, a very worthy gentleman who never forgets a service. I thoroughly recommend him to you, and put him in your hands. In the first place, I hope you will accommodate him in all respects so far as your conscience and dignity will allow and allow they always will, for he will never ask you for anything unbecoming to your character, or for that matter his own. In particular, however, I would recommend to your notice his affairs in the area of the Hellespont with the request that he enjoy rights over cer-

civitas decrevit et dedit et quod semper obtinuit sine ulla
controversia; deinde, si quid habebit cum aliquo Helles-
pontio controversiae, ut in illam διοίκησιν reicias. sed non
mihi videor, cum tibi totum hominem diligentissime com-
mendarim, singulas ad te eius causas perscribere debere.
summa illa sit: quicquid offici, benefici, honoris in Genuci-
lium contuleris, id te existimabo in me ipsum atque in rem
meam contulisse.

131 (XIII.56)

Scr. in Cilicia an. 51 vel 50

CICERO THERMO PRO PR. S.

1   Cluvius Puteolanus valde me observat valdeque est
mihi familiaris. is ita sibi persuadet, quod in tua provincia
negoti habeat, nisi te provinciam obtinente meis commen-
dationibus confecerit, id se in perditis et desperatis habiturum. nunc, quoniam mihi ab amico officiosissimo tantum
oneris imponitur, ego quoque tibi imponam pro tuis in me
summis officiis, ita tamen ut tibi nolim molestus esse.

Mylasis et Alabandis pecuniam Cluvio debent. dixerat
mihi Euthydemus, cum Ephesi essem, se curaturum ut ec-
dici Mylasii Romam mitterentur. id factum non est. legatos
audio missos esse, sed malo ecdicos, ut aliquid confici pos-

---

[1] Not to be distinguished (as in *RE*) from the celebrated
orator, Euthydemus of Mylasa.

tain lands as decreed and granted him by the township of Parium, rights which in the past have always been undisputedly his; further, that if he has any dispute with a native of the Hellespont, you remit it for settlement to that district. But since I am most warmly recommending to you all that he is and has, I do not think I need write in detail of his various concerns. Let this be the long and the short of it: whatever service, kindness, or compliment Genucilius receives at your hands, I shall regard it as rendered to myself and my personal interests.

131 (XIII.56)
CICERO TO MINUCIUS THERMUS

Province of Cilicia, 51 or 50

From Cicero to Thermus, Propraetor, greetings.

Cluvius of Puteoli pays me much attention, and we are on a very familiar footing. He is convinced that unless he settles some business which he has in your province during your period of office through my recommendations, he may as well give it up for lost. Now since a friend of mine, one who never grudges a service, places such a burden on my shoulders, I for my part shall place it on yours in consideration of the very good turns you have done me in the past—but with the proviso that I don't want to put you to any serious trouble.

The towns of Mylasa and Alabanda owe Cluvius money. Euthydemus[1] told me when I was in Ephesus that he would see that Mylasian counsel were sent to Rome. This has not been done. I hear that *envoys* have been dispatched, but prefer counsel so that something can be

53

sit. quare peto a te ut et eos et Alabandis iubeas ecdicos
2 Romam mittere. praeterea Philocles Alabandensis hypo-
thecas¹ Cluvio dedit. eae commissae sunt. velim cures ut
aut de hypothecis decedat easque procuratoribus Cluvi
tradat aut pecuniam solvat; praeterea Heracleotae et Bar-
gyl⟨i⟩etae, qui item debent, aut pecuniam solvant aut
3 fructibus suis satis faciant. Caunii praeterea debent, sed
aiunt se depositam pecuniam habuisse. id velim cognoscas
et, si intellexeris eos neque ex edicto neque ex decreto depositam habuisse, des operam ut usurae Cluvio instituto
tuo conserventur.

His de rebus eo magis laboro quod agitur res Cn. Pompei etiam, nostri necessari, et quod is magis etiam mihi
laborare videtur quam ipse Cluvius; cui satis factum esse a
nobis valde volo. his de rebus te vehementer etiam atque
etiam rogo.

132 (XIII.54)

Scr. Laodiceae inter III *Id. Febr. et Non. Mai. an.* 50
CICERO THERMO PRO PR. S.

1 Cum multa mihi grata sunt quae tu adductus mea
commendatione fecisti tum in primis quod M. Marcilium,
amici atque interpretis mei filium, liberalissime tractavisti.
venit enim Laodiceam et tibi apud me mihique propter te

¹ ὑποθήκας *(SB)*

² It has been plausibly supposed that Cluvius was merely
Pompey's agent.

settled. Accordingly, may I request you to direct both Mylasa and Alabanda to send counsel to Rome? Furthermore, Philocles of Alabanda has given Cluvius a mortgage, which has now expired. I should be grateful if you would see that he either gives up the property and hands it over to Cluvius' agents or else pays the money; also that the towns of Heraclea and Bargylia, which likewise owe money, either pay up or secure the debts on their revenues. The town of Caunus also owes money, but they say they have been keeping it on deposit. Would you please make enquiries, and if you find that they have not been authorized to keep it on deposit by edict or decree, please see that Cluvius does not lose the interest, according to your rule?

I am all the more concerned about these matters because our friend Pompey's interests are also involved and because he seems to me to be even more exercised than Cluvius himself[2] I very much want him to feel content with us. Let me again earnestly beg your assistance in these matters.

132 (XIII.54)
CICERO TO MINUCIUS THERMUS

Laodicea, between 11 February and 7 May 50

From Cicero to Thermus, Propraetor, greetings.

Among the many things you have done as a result of my recommendations I am particularly obliged for your most handsome treatment of M. Marcilius, son of my friend and interpreter. He has come to Laodicea and told me how very grateful he is to you, and to me because of you. For

gratias maximas egit. quare, quod reliquum est, a te peto,
quoniam apud gratos homines beneficium ponis, ut eo
libentius iis commodes operamque des, quoad fides tua
patietur, ut socrus adulescentis rea ne fiat. ego cum antea
studiose commendabam Marcilium tum multo nunc studiosius, quod in longa apparitione singularem et prope
incredibilem patris Marcili fidem, abstinentiam modes-
tiamque cognovi.

133 (XIII.57)

Scr. Laodiceae in. m. Apr., ut vid., an. 50

CICERO THERMO PRO PR. S.

1   Quo magis cottidie ex litteris nuntiisque bellum magnum esse in Syria cognosco eo vehementius a te pro nostra necessitudine contendo ut mihi M. Anneium legatum
primo quoque tempore remittas. nam eius opera, consilio,
scientia rei militaris vel maxime intellego me et rem publicam adiuvari posse. quod nisi tanta res eius ageretur, nec
ipse adduci potuisset ut a me discederet neque ego ut eum
a me dimitterem. ego in Ciliciam proficisci cogito circiter
Kal. Mai. ante eam diem M. Anneius ad me redeat oportet.

2   Illud quod tecum et coram et per litteras diligentissime
egi, id te[1] nunc etiam atque etiam rogo curae tibi sit, ut
suum negotium, quod habet cum populo Sardiano, pro
causae veritate et pro sua dignitate conficiat. intellexi ex
tua oratione, cum tecum Ephesi locutus sum, te ipsius M.

---

[1] et (Lamb.)

the future, let me request you, since your kindness is not falling on stony ground, to be all the readier to accommodate its recipients, and, so far as your conscience will allow, to see that the young man's mother-in-law is not prosecuted. My recommendation of Marcilius is now much more enthusiastic even than before, because I have found Marcilius senior in the course of a long term of service quite remarkably (I might almost say unbelievably) loyal, honest, and well conducted.

133 (XIII.57)
CICERO TO MINUCIUS THERMUS

Laodicea, early April (?) 50

From Cicero to Thermus, Propraetor, greetings.

Every day I learn from letters and reports that a major war is in progress in Syria. That makes me all the more insistent in asking you as a friend to send me back my Legate, M. Anneius, as soon as possible. His services, advice, and military experience may clearly be invaluable to me and to the state. If he had not had so much at stake, nothing would have induced him to leave me or me to let him go. I propose to set out for Cilicia about the Kalends of May. M. Anneius should return to me before that date.

I have already both spoken and written to you very particularly about his business with the people of Sardis, and I would again beg you to see that he settles it in a manner befitting the justice of his case and his personal dignity. From what you said when I talked to you in Ephesus I understood that you were very anxious to oblige M. Anneius

Annei causa omnia velle; sed tamen sic velim existimes te mihi nihil gratius facere posse quam si intellexero per te illum ipsum[2] negotium ex sententia confecisse, idque quam primum ut efficias te etiam atque etiam rogo.

134 (XIII.65)

Scr. in Cilicia an. 51 vel 50

M. CICERO THERMO PRO PR. S.[1]

1   Cum P. Terentio Hispone, qui operas in scriptura pro magistro dat, mihi summa familiaritas consuetudoque est, multaque et magna inter nos officia paria et mutua intercedunt. eius summa existimatio agitur in eo ut pactiones cum civitatibus reliquis conficiat. non me praeterit nos eam rem Ephesi expertos esse neque ab Ephesiis ullo modo impetrare potuisse; sed quoniam, quem ad modum omnes existimant et ego intellego, tua cum summa integritate tum singulari humanitate et mansuetudine consecutus es ut libentissimis Graecis nutu quod velis consequare, peto a te in maiorem modum ut honoris mei causa hac laude Hisponem adfici velis.

2   Praeterea cum sociis scripturae mihi summa necessitudo est, non solum ob eam causam quod ea societas universa in mea fide est sed etiam quod plerisque sociis utor

---

[2] suum *Wes.*
[1] M. CICERO S.D. P. SILIO PRO PR. *(SB, H.M.Cotton secutus)*

---

[1] See Letter 138, n. 1.   [2] I.e. a Roman company which bought the right to collect these rents from the provincials.

for his own sake. But please take it that you can do nothing more agreeable to me than if I understand that thanks to you he has personally settled the business to his satisfaction, and I beg you once again to bring that about as soon as possible.

134 (XIII.65)
CICERO TO MINUCIUS THERMUS

Province of Cilicia, 51 or 50

From Cicero to Thermus,[1] Propraetor, greetings.

With P. Terentius Hispo, who works for the Grazing Rents Company[2] as their local manager, I have a great deal of familiar contact, and each of us is indebted to the other for important services, equal and mutual. His reputation very largely depends on his concluding tax agreements with the communes still outstanding. I do not forget that I tried my own hand at the business in Ephesus and was quite unable to get the Ephesians to oblige. However, according to the universal persuasion and my own observation, your complete integrity combined with your remarkable civility and gentleness have earned you the heartiest compliance of the natives with your every nod. I would therefore particularly request you as a compliment to me to make it your wish that Hispo should get this credit.

Furthermore I am closely connected with the members of the Company, not only because it is under my patronage as a whole but because I am on very close terms with many

familiarissime. ita et Hisponem meum per me ornaris et societatem mihi coniunctiorem feceris tuque ipse et ex huius observantia, gratissimi hominis, et ex sociorum gratia, hominum amplissimorum, maximum fructum capies et me summo beneficio adfeceris. sic enim velim existimes, in[2] tota tua provincia omnique isto imperio nihil esse quod mihi gratius facere possis.

135 (XIII.61)

Scr. in Cilicia an. 51 vel 50

M. CICERO S. D. P. SILIO PRO PR.

T. Pinnio familiarissime me usum esse scire te arbitror, quod quidem ille testamento declaravit, qui me cum tutorem tum etiam secundum heredem instituerit. eius filio mire studioso et erudito et modesto pecuniam Nicaeenses grandem debent, ad sestertium octogies, et, ut audio, in primis ei volunt solvere. pergratum igitur mihi feceris, quoniam non modo reliqui tutores, qui sciunt quanti me facias, sed etiam puer ipse sibi persuasit te omnia mea causa facturum esse, si dederis operam, quoad tua fides dignitasque patietur, ut quam ⟨primum quam⟩[1] plurimum pecuniae Pinnio solvatur Nicaeensium nomine.

[2] ex *(Kleyn)*
[1] *(SB)*

of them individually. So you will both do my friend Hispo a good turn at my instance and strengthen my relations with the Company. You yourself will reap a rich reward from Hispo's attentiveness (he is very appreciative of a service) and from the influence of the Company members, persons of the highest consequence. You will also do me a great kindness. For you may take it that within the whole sphere of your provincial authority you could do nothing that would oblige me more.

135 (XIII.61)
CICERO TO P. SILIUS

Province of Cilicia, 51 or 50

From M. Cicero to P. Silius, Propraetor, greetings.

I think you know that I was on very familiar terms with T. Pinnius, as he himself has testified in his will, under which I am appointed both guardian and second heir. His son, a remarkably studious, erudite, and modest young man, is owed a large sum by the people of Nicaea, about eight million sesterces, and, so I hear, they are particularly desirous to pay him. Not only the other guardians, who know how much you care for me, but the boy himself is convinced that you will do anything for my sake. You will therefore deeply oblige me if you see to it (so far as your conscience and dignity will allow) that as much of the amount as possible is paid to Pinnius as soon as possible on behalf of the people of Nicaea.

136 (XIII.62)

Scr. in Cilicia an. 51 vel 50

M. CICERO S. D. P. SILIO PRO PR.

Et in Atili negotio te amavi (cum enim sero venissem, tamen honestum equitem Romanum beneficio tuo conservavi) et mehercule semper sic in animo habui, te in meo aere esse propter Lamiae nostri coniunctionem et singularem necessitudinem. itaque primum tibi ago gratias quod me omni molestia liberas, deinde impudentia prosequor, sed idem sarciam; te enim semper sic colam et tuebor ut quem diligentissime.

Quintum fratrem meum, si me diligis, eo numero cura ut habeas quo me. ita magnum beneficium tuum magno cumulo auxeris.

137 (XIII.63)

Scr. fort. Laodiceae prid. Non. Apr. an. 50

M. CICERO S. D. P. SILIO PRO PR.

1   Non putavi fieri posse ut mihi verba deessent, sed tamen in M. Laenio commendando desunt. itaque rem tibi exponam paucis verbis, sed[1] tamen ut plane perspicere possis voluntatem meam. incredibile est quanti faciamus

---

[1] ita *Lamb.*: sic *Bengel*

---

[1] Possibly this had to do with the business mentioned in *Letters to Atticus* 94 (V.1).2.

136 (XIII.62)
CICERO TO P. SILIUS

Province of Cilicia, 51 or 50

M. Cicero to P. Silius, Propraetor, greetings.

I was truly beholden to you in the matter of Atilius[1]—thanks to you I saved a respectable Roman Knight from ruin, though I came late upon the scene. And, to be frank, I have always considered you as quite at my command because of your exceptionally close and friendly relations with our good Lamia. So you see that, having thanked you for relieving me of all anxiety, I go on to offer a piece of impertinence! But I shall make amends by ever cultivating your friendship and protecting your interests with all the devotion in the world.

If you care for me, be sure to think of my brother Quintus as you do of myself. In that way you will pile one great favour on top of another.

137 (XIII.63)
CICERO TO P. SILIUS

Laodicea, 4 April 50

From M. Cicero to P. Silius, Propraetor, greetings.

I never thought to find words failing me, but in recommending M. Laenius[1] fail me they do. So I shall explain the case to you briefly, but in terms which will make my sentiments quite clear. You would hardly believe how much I

[1] A friend of Atticus, in Cilicia on business.

et ego et frater meus, qui mihi carissimus est, M. Laenium. id fit cum plurimis eius officiis tum summa probitate et singulari modestia. eum ego a me invitissimus dimisi cum propter familiaritatem et consuetudinis suavitatem tum quod consilio eius fideli ac bono libenter utebar.

2   Sed vereor ne iam superesse mihi verba putes, quae dixeram defutura. commendo tibi hominem sic ut intelle-gis me ⟨eum de⟩[2] quo ea supra scripserim debere com-mendare, a teque vehementer etiam atque etiam peto ut quod habet in tua provincia negoti expedias, quod tibi videbitur rectum esse ipsi dicas. hominem facillimum libe-ralissimumque cognosces. itaque te rogo ut eum solutum liberum confectis eius negotiis per te quam primum ad me remittas. id mihi fratrique meo gratissimum feceris.

138 (XIII.64)

Scr. fort. Laodiceae m. Apr. an. 50

CICERO THERMO PRO PR. S.[1]

1   Nero meus mirificas apud me tibi gratias egit, prorsus incredibilis, ut nullum honorem sibi haberi potuisse dice-ret qui a te praetermissus esset. magnum fructum ex ipso capies; nihil est enim illo adulescente gratius. sed meher-cule mihi quoque gratissimum fecisti; pluris enim ex omni

[2] *(Lamb.)*   [1] M. CICERO S.D. P. SILIO PRO PR. *(SB)*

---

[1] For several reasons I have suggested that this letter is mis-takenly addressed, and that it was really written to the governor of Asia, Minucius Thermus. Cf. Letter 134.

and my dearest brother think of M. Laenius. That arises from his many services, but also from his sterling character and exceptional modesty. I was most reluctant to let him go, both because of the charm of his familiar companionship and because I was glad to avail myself of his sound and loyal advice.

But I am afraid you may be thinking that the words I said would fail me are now all too abundant! I recommend him as you will understand that I am bound to recommend a person of whom I have written the foregoing. And I most earnestly request you to expedite the business he has in your province, and to tell him in person what you consider to be proper. You will find him the soul of good nature and generosity. So I beg you to send him back to me as soon as you can, free and unencumbered, with his affairs settled thanks to you. My brother and I will be very much beholden.

138 (XIII.64)
CICERO TO MINUCIUS THERMUS

Laodicea, April (?) 50

From Cicero to Thermus,[1] Propraetor, greetings.

My friend Nero has told me of his gratitude to you in quite extraordinarily glowing terms, really unbelievable. No compliment, he says, which you could possibly have offered him was overlooked. Nero himself will richly repay you, for nobody has a better memory for a service than this young man. But I do assure you that you have greatly obliged me as well. In the whole range of our aristocracy there is no man I value more. And so you will oblige me

nobilitate neminem facio. itaque, si ea feceris quae ille per me tecum agi voluit, gratissimum mihi feceris: primum de Pausania Alabandensi, sustentes rem dum Nero veniat (vehementer eius causa cupere eum intellexi, itaque hoc valde te rogo); deinde Nysaeos, quos Nero in primis habet necessarios diligentissimeque tuetur ac defendit, habeas tibi commendatissimos, ut intellegat illa civitas sibi in Neronis patrocinio summum esse praesidium. Strabonem Servilium tibi saepe commendavi. nunc eo facio id impensius quod eius causam Nero suscepit. tantum a te petimus ut agas[2] eam rem, ne relinquas hominem innocentem ad alicuius tui dissimilis quaestum. id cum gratum mihi erit, tum etiam existimabo te humanitate tua esse usum.

2   Summa huius epistulae haec est, ut ornes omnibus rebus Neronem sicuti instituisti atque fecisti. magnum theatrum habet ista provincia, non ut haec nostra, ‹ad›[3] adulescentis nobilis, ingeniosi, abstinentis commendationem atque gloriam. quare, si te fautore usus erit, sicut profecto et utetur et usus est, amplissimas clientelas acceptas a maioribus confirmare poterit et beneficiis suis obligare. hoc in genere si eum adiuveris eo studio quo ostendisti, apud ipsum praeclarissime posueris, sed mihi etiam gratissimum feceris.

[2] ‹tu› agas *Baiter*
[3] *(Bengel)*

greatly if you will do certain things which he has asked me to raise with you. First, will you please hold over the matter of Pausanias of Alabanda until Nero arrives—I know he is very anxious to help him and so I beg this favour of you earnestly. Next, will you kindly regard the people of Nysa as specially recommended to your favour? Nero has the closest ties with them and is most active in championing their interests. So please let the commune understand that in Nero's patronage they have a most powerful protection. I have often recommended Strabo Servilius to you, and do so now the more emphatically because Nero has taken up his case. All we ask is that you handle the matter, lest otherwise you leave an innocent man to the rapacity of a successor who may not be like yourself. That will oblige me, and I shall feel that your good nature has had its way.

The sum and substance of this letter is to ask you to continue to confer all possible favours upon Nero, as you have made it your practice to do already. Your province, unlike mine, offers a wide scope to a talented and disinterested young nobleman to recommend himself and advance his reputation. With your backing, which I am sure will be and has already been forthcoming, he will be able to confirm the loyalty of the distinguished body of clients inherited from his ancestors and attach them by favours personal to himself. If you help him in this respect as actively as you have promised, your kindness will be excellently placed with Nero; but I too shall be very greatly beholden.

139 (XIII.9)

Scr. Romae fort. an. 54

CICERO CRASSIPEDI S.

1   Quamquam tibi praesens commendavi ut potui diligentissime socios Bithyniae teque cum mea commendatione tum etiam tua sponte intellexi cupere ei societati quibuscumque rebus posse⟨s⟩ commodare, tamen, cum ii quorum res agitur magni sua interesse arbitrarentur me etiam per litteras declarare tibi qua essem erga ipsos voluntate, non dubitavi haec ad te scribere.

2   Volo enim te existimare me, cum universo ordini publicanorum semper libentissime tribuerim idque magnis eius ordinis erga me meritis facere debuerim, tum in primis amicum esse huic Bithynicae societati, quae societas [ordine][1] ipso[2] hominum genere pars est maxima civitatis (constat enim ex ceteris societatibus); et casu permulti sunt in ea societate valde mihi familiares in primisque is cuius praecipuum officium agitur hoc tempore, P. Rupilius P. f. Men., qui est magister in ea societate.

3   Quae cum ita sint, in maiorem modum a te peto Cn. Pupium, qui est in operis eius societatis, omnibus tuis officiis atque omni liberalitate tueare, curesque ut eius operae,

---

[1] (*Ern.*: '*exspectes* numero' *Watt*)   [2] ipso et χ

---

[1] The letter is usually assigned to the end of 51 or the beginning of 50. Although I believe this to be erroneous, I kept it among the correspondence of the Proconsulate because its date is most conveniently considered (see my Commentary) in that context.

[2] Apparently a consortium of companies operating in Bithynia, where Crassipes was serving as Quaestor.

139 (XIII.9)
CICERO TO CRASSIPES

Rome, 54 (?)[1]

From Cicero to Crassipes greetings.

I have already recommended the Company of Bithynia[2] to you in person as strongly as I could; and it was evident to me that of your own volition as well as in consequence of my recommendation you were anxious to accommodate the Company in any way in your power. However, since those concerned consider it very much to their advantage that I should also declare to you by letter my friendly disposition in their regard, I have not hesitated to write these lines.

I have always been very ready to study the interests of the tax farmers as a class, which is only right in view of the important services they have rendered me. But I should like it to be clear to you that I have a special regard for this Company of Bithynia. The quality of the membership in itself makes the Company an important section of the community (it is a consortium of all the other companies) and, as it happens, it contains a great many very good friends of mine. I would mention one of them in particular who has a special responsibility at the present time, namely the Chairman, P. Rupilius, son of Publius, of the Tribe Menenia.

In view of the above, let me particularly request you to give your most generous support to the Company's agent, Cn. Pupius, assisting him in every way you can. I hope you will ensure, as you easily can, that his employers are thor-

quod tibi facile factu est, quam gratissimae sint sociis, remque et utilitatem sociorum, cuius rei quantam potestatem quaestor habeat non sum ignarus, per te quam maxime defensam et auctam velis. id cum mihi gratissimum feceris tum illud tibi expertus promitto et spondeo, te socios Bithyniae, si iis commodaris, memores esse et gratos cogniturum.

140 (XIII.58)

Scr., ut vid., Laodiceae m. Febr. an. 50

M. CICERO C. TITIO L. F. RUFO PR. URB. S.

L. Custidius est tribulis et municeps et familiaris meus. is causam habet, quam causam ad te deferet. commendo tibi hominem, sicut tua fides et meus pudor postulat, tantum, ut facilis ad te aditus habeat, quae aequa postulabit ut libente te impetret sentiatque meam sibi amicitiam, etiam cum longissime absim, prodesse, in primis apud te.

141 (XIII.59)

Scr. Laodiceae m. Febr. an. 50

M. CICERO M.[1] CURTIO PEDUCAEANO PR. S.

M. Fabium unice diligo summaque mihi cum eo con-

[1] C. *(SB, auct. Münzer)*

---

[1] Gallus; see Letter 114, n. 3.

oughly satisfied with his services, and will be good enough to protect and further their business interests as far as possible—and I am not unaware how much a Quaestor can do in that direction. I shall be greatly beholden. I can also promise and guarantee from experience that if you oblige the Company of Bithynia you will find that its members have good and grateful memories.

140 (XIII.58)
CICERO TO C. TITIUS RUFUS

Laodicea, February 50 (?)

From M. Cicero to C. Titius Rufus, son of Lucius, Praetor Urbanus, greetings.

L. Custidius is a member of my Tribe, a native of my town, and my good friend. He has a case, which he will be submitting to your judgement. Allow me to recommend him to you within the limits imposed by conscience on your side and propriety on mine, merely asking that he find access to you easy and obtain his fair demands with your good will; and that he have reason to feel that my friendship, even at so great a distance, is advantageous to him, especially where you are concerned.

141 (XIII.59)
CICERO TO CURTIUS PEDUCAEANUS

Laodicea, February 50

M. Cicero to M. Curtius Peducaeanus, Praetor, greetings.

I have a unique regard for M. Fabius.[1] My personal

71

suetudo et familiaritas est pervetus. in eius controversiis quid decernas a te non peto (servabis, ut tua fides et dignitas postulat, edictum et institutum tuum), sed ut quam facillimos ad te aditus habeat, quae erunt aequa libente te impetret, ut meam amicitiam sibi, etiam cum procul absim, prodesse sentiat, praesertim apud te. hoc te vehementer etiam atque etiam rogo.

142 (XIII.48)

Scr. in Italia in. an. 49, ut vid.

CICERO C. SEXTILIO RUFO QUAESTORI S. D.

Omnis tibi commendo Cyprios, sed magis Paphios, quibus tu quaecumque commodaris erunt mihi gratissima; eoque facio libentius ut eos tibi commendem quod et tuae laudi, cuius ego fautor sum, conducere arbitror, cum primus in eam insulam quaestor veneris, ea te instituere quae sequantur alii. quod, ut spero, facilius consequere si et P. Lentuli, necessari tui, legem et ea quae a me constituta sunt sequi volueris. quam rem tibi confido magnae laudi fore.

intercourse with him is of the closest, and our friendship goes back a very long way. I do not make any request as to your verdict on the matters he has at issue (you will follow your edict and rule, as your conscience and dignity require), but only ask that he find access to you as easy as possible and obtain such points as shall appear just with your good will, so that he may feel that my friendship, even at a long distance, is of advantage to him, particularly where you are concerned. This I beg of you as a special favour.

142 (XIII.48)
CICERO TO C. SEXTILIUS RUFUS

Italy, beginning of 49 (?)

From Cicero to C. Sextilius Rufus, Quaestor, greetings.

I recommend all the inhabitants of Cyprus to your favour, but more especially those of Paphos. Anything you do for them I shall greatly appreciate. I am all the more ready to recommend them to you because I think it is to the advantage of your own reputation (which I have much at heart) that on your first arrival in the island as Quaestor you should set a pattern for others to follow. This I think you will the more easily achieve if you see fit to follow the enactment of your friend P. Lentulus and my own ordinances. I am confident that this will tend much to your credit.

143 (XVI.11)

Scr. ad urbem prid. Id. Ian. an. 49

TULLIUS ET CICERO, TERENTIA, TULLIA, QQ. TIRONI
S. P. D.

1   Etsi opportunitatem operae tuae omnibus locis desidero, tamen non tam mea quam tua causa doleo te non
valere. sed quoniam in quartanam conversa vis est morbi
(sic enim scribit Curius), spero te diligentia adhibita iam[1]
firmiorem fore. modo fac, id quod est humanitatis tuae, ne
quid aliud cures hoc tempore nisi ut quam commodissime
convalescas. non ignoro quantum ex desiderio labores; sed
erunt omnia facilia si valebis. festinare te nolo, ne nauseae
molestiam suscipias aeger et periculose hieme naviges.

2   Ego ad urbem accessi prid. Non. Ian. obviam mihi sic
est proditum ut nihil posset fieri ornatius. sed incidi in
ipsam flammam civilis discordiae, vel potius belli; cui cum
cuperem mederi et, ut arbitror, possem, cupiditates certorum hominum (nam ex utraque parte sunt qui pugnare
cupiant) impedimento mihi fuerunt. omnino et ipse Caesar, amicus noster, minacis ad senatum et acerbas litteras
miserat et erat adhuc impudens, qui exercitum et provinciam invito senatu teneret, et Curio meus illum incitabat.
Antonius quidem noster et Q. Cassius nulla vi expulsi ad
Caesarem cum Curione profecti erant, postea quam senatus consulibus, praetoribus, tribunis pl. et nobis qui pro

---

[1] etiam *(C.F.W.Mueller)*

---

[1] It had previously been a tertian.
[2] Both Tribunes.

143 (XVI.11)
CICERO TO TIRO

Outside Rome, 12 January 49

From Tullius and Marcus, Terentia, Tullia, and the Quinti to Tiro best greetings.

Although I miss your timely service at every turn, your continued ill health distresses me for your sake more than for my own. But seeing that the violence of the disease has turned into a quartan[1] fever (so Curius writes), I trust that with care you will soon be stronger. Only be considerate of others as you always are, and think of nothing at the present time except how best to get well. I know well enough how painfully you are missing us. But all will be easy if you regain your health. I don't want you to hurry for fear of your exposing yourself to the miseries of sea sickness while you are still an invalid, and of your having a dangerous winter voyage.

I arrived outside Rome on 4 January. They streamed out to meet me on the road—no welcome could have been warmer. But I have fallen right into the flames of civil conflict, or rather war. I should dearly have liked to heal the mischief, and I believe I could, had not the personal desires of certain people (there are warmongers on both sides) stood in my way. To be sure, our friend Caesar has sent a threatening, harsh letter to the Senate, and persists in his shameless determination to hold his army and province in defiance of the Senate, and my friend Curio is egging him on. Our friend Antony and Q. Cassius[2] have gone to join Caesar along with Curio. They were not expelled by violence of any kind but left after the Senate had charged the Consuls, Praetors, Tribunes, and us Proconsuls to see

consulibus sumus, negotium dederat ut curaremus ne quid
3   res publica detrimenti caperet. numquam maiore in periculo civitas fuit, numquam improbi cives habuerunt para-
tiorem ducem. omnino ex hac quoque parte diligentissime
comparatur. id fit auctoritate et studio Pompei nostri, qui
Caesarem sero coepit timere.

Nobis inter has turbas senatus tamen frequens flagi-
tavit triumphum; sed Lentulus consul, quo maius suum
beneficium faceret, simul atque expedisset quae essent
necessaria de re publica dixit se relaturum. nos agimus
nihil cupide eoque est nostra pluris auctoritas. Italiae
regiones discriptae sunt, quam quisque partem tueretur.
nos Capuam sumpsimus.

Haec te scire volui. tu etiam atque etiam cura ut valeas
litterasque ad me mittas quotienscumque habebis cui des.

Etiam atque etiam vale.

D. prid. Id. Ian.

144 (XIV.18)

Scr. Formiis IX *Kal. Febr. an. 49*

TULLIUS TERENTIAE SUAE ET PATER SUAVISSIMAE
FILIAE ⟨ET⟩[1] CICERO MATRI ET SORORI S. D. P.

1   Considerandum vobis etiam atque etiam, animae

[1] *(Lamb.)*

---

[3] The so-called Ultimate Decree of the Senate, amounting to a
declaration of martial law.

[4] The controversial matter of Cicero's command in Campania

that the state took no harm.[3] Never was the community in greater peril, never did bad citizens have a leader more ready to strike. Not but what preparations are going forward actively, on our side too. This is taking place by the authority and zeal of our friend Pompey, who late in the day has begun to be afraid of Caesar.

Despite these commotions the Senate in large numbers has demanded a Triumph for me. But Consul Lentulus, to make it a bigger favour on *his* part, said he would put the matter before the House as soon as he had cleared up necessary state business. I am showing no undue eagerness, which makes my public influence the greater. Italy has been divided into districts, each under an appointed supervisor. I am taking Capua.[4]

I wanted you to know these facts. On your side, once again, see that you get well, and send me a letter as often as you have anybody to bring one.

Again, good-bye.

Dispatched 12 January.

144 (XIV.18)
CICERO TO TERENTIA AND TULLIA

Formiae, 22 January 49

From Tullius to his dear Terentia, and her father to his darling daughter, and Marcus to his mother and sister best greetings.

My dear hearts, I think you should yet again carefully

is discussed in my Cambridge edition of *Letters to Atticus,* Vol. IV, App. II.

meae, diligenter puto quid faciatis, Romaene sitis an mecum an aliquo tuto loco. id non solum meum consilium est
sed etiam vestrum.

Mihi veniunt in mentem haec: Romae vos esse tuto
posse per Dolabellam eamque rem posse nobis adiumento
esse si quae vis aut si quae rapinae fieri coeperint; sed rursus illud me movet, quod video omnis bonos abesse Roma
et eos mulieres suas secum habere. haec autem regio in
qua ego sum nostrorum est cum oppidorum tum etiam
praediorum, ut et multum esse mecum et, cum aberitis,[2]
2   commode et in nostris esse possitis. mihi plane non satis
constat adhuc utrum sit melius. vos videte quid aliae faciant isto loco feminae et ne, cum velitis, exire non liceat.
id velim diligenter etiam atque etiam vobiscum et cum
amicis consideretis. domus ut propugnacula et prae-
<si>dium habeat Philotimo dicetis. et velim tabellarios in-
stituatis certos ut cottidie aliquas a vobis litteras accipiam.
maxime autem date operam ut valeatis, si nos vultis valere.

VIIII Kal. Formi<i>s.

145 (XIV.14)

Scr. Minturnis VIII *Kal. Febr. an.* 49

TULLIUS TERENTIAE ET PATER TULLIAE, DUABUS
ANIMIS SUIS, ET CICERO MATRI OPTIMAE, SUAVIS-
SIMAE SORORI S. P. D.

---

[2] abieritis *vel sim.* (SB)

---

[1] Now one of Caesar's supporters.   [2] Cicero and his son.

consider what you are to do—whether you should stay in Rome or with me or in some place of safety. The decision is yours as well as mine.

The points that occur to me are these: Thanks to Dolabella[1] you can stay in Rome safely, and your doing so might help us if there is any outbreak of violence or looting. But on the other hand I am concerned when I observe that all honest men have left Rome and have their womenfolk with them. Moreover, this district where I am is full of towns friendly to me and also of properties of mine, so that you could be with me a good deal, and when we are separated could live comfortably in places of our own. Frankly I have not yet made up my mind which is the better course. You must observe what other ladies of your rank are doing, and take care that when and if you do want to leave you don't find the way barred. Do please consider the matter again together and with our friends. Tell Philotimus to see that the house is barricaded and guarded and please arrange reliable couriers, so that I get some sort of a letter from you every day. But your chief care must be for your health, if you want us[2] to keep ours.

22nd, from Formiae.

145 (XIV.14)
CICERO TO TERENTIA AND TULLIA

Minturnae, 23 January 49

From Tullius to Terentia, and from her father to Tullia, his two dear hearts, and from Marcus to his best of mothers and darling sister best greetings.

79

1   Si vos valetis, nos valemus.

Vestrum iam consilium est, non solum meum, quid sit vobis faciendum. si ille Romam modeste venturus est, recte in praesentia domi esse potestis; sin homo amens diripiendam urbem daturus est, vereor ut Dolabella ipse satis nobis prodesse possit. etiam illud metuo, ne iam intercludamur, ut, cum velitis, exire non liceat. reliquum est, quod ipsae optime considerabitis, vestri similes feminae sintne Romae. si enim non sunt, videndum est ut honeste vos esse possitis. quo modo quidem nunc se res habet, modo ut haec nobis loca tenere liceat, bellissime vel mecum vel in nostris praediis esse poteritis. etiam illud verendum est, ne brevi tempore fames in urbe sit. his de rebus velim cum Pomponio, cum Camillo, cum quibus vobis videbitur, consideretis, ad summam animo forti sitis. Labienus rem meliorem fecit; adiuvat etiam Piso, quod ab urbe discedit et sceleris condemnat generum suum.

Vos, meae carissimae animae, quam saepissime ad me scribite et vos quid agatis et quid istic agatur. Quintus pater et filius et Rufus vobis s. d.

Valete.

VIII Kal. Febr.[1] Minturnis.

---

[1] Quin(c)t. *(Rut.: del. Bengel)*

If you are well, we are well.

The decision as to what you should do is now yours, not mine only. If Caesar is going to come back to Rome in civilized fashion, you can safely stay at home for the present. But if in his madness he is going to give the city over to plunder, I am afraid that even Dolabella's protection may not be enough for us. I also have the fear that we may soon be cut off, so that when and if you want to leave you may not be able. There remains the question, on which you yourselves will be the best judges, whether other ladies in your position are staying in Rome. If they are not, you should consider whether *you* can do so without discredit. As things now stand, provided that we can hold this area, you can stay very nicely with me or at my little properties in the country. There is also the danger of a food shortage in Rome in the near future. I should like you to discuss these points with Pomponius and Camillus and any others you think proper, and, in fine, to keep stout hearts. Labienus[1] has improved the situation, and Piso[2] too helps by leaving Rome and branding his son-in-law as a criminal.

My dearest hearts, write to me as often as you can to tell me how you are and what is going on in Rome. Quintus senior and junior and Rufus send you their greetings.

Good-bye.

23 January, from Minturnae.

[1] Caesar's principal lieutenant, who went over to Pompey on the outbreak of war.

[2] L. Piso Caesoninus, Consul in 58, whose daughter Calpurnia was married to Caesar.

146 (XVI.12)

Scr. Capuae IV *Kal. Febr. an. 49*

TULLIUS S. D. TIRONI SUO

1   Quo in discrimine versetur salus mea et bonorum omnium atque universae rei publicae ex eo scire potes quod
domos nostras et patriam ipsam vel diripiendam vel in-
flammandam reliquimus. in eum locum res deducta est ut,
nisi qui deus vel casus aliquis subvenerit, salvi esse ne-
queamus.

2   Equidem, ut veni ad urbem, non destiti omnia et sentire et dicere et facere quae ad concordiam pertinerent.
sed mirus invaserat furor non solum improbis sed etiam iis
qui boni habentur, ut pugnare cuperent, me clamante nihil
esse bello civili miserius. itaque, cum Caesar amentia quadam raperetur et oblitus nominis atque honorum suorum
Ariminum, Pisaurum, Anconam, Arretium occupavisset,
urbem reliquimus, quam sapienter aut quam fortiter nihil
attinet disputari.

3   Quo quidem in casu simus vides. feruntur omnino
condiciones ab illo, ut Pompeius eat in Hispaniam, dilectus qui sunt habiti et praesidia nostra dimittantur; se ulte-
riorem Galliam Domitio, citeriorem Considio Noniano
(his enim obtigerunt) traditurum; ad consulatus petitio-
nem se venturum, neque se iam velle absente se rationem
haberi suam; se praesentem trinum nundinum petiturum.
accepimus condiciones, sed ita ut removeat praesidia ex iis
locis quae occupavit, ut sine metu de his ipsis condicioni-
4   bus Romae senatus haberi possit. id ille si fecerit, spes est

146 (XVI.12)
CICERO TO TIRO

Capua, 27 January 49

From Tullius to his dear Tiro greetings.

My existence and that of all honest men and the entire commonwealth hangs in the balance, as you may tell from the fact that we have left our homes and the mother city herself to plunder or burning. We have reached the point when we cannot survive unless some God or accident comes to our rescue.

From the day I arrived outside Rome all my views, words, and actions were unceasingly directed towards peace. But a strange madness was abroad. Not only the rascals but even those who pass for honest men were possessed with the lust of battle, while I cried aloud that civil war is the worst of calamities. Swept along by some spirit of folly, forgetting the name he bears and the honours he has won, Caesar seized Ariminum, Pisaurum, Ancona, and Arretium. So we abandoned Rome—how wisely or how courageously it is idle to argue.

You see our predicament. To be sure, he is offering terms: that Pompey go to Spain, that the levies already raised and the forces at our disposal be dismissed. On his side he will hand over Further Gaul to Domitius and Hither Gaul to Considius Nonianus, their appointed governors; he will come to Rome to stand for the Consulship, and no longer desires his candidature to be accepted *in absentia;* he will canvass for the period of three market days in person. We have accepted the terms, on condition that he withdraws his forces from the places he has occupied so that a meeting of the Senate may be called in Rome, free of

pacis, non honestae (leges enim imponuntur), sed quidvis
est melius quam sic esse ut sumus. sin autem ille suis
condicionibus stare noluerit, bellum paratum est, eius
modi tamen quod sustinere ille non possit, praesertim cum
a suis condicionibus ipse fugerit; tantum modo ut eum
intercludamus ne ad urbem possit accedere, quod spera-
bamus fieri posse. dilectus enim magnos habebamus puta-
bamusque illum metuere, si ad urbem ire coepisset, ne
Gallias amitteret, quas ambas habet inimicissimas praeter
Transpadanos, ex Hispaniaque sex legiones et magna auxi-
lia Afranio et Petreio ducibus habet a tergo. videtur, si
insaniet, posse opprimi, modo ut urbe salva. maximam
autem plagam accepit quod is qui summam auctoritatem
in illius exercitu habebat, T. Labienus, socius sceleris esse
noluit. reliquit illum et ⟨est⟩[1] nobiscum, multique idem
facturi esse dicuntur.

5   Ego adhuc orae maritimae praesum a Formiis. nullum
maius negotium suscipere volui, quo plus apud illum meae
litterae cohortationesque ad pacem valerent. sin autem
erit bellum, video me castris et certis legionibus praefutu-
rum. habeo etiam illam molestiam, quod Dolabella noster
apud Caesarem est.

       Haec tibi nota esse volui; quae cave ne te perturbent et
6   impediant valetudinem tuam. ego A. Varroni, quem cum
amantissimum mei cognovi tum etiam valde tui studiosum, diligentissime te commendavi, ut et valetudinis tuae
rationem haberet et navigationis et totum te susciperet ac

---

[1] (*R. Klotz*: post nobiscum ⌐)

---

[1] Cisalpine and Transalpine Gaul.
[2] Pompey's Legates.

duress, to discuss these same terms. If he complies, there is hope of peace, though not peace with honour, since the conditions are dictated; but anything is better than to be as we are. On the other hand, if he refuses to abide by his own terms, war is ready to hand. Caesar, however, will not be able to bear the brunt of it, especially having run away from his own terms. Only we must cut him off so that he cannot get to Rome, which we trust can be done. For we are raising levies on a large scale, and think he is afraid that if he advances on the capital he will lose the Gallic provinces. Both,[1] except for the Transpadanes, are thoroughly disaffected towards him, and he has six legions and large auxiliary forces to his rear in Spain, commanded by Afranius and Petreius.[2] If he does not come to his senses, it looks as though he can be crushed—let us only hope without harm to the capital. He has had a body blow in the defection of T. Labienus, the most distinguished of his officers; who has refused to be party to his criminal enterprise and joined us. Many are said to be about to follow Labienus' example.

I am still in command of the coast, which I exercise from Formiae. I did not wish to take a more important charge, in order that my letters and exhortations to peace may carry the greater weight with Caesar. But if war is to be, I envisage myself as commanding an army and specified legions. To add to my vexations, my son-in-law Dolabella is with Caesar.

I wanted you to be aware of these facts. Mind you don't let them upset you and hinder your recovery. I have very particularly recommended you to A. Varro, whom I know to be very fond of me and anxious to assist you, asking him to interest himself in your health and sailing arrangements

tueretur. quem omnia facturum confido; recepit enim et
mecum locutus est suavissime.

Tu, quoniam eo tempore mecum esse non potuisti quo
ego maxime operam et fidelitatem desideravi tuam, cave
festines aut committas ut aut aeger aut hieme naviges.
numquam sero te venisse putabo si salvus veneris. adhuc
neminem videram qui te postea vidisset quam M. Volusius, a quo tuas litteras accepi. quod non mirabar; neque
enim meas puto ad te litteras tanta hieme perferri. sed da
operam ut valeas et, si valebis, cum recte navigari poterit,
tum naviges. Cicero meus in Formiano erat, Terentia et
Tullia Romae.

Cura ut valeas.

IIII Kal. Febr. Capua.

147 (XVI.8)

Scr., ut vid., in Formiano in. Ian. an. 49

Q. CICERO TIRONI S. D.

1   Magnae nobis est sollicitudini valetudo tua. nam tametsi qui veniunt ἀκίνδυνα μὲν χρονιώτερα δὲ nuntiant,
tamen in magna consolatione ingens inest sollicitudo, si
diutius nobis ⟨a⟩futurus es, is cuius usum et suavitatem
desiderando sentimus. ac tamen,[1] quamquam videre te
tota cogitatione cupio, tamen te penitus rogo ne te tam
longae navigationi et viae per hiemem nisi bene firmum
2   committas neve naviges nisi explorate. vix in ipsis tectis et

[1] attamen *(Wes.)*

and in general to take you under his wing. I am sure he will do everything. He gave his word, and spoke to me very nicely.

Since you could not be with me when I most needed your services and loyalty, mind you do not hurry or be so foolish as make the voyage either as an invalid or in winter. I shall never think you have been too long in coming if you come safe and sound. I have not yet met anyone who had seen you later than M. Volusius, from whom I received your letter. That does not surprise me. I don't suppose that my letters either are getting through to you in the depth of winter. But do your best to get well, and once you *are* well and the voyage can be made safely, make it then. My son Marcus is at Formiae, Terentia and Tullia are in Rome.

Take care of your health.

27 January, from Capua.

147 (XVI.8)
Q. CICERO TO TIRO

Formiae, January 49 (?)

From Q. Cicero to Tiro greetings.

Your health makes us terribly anxious. Travellers report 'no danger, but it will take time,' which is a great consolation. Still it's a huge anxiety, if you are going to be away from us for long. Missing you brings home to us how useful and pleasant it is to have you. But though I long to see you with my every thought, I do ask you in all sincerity not to venture upon so long a journey by water and land in winter unless you are thoroughly strong, and not to take ship without careful preliminary enquiries. Cold is hard enough for

oppidis frigus infirma valetudine vitatur, nedum in mari et
via sit facile abesse ab iniuria temporis.

ψῦχος δὲ λεπτῷ χρωτὶ πολεμιώτατον,

inquit Euripides. cui tu quantum credas nescio; ego certe
singulos eius versus singula testimonia puto. effice, si me
diligis, ut valeas et ut ad nos firmus ac valens quam primum venias.

Ama nos et vale. Quintus filius tibi salutem dicit.

148 (VII.27)

Scr. an. 49 ante m. Apr.

M. CICERO S. D. T. FADIO[1]

1   Miror cur me accuses cum tibi id facere non liceat.
quod si liceret, tamen non debebas. 'ego enim te in consulatu observaram,' ais, et[2] fore ut te Caesar restituat: multa
tu quidem dicis, sed tibi nemo credit. tribun⟨at⟩um plebi
dicis te mea causa petisse: utinam semper esses tribunus!
intercessorem non quaereres. negas me audere quod sentiam dicere: quasi tibi, cum impudenter me rogares, parum fortiter responderim.

[1] S. D. GALLO *(SB)*
[2] et ais *(SB)*

---

[1] From one of the lost plays.
[1] From exile; cf. Letter 51.
[2] Latin *credit* means (a) 'believes,' and (b) 'lends money to.'
Fadius had apparently asked Cicero to stand surety and, on re-

an invalid to avoid in town houses; how much more difficult to escape the inclemency of the weather at sea or on the road! As Euripides says, 'Cold is a tender skin's worst enemy.'[1] How much trust you put in him I don't know, but *I* look upon every verse he wrote as an affidavit. Mind you get well, if you love me, and come back to us as soon as possible hale and hearty.

Love us and good-bye. Young Quintus sends you his love.

148 (VII.27)
CICERO TO T. FADIUS

Early 49

From M. Cicero to T. Fadius greetings.

I am surprised that you should reproach me, when you have no right to do so; but even, if you *had* the right, it would ill become you. You say you paid me many attentions when I was Consul, and that Caesar will restore you.[1] You say a great deal, but nobody gives you credit.[2] You say you stood for the Tribunate on my account. A pity you are not Tribune all the time, then you would not be looking for an intercessor![3] You say I don't dare to speak my mind—as though my answer to your impudent request smacked of timidity!

ceiving a negative answer, written again in terms which put Cicero in a rage. The harsh, offensive tone of this letter is unique in his correspondence.

3 I*ntercessor* means (a) 'one who (as Tribune) casts a veto,' and (b) 'surety.'

2   Haec tibi scripsi ut isto ipso in genere in quo aliquid
posse vis te nihil esse cognosceres. quod si humaniter mecum questus esses, libenter tibi me et facile purgassem;
non enim ingrata mihi sunt quae fecisti, sed quae scripsisti
molesta. me autem, propter quem ceteri liberi sunt, tibi
liberum non visum demiror. nam si falsa fuerunt quae tu
ad me, ut ais, detulisti, quid tibi ego debeo? si vera, tu es
optimus testis quid mihi populus Romanus debeat.

149 (VIII.15)

Scr. in itinere ad Liguriam c. VII Id. Mart. an. 49
CAELIUS CICERONI S.

1   Ecquando tu hominem ineptiorem quam tuum Cn.
Pompeium vidisti, qui tantas turbas, qui tam nugas esset,
commorit? ecquem autem Caesare nostro acriorem in rebus gerendis, eodem in victoria temperatiorem aut legisti
aut audisti? quid est? nunc tibi nostri milites, qui durissi-
mis et frigidissimis locis, taeterrima hieme, bellum ambu-
lando confecerunt, malis orbiculatis esse pasti videntur?
'quid? tam'[1] inquis 'gloriose omnia?' si[2] scias quam sollicitus sim, tum hanc meam gloriam, quae ad me nihil pertinet, derideas. quae tibi exponere nisi coram non possum,

---

[1] iam *(Man.)*
[2] omnia? ‹immo› si *Wes.*: ‹immo› si *Rut.*

---

[4] Evidently in connection with Catiline's conspiracy.
[1] Literally 'rounded apples,' a variety mentioned by Varro,
Columella, and others. Such things were served at dessert, not the

The above is just to let you see that even in the style in which you aspire to shine you are a total failure. If you had expostulated with me in civil fashion, I should willingly and easily have cleared myself. I am not ungrateful for what you did, but I *am* vexed at what you wrote. And I am much surprised that you take me, to whom my fellows owe their freedom, for no better than a slave. If the information[4] you say you gave me was false, what do I owe you? If it was true, you are in an excellent position to testify what the Roman People owes *me*.

149 (VIII.15)
CAELIUS RUFUS TO CICERO

En route to Liguria, ca. 9 March 49

From Caelius to Cicero greetings.

Have you ever seen a more egregious ass than your Cn. Pompeius? What a commotion he has created, and he such a fraud! And have you ever read or heard tell of a leader more energetic in action or more moderate in victory than our Caesar? And what about these troops of ours who have finished a war by the use of their legs, in the roughest and coldest country and the filthiest winter weather—do you think they feed on sugar plums?[1] 'What's all this brag?' you may say. If you only knew how I am beset with anxieties, you would find this bragging of mine, which has nothing to do with *me*, quite funny. I cannot explain to you what I mean otherwise than in person, and I hope this will shortly

kind of fare to interest tough soldiers (like Agesilaus of Sparta; see Plutarch's Life of him, 36).

idque celeriter fore spero. nam me, cum expulisset ex Italia Pompeium, constituit ad urbem vocare, id quod iam
existimo confectum, nisi si maluit Pompeius Brundisi cir-
2   cumsederi.[3] peream si minima causa est properandi isto
mihi quod te videre et omnia intima conferre discupio;
habeo autem quam multa. hui, vereor, quod solet fieri, ne
cum te videro omnia obliviscar.

Sed tamen, qu⟨odn⟩am[4] ob scelus iter mihi necessa-
rium retro ad Alpis versus incidit? ideo[5] quod Intimilii[6] in
armis sunt, neque de magna causa. Bellieni verna Demetrius,[7] qui ibi cum praesidio erat, Domitium quendam, no-
bilem illi, Caesaris hospitem, a contraria factione nummis
acceptis comprehendit et strangulavit; civitas ad arma iit.
eo nunc[8] ⟨cum⟩ *[9] cohortibus mihi per nivis eundum est.
'usque quaque' inquis 'se Domitii male dant.' vellem quidem Venere prognatus[10] tantum animi habuisset in vestro
Domitio quantum Psecade natus[11] in hoc habuit.

Ciceroni f. s. d.

3 -dere *(Rut.)*
4 tum quam*
5 adeo *(Rut.:* ⟨atque⟩ adeo *coni. SB)*
6 intimidi *(Mommsen)*
7 Bellienus verna Demetri *(C.F.Hermann, re non intellecta)*
8 num *(Man.)*
9 quattuor *suppl.* ⌐
10 Venerem propugnatus *(Vict.)*
11 ipsa *(ex* ipse?*)* cadenatus *(Man.)*

be possible—he has decided to call me to Rome when he has driven Pompey out of Italy. That business, I imagine, is already done, unless Pompey has preferred to stand siege in Brundisium. Hang me if my mortal impatience to see you and exchange all our most intimate thoughts is the least important reason for my hurry to be back! I have a great many such thoughts, but I'm terribly afraid that when I see you the usual thing will happen—I'll forget the lot!

Be that as it may, what have I ever done to deserve the bad luck of this compulsory journey back to the Alps? The Intimilii[2] are up in arms, for no very momentous reason: Demetrius, Bellienus' slave boy,[3] being stationed there with a detachment of troops, was bribed by the opposite party to seize and strangle one Domitius, a notable of the district and a host of Caesar's. The people rushed to arms. Now I have to trudge there through the snow with *[4] cohorts. You'll remark that the Domitii[5] are coming to grief all along the line. Well, I could wish our scion of Venus had shown as much spirit in dealing with *your* Domitius as Psecas'[6] offspring showed with this one!

Please give my regards to your son.

2 A people in Liguria.

3 The man was no doubt a freedman.

4 A number is missing.

5 An allusion to the capture of L. Domitius Ahenobarbus and his army at Corfinium. Caesar ('our scion of Venus,' the supposed ancestor of the Julian clan) let him go free.

6 Typical name for a slave woman (cf. Juvenal, 6.491).

150 (IV.1)

Scr. in Cumano c. x Kal. Mai. an. 49

M. CICERO S. D. SER. SULPICIO

1   C. Trebatius, familiaris meus, ad me scripsit te ex se quaesisse quibus in locis essem, molesteque te ferre quod me propter valetudinem tuam, cum ad urbem accessissem, non vidisses, et hoc tempore velle te mecum, si propius accessissem, de officio utriusque nostrum communicare.

Utinam, Servi, salvis rebus (sic enim est dicendum) colloqui potuissemus inter nos! profecto aliquid opis occidenti rei publicae tulissemus. cognoram enim iam absens te haec mala multo ante providentem defensorem pacis et in consulatu tuo et post consulatum fuisse. ego autem, cum consilium tuum probarem et idem ipse sentirem, nihil proficiebam. sero enim veneram, solus eram, rudis esse videbar in causa, incideram in hominum pugnandi cupidorum insanias. nunc, quoniam nihil iam videmur opitulari posse rei publicae, si quid est in quo nobismet ipsis consulere possimus, non ut aliquid ex pristino statu nostro retineamus sed ut quam honestissime lugeamus, nemo est omnium quicum potius mihi quam tecum communicandum putem. nec enim clarissimorum virorum, quorum similes esse debemus, exempla neque doctissimorum, quos semper coluisti, praecepta te fugiunt. atque ipse antea ad te scripsissem te frustra in senatum, sive potius in

---

[1] Cicero had stayed outside the old city boundary so as not to lose his *imperium* and so forfeit the hoped-for Triumph.

150 (IV.1)

CICERO TO SERVIUS SULPICIUS RUFUS

Cumae, ca. 21 April 49

M. Cicero to Ser. Sulpicius greetings.

My friend C. Trebatius has written informing me that you enquired of him as to my present whereabouts. He says you are sorry your health did not permit you to see me when I came to the neighbourhood of Rome,[1] and that you would like to take counsel with me at the present time, if I come nearer, on what both of us ought to do.

My dear Servius, if only we could have conferred together before the disaster (one has to use such words)! Surely we should have lent some succour to the foundering commonwealth. Even before my return I knew you to be a champion of peace both during and after your Consulship, foreseeing these calamities, as you did, long in advance. As for me, though I approved your policy and shared your views, it was no use. I arrived on the scene too late and stood alone, regarded as a newcomer to the situation, finding myself surrounded by an atmosphere of insensate bellicosity. Now that it no longer seems in our power to be of any assistance to the commonwealth, if there is any step we can take for our personal benefit (not with the object of retaining any part of our former status, but so as to mourn with what dignity we may), there is no man in the world with whom I should think it more appropriate to take counsel than yourself: You do not need to be reminded of the examples of famous men, whom we should resemble, or of the precepts of learned men, to whom you have always been devoted. Indeed I should myself have written to you earlier expressing the opinion that your attendance in

conventum senatorum, esse venturum, ni veritus essem ne eius animum offenderem qui a me ut te imitarer petebat. cui quidem ego, cum me rogaret ut adessem in senatu, eadem omnia quae a te de pace et de Hispaniis dicta sunt ostendi me esse dicturum.

2   Res vides quo modo se habeat: orbem terrarum imperiis distributis ardere bello, urbem sine legibus, sine iudiciis, sine iure, sine fide relictam direptioni et incendiis. itaque mihi venire in mentem nihil potest non modo quod sperem sed vix iam quod audeam optare. sin autem tibi, homini prudentissimo, videtur utile esse nos colloqui, quamquam longius etiam cogitabam ab urbe discedere, cuius iam etiam nomen invitus audio, tamen propius accedam; Trebatioque mandavi ut, si quid tu eum velles ad me mittere, ne recusaret, idque ut facias velim, aut, si quem tuorum fidelium voles, ad me mittas, ne aut tibi exire ex urbe necesse sit aut mihi accedere. ego tantum tibi tribuo quantum mihi fortasse adrogo, ut exploratum habeam quicquid nos communi sententia statuerimus id omnis homines probaturos.

Vale.

the Senate, or rather the meeting of Senators,[2] would serve no useful purpose, but that I was afraid of offending one who desired me to follow your example. When the person to whom I refer asked me to come to the Senate, I made it plain that I should say exactly what you have said on the subject of peace and the Spanish provinces.[3]

You see the situation. The whole world is ablaze with war, distributed into military commands: Rome lies abandoned to fire and plunder; statutes, courts, law, credit have ceased to exist. I cannot imagine anything to hope for, I can scarcely any longer imagine anything I dare to pray for. But if you in the fullness of your wisdom think it useful for us to confer, I will come nearer Rome, though I have it in mind to go still further away and hate to hear the very name of the city. I have asked Trebatius to be good enough to forward any communication you may wish to send me, and would request you to do this, or else, if you prefer, to send me some trustworthy person from your entourage. That way it may not be necessary for you to leave Rome or for me to go there. I feel well assured (in saying which I allow you no less than, perhaps presumptuously, I claim for myself) that whatever we decide by mutual consent will be universally approved.

Good-bye.

[2] Convened at the beginning of April 49, when Caesar returned to Rome. The Consuls and many other magistrates having left Italy with Pompey, Cicero considered the meetings to be irregular, even though the Senate could constitutionally be summoned by a Praetor in default of Consuls.

[3] Cicero's interview with Caesar on 28 March is described in *Letters to Atticus* 187 (IX.18).

151 (IV.2)

Scr. in Cumano III *vel prid. Kal. Mai. an. 49*

M. CICERO S. D. SER. SULPICIO

1   A. d. III Kal. Mai., cum essem in Cumano, accepi tuas
litteras; quibus lectis cognovi non satis prudenter fecisse
Philotimum, qui, cum abs te mandata haberet, ut scribis,
de omnibus rebus, ipse ad me non venisset, litteras tuas
misisset, quas intellexi breviores fuisse quod eum per-
laturum putasses. sed tamen, postquam tuas litteras legi,
Postumia tua me convenit et Servius noster. his placuit ut
tu in Cumanum venires, quod etiam mecum ut ad te scriberem egerunt.

2   Quod meum consilium exquiris, id est tale ut capere
facilius ipse possim quam alteri dare. quid enim est quod
audeam suadere tibi, homini summa auctoritate summaque prudentia? si quid rectissimum sit quaerimus, perspi-
cuum est; si quid maxime expediat, obscurum. sin ii sumus
qui profecto esse debemus, ut nihil arbitremur expedire
nisi quod rectum honestumque sit, non potest esse dubium quid faciendum nobis sit.

3   Quod existimas meam causam coniunctam esse cum
tua, certe similis in utroque nostrum, cum optime sentire-
mus, error fuit. nam omnia utriusque consilia ad concordiam spectaverunt; qua cum ipsi Caesari nihil esset utilius,
gratiam quoque nos inire ab eo defendenda pace arbitra-
bamur. ⟨quod⟩[1] quantum nos fefellerit et quem in locum

---

[1] *(SB)*

151 (IV.2)
CICERO TO SERVIUS SULPICIUS RUFUS

Cumae, 28 or 29 April 49

M. Cicero to Ser. Sulpicius greetings.

On 28 April I received your letter at my house near
Cumae. Having read it, I apprehend that Philotimus has
not acted very sensibly in forwarding the letter to me
instead of coming in person, when he had, as you say, a
message from you covering all points. I realize that your
letter would have been longer if you had not expected him
to carry it to its destination. However, after I read it, your
lady wife Postumia and our dear Servius[1] met me. They
thought you should come to Cumae, and urged me to write
to you to that effect.

You ask my advice. It is such as I can more easily take
myself than offer to another. What course could I venture
to recommend to one so respected and wise as yourself? If
we ask which is the most clearly right, the answer is obvious. If we ask which is the most expedient, it is doubtful.
But if we are the men we surely should be and judge nothing to be expedient except what is right and honourable,
there can be no question how we ought to act.

You judge that your situation and mine are allied, and it
is assuredly true that with the best intentions we both went
astray in much the same way. Both of us made concord the
sole object of our policy; and as nothing could have been
more to Caesar's own advantage, we expected actually to
earn his gratitude by defending peace. You see the extent
of our miscalculation, and the point to which the situa-

---

[1] Sulpicius' son.

res deducta sit vides. neque solum ea perspicis quae geruntur quaeque iam gesta sunt sed etiam qui cursus rerum,
qui exitus futurus sit. ergo aut probare oportet ea quae
fiunt aut interesse etiam si non probes; quorum altera mihi
4 turpis, altera etiam periculosa ratio videtur. restat ut disce-
dendum putem; in quo reliqua videtur esse deliberatio,
quod consilium in discessu, quae loca sequamur. omnino
cum miserior res numquam accidit tum ne deliberatio quidem difficilior. nihil enim constitui potest quod non incurrat in magnam aliquam difficultatem.

Tu, si videbitur, ita censeo facias ut, si habes iam statutum quid tibi agendum putes, in quo non sit coniunctum
consilium tuum cum meo, supersedeas hoc labore itineris.
sin autem est quod mecum communicare velis, ego te ex-
spectabo. tu, quod tuo commodo fiat, quam primum velim
venias, sicut intellexi et Servio et Postumiae placere.

Vale.

152 (V.19)

Scr. in Cumano c. III Kal. Mai. an. 49

CICERO RUFO

1   Etsi mihi numquam dubium fuit quin tibi essem carissimus, tamen cottidie magis id perspicio exstatque id quod
mihi ostenderas quibusdam litteris, hoc te studiosiorem in
me colendo fore quam in provincia fuisses (etsi meo iudi-

---

[2] The interview took place, but led to nothing; cf. *Letters to Atticus* 206 (X.14) and 207 (X.15).2.

tion has deteriorated. And you perceive not only the steps which are being, and have already been, taken but the future course and issue of affairs. So one must either approve current proceedings or live amongst them, even though one disapproves. The first plan seems to me dishonourable, the second dangerous as well. I am left to conclude that the right course is to go abroad. That would seem to leave two questions, what plan of departure to adopt and what part of the world to head for. To be sure there was never a sadder business, or a more difficult problem either. Every possible decision runs into some major difficulty.

As for yourself, the advice which I venture to offer is this: if you have already settled what you think you ought to do and your plan is not of a nature to fit in with mine, you should spare yourself this troublesome journey. If, on the other hand, you have something on which you wish to confer with me, I shall wait for you. I beg you will come as soon as you conveniently can; I gathered that both Servius and Postumia would like you to do so.[2]

Good-bye.

152 (V.19)
CICERO TO MESCINIUS RUFUS

Cumae, ca. 28 April 49

Cicero to Rufus.

Although I never doubted your warm regard for me, I see it every day more plainly. This is the fulfilment of the promise you made in one of your letters, that you would be more zealous in your attentions to me than you had been in Cilicia (not that in my judgement the solicitude you

cio nihil ad tuum provinciale officium addi potest) quo
liberius iudicium esse posset tuum. itaque me et superiores litterae tuae admodum delectaverunt, quibus et ex-
spectatum meum adventum abs te amanter videbam
et, cum aliter res cecidisset ac putasses, te meo consilio
magno opere esse laetatum, et ex his proximis litteris
magnum cepi fructum et iudici et offici tui: iudici, quod intellego te, id quod omnes fortes ac boni viri facere debent,
nihil putare utile esse nisi quod rectum honestumque sit;
offici, quod te mecum, quodcumque cepissem consili, pol-
liceris fore, quo neque mihi gratius neque, ut ego arbitror,
tibi honestius esse quicquam potest.

2   Mihi consilium captum iam diu est. de quo ad te non
quo celandus esses nihil scripsi antea sed quia communica-
tio consili tali tempore quasi quaedam admonitio videtur
esse offici, vel potius efflagitatio ad coeundam societatem
vel periculi vel laboris. cum vero ea tua sit voluntas, huma-
nitas, benevolentia erga me, libenter amplector talem animum, sed ita (non enim dimittam pudorem in rogando
meum): si feceris id quod ostendis, magnam habebo gratiam; si non feceris, ignoscam et alterum timori, alterum
mihi te negare non potuisse arbitrabor. est enim res profecto maxima. quid rectum sit apparet; quid expediat obscurum est, ita tamen ut, si nos ii sumus qui esse debemus,
id est studio digni ac litteris nostris, dubitare non possimus
quin ea maxime conducant quae sunt rectissima.

---

[1] To join the republicans overseas.

showed out there admits of any addition) in proportion as your choice in friendship could be more freely exercised. Your earlier letter gave me great pleasure. I found that you had waited for my coming, which was friendly of you, and that, when the matter turned out otherwise than you had expected, you were heartily glad of my advice. And from this last letter of yours I appreciate with satisfaction your sound principles and your sense of friendly obligation. As for the first, I perceive that you hold, as all brave and good men ought to hold, nothing expedient but what is right and honourable. As for the second, you promise that you will be my companion in whatever I decide to do; nothing can be more agreeable to me, nor, I fancy, more creditable to you.

My resolution[1] was taken long ago. If I did not write to you about it earlier, it was not that it seemed best to keep you in the dark, but because its communication at such a time has somewhat the air of a reminder of obligation, or rather of an urgent demand of the recipient to take a share in hazard and toil. But since your friendly disposition, kindness, and good will towards me are what they are, I gladly welcome such a spirit—but with one qualification (for I am not going to put aside my feeling of delicacy in making a request): if you carry out your promise, I shall be deeply grateful, and if you do not, I shall understand. I shall take it that you could not bring yourself to deny me (hence the promise), nor yet to deny your fears (hence the withdrawal). To be sure the matter is of great moment. The right course is plain, the expedient doubtful; and yet, if we are the men we ought to be, worthy of our studies and our books, we cannot doubt that whatever is most right is also most advantageous.

Qua ⟨r⟩e tu, si simul placebit, statim ad me venies; sin idem placebit atque eodem, nec continuo poterit, omnia tibi ut nota sint faciam. quicquid statueris, te mihi amicum, sin id quod opto, etiam amicissimum iudicabo.

153 (VIII.16)

Scr. in Liguria (?) c. xv Kal. Mai. an. 49

CAELIUS CICERONI SAL.

1   Exanimatus tuis litteris, quibus te nihil nisi triste cogitare ostendisti neque id quid esset perscripsisti neque non tamen quale esset quod cogitares aperuisti, has ad te ilico litteras scripsi.

    Per fortunas tuas, Cicero, per liberos te oro et obsecro ne quid gravius de salute et incolumitate tua consulas. nam deos hominesque amicitiamque nostram testificor me tibi praedixisse neque temere monuisse sed, postquam Caesarem convenerim sententiamque eius qualis futura esset parta victoria cognorim, te certiorem fecisse. si existimas eandem rationem fore Caesaris in dimittendis adversariis et condicionibus ferendis, erras. nihil nisi atrox et saevum cogitat atque etiam loquitur. iratus senatui exiit, his intercessionibus plane incitatus est; non mehercules erit deprecationi locus.

2   Qua re si tibi tu, si filius unicus, si domus, si spes tuae

---

[1] This letter is also included in the correspondence with Atticus (200A (X.9A)), to whom Cicero sent a copy.

[2] Not extant.   [3] The Tribune L. Metellus had been obstructing Caesar in the Senate.

So, if it is to be you and I together, you will join me immediately. If, however, you concur in my plan and destination, but cannot manage it straight away, I shall keep you fully informed. I shall count you as my friend, whatever you decide; but if you decide the way I would fain hope, as a friend indeed.

153 (VIII.16)
CAELIUS RUFUS TO CICERO

Liguria (?), ca. 16 April 49

From Caelius to Cicero greetings.[1]

Much agitated as I am by your letter,[2] in which you make it plain that you have none but gloomy ideas in mind but do not say in detail what they are, and yet do not conceal the general nature of your intentions, I am writing this letter to you straight away.

I beg and implore you, Cicero, in the name of your fortunes and your children, to take no step which will jeopardize your well-being and safety. I call Gods and men and our friendship to witness that I have told you how it will be, and that it is no casual warning I give; having met Caesar and found what his disposition is likely to be once victory is won, I am telling you what I know. If you suppose that Caesar will continue his policy of letting opponents go free and offering terms, you are making a mistake. He thinks and even talks of nothing but ruthless severity. He left Rome angry with the Senate, he is thoroughly incensed by these vetoes.[3] Believe me, the time for intercession will be past.

Accordingly, if you care for yourself, for your only son,

reliquae tibi carae sunt, si aliquid apud te nos, si vir optimus, gener tuus, valemus, quorum fortunam non debes
velle conturbare, ut eam causam in cuius victoria salus
nostra est odisse aut relinquere cogamur aut impiam cupiditatem contra salutem tuam habeamus * * *[1] denique
illud cogita, quod offensae fuerit in ista cunctatione te
subisse. nunc te contra victorem Caesarem facere quem
dubiis rebus laedere noluisti et ad eos fugatos accedere
quos resistentis sequi nolueris summae stultitiae est. vide
ne, dum pudet te parum optimatem esse, parum diligenter
3   quid optimum sit eligas. quod si totum tibi persuadere
non possum, saltem dum quid de Hispaniis agamus scitur
exspecta; quas tibi nuntio adventu Caesaris fore nostras.
quam isti spem habeant amissis Hispaniis nescio; quod
porro tuum consilium sit ad desperatos accedere non me
dius fidius reperio.

4   Hoc quod tu non dicendo mihi significasti Caesar au-
dierat ac, simul atque 'have' mihi dixit, statim quid de te
audisset exposuit. negavi me scire, sed tamen ab eo petii
ut ad te litteras mitteret quibus maxime ad remanendum
commoveri posses. me secum in Hispaniam ducit; nam
nisi ita faceret, ego, prius quam ad urbem accederem, ubicumque esses, ad te percurrissem et hoc a te praesens
contendissem atque omni vi te retinuissem.

5   Etiam atque etiam, Cicero, cogita ne te tuosque omnis
funditus evertas, ne te sciens prudensque eo demittas
unde exitum vides nullum esse. quod si te aut voces opti-

---

[1] haec omnia etiam atque etiam cogitabimus *vel. sim. sup-
plenda coni. SB,* noli committere *supra post* conturbare *Lehmann*

for your household, for your remaining hopes, if I and your excellent son-in-law have any influence with you, whose careers you surely do not wish to ruin by forcing us to hate or abandon the cause with which our welfare is bound up or else to harbour an undutiful wish contrary to *your* welfare * * *. Finally, consider that any odium which may attach to your hesitancy has already been incurred. When Caesar's prospects were doubtful, you were unwilling to harm him; to go against him now, in his hour of victory, and to join a routed party which you did not choose to follow when they were fighting back, is the acme of folly. Don't be so much afraid of failing the 'right' side as to think too little about making the right choice. But if I cannot persuade you altogether, do at least wait until it is known how things go with us in Spain. You may take my word for it that these provinces will be ours as soon as Caesar arrives. What hope your friends will have with Spain lost I do not know, and what sense it makes for you to join a hopeless party on my honour I cannot imagine.

What you conveyed to me without putting it into words Caesar had heard already. He scarcely said good day to me before he told me what he had heard about you. I professed ignorance, but asked him all the same to write to you in terms best adapted to induce you not to leave. He is taking me with him to Spain. Otherwise, before returning to Rome, I should have hurried to you wherever you were, and urged my plea in person, and held you back with all my might.

Think, Cicero, again and yet again before you bring utter ruin on yourself and your family, before you plunge with your eyes wide open into a situation from which you see there is no escape. If, however, you are worried by what

107

matium commovent aut non nullorum hominum insolentiam et iactationem ferre non potes, eligas censeo aliquod
oppidum vacuum a bello dum haec decernuntur; quae iam
erunt confecta. id si feceris, et ego te sapienter fecisse
iudicabo et Caesarem non offendes.

154 (II.16)

Scr. in Cumano VI *vel* V *Non. Mai. an. 49*

M. CICERO IMP. S. D. M. CAELIO

1   Magno dolore me adfecissent tuae litterae nisi iam et
ratio ipsa depulisset omnis molestias et diuturna desperatione rerum obduruisset animus ad dolorem novum. sed
tamen qua re acciderit ut ex meis superioribus litteris id
suspicarere quod scribis nescio. quid enim in illis fuit praeter querelam temporum, quae non meum animum magis
sollicitum habere⟨n⟩t[1] quam tuum? nam non eam cognovi
aciem ingeni tui quod ipse videam te id ut non putem
videre. illud miror, adduci potuisse te, qui me penitus
nosse deberes, ut existimares aut me tam improvidum qui
ab excitata fortuna ad inclinatam et prope iacentem descis-
cerem aut tam inconstantem ut collectam gratiam floren-
tissimi hominis effunderem a meque ipse deficerem et,
quod initio semperque fugi, civili bello interessem.

2   Quod est igitur meum triste consilium? ut discederem
fortasse in aliquas solitudines. nosti enim non modo sto-

---

[1] (*Calderius*: habent *Man.*)

the optimates may be saying, or if you find the arrogance and bounce of certain people too much for you, my advice is to choose some town well away from the war while these issues are deciding. It will not be long before they are settled. If you do that, I shall judge you to have acted wisely and you will not offend Caesar.

154 (II.16)
CICERO TO CAELIUS RUFUS

Cumae, 2 or 3 May 49

From M. Cicero, Imperator, to M. Caelius, greetings.

Your letter would have given me great distress, were it not that by now the power of reason has dispelled all vexations and inveterate despair of the world has hardened my mind against new sorrows. All the same, I do not know how you came to form the suspicion of which you write from my last letter. What did that contain apart from complaint against the times we live in? And they surely weighed no less upon your mind than upon mine. I have not formed so poor an opinion of your intellectual acumen as to suppose you blind to what I see myself. But I *am* surprised that you, who ought to know me thoroughly, could have been led to believe me so improvident as to desert the rising sun for the setting and almost set, or so unstable as to throw away the hard-won favour of an eminently successful personage, to turn false to myself, and to take part in civil war, a course which I have always shunned from the very first.

Well then, what is this 'melancholy' project of mine? To withdraw, it may be, to some place of solitude. You must know how the unseemly behaviour of insolent upstarts

machi mei, cuius tu similem quondam habebas, sed etiam
oculorum in hominum insolentium indignitate fastidium.
accedit etiam molesta haec pompa lictorum meorum no-
menque imperi quo appellor. eo si onere carerem, quamvis parvis Italiae latebris contentus essem. sed incurrit
haec nostra laurus non solum in oculos sed iam etiam in vo-
culas malevolorum. quod cum ita esset, nil tamen umquam
de profectione nisi vobis approbantibus cogitavi. sed mea
praediola tibi nota sunt; in his mihi necesse est esse, ne
amicis molestus sim. quod autem in maritimis facillime
sum, moveo non nullis suspicionem velle me navigare.
quod tamen fortasse non nollem si possem ad otium. nam
ad bellum quidem, qui convenit? praesertim contra eum
cui spero me satis fecisse ab eo cui iam satis fieri nullo
modo potest.

3   Deinde sententiam meam tu facillime perspicere potuisti iam ab illo tempore cum in Cumanum mihi obviam
venisti. non enim te celavi sermonem T. Ampi. vidisti
quam abhorrerem ab urbe relinquenda, cum audissem.
nonne tibi adfirmavi quidvis me potius perpessurum quam
ex Italia ad bellum civile exiturum? quid ergo accidit cur
consilium mutarem? nonne omnia potius ut in sententia
permanerem? credas hoc mihi velim, quod puto te existimare, me ex his miseriis nihil aliud quaerere nisi ut homines aliquando intellegant me nihil maluisse quam pacem,
ea desperata nihil tam fugisse quam arma civilia. huius
me constantiae puto fore ut numquam paeniteat. etenim
memini in hoc genere gloriari solitum esse familiarem

---

[1] Imperator.

[2] On the lictors' fasces, in token of victory.

irritates my spleen (you used to have a similar organ), even my eyes. Then there is this tiresome parade of my lictors and the military title[1] by which I am addressed. If I could shed this load, I should be content with a hiding place in Italy, however exiguous. But these laurels[2] of mine obtrude themselves upon the eyes of my ill-wishers, even on their petty little tongues. And yet I never entertained a thought of leaving without your and your associates' approval. But you know my little properties. I must stay on them, so as not to be a nuisance to my friends. The fact that I find it most convenient to stay on those which are near the coast makes some people suspect that I want to take ship. After all, perhaps I should not mind doing that if I could sail to peace. As for war, the idea is incongruous—especially to fight against one who I trust is satisfied with my conduct, on the side of one who cannot now be satisfied whatever I do.

Furthermore, you have been in a particularly good position to see into my mind ever since you visited me at Cumae. I did not conceal from you what T. Ampius had said. You saw how much I disliked the idea of abandoning the capital after I heard of it. Did I not assure you that I would put up with anything rather than leave Italy to join in civil war? Well then, what has occurred to change my decision? Has not everything rather tended to confirm me in my views? I hope you will believe my assurance, which I think conforms to your own opinion, that I seek nothing from this unhappy situation except to convince the world at last that peace was my chief desire and that, since all hope of peace disappeared, civil war has been my chief aversion. I do not think I shall ever wish to change this resolution. I remember how our old friend Q. Hortensius

111

nostrum Q. Hortensium, quod numquam bello civili inter-
fuisset. hoc nostra laus erit illustrior quod illi tribuebatur
ignaviae, de nobis id existimari posse non arbitror.

4   Nec me ista terrent quae mihi a te ad timorem fid⟨e-
l⟩issime atque amantissime proponuntur. nulla est enim
acerbitas quae non omnibus hac orbis terrarum perturba-
tione impendere videatur. quam quidem ego a re publica
meis privatis et domesticis incommodis libentissime, vel
istis ipsis quae tu me mones ut caveam, redemissem. filio
5 meo, quem tibi carum esse gaudeo, si erit ulla res publica,
satis amplum patrimonium relinquam in memoria nominis
mei; sin autem nulla erit, nihil accidet ei separatim a
reliquis civibus. nam quod rogas ut respiciam generum
meum, adulescentem optimum mihique carissimum, an
dubitas, qui[2] scias quanti cum illum tum vero Tulliam
meam faciam, quin ea me cura vehementissime sollicitet
et eo magis quod in communibus miseriis hac tamen ob-
lectabar specula, Dolabellam meum, vel potius nostrum,
fore ab iis molestiis quas liberalitate sua contraxerat liberum? velim quaeras quos ille dies sustinuerit in urbe dum
fuit, quam acerbos sibi, quam mihimet[3] ipsi socero non
honestos.

6   Itaque neque ego hunc Hispaniensem casum exspecto,
de quo mihi exploratum est ita esse ut tu scribis, neque
quicquam astute cogito. si quando erit civitas, erit profecto
nobis locus; sin autem non erit, in easdem solitudines tu
ipse, ut arbitror, venies in quibus nos consedisse audies.

[2] quin (*Or.*)
[3] mihi fuit (*Or.*)

used to plume himself in this connection, because he had never taken part in a civil war. Mine will be the brighter glory in that *his* conduct was put down to lack of spirit, whereas I do not think the same can be thought of me.

Nor am I alarmed by the bogies which you, in all loyalty and affection, bring out to frighten me. In this worldwide commotion every sort of distress can be seen hanging over every head. For my part, I should have been only too glad to have saved the country from this fate at the cost of private and domestic misfortunes of my own, even those of which you warn me to beware. I am glad you care for my son. If a free constitution survives in any form, I shall leave him a sufficient inheritance in the memory of my name. If there is to be none, nothing will happen to him outside the general lot of his countrymen. You also ask me to think of my son-in-law. He is a fine young man and very dear to me. Knowing as you do my affection for him, and still more for my Tullia, can you doubt that I am most keenly concerned on his behalf?—all the more so because I was flattering myself with one ray of hope amidst the general misery, that my dear Dolabella (*our* dear Dolabella, I should say) would free himself from the difficulties in which his open-handed ways had involved him. You should inform yourself what sort of days he went through while he was in Rome, how painful to himself and how embarrassing even for me as his father-in-law.

Accordingly, I am not waiting for the outcome of this Spanish affair, which I am sure is going exactly as you say, and I am making no shrewd calculations. If there is to be a civic community, one day, there will presumably be a place in it for me. If not, I expect you yourself will come and join me in the lonely retreat in which you will hear that I have

sed ego fortasse vaticinor et haec omnia meliores habebunt exitus. recordor enim desperationes eorum qui senes erant adulescente me. eos ego fortasse nunc imitor et utor aetatis vitio. velim ita sit; sed tamen.

7   Togam praetextam texi Oppio puto te audisse; nam Curtius noster dibaphum cogitat, sed eum infector moratur. hoc aspersi ut scires me tamen in stomacho solere ridere.

⟨De⟩ Dolabella quod scripsi suadeo videas tamquam si tua res agatur.

Extremum illud erit: nos nihil turbulenter, nihil temere faciemus. te tamen oramus, quibuscumque erimus in terris, ut nos liberosque nostros ita tueare ut amicitia nostra et tua fides postulabit.

155 (XIV.7)

Scr. in portu Caietano nave conscensa VII *Id. Iun. an.* 49

TULLIUS TERENTIAE SUAE S. P.

1   Omnis molestias et sollicitudines quibus et te miserrimam habui, id quod mihi molestissimum est, et Tulliolam, quae nobis nostra vita dulcior est, deposui et eieci. quid causae autem fuerit postridie intellexi quam a vobis discessi. χολὴν ἄκρατον noctu eieci. statim ita sum levatus ut mihi deus aliquis medicinam fecisse videatur. cui

---

³ The purple-bordered gown *(toga praetexta)* was worn by, among others, members of the four principal priestly colleges. One of these, the Augurs, also wore a distinctive gown, the *trabea,* of purple and yellow. Oppius and Curtius Postumus were friends

settled down. But perhaps I am just a prophet of woe and all this will have a happier ending. I remember how despairingly old men talked when I was young. Perhaps I am doing as they did and indulging the weakness of my age. I wish it may be so; but I doubt it.

I expect you have heard that Oppius' purple-bordered gown is a-weaving. Our friend Curtius has a double-dyed one in mind, but the dyer is keeping him waiting.[3] There's a pinch of seasoning, just to show that I like to laugh even when I am exasperated.

I recommend you to pay attention to what I have written about Dolabella as though it were your own affair.

Now this is my final word: I shall do nothing wildly or hastily. All the same, I beg you to stand by me and my children, in whatever part of the world we may be, as our friendship and your honour shall require.

155 (XIV.7)
CICERO TO TERENTIA

Aboard ship, Caieta harbour, 7 June 49

From Tullius to his dear Terentia best greetings.

All the miseries and cares with which I plagued you to desperation (and very sorry I am for it) and Tulliola too, who is sweeter to me than my life, are dismissed and ejected. I understood what lay behind them the day after our parting. I threw up pure bile during the night, and felt an instantaneous relief as though a God had cured me. To

of Caesar ('the dyer'), and apparently expecting priestly office as indicated.

quidem tu deo, quem ad modum soles, pie et caste satis facies [id est Apollini et Aesculapio].[1]

2   Navem spero nos valde bonam habere. in eam simul atque conscendi, haec scripsi. deinde conscribam ad nostros familiaris multas epistulas, quibus te et Tulliolam nostram diligentissime commendabo. cohortarer vos quo animo fortiores essetis nisi vos fortiores cognossem quam quemquam virum. et tamen eius modi spero negotia esse ut et vos istic commodissime sperem esse et me aliquando
3   cum similibus nostri rem publicam defensuros. tu primum valetudinem tuam velim cures; deinde, si tibi videbitur, villis iis utere quae longissime aberunt a militibus. fundo Arpinati bene poteris uti cum familia urbana si annona carior fuerit.

Cicero bellissimus tibi salutem plurimam dicit. etiam atque etiam vale.

D. VII Id. Iun.

156 (VIII.17)

Scr. Romae fort. ex. m. Ian. 48

CAELIUS CICERONI S.

1   Ergo me potius in Hispania fuisse tum quam Formi‹i›s cum tu profectus es ad Pompeium! quod utinam aut Appius Claudius in ‹hac parte fuisset aut in›[1] ista parte C. Curio, cuius amicitia me paulatim in hanc per‹di›tam[2] causam imposuit! nam mihi sentio bonam mentem iracundia et amore ablatam. tu [tu] porro, cum ad te proficiscens

----

[1] *(Man.)*   [1] *(R. Klotz)*   [2] portam *(Man.)*

that God you will make due acknowledgement in piety and purity after your custom.

I trust we have a very good ship—I am writing this directly after coming aboard. I shall next write many letters to our friends, commending you and our Tulliola most earnestly to their care. I should give you words of encouragement to make you both braver if I had not found you braver than any man. And after all, I trust things are now in better train. You, I hope, will be as well off as possible where you are, and I shall at last be fighting for the commonwealth alongside my peers. First and foremost, I want you to take care of your health. Second, if you agree, please use the country houses which will be farthest away from army units. The farm at Arpinum with the servants we have in town will be a good place for you if food prices go up.

Darling Marcus sends you his best love. Once again good-bye.

Dispatched 7 June.

156 (VIII.17)
CAELIUS RUFUS TO CICERO

Rome, end of January (?) 48

From Caelius to Cicero greetings.

To think then that I was in Spain instead of at Formiae when you left to join Pompey! If only Appius Claudius had been on our side or C. Curio on yours! It was my friendship with him that little by little landed me in this god-forsaken camp. I realize now that pique and affection robbed me of my good sense. And then, you, when I visited you that

Ariminum noctu venissem, dum mihi pacis mandata das
ad Caesarem et mirificum civem agis, amici officium ne-
glexisti neque mi consuluisti. neque haec dico quod
diffidam huic causae, sed, crede mihi, perire satius est
quam hos videre.

2   Quod si timor vestrae crudelitatis non esset, eiecti iam
pridem hinc essemus. nam hic nunc praeter faeneratores
paucos nec homo nec ordo quisquam est nisi [est] Pom-
peianus. equidem iam effeci ut maxime plebs et, qui antea
noster fuit, populus vester esset. 'cur hoc?' inquis. immo
reliqua exspectate;[3] vos invitos vincere coegero. †arrunta-
num me Catonem†.[4] vos dormitis nec haec adhuc mihi
videmini intellegere, qua nos pateamus et qua<m> simus
imbecilli. atque hoc nullius praemi spe faciam sed, quod
apud me plurimum solet valere, doloris atque indignitatis
causa.

    Quid istic facitis? proelium exspectatis, quod firmissi-
mum hac?[5] vestras copias non novi; nostri valde depugnare
et facile algere et esurire consuerunt.

---

[3] expectant (*Or.*)
[4] arridebunt tamen mi Catones *coni. SB, alii alia*
[5] haec (*Becher*)

night as I was leaving for Ariminum[1] and you gave me a peace message for Caesar, and played your fine patriotic role—you neglected the duty of a friend, you did not think of me! I don't say all this because I doubt our party's success. But, believe me, death is better than the spectacle of these people.

But for the fear of your party's ferocity we should have been thrown out of here long ago, for apart from a few capitalists there's not a man or a class here that is not for Pompey. Thanks to me, the lower classes especially, and the general public, which used to be on our side, are now on yours.[2] You ask why. No, you and your friends must wait and see. I'll make you win in spite of yourselves. Cato and company will be smiling on me yet! You folk are fast asleep. You don't seem to me to understand conditions over here as yet—where we are vulnerable, how weak we are. And I shall not be doing this in the hope of any reward, but from what is apt to be the most powerful motive with me— indignation and outrage.

What are you and your friends doing over there? Waiting for a battle? There lies Caesar's *forte*. I don't know about your army, but our fellows are desperate fighters and accustomed to take cold and hunger in their day's work.

---

[1] On 7 January, along with Curio and the Tribunes Mark Antony and Q. Cassius. This is the only record of Caelius' interview with Cicero.   [2] As Praetor Caelius had started an agitation for the relief of debtors. *Plebs et populus* here seems to be an amalgamation with no clear distinction between the two components; see my Commentary, adding Manilius 5.737 *populumque equiti populoque subire / vulgus iners,* where *vulgus* evidently includes noncitizens and slaves.

157 (IX.9)

Scr. in castris Caesaris ante Dyrrachium m. Mai., ut vid., an. 48

DOLABELLA S. D. CICERONI

1   S. v. g.; v. et Tullia nostra recte v. Terentia minus belle habuit, sed certum scio iam convaluisse eam. praeterea rectissime sunt apud te omnia.

Etsi nullo tempore in suspicionem tibi debui venire partium causa potius quam tua tibi suadere ut te aut cum Caesare nobiscumque coniungeres aut certe in otium referres, praecipue nunc, iam inclinata victoria, ne possum quidem in ullam aliam incidere opinionem nisi in eam in[1] qua scilicet tibi suadere videar quod pie tacere non possim. tu autem, mi Cicero, sic haec accipies ut, sive probabuntur tibi sive non probabuntur, ab optimo certe animo ac deditissimo tibi et cogitata et scripta esse iudices.

2   Animadvertis Cn. Pompeium nec nominis sui nec rerum gestarum gloria neque etiam regum ac nationum clientelis, quas ostentare crebro solebat, esse tutum, et hoc etiam quod infimo cuique contigit illi non posse contingere, ut honeste effugere possit, pulso Italia, amissis Hispaniis, capto exercitu veterano, circumvallato nunc denique, quod nescio an nulli umquam nostro acciderit imperatori. quam ob rem quid aut ille sperare possit aut ⟨tu illi prodesse⟩[2] tu animadverte pro tua prudentia; sic

[1] *del. Wes.*
[2] *(coni. Watt, auct. SB, qui nos timere)*

157 (IX.9)
DOLABELLA TO CICERO

Caesar's camp near Dyrrachium, May (?) 48

From Dolabella to Cicero greetings.

If you are well I am glad. I myself am well and so is our Tullia. Terentia has been rather out of sorts, but I know for certain that she has now recovered. Otherwise all your domestic affairs are in excellent shape.

You did me an injustice if at any time you suspected that in advising you to throw in your lot with Caesar and with me, or at least to retire into private life, I was thinking of party interests rather than of yours. But now, when the scales are coming down on our side, I imagine that only one thing can possibly be thought of me, namely, that I am proffering advice to you which it would be contrary to my duty as your son-in-law to withhold. On your side, my dear Cicero, you must take what follows, whether it meets with your approval or not, in the persuasion that I have thought and written it out of the most sincere loyalty and devotion to yourself.

You see Cn. Pompeius' situation. Neither the glory of his name and past nor yet the kings and nations of whose dependence he used so often to boast can protect him. Even the door of an honourable retreat, which humble folk find open, is closed to him. Driven out of Italy, Spain lost, his veteran army taken prisoner, he is now to crown all blockaded in his camp, a humiliation which I fancy has never previously befallen a Roman general. Do therefore, as a man of sense, consider what he can have to hope or what good you can do him; so you will find it easiest to take the decision most expedient for you. One thing I beg of

121

enim facillime quod tibi utilissimum erit consili capies. illud autem ⟨a⟩ te peto, ut, si iam ille evitaverit hoc periculum et se abdiderit in classem, tu tuis rebus consulas et aliquando tibi potius quam cuivis sis amicus. satis factum est iam a te vel officio vel familiaritati, satis factum etiam parti-
3 bus et ei rei publicae quam tu probabas. reliquum est, ubi nunc est res publica, ibi simus potius quam, dum illam veterem sequamur, simus in nulla.

Qua re velim, mi iucundissime Cicero, si forte Pompeius pulsus his quoque locis rursus alias regiones petere cogatur, ut tu te vel Athenas vel in quamvis quietam recipias civitatem. quod si eris facturus, velim mihi scribas, ut ego, si ullo modo potero, ad te advolem. quaecumque de tua dignitate ab imperatore erunt impetranda, qua est humanitate Caesar, facillimum erit ab eo tibi ipsi impetrare, et meas tamen preces apud eum non minimum auctoritatis habituras puto.

Erit tuae quoque fidei et humanitatis curare ut is tabellarius quem ad te misi reverti possit ad me et a te mihi litteras referat.

158 (XIV.6)

Scr. in Pompeii castris, ut vid., Id. Quint. an. 48
SUIS S. D.

Nec saepe est cui litteras demus nec rem habemus ullam quam scribere velimus. ex tuis litteris quas proxime accepi cognovi praedium nullum venire potuisse. qua re

you; if he does manage to escape from his present dangerous position and takes refuge with his fleet, consult your
own best interests and at long last be your own friend
rather than anybody else's. You have done enough for
obligation and friendship; you have done enough for your
party too and the form of commonwealth of which you
approved. It is time now to take our stand where the
commonwealth actually is rather than, by following after
its old image, to find ourselves in a political vacuum.

Therefore, my most delightful Cicero, if it turns out
that Pompey is driven from this area too and forced to seek
yet other regions of the earth, I hope you will retire to
Athens or to any peaceful community you please. If you
decide to do that, please write and tell me, so that if I possibly can I may hasten to your side. Any concessions that you
need from the Commander-in-Chief to safeguard your
dignity you will yourself obtain with the greatest ease from
so kindly a man as Caesar; but I believe that *my* petitions
will carry more than negligible weight with him.

I trust to your honour and kindness to see that the
courier I am sending you is able to return to me and brings
a letter from you.

158 (XIV.6)
CICERO TO TERENTIA

Pompey's camp (?), 15 July 48

To my family, greetings.

It is not often that I have anyone to take a letter, nor
have I anything I want to write about. From the last letter I
received from you I learned that it was impossible to sell

videatis velim quo modo satis fiat ei cui scitis me satis fieri
velle. quod nostra tibi gratias agit, id ego non miror, te
mereri ut ea tibi merito tuo gratias agere possit. Pollicem,
si adhuc non est profectus, quam primum fac extrudas.

Cura ut valeas.

Id. Quint.

159 (XIV.12)

Scr. Bundisii prid. Non. Nov. an. 48

TULLIUS TERENTIAE SUAE S. D.

Quod nos in Italiam salvos venisse gaudes, perpetuo
gaudeas velim. sed perturbati dolore animi magnisque
⟨meorum⟩[1] iniuriis metuo ne id consili ceperimus quod
non facile explicare possimus. qua re, quantum potes,
adiuva; quid autem possis mihi in mentem non venit. in
viam quod te des hoc tempore nihil est. et longum est iter
et non tutum; et non video quid prodesse possis si veneris.

Vale.

D. prid. Non. Nov. Brundisio.

[1] *(SB)*

124

any property. So I shall be grateful if you and the others will consider how to meet the claims of the person[1] whose claims you know I want met. As to what you say about our girl thanking you, I am not surprised that you should give her good reason to do that. If Pollex has not yet left, please pack him off as soon as possible.

Take care of your health.

Ides of July.

159 (XIV.12)
CICERO TO TERENTIA

Brundisium, 4 November 48

From Tullius to his dear Terentia greetings.

I hope your joy at our safe arrival in Italy may be a lasting one. But distracted as I was by my unhappiness and the cruel ill treatment of my family, I am afraid I may have taken a road with no easy outcome. So help me as far as you can—though what you can do I cannot imagine. There is no reason for you to leave home at present. It is a long, unsafe journey, and I do not see what good you can do if you come.

Good-bye.

Dispatched 4 November from Brundisium.

[1] Dolabella, to whom money was due for Tullia's dowry; cf. *Letters to Atticus* 212 (XI.2).2.

160 (XIV.19)

Scr. Brundisii IV *Kal. Dec. an. 48*

TULLIUS TERENTIAE SUAE S. D.

In maximis meis doloribus excruciat me valetudo Tulliae nostrae, de qua nihil est quod ad te plura scribam; tibi
enim aeque magnae curae esse certo scio. quod me propius vultis accedere, video ita esse faciendum et iam ante
fecissem, sed me multa impediverunt, quae ne nunc quidem expedita sunt. sed a Pomponio exspecto litteras, quas
ad me quam primum perferendas cures velim.

Da operam ut valeas.

161 (XIV.9)

Scr. Brundisii a. d. XIV *Kal. Ian., ut vid., an. 48*

TULLIUS TERENTIAE SUAE S. P.

Ad ceteras meas miserias accessit dolor et de Dolabellae valetudine et de Tulliae. omnino de omnibus rebus
nec quid consili capiam nec quid faciam scio. tu velim
tuam et Tulliae valetudinem cures.

Vale.

160 (XIV.19)
CICERO TO TERENTIA

Brundisium, 27 November 48

From Tullius to his dear Terentia greetings.

In my own deep distresses our Tullia's illness is an agony to me. There is no need for me to write any more to you on the subject, for I am sure that you are no less gravely concerned. As for your joint wish that I should come nearer Rome, I see that I ought to do so; and I should have done so already, but have been held up by various obstacles which even now have not been cleared. However, I am expecting a letter from Pomponius, and shall be grateful if you will see that it is forwarded as quickly as possible.

Take care of your health.

161 (XIV.9)
CICERO TO TERENTIA

Brundisium, 17 (?) December 48

Tullius to his dear Terentia best greetings.

In addition to my other distresses I am now worried about Dolabella's and Tullia's illnesses. In general, I just don't know what plans to make or what to do about anything. I hope you will take care of your own health and Tullia's.

Good-bye.

162 (XIV.17)

Scr. Brundisii fort. VIII *Kal. Ian. an. 48*

TULLIUS TERENTIAE SUAE S. D.

S. v. b.; e. v.

Si quid haberem quod ad te scriberem, facerem id et pluribus verbis et saepius. nunc, quae sint negotia vides. ego autem quo modo sim adfectus ex Lepta et Trebatio poteris cognoscere. tu fac ut tuam et Tulliae valetudinem cures.

Vale.

163 (XIV.16)

Scr. Brundisii prid. Non. Ian. an. 47

TULLIUS TERENTIAE SUAE S. D.

S. v. b.; e. v.

Etsi eius modi tempora nostra sunt ut nihil habeam quod aut a te litterarum exspectem aut ipse ad te scribam, tamen nescio quo modo et ipse vestras litteras exspecto et scribo ad vos cum habeo qui ferat.

Volumnia debuit in te officiosior esse quam fuit et id ipsum quod fecit potuit diligentius facere et cautius. quamquam alia sunt quae magis curemus magisque doleamus; quae me ita conficiunt ut ii voluerunt qui me de mea sententia detruserunt.

Cura ut valeas. Vale.

Prid. Non. Ian.

162 (XIV.17)
CICERO TO TERENTIA

Brundisium, 23 (?) December 48

From Tullius to his dear Terentia greetings.

I hope you are well, as I am.

I should write to you at greater length and more often if I had anything to say. As it is, you see how matters stand. Of my own sorry state Lepta and Trebatius will tell you. Be sure to take care of your health and Tullia's.

Good-bye.

163 (XIV.16)
CICERO TO TERENTIA

Brundisium, 4 January 47

From Tullius to his dear Terentia greetings.

I hope you are well, as I am.

In my present circumstances I have no reason to expect anything in the way of a letter from you or to write to you myself. And yet somehow I do expect letters from home and write when I have a bearer.

Volumnia[1] ought to have been more ready to oblige you than she was; and what she did do might have been done with more care and circumspection. However, we have more important matters to occupy and vex us. They are overwhelming me, as was the purpose of those who forced me away from my original intention.

Take care of your health. Good-bye.

4 January.

---

[1] Probably Volumnia Cytheris, actress and mistress of Mark Antony; cf. Letter 197.2.

164 (XIV.8)

Scr. Brundisii IV *Non. Iun. an. 47*

TULLIUS TERENTIAE SUAE S.

Si vales, bene est; ego valeo.

Valetudinem tuam velim cures diligentissime. nam mihi et scriptum et nuntiatum est te in febrim subito incidisse. quod celeriter me fecisti de Caesaris litteris certiorem, fecisti mihi gratum. item posthac, si quid opus erit, si quid acciderit novi, facies ut sciam

Cura ut valeas. Vale.

D. IIII Non. Iun.

165 (XIV.21)

Scr. Brundisii c. III *Non. Iun. an. 47*

TULLIUS TERENTIAE SUAE S. D.

S. v. b.; e. v.

Da operam ut convalescas; quod opus erit, ut res tempusque postulat, provideas atque administres, et ad me de omnibus rebus quam saepissime litteras mittas.

Vale.

164 (XIV.8)
CICERO TO TERENTIA

Brundisium, 2 June 47

From Tullius to his dear Terentia greetings.

I hope you are well, as I am.

I want you to take the greatest care of your health, for I have been told both by letter and word of mouth that you had a sudden attack of fever. Thank you for informing me so promptly about Caesar's letter.[1] In future too, please let me know if there is anything needful or any new development. Take care of your health.

Good-bye.

Dispatched 2 June.

165 (XIV.21)
CICERO TO TERENTIA

Brundisium, ca. 3 June 47

From Tullius to his dear Terentia greetings.

I hope you are well, as I am.

Do your best to regain your health. Please make all necessary provisions and arrangements as circumstances require and write to me as often as possible on all points.

Good-bye.

[1] Cf. *Letters to Atticus* 227 (XI.16).1.

166 (XIV.11)

Scr. Brundisii XVII *Kal. Quint. an. 47*

TULLIUS S. D. TERENTIAE SUAE

S. v. b.; e. v.

Tullia nostra venit ad me prid. Id. Iun. cuius summa virtute et singulari humanitate graviore etiam sum dolore adfectus nostra factum esse neglegentia ut longe alia in fortuna esset atque eius pietas ac dignitas postulabat.

Nobis erat in animo Ciceronem ad Caesarem mittere et cum eo Cn. Sallustium. si profectus erit, faciam te certiorem. valetudinem tuam cura diligenter.

Vale.

XVII Kal. Quint.

167 (XIV.15)

Scr. Brundisii XII *Kal. Quint. an. 47*

TULLIUS S. D. TERENTIAE

Si vales, bene est.

Constitueramus, ut ad te antea scripseram, obviam Ciceronem Caesari mittere; sed mutavimus consilium quia de illius adventu nihil audiebamus. de ceteris rebus, etsi nihil erat novi, tamen quid velimus et quid hoc tempore putemus opus esse ex Sicca poteris cognoscere. Tulliam adhuc mecum teneo. valetudinem tuam cura diligenter.

Vale.

XII Kal. Quint.

166 (XIV.11)
CICERO TO TERENTIA

Brundisium, 14 June 47

From Tullius to his dear Terentia greetings.

I hope you are well, as I am.

Our Tullia joined me on 12 June. She is so wonderfully brave and kind that it gives me even greater pain to think that through my carelessness she is placed far otherwise than befitted a girl of her station and so good a daughter.

I am thinking of sending Marcus to Caesar, and Cn. Sallustius with him. I shall send you word when he leaves. Take good care of your health.

Good-bye.

14 June.

167 (XIV.15)
CICERO TO TERENTIA

Brundisium, 19 June 47

Tullius to Terentia greetings.

I hope you are well.

As I wrote to you earlier, I had decided to send Marcus to Caesar, but changed my mind because there are no reports of his coming home. On other matters there is nothing new, but Sicca will tell you what I wish and think expedient at this time. I still have Tullia with me. Take good care of your health.

Good-bye.

19 June.

168 (XIV.10)

Scr. Brundisii VII *Id. Quint. an. 47*

TULLIUS S. D. TERENTIAE SUAE

Quid fieri placeret scripsi ad Pomponium, serius quam oportuit. cum eo si locuta eris, intelleges quid fieri velim. apertius scribi, quoniam ad illum scripseram, necesse non fuit. de ea re et de ceteris rebus quam primum velim nobis litteras mittas. valetudinem tuam cura diligenter.

Vale.

VII Id. Quint.

169 (XIV.13)

Scr. Brundisii VI *Id. Quint. an. 47*

TULLIUS S. D. TERENTIAE SUAE

Quod scripsi ad te proximis litteris de nuntio remittendo, quae sit istius vis hoc tempore et quae concitatio multitudinis ignoro. si metuendus iratus est, quiesces. tamen ab illo fortasse nascetur. totum iudicabis quale sit, et quod in miserrimis rebus minime miserum putabis id facies.

Vale.

VI Id. Quint.

---

[1] Concerning Tullia's divorce from Dolabella.

168 (XIV.10)
CICERO TO TERENTIA

Brundisium, 9 July 47

From Tullius to his dear Terentia greetings.

I wrote to Pomponius, later than I ought, telling him what I thought should be done.[1] When you have had a talk with him, you will understand my wishes. There is no need to write more explicitly, since I have written to him. Please send me a letter as soon as possible on this and other matters. Take good care of your health.

Good-bye.

9 July.

169 (XIV.13)
CICERO TO TERENTIA

Brundisium, 10 July 47

From Tullius to his dear Terentia greetings.

As regards what I wrote in my last letter about sending notice of divorce, I don't know how powerful he is at the present time[1] nor how excited the state of popular feeling. If he is likely to be a formidable enemy, don't do anything—perhaps he will take the initiative even so. You must judge of the whole position and choose whatever you think the least of evils in this wretched situation.

Good-bye.

10 July.

[1] Dolabella was Tribune in 47 and like Caelius in 48 was agitating for a cancellation of debts.

170 (XIV.24)

Scr. Brundisii III *Id. Sext. an. 47*

TULLIUS TERENTIAE SUAE S. D.

S. v. b.; e. v.

Nos neque de Caesaris adventu neque de litteris quas Philotimus habere dicitur quicquam adhuc certi habemus. si quid erit certi, faciam te statim certiorem. valetudinem tuam fac ut cures.

Vale.

III Id. Sext.

171 (XIV.23)

Scr. Brundisii prid. Id. Sext. an. 47

TULLIUS TERENTIAE SUAE S. D.

S. v. b.; e. v.

Redditae mihi tandem sunt a Caesare litterae satis liberales et ipse opinione celerius venturus esse dicitur; cui utrum obviam procedam an hic eum exspectem cum constituero, faciam te certiorem. tabellarios mihi velim quam primum remittas. valetudinem tuam cura diligenter.

Vale.

D. prid. Id. Sext.

170 (XIV.24)
CICERO TO TERENTIA

Brundisium, 11 August 47

From Tullius to his dear Terentia greetings.

I hope you are well, as I am.

I have nothing definite yet either about Caesar's arrival or the letter which Philotimus is said to have.[1] If anything definite comes along, I shall let you know at once. Take good care of your health.

Good-bye.

11 August.

171 (XIV.23)
CICERO TO TERENTIA

Brundisium, 12 August 47

From Tullius to his dear Terentia greetings.

I hope you are well, as I am.

I have at last received a letter from Caesar, quite a handsome one. He is said to be arriving in person sooner than was expected. I shall let you know when I have decided whether to go to meet him or to wait for him here. Please send the couriers back to me as soon as possible. Take good care of your health.

Good-bye.

Dispatched 12 August.

[1] Cf. *Letters to Atticus* 232 (XI.23).2.

172 (XIV.22)

Scr. Brundisii Kal. Sept. an. 47

TULLIUS S. D. TERENTIAE SUAE

S. v. b.; e. v.

Nos cottidie tabellarios nostros exspectamus; qui si venerint, fortasse erimus certiores quid nobis faciendum sit faciemusque te statim certiorem. valetudinem tuam cura diligenter.

Vale.

Kal. Sept.

173 (XIV.20)

Scr. in Venusino Kal. Oct. an. 47

TULLIUS S. D. TERENTIAE SUAE

In Tusculanum nos venturos putamus aut Nonis aut postridie. ibi ut sint omnia parata. plures enim fortasse nobiscum erunt et, ut arbitror, diutius ibi commorabimur. labrum si in balineo non est, ut sit; item cetera quae sunt ad victum et ad valetudinem necessaria.

Vale.

Kal. Oct. de Ven‹u›sino.[1]

---

[1] *(Vict.)*

172 (XIV.22)
CICERO TO TERENTIA

Brundisium, 1 September 47

From Tullius to his dear Terentia greetings.

I hope you are well, as I am.

I am expecting our couriers any day. When they arrive, perhaps I shall know better what to do, and I shall at once inform you. Take good care of your health.

Good-bye.

Kalends of September.

173 (XIV.20)
CICERO TO TERENTIA

Near Venusia, 1 October 47

From Tullius to his dear Terentia greetings.

I think I shall get to Tusculum either on the Nones or on the following day. Kindly see that everything there is ready. I may have a number of people with me, and shall probably make a fairly long stay there. If there is no tub in the bathroom, get one put in; likewise whatever else is necessary for health and subsistence.

Good-bye.

Kalends of October, from the district of Venusia.

174 (XV.15)

Scr. Brundisii m. Sext. an. 47

M. CICERO S. D. C. CASSIO

1   Etsi uterque nostrum spe pacis et odio civilis sanguinis
abesse a belli ⟨non⟩[1] necessari[a][2] pertinacia voluit, tamen, quoniam eius consili princeps ego fuisse videor, plus
fortasse tibi praestare ipse debeo quam a te exspectare;
etsi, ut saepe soleo mecum recordari, sermo familiaris
meus tecum et item mecum tuus adduxit utrumque nostrum ad id consilium ut uno proelio putaremus, si non totam causam, at certe nostrum iudicium definiri convenire.
neque quisquam hanc nostram sententiam vere umquam
reprehendit praeter eo⟨s⟩ qui arbitrantur melius esse
deleri omnino rem publicam quam imminutam et debili-
tatam manere. ego autem ex interitu eius nullam spem
scilicet mihi proponebam, ex reliqui⟨i⟩s magnam.

2   Sed ea sunt consecuta ut magis mirum sit accidere illa
potuisse quam nos non vidisse ea futura nec, homines cum
essemus, divinare potuisse. equidem fateor meam coniecturam hanc fuisse, ut illo quasi quodam fatali proelio facto
et victores communi saluti consuli[3] vellent et victi suae;
utrumque autem positum esse arbitrabar in celeritate victoris. quae si fuisset, eandem clementiam experta esset
Africa quam cognovit Asia, quam etiam Achaia te,[4] ut opinor, ipso legato ac deprecatore. amissis autem temporibus,
quae plurimum valent, praesertim in bellis civilibus, inter-

---

[1] *(Madvig)*   [2] *(Graevius)*
[3] consule *(Man.)*
[4] et *(Gron.)*

174 (XV.15)
CICERO TO CASSIUS

Brundisium, August 47

M. Cicero to C. Cassius greetings.

Both of us, hoping for peace and hating civil bloodshed, decided to hold aloof from persistence in an unnecessary war. But as I am regarded as having taken the lead in that course, perhaps my feeling towards you in this context should hold more of responsibility than of expectation. And yet I often recall how in talking familiarly to each other, you to me no less than I to you, we were both led to the persuasion that our verdict, if not the entire issue, might properly be decided by the result of a single battle. Nor has anyone ever fairly blamed us for taking this view, excepting those who think the commonwealth had better be wiped out altogether than survive in an enfeebled and attenuated form. For my part I saw no hope (obviously) from its destruction, but great hope from its remnants.

The sequel, however, was unexpected—the wonder is that such events could happen rather than that we did not see them coming and, being but human, could not divine them. For my part, I confess my forecast was that, once the fated and fatal battle, so to speak, had been fought, the victors would turn their attention to the general survival and the vanquished to their own. At the same time I thought that both the one and the other depended upon swift action by the victorious leader. Had that been forthcoming, Africa would have experienced the clemency which Asia came to know, as did Achaea also, whose ambassador and intercessor was, I believe, none other than yourself. But the crucial moments were lost, the moments which matter

positus annus alios induxit ut victoriam sperarent, alios ut ipsum vinci contemnerent. atque horum malorum omnium culpam Fortuna sustinet. quis enim aut Alexandrini belli tantam moram huic bello adiunctum iri aut nescio quem istum Pharnacem Asiae terrorem illaturum putaret?

3   Nos tamen in consilio pari casu dissimili usi sumus. tu enim eam partem petisti ut et consiliis interesses et, quod maxime curam levat, futura animo prospicere posses; ego, qui festinavi ut Caesarem in Italia viderem (sic enim arbitra<ba>mur) eumque multis honestissimis viris conservatis redeuntem ad pacem currentem, ut aiunt, incitarem, ab illo longissime et absum et afui. versor autem in gemitu Italiae et in urbis miserrimis querelis; quibus aliquid opis fortasse ego pro mea, tu pro tua, pro sua quisque parte ferre potuisset si a<u>ctor adfuisset.

4   Qua re velim pro tua perpetua erga me benevolentia scribas ad me quid videas, quid sentias, quid exspectandum, quid agendum nobis existimes. magni erunt mihi tuae litterae. atque utinam primis illis quas Luceria miseras paruissem! sine ulla enim molestia dignitatem meam retinuissem.

most, especially in civil warfare. A year intervened, leading
some to hope for victory and others to care nothing even
for defeat. The blame for all these calamities lies at Fortune's door. Who could have expected that the main hostilities would have been so long held up by the fighting
at Alexandria, or that this what's-his-name, Pharnaces,
would menace Asia so formidably?

We thought alike, but we fared differently. *You* made
for a quarter[1] where you would be present at the making of
decisions and able to foresee events to come, the best comfort for an anxious mind. *I* made haste to meet Caesar in
Italy (so we thought), on his way home after sparing many
valuable lives, and to urge him to peace—spurring a willing horse, as they say. The consequence was that I have
been, and still am, at a vast distance away from him. I am
living amidst the groans of Italy and the pitiful plaints of
Rome. Perhaps I and you and every man, each according
to his powers, might have done something to help, if au-
thoritative backing had been available.

So I would ask you, in virtue of your unfailing kindliness
toward me, to write to me and tell me what you see and
feel, what you think I have to expect and ought to do. A
letter from you will mean a great deal to me. I only wish I
had followed the advice in that first letter of yours from
Luceria.[2] I should have kept my standing and avoided all
unpleasantness.

[1] Cassius had joined Caesar in the East.
[2] The letter here referred to must have advised Cicero to stay
out of the war. It was probably written in February 49, just before
the fall of Corfinium. Pompey set up his headquarters at Luceria
about 25 January.

175 (IX.1)

Scr. Romae ex. an. 47 aut in. an. 46

CICERO M. VARRONI S.

1   Ex iis litteris quas Atticus a te missas mihi legit quid
ageres et ubi esses cognovi; quando autem te visuri essemus, nihil sane ex isdem litteris potui suspicari. in spem
tamen venio appropinquare tuum adventum. qui mihi utinam solacio sit! etsi tot tantisque rebus urgemur ut nullam
adlevationem quisquam non stultissimus sperare debeat.
sed tamen aut tu potes me aut ego te fortasse aliqua re
2   iuvare. scito enim me, postea quam in urbem venerim,
redisse cum veteribus amicis, id est cum libris nostris, in
gratiam. etsi non idcirco eorum usum dimiseram quod
iis suscenserem sed quod eorum me suppudebat; videbar
enim mihi, cum me in res turbulentissimas infidelissimis
sociis demi‹si›ssem, praeceptis illorum non satis paruisse.
ignoscunt mihi, revocant in consuetudinem pristinam
teque, quod in ea permanseris, sapientiorem quam me dicunt fuisse. quam ob rem, quoniam placatis iis utor, videor
sperare debere, si te viderim, et ea quae premant et ea
quae impendeant me facile laturum.

Quam ob rem, sive in Tusculano sive in Cumano, ‹sive
ad me sive›[1] ad te placebit, sive, quod minime velim,
Romae, dum modo simul simus, perficiam profecto ut id
utrique nostrum commodissimum esse videatur.

[1] *(SB)*

---

[1] Varro may not yet have returned to Italy.
[2] Both Cicero and Varro had villas in both areas.

175 (IX.1)
CICERO TO VARRO

Rome, 47 (end) or 46 (beginning)

From Cicero to M. Varro greetings.

The letter which you sent to Atticus and which he read to me informed me of your doings and whereabouts, but as to when we are to see you, I could not so much as make a guess from that letter. However, I am coming to hope that your advent is not far away.[1] I wish I may find some comfort in it, though our afflictions are so many and so grievous that nobody but an arrant fool ought to hope for any relief. And yet either you may be able to help me or perhaps I may in some way be able to help you. For I should tell you that since my return I have restored my relations with my old friends, that is to say my books. Not that I had renounced their companionship because I was annoyed with them—it was because they gave me a sense of shame. I felt that in casting myself into a turmoil of events with altogether untrustworthy associates I had failed in obedience to their precepts. They forgive me. They call me back to the old intercourse and tell me that you in staying faithful to it were wiser than I. And so I have made my peace with them and we are together again. That is why I think I may properly hope that once I see you I shall find both present and impending troubles easy to bear.

So whatever rendezvous you favour, be it Tusculum or Cumae,[2] my house or yours, or (what would be my last choice) Rome, you may be sure I shall make it appear the most convenient for both of us, only provided we are together.

176 (IX.3)

Scr. Romae c. XIII *Kal. Mai. an. 46*

CICERO VARRONI

1   Etsi quid scriberem non habebam, tamen Caninio ad te euenti non potui nihil dare. quid ergo potissimum scribam? quod velle te puto, cito me ad te esse venturum. etsi vide, quaeso, satisne rectum sit nos hoc tanto incendio civitatis in istis locis esse; dabimus sermonem iis qui nesciunt nobis, quocumque in loco simus, eundem cultum, eundem victum esse. <sed>[1] quid refert? tamen in sermonem incidemus. valde id, credo, laborandum est, ne, cum omnes in omni genere et scelerum et flagitiorum volutentur, nostra 2 nobiscum aut inter nos cessatio vituperetur! ego vero neglecta barbarorum inscitia persequar. quamvis enim sint haec misera, quae sunt miserrima, tamen artes nostrae nescio quo modo nunc uberiores fructus ferre videntur quam olim ferebant, sive quia nulla nunc in re alia acquiescimus sive quod gravitas morbi facit ut medicinae egeamus eaque nunc appareat, cuius vim non sentiebamus cum valebamus.

Sed quid ego nunc haec ad te, cuius domi nascuntur, γλαῦκ᾽ εἰς Ἀθήνας? nihil scilicet nisi ut rescriberes aliquid, me exspectares. sic igitur facies.

[1] *(T.–P.)*

---

[1] No doubt L. Caninius Gallus.
[2] On the coast of Campania.
[3] Down to Cumae.
[4] Like 'coals to Newcastle.'

176 (IX.3)
CICERO TO VARRO

Rome, ca. 18 April 46

From Cicero to Varro.

   Although I have nothing to write about, I could not let Caninius[1] go to you without giving him something. So what *should* I write? What I think you want to read, that I shall be coming to visit you soon. But pray ask yourself whether it is quite proper for us to be down there[2] at such a time of national conflagration. We shall be giving a chance for gossip to those who don't know that, wherever we are, our style and way of living remain the same. And yet, what does it matter? They will gossip about us anyway. When all mankind is wallowing in every sort of crime and outrage, I hardly suppose we need concern ourselves overmuch about possible aspersions on our idleness, whether by ourselves or in one another's company. Yes, I shall follow you[3] and take no notice of these ignorant barbarians. However melancholy the times, and melancholy indeed they are, our pursuits seem somehow to yield more generous rewards now than they did in days gone by. Perhaps it is because we have no other means of relief; or perhaps the severity of the disease puts us in need of the medicine, and its strength, which we did not perceive when we were well, is now manifest.

   But why am I now sending such reflections to *you,* who have them home-grown—an owl to Athens?[4] No reason, to be sure, except for you to write a line in return, and to expect me. So please do.

177 (IX.2)

Scr. Romae c. IX *Kal. Mai. an. 46*

CICERO VARRONI

1   Caninius ‹tuus›[1] et idem noster cum ad me pervesperi
venisset et se postridie mane ad te iturum esse dixisset, dixi
ei me daturum litterarum aliquid; mane ut peteret rogavi.
conscripsi epistulam noctu, nec ille ad me rediit; oblitum
credidi. ac tamen eam ipsam tibi epistulam misissem per
meos nisi audissem ex eodem postridie te mane e Tusculano exiturum. at tibi repente paucis post diebus, cum minime exspectarem, venit ad me Caninius mane; proficisci
ad te statim dixit. etsi erat ἕωλος illa epistula, praesertim
tantis postea novis rebus adlatis, tamen perire lucubratio-
nem meam nolui et eam ipsam Caninio dedi; sed cum eo ut
cum homine docto et amantissimo tui locutus ea sum quae
pertulisse illum ad te existimo.

2   Tibi autem idem consili do quod mihimet ipsi, ut vite-
mus oculos hominum, si linguas minus facile possimus; qui
enim victoria se efferunt quasi victos nos intuentur, qui
autem victos nostros moleste ferunt nos dolent vivere.
quaeres fortasse cur, cum haec in urbe sint, non absim
quem ad modum tu. tu enim ipse, qui et me et alios prudentia vincis, omnia, credo, vidisti, nihil te omnino fefellit!

---

[1] -ius idem et idem *(Man.)*

---

[1] Letter 176.

[2] For Cumae. In fact, Varro's departure was postponed.

[3] The news of Caesar's victory over the republicans at Thapsus
reached Rome about 20 April.

177 (IX.2)
CICERO TO VARRO

Rome, ca. 22 April 46

From Cicero to Varro.

Your (and our) friend Caninius called upon me late one evening and told me that he would be leaving betimes next day to join you; so I said I would give him something to carry, and asked him if he would kindly call for it in the morning. I wrote a letter[1] that night; but he did not come back after all and I assumed he had forgotten. I should have sent you the letter all the same by messengers of my own, had I not heard from Caninius that you would be leaving Tusculum[2] early the following day. Well, a few days later who should arrive at my house early in the morning out of the blue, when I was least expecting him, but Caninius? He said he was just off to join you. My letter was by now out of date, particularly as such important news had come in since I wrote it; but still I did not want my midnight oil to be wasted, and so I gave it to Caninius as it stood. But I also said certain things to him, knowing him to be a man of culture and a very warm friend of yours, which I expect he has passed on to you.

To you I have the same advice to offer as to myself. Let us avoid men's eyes, even if we cannot easily escape their tongues. The jubilant victors[3] regard us as among the defeated, whereas those who are sorry for the defeat of our friends feel aggrieved that we are still among the living. Perhaps you will wonder why, with this going on in Rome, I am not elsewhere like you. Well, and have you yourself, a shrewder man than I or any other, foreseen everything, has *nothing* turned out contrary to your expectations? I

quis est tam Lynceus qui in tantis tenebris nihil offendat,
3   nusquam incurrat? ac mihi quidem iam pridem venit in
mentem bellum esse aliquo exire, ut ea quae agebantur hic
quaeque dicebantur nec viderem nec audirem. sed calum-
niabar ipse; putabam qui obviam mihi venisset, ut cuique
commodum esset, suspicaturum, aut dicturum etiam si
non suspicaretur: 'hic aut metuit et ea re fugit aut aliquid
cogitat et habet navem paratam.' denique levissime qui
suspicaretur et qui fortasse me optime novisset putaret me
idcirco discedere quod quosdam homines oculi mei ferre
non possent. haec ego suspicans adhuc Romae maneo; et
tamen λεληθότως consuetudo diu‹tu›rna callum iam
obduxit stomacho meo.

4   Habes rationem mei consili. tibi igitur hoc censeo, la-
tendum tantisper ibidem dum effervescit haec gratulatio
et simul dum audiamus quem ad modum negotium confectum sit; confectum enim esse existimo. magni autem
intererit qui fuerit victoris animus, qui exitus rerum;
quamquam quo me coniectura ducat habeo, sed exspecto
tamen.

5   Te vero nolo, nisi ipse rumor iam raucus erit factus, ad
Baias venire. erit enim nobis honestius, etiam cum hinc
discesserimus, videri venisse in illa loca ploratum potius
quam natatum. sed haec tu melius, modo nobis stet illud,
una vivere in studiis nostris, a quibus antea delectationem
modo petebamus, nunc vero etiam salutem; non deesse si
quis adhibere volet, non modo ut architectos verum etiam
ut fabros, ad aedificandam rem publicam, et potius liben-

---

4 Literally 'who is such a Lynceus?' The Argonaut Lynceus
could see in the dark.   5 At Tusculum.   6 The fashion-
able resort (as distinct from Varro's own villa at Cumae).

can hardly believe that. Whose eyes are so preternaturally sharp[4] as to avoid every obstacle, every pitfall, in darkness such as this? In point of fact it did cross my mind long ago that it would be nice to get away somewhere, so as not to see or hear what was being done and said in Rome. But I made difficulties for myself. I thought that whoever came my way would suspect or, even if he did not suspect, would say, as might suit his individual purpose, 'Aha! He took fright, that's why he ran away; or else he's up to something, has a boat all ready.' Even the most charitable (and perhaps best acquainted with the kind of man I am) would have thought that I was leaving because I could not stand the sight of certain persons. With all this in mind I stay on in Rome. And after all, long custom has imperceptibly anaesthetized my spleen.

So my conduct is explained. Now my counsel to you is to lie low for the present where you are,[5] while these rejoicings are at boiling point and also until we hear just how the affair has been settled—for settled I believe it is. A great deal will depend on the victor's disposition and the way things turned out. I have my own guess to be sure, but am waiting for news.

No, I don't think you ought to go to Baiae,[6] unless rumour itself grows hoarse. Even when we go away from here, it will be more seemly to appear to have chosen that part of the world for weeping rather than for bathing. But you will judge better than I. Only let us be firm on one point—to live together in our literary studies. We used to go to them only for pleasure, now we go for salvation. If anybody cares to call us in as architects or even as workmen to help build a commonwealth, we shall not say no,

ter accurrere; si nemo utetur opera, tamen et scribere et legere πολιτείας, et, si minus in curia atque in foro, at in litteris et libris, ut doctissimi veteres fecerunt, gnavare[2] rem publicam et de moribus ac legibus quaerere.

Mihi haec videntur. tu quid sis acturus et quid tibi placeat pergratum erit si ad me scripseris.

178 (IX.7)

Scr. Romae m. Mai. parte post. an. 46

CICERO VARRONI

1   Cenabam apud Seium, cum utrique nostrum redditae sunt a te litterae. mihi vero iam maturum videtur. nam quod ante[a te][1] calumniatus sum, indicabo malitiam meam: volebam prope alicubi esse t⟨e⟩,[2] si quid bonae salutis; σύν τε δύ' ἐρχομένω. nunc, quoniam confecta sunt omnia, dubitandum non est quin equis viris. nam ut audivi de L. Caesare filio, mecum ipse 'quid hic mihi faciet patri?' itaque non desino apud istos qui nunc dominantur cenitare. quid faciam? tempori serviendum est.

---

[2] gravare *(Mend.)*
[1] anteate *(Mend.*: antea *Man.)*   [2] *(Man.)*

---

[7] Cicero may have resumed work on his unfinished treatise *On Laws.*

[1] To go to Campania.   [2] *Iliad* 10.224: 'When two go together, one notices before the other.'

[3] Literally 'with horse and foot,' i.e. without any holding back. 'We must make friends with the winning party' is implied.

rather we shall hasten cheerfully to the task. If our services are not required, we must still read and write 'Republics.' Like the learned men of old, we must serve the state in our libraries, if we cannot in Senate House and Forum, and pursue our researches into custom and law.[7]

Such are my sentiments. You will oblige me greatly if you will write and tell me what you are going to do and what you think best.

178 (IX.7)
CICERO TO VARRO

Rome, latter May 46

Cicero to Varro.

I was at dinner with Seius when a letter from you was delivered to each of us. Yes, I think it's seasonable now.[1] As for the difficulties I put up previously, I'll confess my craftiness. I wanted to have you nearby in case some chance of good turned up. 'Two heads,'[2] you know. Now, since all is settled, we must hesitate no longer—full speed ahead.[3] When I heard about L. Caesar junior,[4] I said to myself 'What can I, his father, look for?'[5] So I go dining every night with our present rulers. What am I to do? One must go with the times.

[4] About his death in Africa. Cicero, perhaps mistakenly, implies that this took place by Caesar's orders.

[5] I.e. 'what have *I* got to expect?' Cicero recalls this scrap of Terence's *Girl from Andros* (112) (probably without remembering its dramatic context, which is foreign to his point) because 'father' suggests an old man as compared to a young one.

2   Sed ridicula missa, praesertim cum sit nihil quod rideamus.

Africa terribili tremit horrida terra tumultu.

itaque nullum est ἀποπροηγμένον quod non verear.

Sed quod quaeris quando, qua, quo, nihil adhuc scimus. istuc ipsum de Baiis,[3] non nulli dubitant an per Sardiniam veniat. illud enim adhuc praedium suum non inspexit; nec ullum habet deterius, sed tamen non contemnit. ego omnino magis arbitror per Siciliam, sed iam[4] sciemus; adventat enim Dolabella. eum puto magistrum fore.

πολλοὶ μαθηταὶ κρείσσονες διδασκάλων.

sed tamen, si sciam quid tu constitueris, meum consilium accommodabo potissimum ad tuum. qua re exspecto tuas litteras.

179 (IX.5)

Scr. Romae ex. m. Mai. an. 46

CICERO VARRONI

1   Mihi vero ad Nonas bene maturum videtur fore, neque

[3] scimus, ⟨ut⟩ . . . Baiis; non nulli *coni. SB*
[4] veliam *(Wes.)*

---

[6] From Ennius' *Annals.*
[7] A Greek term from Stoic philosophy, which recognized virtue as the only good but allowed that other things (e.g. health,

But joking aside (especially as we have nothing to laugh about), 'Africa, grim land's a-tremble in terrific tumult tossed.'[6] There is nothing 'negative'[7] that I don't apprehend.

But in answer to your questions as to date, route, and destination, we know nothing yet. Even as to Baiae,[8] some think he may come by way of Sardinia. That is one of his properties that he has not yet inspected. It's the worst he owns, but he doesn't despise it. I myself, to be sure, think he's more likely to travel by way of Sicily. But we shall soon know. Dolabella is coming, and I expect he will be our schoolmaster. 'The teacher's oft inferior to the taught.'[9] However, as soon as I know what you have decided, I shall try to accommodate my plans to yours. So I expect to hear from you.

179 (IX.5)

CICERO TO VARRO

Rome, end of May 46

From Cicero to Varro.

The Nones? Yes, that will be very seasonable, I think,

wealth, and their opposites) were on one side or other of complete indifference. Varro was an expert on Greek philosophy.

[8] There seems to have been a rumour that Caesar would land at Baiae. He did in fact come by way of Sardinia and landed at Ostia.

[9] A Greek line from an unknown dramatic source. Cicero had given Dolabella lessons in rhetoric (cf. Letter 192.2).

solum propter rei publicae sed etiam propter anni tempus.
qua re istum diem probo; itaque eundem ipse sequar.

2   Consili nostri, ne si eos quidem qui id secuti non sunt
non paeniteret, nobis paenitendum putarem. secuti enim
sumus non spem sed officium, reliquimus autem non
officium sed desperationem. ita verecundiores fuimus
quam qui se domo non commoverunt, saniores quam qui
amissis opibus domum non reverterunt. sed nihil minus
fero quam severitatem otiosorum et, quoquo modo se res
habet, magis illos vereor qui in bello occiderunt quam hos
curo quibus non satis facimus quia vivimus.

3   Mihi si spatium fuerit in Tusculanum ante Nonas ve-
niendi, istic te videbo; si minus, persequar in Cumanum et
ante te certiorem faciam, ut lavatio parata sit.

180 (IX.4)

Scr. in Tusculano, ut vid., ex. m. Mai. vel in. m. Iun. an. 46
CICERO VARRONI

Περὶ δυνατῶν me scito κατὰ Διόδωρον κρίνειν. quapropter, si venturus es, scito necesse esse te venire; sin

---

1 Literally 'not only because of the circumstances *(tempus)* of
the commonwealth but because of the time *(tempus)* of year.' The
date 5 June by the calendar in 46 represented 7 April, a pleasant
time for a visit to the Bay of Naples. The reference to politics
means, I think, that it would be wise to take the proposed holiday
before Caesar's return.   2 In supporting Pompey in the first
place and in withdrawing from the war after Pharsalia.

1 Fourth-century philosopher. His so-called Master Argument sought to prove that what is or will be actual is possible, and

literally as well as politically speaking.[1] So I approve your date and shall keep it in view myself.

As for our line of conduct,[2] we ought not in my opinion to regret it, even if those who took a different line were not regretting *that*. It was not hope, but duty, whose call we followed; and it was not duty, but despair, that we abandoned. We had a tenderer conscience than those who never stirred from home and a sounder sense of reality than those who, after the loss of our resources, did not return there. But what I find hardest to stomach is the censure of do-nothings. However things stand, I have more respect for the men who perished in the war than time for persons who cannot forgive us for being alive.

If I have leisure for a visit to Tusculum before the Nones, I shall see you there. If not, I shall follow you to Cumae, and let you know in advance, so that the bath be ready.

180 (IX.4)
CICERO TO VARRO

Tusculum (?), end of May or beginning of June 46

From Cicero to Varro.

'Concerning things possible,' let me tell you that I pronounce with Diodorus.[1] So if you are coming, you may be sure that it is necessary for you to come; if you are not com-

that what is not going to be actual is not possible. It was controverted by the great third-century Stoic Chrysippus, who defined the possible as that which was capable of being actual (if circumstances did not prevent it).

autem non es, τ⟨ῶν⟩ ἀδυνάτων[1] est te venire. nunc vide
utra te κρίσις magis delectet, Chrysippi an[2] haec quam
noster Diodotus non concoquebat. sed de his etiam rebus,
otiosi cum erimus, loquemur. hoc etiam κατὰ Χρύσιππον
δυνατὸν est.

De †coctio†[3] mihi gratum est; nam id etiam Attico mandaram. tu si minus ad nos, accurremus ad te. si hortum in
bibliotheca habes, deerit nihil.

181 (IX.6)

Scr. Romae post. parte m. Iun. an. 46

CICERO VARRONI

1   Caninius noster me tuis verbis admonuit ut scriberem
ad te si quid esset quod putarem te scire oportere. est igitur adventus [Caesaris scilicet][1] in exspectatione; neque tu
id ignoras. sed tamen, cum ille scripsisset, ut opinor, se in
Alsiense venturum, scripserunt ad eum sui ne id faceret;
multos ei molestos fore ipsumque multis; Ostiae videri
commodius eum exire posse. id ego non intellegebam quid
interesset; sed tamen Hirtius mihi dixit et se ad eum et

---

[1] est αδυν- (*SB ex Vict. et* ⌐)
[2] chrysippias *(Man.)*
[3] Cocceio *Corr.*: Coccio *Sjögren*: Cottio *coni. SB*
[1] *(Vict.)*

---

[2] 'Coctius' in the manuscripts is not attested as a Roman name.
Perhaps it should be 'Cottius.'

158

ing, it is impossible for you to come. Now ask yourself which pronouncement you prefer, Chrysippus' or this— which our friend Diodotus used to be unable to stomach. But we will talk of these matters as well as others when we have time to spare. This too is possible according to Chrysippus.

Thank you for what you have done about *[2]—I had asked Atticus too to attend to that matter. If you don't come to me I shall run over to you. If you have a kitchen garden in your library we shall lack for nothing.[3]

181 (IX.6)
CICERO TO VARRO

Rome, latter June 46

From Cicero to Varro.

Our friend Caninius told me from you to write if there should be anything which I thought you ought to know. Well, the arrival is awaited—that is no news to you. But when he wrote, as I suppose, that he would be coming to his place at Alsium,[1] his friends wrote to dissuade him, telling him that there were many people thereabouts whose presence would be annoying to him, and many whom his presence would annoy; Ostia, in their opinion, would make a more convenient landing place. I do not myself see what odds it makes, but Hirtius told me that both he and Balbus

---

[3] Having food for both mind and body. Even so a rather obscure remark.

[1] Or 'the district of Alsium.'

Balbum et Oppium scripsisse ut ita faceret, homines, ut cognovi, amantis tui.

2   Hoc ego idcirco nosse te volui ut scires hospitium tibi ubi parares, vel potius ⟨ut⟩[2] utrubique; quid enim ille facturus sit incertum est. et simul ostentavi tibi me istis esse familiarem et consiliis eorum interesse. quod ego cur nolim nihil video. non enim est idem ferre si quid ferendum est et probare si quid non probandum est. etsi ⟨ne⟩[3] quid non probem quidem iam scio, praeter initia rerum; nam haec in voluntate fuerunt. vidi enim (nam tu aberas) nostros amicos cupere bellum, hunc autem non tam cupere quam non timere. ergo haec consili fuerunt, reliqua necessaria. vincere autem aut hos aut illos necesse erat.[4]

3   Scio te semper mecum in luctu fuisse cum videremus cum[5] illud ingens malum, alterius utrius exercitus et ducum interitum, tum vero extremum malorum omnium esse civilis belli victoriam, quam quidem ego etiam illorum timebam ad quos veneramus; crudeliter enim otiosis minabantur, eratque iis et tua invisa voluntas et mea oratio. nunc vero, si essent nostri potiti, valde intemperantes fuissent; erant enim nobis perirati, quasi quicquam de nostra salute decrevissemus quod non idem illis censuissemus aut quasi utilius rei publicae fuerit eos etiam ad bestiarum auxilium confugere quam vel emori[6] vel cum spe, si non optima, at aliqua tamen vivere.

---

[2] *(Schütz)*   [3] *(Gul.)*   [4] esse *(SB: del. Watt)*
[5] quam *(Lamb.)*
[6] velle mori *(Vict.)*

---

[2] The elephants of King Juba of Numidia, an ally of the republicans.

and Oppius wrote advising him in this sense—persons whom I know to be fond of you.

I wanted you to hear of this so you should know where to arrange to stay, or rather so you should make arrangements in both localities, since what *he* will do is uncertain. At the same time I have shown off to you the familiar footing on which I stand with these gentry, and how I am taken into their counsels. I see no reason why I should object to that. It is one thing to put up with what has to be put up with, another to approve what ought to be disapproved— though for my part I don't any longer know what to disapprove of, except the beginnings of it all, which were a matter of volition. I saw (you were away) that our friends were desirous of war, whereas the person we are expecting was not so much desirous as unafraid of it. That then came within the scope of design, all else followed inevitably. And victory had to fall to one side or the other.

I know that your heart was always as heavy as mine. Not only did we foresee the destruction of one of the two armies and its leader, a vast disaster, but we realized that victory in civil war is the worst of all calamities. I dreaded the prospect, even if victory should fall to those we had joined. They were making savage threats against the do-nothings, and your sentiments and my words were alike abhorrent to them. As for the present time, if our friends had gained the mastery, they would have used it very immoderately. They were infuriated with us. One might have supposed that we had taken some resolution for our own safety which we had not advised them to take for theirs, or that it was to the advantage of the state that they should go to brute beasts[2] for help rather than die outright or live in hope—admittedly no very bright hope, but still hope.

4 At in perturbata re publica vivimus. quis negat? sed hoc
viderint ii qui nulla sibi subsidia ad omnis vitae status para-
verunt. huc enim ut venirem superior longius quam volui
fluxit oratio. cum enim te semper magnum hominem duxi
tum[7] quod his tempestatibus es prope solus in portu, fruc-
tusque doctrinae percipis eos qui maximi sunt, ut ea con-
sideres eaque tractes quorum et usus et delectatio est
omnibus istorum et actis et voluptatibus anteponenda.
equidem hos tuos Tusculanensis dies instar esse vitae puto
libenterque omnibus omnis opes concesserim ut mihi
5 liceat vi nulla interpellante isto modo vivere. quod nos
quoque imitamur, ut possumus, et in nostris studiis libentissime conquiescimus. quis enim hoc non dederit nobis,
ut, cum opera nostra patria sive non possit uti sive nolit, ad
eam vitam revertamur quam multi docti homines, fortasse
non recte sed tamen multi, etiam rei publicae praeponen-
dam putaverunt? quae igitur studia magnorum hominum
sententia vacationem habent quandam[8] publici muneris,
iis concedente re publica cur non abutamur?
6 Sed plus facio quam Caninius mandavit. ille[9] enim si
quid ego scirem rogarat quod tu nescires; ego tibi ea narro
quae tu melius scis quam ipse qui narro. faciam ergo illud
quod rogatus sum, ut eorum quae temporis huius sunt,
quaecumque[10] audiero, ne quid ignores.

[7] duxerim *(Man.)*
[8] eandem *(Iac. Gron.)*
[9] iure *(R. Klotz)*
[10] qu(a)etua *(Madvig: alii alia)*

We live, it may be said, in a state that has been turned upside down. Undeniably true. But that is a problem for persons who have not prepared resources for themselves against all life's contingencies. Here is the point to which the flow of these remarks, more prolix than I wished, has been tending. I have always thought you a great man and I think you so now, because in this stormy weather you almost alone are safe in harbour. You reap the most precious fruits of learning, devoting your thoughts and energies to pursuits which yield a profit and a delight far transcending the exploits and pleasures of these worldlings. These days you are now spending down at Tusculum are worth a lifetime by my reckoning. Gladly would I leave all earthly wealth and power to others, and take in exchange a licence to live thus, free from interruption by any outside force. I am following your example as best I can, and most gladly find repose in literary studies. Surely nobody would begrudge us this. Our country will not or cannot use our services, so we return to a mode of life which many philosophers (mistakenly perhaps, but many) have considered actually to be preferred to the political. The state now grants its permission. Are we not then at liberty to give full rein to pursuits which in the judgement of great thinkers carry a sort of exemption from public employment?

However, I am going beyond Caninius' commission. *He* asked me to write if anything came to my knowledge of which you were unaware; and here am I telling you what you know better than I, your informant. So I shall do what I was asked, and see that you are not left in ignorance of any items relevant to the present situation that may come my way.

Scr. Romae med. m. Apr. an. 46

M. CICERO S. D. L. MESCINIO

1   Gratae mihi tuae litterae fuerunt; ex quibus intellexi,
quod etiam sine litteris arbitrabar, te summa cupiditate
adfectum esse videndi mei. quod ego ita libenter accipio ut
tamen tibi non concedam; nam tecum esse ita mihi commoda[1] omnia quae opto contingant ut vehementer velim!
tum enim cum esset maior et virorum et civium bonorum
et iucundorum hominum et amantium mei copia, tamen
erat nemo quicum essem libentius quam tecum et pauci
quibuscum essem aeque libenter; hoc vero tempore, cum
alii interierint, alii absint, alii mutati voluntate sint, unum
me dius fidius tecum diem libentius posuerim quam hoc
omne tempus cum plerisque eorum quibuscum vivo necessario. noli enim existimare mihi non solitudinem iucundiorem esse, qua tamen ipsa uti non licet, quam sermones
eorum qui frequentant domum meam, excepto uno aut
summum altero.

2   Itaque utor eodem perfugio quo tibi utendum censeo,
litterulis nostris, praeterea conscientia etiam consiliorum
meorum. ego enim is sum, quem ad modum tu facillime
potes existimare, qui nihil umquam mea potius quam meorum civium causa fecerim. cui nisi invidisset is quem tu
numquam amasti (me enim amabas), et ipse beatus esset
et omnes boni. ego sum qui nullius vim plus valere volui
quam honestum otium, idemque, cum illa ipsa arma quae
semper timueram plus posse sensi quam illum consensum

---

[1] communia (⊊: *del. Vict.*)

182 (V.21)
CICERO TO MESCINIUS RUFUS

Rome, mid April 46

From M. Cicero to L. Mescinius greetings.

Many thanks for your letter. It told me what I thought even before I read it, that you have a great desire to see me. That I welcome, but at the same time I don't allow you any priority in such a feeling. To be with you is my ardent wish, by all my hopes I swear it. Even when there was a greater plenty of good men and good citizens and of pleasant and friendly company, I liked nobody's society better than yours and few people's so well. But now, when some are dead, others away, others changed towards me, upon my soul I would rather spend a day with you than this whole period with most of those whose company I keep perforce. Don't imagine that solitude is not more agreeable to me (though I am not allowed it) than the talk of my usual visitors, one or two at most excepted.

And so I take refuge, as I would advise you to do, in my literary dabbling, and also in my political conscience. I am one, as you are in an excellent position to judge, that never put his own interest before his countrymen's. Had a personage[1] for whom you never much cared (you cared for *me*) not been jealous of me, it would be well with him and with all honest men today. I am one that wished no man's violence to prevail over public tranquillity and honour; but when I found the armed might which I had always dreaded

[1] Pompey.

bonorum quem ego idem effeceram, quamvis ‹inius›ta[2] condicione pacem accipere malui quam viribus cum valentiore pugnare. sed et haec et multa alia coram brevi tempore licebit.

3   Neque me tamen ulla res alia Romae tenet nisi exspectatio rerum Africanarum. videtur enim mihi res in propinquum adducta discrimen. puto autem mea non nihil interesse (quamquam id ipsum, quid intersit, non sane intellego, verum tamen), quicquid illinc nuntiatum sit, non longe abesse a consiliis amicorum. est enim res iam in eum locum adducta ut, quamquam multum intersit inter eorum causas qui dimicant, tamen inter victorias non multum interfuturum putem.

Sed plane animus ‹meus›,[3] qui dubiis rebus forsitan fuerit infirmior, desperatis confirmatus est multum. quem etiam tuae superiores litterae confirmarunt, quibus intellexi quam fortiter iniuriam ferres; iuvitque me tibi cum summam humanitatem tum etiam tuas litteras profuisse. verum enim scribam: teneriore mihi animo videbare, sicut omnes fere qui vitam ingenuam[4] in beata civitate et in libe-

4   ra ‹re publica›[5] viximus. sed ut illa secunda moderate tulimus, sic hanc non solum adversam sed funditus eversam fortunam fortiter ferre debemus, ut hoc saltem in maximis malis boni consequamur, ut mortem, quam etiam beati contemnere debe‹b›amus propterea quod nullum sensum esset habitura, nunc sic adfecti non modo contemnere

---

[2] quavis (quamvis GR) tota *(SB)*
[3] *(Wes.)*
[4] vita ingenua *(Or.)*
[5] *(Wes.)*

more potent than the union of honest men of which I had myself been the architect, I was for peace on terms however unfair rather than a trial of force against a stronger adversary. But of this and much besides we shall soon be able to talk together.

The only thing that keeps me in Rome, however, is the expectation of events in Africa, where a crisis seems to be imminent. I feel it is of some moment to me (though what actual difference it makes I hardly see, but even so) not to be far away from my friends' advice, whatever news comes in from that quarter. The situation is now such that, although there may be a good deal to choose between the causes of the combatants, I think the victory of either will amount to pretty much the same.

But the fact is that my spirit, which was perhaps inclined to frailty when the issue was in doubt, has been much stronger in despair. Your earlier letter strengthened it still further, for it showed how bravely you bore your ill usage;[2] and it did me good to see how your fine culture, and especially your literary work, stood you in good stead. For, to tell the truth, I thought you a trifle too easily hurt, like nearly all of us who have lived an independent life in a happy community under a free constitution. But as we observed moderation in the good days gone by, so we ought to take our present adversity, or rather utter ruin, with fortitude. In the midst of disaster we gain one advantage at least: death, which even in the days of our happiness it was incumbent on us to despise on the ground that it would be devoid of consciousness, we ought in our present plight

---

[2] Though back in Italy, Mescinius had been in some way penalized by Caesar, perhaps forbidden to return to Rome.

debeamus sed etiam optare.

5   Tu, si me diligis, fruere isto otio tibique persuade praeter culpam ac peccatum, qua semper caruisti et carebis,
homini accidere nihil posse quod sit horribile aut per-
timescendum. ego, si videbitur recte fieri posse, ad te veniam brevi; si quid acciderit ut mutandum consilium sit, te
certiorem faciam statim. tu ita fac cupidus mei videndi sis
ut istinc te ne moveas tam infirma valetudine nisi ex me
prius quaesieris per litteras quid te velim facere. me velim,
ut facis, diligas valetudinique tuae et tranquillitati animi
servias.

183 (VII.3)

Scr. Romae med. m. Apr., ut vid., an. 46

M. CICERO S. D. M. MARIO

1   Persaepe mihi cogitanti de communibus miseriis in
quibus tot annos versamur et, ut video, versabimur solet in
mentem venire illius temporis quo proxime fuimus una;
quin etiam ipsum diem memoria teneo. nam a. d. III⟨I⟩[1]
Id. Mai. Lentulo et Marcello consulibus, cum in Pompeianum vesperi venissem, tu mihi sollicito animo praesto
fuisti. sollicitum autem te habebat cogitatio cum offici tum
etiam periculi mei. si manerem in Italia, verebare ne
officio deessem; si proficiscerer ad bellum, periculum te
meum commovebat. quo tempore vidisti profecto me

[1] *(Wes.)*

not merely to despise but positively to pray for.

If you care for me, enjoy your present leisure, and persuade yourself that no matter for fear or trembling can befall a man apart from fault and wrongdoing; and of this you are free, and always will be. If I feel I can safely do so, I shall join you shortly, and if anything occurs to alter my intention, I shall let you know immediately. Eager to see me as I should like you to be, in your poor state of health you must not stir from where you are without first writing to me and asking what I wish you to do. I hope you will continue to care for me, and pay proper regard to your health and peace of mind.

183 (VII.3)
CICERO TO M. MARIUS

Rome, mid April (?) 46

From M. Cicero to M. Marius greetings.

Considering, as I very often do, the general miseries in which we have been living for so many years and, as I see it, shall continue to live, I am apt to call to mind the last time we were together. I remember the very day—12 May in the Consulship of Lentulus and Marcellus.[1] I had come down to my place near Pompeii that evening, and found you there to meet me in a troubled state of mind—troubled by the thought of my duty, and my danger too. You were afraid that if I stayed in Italy I should be failing in my duty, whereas if I set off for the war you were disturbed by the risk I should run. No doubt you saw on that occasion

---

[1] I.e. 49; see *Letters to Atticus* 208 (X.16).4.

quoque ita conturbatum ut non explicarem quid esset optimum factu. pudori tamen malui famaeque cedere quam
salutis meae rationem ducere.

2   Cuius me mei facti paenituit, non tam propter periculum meum quam propter vitia multa quae ibi offendi quo
veneram: primum neque magnas copias neque bellicosas;
deinde, extra ducem paucosque praeterea (de principibus
loquor), reliquos primum in ipso bello rapacis, deinde in
oratione ita crudelis[2] ut ipsam victoriam horrerem; maximum autem aes alienum amplissimorum virorum. quid
quaeris? nihil boni praeter causam. quae cum vidissem,
desperans victoriam primum coepi suadere pacem, cuius
fueram semper auctor; deinde, cum ab ea sententia Pompeius valde abhorreret, suadere institui ut bellum duceret.
hoc interdum probabat et in ea sententia videbatur fore, et
fuisset fortasse nisi quadam ex pugna coepisset suis militibus confidere. ex eo tempore vir ille summus nullus
imperator fuit. signa tirone et collecticio exercitu cum
legionibus robustissimis contulit. victus turpissime amissis
etiam castris solus fugit.

3   Hunc ego mihi belli finem feci nec putavi, cum integri
pares non fuissemus, fractos superiores fore. discessi ab eo
bello in quo aut in acie cadendum fuit aut in aliquas in-
sidias incidendum aut deveniendum in victoris manus aut
ad Iubam confugiendum aut capiendus tamquam exsilio
locus aut consciscenda mors voluntaria. certe nihil fuit

---

[2] reliqui . . . rapaces . . . crudeles *(Man.)*

---

[2] At Dyrrachium in July 48.

that I too was in such a state of mental turmoil that I could not work out what was best to do. However, I preferred to yield to the claims of honour and reputation than to calculate for my own safety.

I came to regret my action, not so much on account of my personal hazard as of the many deplorable aspects of the situation which confronted me on arrival. To begin with, the forces fell short both in numbers and in fighting spirit. Secondly, apart from the Commander-in-Chief and a few besides, all (I am referring to the principal figures) showed their greed for plunder in the war itself, and talked in so bloodthirsty a style that I shuddered at the prospect of victory. Moreover, those of the highest rank were up to their ears in debt. In a phrase, nothing good except the cause. With these things before my eyes, I started by recommending peace, of which I had always been an advocate. When Pompey showed himself strongly averse to that policy, I set myself to recommend delaying tactics. At times he tended to favour this course and seemed likely to make it his policy. Perhaps he would have done so, had not the result of a particular engagement[2] given him confidence in his troops. From then on that great man ceased to be a general. With his raw medley of an army he fought a pitched battle against the hardiest of legions, and was defeated. Even his camp was lost. He fled shamefully, alone.

For me that was the end of the war. Our full strength had proved no match for the enemy. I saw no prospect of getting the upper hand after a shattering reverse. I withdrew from the conflict. What were the choices? To die on the battlefield, or to fall into some trap, or to come into the hands of the victor, or to take refuge with Juba, or to select a place of virtual exile, or suicide. Nothing else surely, if

praeterea, si te victori nolles aut non auderes committere. ex omnibus autem iis quae dixi incommodis nihil tolerabilius exsilio, praesertim innocenti, ubi nulla adiuncta est turpitudo; addo etiam, cum ea urbe careas in qua nihil sit quod videre possis sine dolore.

Ego cum meis ⟨et⟩,[3] si quicquam nunc cuiusquam est, etiam in meis esse malui. quae acciderunt omnia dixi futura. veni domum, non quo optima vivendi condicio esset, sed tamen, si esset aliqua forma rei publicae, tamquam[4] in patria ut essem, si nulla, tamquam in exsilio. mortem mihi cur consciscerem causa non visa est, cur optarem multae causae. vetus est enim, ubi non sis qui fueris, non esse cur velis vivere. sed tamen vacare culpa magnum est solacium, praesertim cum habeam duas res quibus me sustentem, optimarum artium scientiam et maximarum rerum gloriam; quarum altera mihi vivo numquam eripietur, altera ne mortuo quidem.

Haec ad te scripsi verbosius et tibi molestus fui quod te cum mei tum rei publicae cognovi amantissimum. notum tibi omne meum consilium esse volui, ut primum scires me numquam voluisse plus quemquam posse quam universam rem publicam, postea autem quam alicuius culpa tantum valeret unus ut obsisti non posset, me voluisse pacem; amisso exercitu et eo duce in quo spes fuerat uno me voluisse etiam reliquis omnibus, postquam non potuerim, mihi ipsi finem fecisse belli; nunc autem, si haec civitas est, civem esse me, si non, exsulem esse non incommodiore

4

5

---

[3] (*Schütz*)   [4] *del. Frederking*

---

[3] Pompey.

one would not, or dared not, trust oneself to the victor. Of all the aforesaid evils exile is as tolerable as any—especially an innocent exile, with no stain of discredit, and (let me add) exile from a country that holds nothing one can look upon without distress.

For my part, I preferred to be with my own people, and my own belongings too—if anything belongs to anybody nowadays. All that has happened I foretold. I came home, not that the life there offered was particularly attractive, but still, if there was to be some shape or form of free constitution, I wanted to feel as though I was living in my country; and if not, it would serve as a place of exile. I saw no reason to take my life, though many reasons to pray for its ending. It's an old saying that when a man is no longer what he was he has nothing to live for. However, there's a great comfort in having nothing with which to reproach oneself; and I have two further supports, conversance with noble arts and the glory of great achievements. Of the first I shall never be deprived in life, of the second not even in death.

In writing all this I have not spared words. I have thus imposed upon you because I know how deeply you care for me and for the commonwealth. I wanted you to be acquainted with my whole mind and purpose, to know in the first place that I never wished any man to have more power than the state entire; but when by the fault of somebody or other[3] a single person became too strong to resist, I was for peace. With the loss of the army and of the leader upon whom all our hopes were pinned I wanted an end to the war for all concerned; unable to bring that to pass, I made an end for myself individually. At present, if this is a body politic, I am a citizen; if it is not, I am an exile in no worse a

173

loco quam si Rhodum ‹me›[5] aut Mytilenas contulissem.

6   Haec tecum coram malueram; sed quia longius fiebat, volui per litteras eadem, ut haberes quid diceres si quando in vituperatores meos incidisses. sunt enim qui, cum meus interitus nihil fuerit rei publicae profuturus, criminis loco putent esse quod vivam; quibus ego certo scio non videri satis multos perisse. qui si me audissent, quamvis iniqua pace, honeste tamen viverent. armis enim inferiores, non causa, fuissent.

Habes epistulam verbosiorem fortasse quam velles; quod tibi ita videri putabo nisi mihi longiorem remiseris. ego si quae volo expediero, brevi tempore te, ut spero, videbo.

184 (XVI.19)

Scr. in Tusculano fort. m. Quint. an. 46

TULLIUS TIRONI SUO S.

Exspecto tuas litteras de multis rebus, te ipsum multo magis. Demetrium redde nostrum, et aliud si quid potest boni. de Aufidiano nomine nihil te hortor. scio tibi curae esse, sed confice. et si ob eam rem moraris, accipio causam; si id te non tenet, advola. litteras tuas valde exspecto.

Vale.

[5] (*Ern.: post* Myt- R)

place than if I had betaken myself to Rhodes or Mytilene.

I would rather have discussed all this with you in person; but since time was dragging on, I thought it desirable to do so by letter, in order to give you something to say if you should happen to fall in with people who speak ill of me. There are those who hold it an offence in me to be alive, even though my destruction would have brought no advantage to the commonwealth. I am well aware that they think the death roll not long enough. Had those upon it listened to me, they would at least be living honourably, however harsh the terms of peace, proved weaker in military strength but not in the justice of their cause.

So here you have a wordier letter, it may be, than you would have wished. I shall believe you think so, unless you send me a longer one in return. I have certain matters I want to clear up; that done, I hope I shall see you shortly.

184 (XVI.19)
CICERO TO TIRO

Tusculum, July (?) 46

From Tullius to his dear Tiro greetings.

I am looking forward to a letter from you on many topics, but to you in person even more. Make Demetrius my friend, and do any other good work you can. I won't urge you about Aufidius' debt, for I know you have it in mind. But get a settlement. If you are taking time on that account, I accept your excuse; but if that is not detaining you, hurry. I am impatiently looking forward to a letter from you.

Good-bye.

185 (XVI.22)

Scr. in Tusculano fort. m. Quint. an. 46

TULLIUS TIRONI SUO S.

1   Spero ex tuis litteris tibi melius esse, cupio certe. cui quidem rei omni ratione cura ut inservias et cave suspiceris contra meam voluntatem te facere quod non sis mecum. mecum es si te curas. qua re malo te valetudini tuae servire quam meis oculis et auribus. etsi enim et audio te et video libenter, tamen hoc multo erit si valebis iucundius.

Ego hic cesso, quia ipse nihil scribo; lego autem libentissime. tu istic, si quid librarii mea manu non intellegent, monstrabis. una omnino interpositio difficilior est, quam ne ipse quidem facile legere soleo, de quadrimo Catone. de triclinio cura, ut facis. Tertia[1] aderit, modo ne Publi‹li›us rogatus sit.

2   Demetrius iste numquam omnino Phalereus fuit, sed nunc plane Bellienus[2] est. itaque te do vicarium; tu eum observabis. 'etsi—,' 'verum tamen—,' 'de illis—'; nosti cetera. sed tamen, si quem cum eo sermonem habueris, scribes ad me, ut mihi nascatur epistulae argumentum et ut

[1] Terentia *Böhm**
[2] Belli- V: Billi- MD: Bibli- H*

---

[1] Cicero had recently written a Eulogy of Cato (now lost). The story of the four-year-old Cato's defiance of Poppaedius the Marsian is told by Valerius Maximus (3.1.2) and Plutarch in his Life (2).

[2] Brother (?) of Cicero's second wife. The manuscripts have *Publius,* a routine error. (Junia) Tertia may have been a friend of

185 (XVI.22)
CICERO TO TIRO

Tusculum, July (?) 46

From Tullius to his dear Tiro greetings.

From your letter I trust that you are better, certainly I very much hope so. Mind you consider that in every way, and don't take it into your head that you are acting against my wishes in not being with me. You *are* with me if you are looking after yourself. So I want you to care for your health rather than for my eyes and ears. Of course I enjoy hearing and seeing you, but that will be a much greater pleasure if you are fit and well.

I am idling here because I don't write anything myself, though I am reading with great gusto. If the copyists up there can't make out my handwriting, you will put them right. There *is* a rather difficult inset which I don't find easy to read myself, the story about Cato as a four-year-old.[1] See about the dining room, as you are doing. Tertia will be there, provided that Publilius[2] is not invited.

That fellow Demetrius was never a Phalereus[3] but now he is an absolute Bellienus![4] So I appoint you my deputy— you show him the courtesies. 'Though to be sure . . . ,' 'All the same . . . ,' 'As to that . . .'—you know how it goes on. Still, if you have any talk with him, please write and tell me,

Terentia's, whose divorce had probably gone through early in 46. The conjecture *Terentia* (Boehm) is doubtful at best, especially as Cicero and his ex-wife were not on good terms.

[3] I.e. a man of polish and wit, qualities for which Demetrius of Phalerum was celebrated.   [4] I.e. an assassin; cf. Letter 149.2. He could bore his company to death.

tuas quam longissimas litteras legam.

Cura, mi Tiro, ut valeas; hoc gratius mihi facere nihil potes.

Vale.

186 (XVI.17)

Scr. in Tusculano fort. m. Quint. an. 46

1 TULLIUS TIRONI S.

Video quid agas; tuas quoque epistulas vis referri in volumina. sed heus tu, qui κανών esse meorum scriptorum soles, unde illud tam ἄκυρον 'valetudini fideliter inserviendo'? unde in istum locum 'fideliter' venit? cui verbo domicilium est proprium in officio, migrationes in alienum multae. nam et doctrina et domus et ars et ager etiam fidelis dici potest, ut sit, quo modo Theophrasto placet, vere-

2 cunda tralatio. sed haec coram.

Demetrius venit ad me; quo quidem comitatu ἀφωμίλησα satis scite. tu eum videlicet non potuisti videre. cras aderit; videbis igitur. nam ego hinc perendie mane cogito.

Valetudo tua me valde sollicitat; sed inservi et fac omnia. tum te mecum esse, tum mihi cumulatissime satis facere putato.

---

1 *Fideliter.* Tiro no doubt meant 'conscientiously.' Cicero seems to have taken him to mean that he was giving his health *its* due.

so that I get a theme for a letter and as long as possible a letter of yours to read.

Look after your health, my dear Tiro. You can do nothing to please me more.

Good-bye.

186 (XVI.17)
CICERO TO TIRO

Tusculum, July (?) 46

From Tullius to Tiro greetings.

I see your game! You want your letters too put into rolls. But just a moment, you yardstick of my literary style, where did you come by so bizarre a phrase as 'faithfully[1] studying my health'? What is 'faithfully' doing in such a context? The home territory of the word is the performance of a duty, but it makes many excursions into other fields. For example, it can be applied to acquired knowledge or a house or a vocation or a piece of land within the bounds of decent metaphor as approved by Theophrastus.[2] But of this when we are together.

I have had a visit from Demetrius, from whose company on the road I disengaged myself rather neatly. Of course you could not have seen him. He will be in Rome tomorrow, so see him you will. For my part, I intend leaving here early the day after.

Your health makes me very anxious, but pamper it and leave nothing undone. *Then* you may feel that you are with me and that I am more than satisfied.

---

[2] He had discussed metaphor in his treatise *On Speech*.

Cuspio quod operam dedisti mihi gratum est. valde enim eius causa volo.

Vale.

187 (V.16)

Scr. Romae aestate vel autumno, ut vid., an. 46

M. CICERO S. D. TITIO

1 Etsi unus ex omnibus minime sum ad te consolandum accommodatus, quod tantum ex tuis molestiis cepi doloris ut consolatione ipse egerem, tamen, cum longius a summi luctus acerbitate meus abesset dolor quam tuus, statui nostrae necessitudinis esse meaeque in te benevolentiae non tacere tanto in tuo maerore tam diu sed adhibere aliquam modicam consolationem, quae levare dolorem tuum posset si minus sanare potuisset.

2 Est autem consolatio pervulgata quidem illa maxime, quam semper in ore atque in animo habere debemus, homines nos ut esse meminerimus, ea lege natos ut omnibus telis Fortunae proposita sit vita nostra, neque esse recusandum quo minus ea qua nati sumus condicione vivamus, neve tam graviter eos casus feramus quos nullo consilio vitare possimus eventisque aliorum memoria repetendis

3 nihil accidisse novi nobis cogitemus. ⟨sed⟩[1] neque hae neque ceterae consolationes quae sunt a sapientissimis viris usurpatae memoriaeque litteris proditae tantum viden-

[1] *(Wes.)*

---

[1] Not certainly identifiable with any of the other Titii who crop

Thank you for helping Cuspius, whose hearty well-wisher I am.

Good-bye.

187 (V.16)
CICERO TO TITIUS

Rome, summer or autumn 46 (?)

From M. Cicero to Titius[1] greetings.

Of all men I am the least suited to console you, since I am so grieved by your distress that I stand in need of consolation myself. But seeing that my grief falls shorter than yours of the ultimate bitterness of sorrow, I have concluded that our friendship and my anxiety for your welfare make it wrong to be silent so long in your heavy affliction, and require me to proffer a measure of comfort, which may alleviate, if it cannot heal, your pain.

There is a very well-worn form of consolation which we should always have on our lips and in our minds. We must remember that we are but men, the law of whose birth requires that our lives be a target for all the darts of Fortune. We must not rebel against the condition to which we are born. We must bear less hard those misfortunes which we cannot by any prudence avoid. We must recall the experiences of our fellows, and reflect that nothing new has befallen us. But more efficacious perhaps than these and other forms of consolation employed by the wisest of mankind and consigned to memory in their writings should be

up at this period. He had apparently lost two or more sons in an epidemic; cf. the reference in *Letters to Atticus* 247 (XII.10).

tur proficere debere quantum status ipse nostrae civitatis
et haec per‹tur›batio temporum perditorum, cum beatis-
simi sint qui liberos non susceperunt, minus autem miseri
qui his temporibus amiserunt quam si eosdem bona aut
denique aliqua re publica perdidissent.

4   Quod si tuum te desiderium movet aut si tuarum rerum
cogitatione maeres, non facile exhauriri tibi istum dolorem
posse universum puto; sin illa te res cruciat quae magis
amoris est, ut eorum qui occiderunt miserias lugeas, ut ea
non dicam quae saepissime et legi et audivi, nihil mali esse
in morte, ex qua si[2] resideat sensus immortalitas illa potius
quam mors ducenda sit, sin sit amissus nulla videri miseria
debeat quae non sentiatur, hoc tamen non dubitans confirmare possum, ea misceri, parari, impendere rei publicae
quae qui reliquerit nullo modo mihi quidem deceptus esse
videatur. quid est enim iam non modo pudori, probitati,
virtuti, rectis studiis, bonis artibus sed omnino libertati ac
saluti loci? non mehercule quemquam audivi hoc gravissimo et pestilentissimo anno adulescentulum aut puerum
mortuum qui mihi non a dis immortalibus ereptus ex his
miseriis atque ex iniquissima condicione vitae videretur.

5   Qua re, si tibi unum hoc detrahi potest, ne quid iis quos
amasti mali putes contigisse, permultum erit ex maerore
tuo deminutum. relinquetur enim simplex illa iam cura

[2] et quasi (*Iac. Gron.*)

the actual state of our community in these chaotic and desperate times. In the world of today those who have never raised children are most to be envied, and those who have lost them less to be commiserated than if they had been thus bereaved in a well-ordered commonwealth, or indeed in any commonwealth properly so called.

If it is the sense of your own loss that grieves you, if it is your own fate you lament, then I think your pain cannot easily exhaust itself altogether. On the other hand, if the sting lies in your grief for the sad lot of the departed, a sentiment more closely in keeping with affection, it is another matter. I will not dwell on the arguments I have often heard and read in books to the effect that there is no evil in death, because if any consciousness remains thereafter, we should not think of it as death but as immortality, whereas if all consciousness disappears, misery unfelt should not be deemed misery at all; but this I can declare without hesitation, that to my mind at any rate whoever has left behind him the present political turmoil, and all that is in preparation, looming ahead of us, has been cheated of *nothing*. There is no place any more for honour, uprightness, manliness, honest pursuits and liberal accomplishments; none even for personal independence and existence as a citizen. I give you my word that whenever in this terrible year of pestilence I have heard of the death of a young man or a boy, I have considered him as snatched by the Immortal Gods from these calamities and from a life of which all the terms were in his disfavour.

If only you can be divested of the idea that some evil has befallen those dear to you, that in itself will very sensibly diminish the sum of your sorrow. There will then remain the simple burden of your own grief, in which *they* will

183

doloris tui, quae non cum illis communicabitur sed ad te
ipsum proprie referetur; in qua non est iam gravitatis et
sapientiae tuae, quam tu a puero praestitisti, ferre immo-
deratius casum incommodorum tuorum, qui sit ab eorum
quos dilexeris miseria maloque seiunctus. etenim eum
semper te et privatis in rebus et publicis praestitisti tuenda
tibi ut sit gravitas et constantiae serviendum. nam quod
adlatura est ipsa diuturnitas, quae maximos luctus vetustate tollit, id nos praecipere consilio prudentiaque debe-
6   mus. etenim si nulla fuit umquam [si] liberis amissis tam
imbecillo mulier animo quae non aliquando lugendi modum fecerit, certe nos, quod est dies adlatura, id consilio
ante ferre[3] debemus neque exspectare temporis medicinam, quam repraesentare ratione possimus.

His ego litteris si quid profecissem existimabam optan-
dum quiddam me esse adsecutum; sin minus forte valuis-
sent, officio tamen esse functum viri[4] benevolentissimi
atque amicissimi. quem me tibi et fuisse semper existimes
velim et futurum esse confidas.

188 (IX.21)

Scr. Romae anno incerto

CICERO PAETO S.

1   Ain tandem? insanire tibi videris quod imitere verbo-

[3] anteferre *(Baiter)*
[4] functurum *(Wes.)*

have no part; it will pertain to you individually. Now to bear the troubles chance has brought upon you more hardly than is fitting, when they involve no unhappiness or evil for those you loved, is really unworthy of the responsibility and sound sense which you have shown since your childhood days. The character you have always presented in public and in private requires you to maintain your dignity and faithfully to follow the pattern you have set. For it is our duty by reason and wisdom to anticipate the effects of time, which by its mere efflux cancels our deepest sorrows. After all, there was never a woman bereaved of children so frail of spirit that she did not in the end set a term to her mourning. Surely then *we* should apply in advance by using our reason what the passing of the days will bring; we ought not to wait for time to produce the medicine which our intelligence can supply to hand.

If this letter has done you good, I feel that I have achieved something worth praying for. But perhaps it has had but little effect, in which case I have at least discharged the duty of a sincere friend and well-wisher. That I have ever been such to you I hope you believe, and are confident that I shall so remain.

188 (IX.21)
CICERO TO PAPIRIUS PAETUS

Rome, date uncertain

From Cicero to Paetus greetings.

Really? You think you are out of your mind to be imitat-

rum meorum, ut scribis, fulmina? tum insanires si consequi non posses; cum vero etiam vincas, me prius irrideas
quam te oportet. qua re nihil tibi opus est illud a Trabea,
sed potius ἀπότευγμα meum. verum tamen quid tibi ego
videor in epistulis? nonne plebeio sermone agere tecum?
nec enim semper eodem modo. quid enim simile habet
epistula aut iudicio aut contioni? quin ipsa iudicia non
solemus omnia tractare uno modo. privatas causas et eas
tenuis agimus subtilius, capitis aut famae scilicet ornatius.
epistulas vero cottidianis verbis texere solemus.

2   Sed tamen, mi Paete, qui tibi venit in mentem negare
Papirium quemquam umquam nisi plebeium fuisse? fuerunt enim patricii minorum gentium, quorum princeps L.
Papirius Mugillanus, qui censor cum L. Sempronio Atrati-
no fuit, cum ante consul[1] cum eodem fuisset, annis post
Romam conditam CCCXII; sed tum Papisii dicebamini.
post hunc XIII fuerunt[2] sella curuli ante L. Papirium Crassum, qui primum Papi⟨s⟩ius est vocari desitus. is dictator
cum L. Papirio Cursore magistro equitum factus est annis
post Romam conditam CCCCXV, et quadriennio post consul cum K.[3] Duilio. hunc secutus est Cursor, homo valde

[1] consul . . . censor *(Man.)*
[2] sederunt ⟨in⟩ *(sed* in *praeter necessitatem) Wes.*
[3] c.

---

[1] The context can only be guessed. Perhaps Paetus had been
sent a copy of a Ciceronian speech and tried to produce something
in the same vein. Cicero writes more than once of Demosthenes'
'thunderbolts' *(fulmina).*
[2] Perhaps the quotation warned against reaching beyond one's
grasp.

ing my 'verbal thunderbolts'?[1] You would be if you could not make a success of it. Since in fact you actually go one better, you should make fun of me rather than yourself. So you don't need that quotation from Trabea.[2] The 'miss' was rather mine. But tell me now, how do you find me as a letter writer? Don't I deal with you in colloquial style? The fact is that one's style has to vary. A letter is one thing, a court of law or a public meeting quite another. Even for the courts we don't have just one style. In pleading civil cases, unimportant ones, we put on no frills, whereas cases involving status or reputation naturally get something more elaborate. As for letters, we weave them out of the language of everyday.

Be that as it may, my dear Paetus, what possessed you to say that all the Papirii without exception were plebeians? They were in fact patricians, one of the Lesser Clans.[3] The roll begins with L. Papirius Mugillanus, who was Censor along with L. Sempronius Atratinus, having previously been his colleague in the Consulship in the year 312 after the foundation of Rome.[4] But in those days you used to be called Papisii. Thirteen held curule office between him and L. Papirius Crassus, the first of the race not to be called Papisius. He was appointed Dictator with L. Papirius Cursor as his Master of the Horse in the year 415 after the foundation,[5] and four years later became Consul with Kaeso Duilius. Cursor[6] followed him, a very distin-

---

[3] According to tradition King Tarquinius Priscus appointed a number of new Senators whose clans were called *gentes minores*.

[4] By inclusive reckoning from a foundation date 754 = 443 B.C.

[5] 340 B.C.

[6] Son of the Cursor just mentioned.

honoratus, deinde L. Masso aedilicius, inde multi Massones. quorum quidem tu omnium patriciorum imagines habeas volo.

3   Deinde Carbones et Turdi insequuntur. hi plebeii fuerunt, quos contemnas censeo; nam praeter hunc C. Carbonem quem Damasippus occidit civis e re publica Carbonum nemo fuit. cognovimus Cn. Carbonem et eius fratrem scurram; quid iis improbius? de hoc amico meo, Rubriae filio, nihil dico. tres illi fratres fuerunt, C., Cn., M. Carbones. Marcus P. Flacco accusante condemnatus, fur magnus, ex Sicilia. Gaius accusante L. Crasso cantharidas sumpsisse dicitur. is et tribunus pl. seditiosus et P. Africano vim attulisse existimatus est. hoc vero qui Lilybaei a Pompeio nostro est interfectus improbior nemo meo iudicio fuit. iam pater eius accusatus a M. Antonio sutorio atramento absolutus putatur.

Qua re ad patres censeo revertare; plebeii quam fuerint importuni vides.

---

7 Surnamed Arvina. He was killed by the Marian leader L. Junius Brutus Damasippus in 82.

8 Probably not the Marian leader mentioned below, but a person otherwise unknown, perhaps son of the 'great thief' Marcus. His brother can be identified with a C. Carbo who seems to have been Tribune in 89 and a supporter of Sulla.

9 Another Gaius, perhaps son of the 'wag,' who was condemned (probably in 58) for extortion in his province of Bithynia. Caesar may have brought him back from exile.

10 Father of Arvina.

11 Gnaeus, the Marian leader, son of the second of the three brothers. Pompey executed him in 81. His father, also Gnaeus, was Consul in 113.

12 Generally supposed to mean that he poisoned himself like

guished official career. Then came L. Masso, of aedilician rank, and many Massos after him. All the foregoing were patricians, and I hope you will have their portraits in your hall.

Then follow the Carbos and the Turdi. These were plebeians, and I advise you to ignore them. For with the exception of the C. Carbo[7] who was killed by Damasippus, not one of the Carbos was an asset to his country. We knew Cn. Carbo[8] and his brother the wag—a pair of rascals if ever there was one. Of my friend who is still with us,[9] Rubria's son, I say nothing. There were the three famous brothers, C., Cn., and M. Carbo. Marcus, a great thief, was condemned after his career in Sicily on a charge brought by P. Flaccus. Gaius[10] is said to have swallowed Spanish fly when prosecuted by Crassus. He was a seditious Tribune of the Plebs and was believed to have murdered P. Africanus. As for the man[11] who was put to death at Lilybaeum by our friend Pompey, he was in my opinion as arrant a rascal as ever breathed. His father before him was prosecuted by M. Antonius and is thought to have been acquitted by shoe-blacking.[12]

So I recommend you to 'revert to the *patres.*'[13] The plebeians were an unconscionable lot, as you see.

his brother Gaius, but such a coincidence could hardly have failed to attract notice in our sources. Probably the reference is to some sort of tampering with the voting tablets at the trial. The charge probably concerned his defeat by the Cimbri in 113.

[13] Probably a facetious echo of a technical phrase. In default of patrician magistrates the auspices were said to 'revert to the Fathers' (i.e. the patrician members of the Senate); cf. *Letters to Marcus Brutus* 9 (I.5).3.

189 (IX.22)

Scr. Romae an. incerto sed, ut vid., inter 46 et 44

CICERO PAETO

1   Amo verecundiam!—vel potius libertatem loquendi.[1] atqui hoc Zenoni placuit, homini mehercule acuto, etsi Academiae nostrae cum eo magna rixa est. sed, ut dico, placet Stoicis suo quamque rem nomine appellare. sic enim disserunt, nihil esse obscenum, nihil turpe dictu; nam, si quod sit in obscenitate flagitium, id aut in re esse aut in verbo; nihil esse tertium. in re non est. itaque non modo in comoediis res ipsa narratur (ut ille in 'Demiurgo'

modo forte—

nosti canticum. meministi Roscium:

ita me destituit nudum.

totus est sermo verbis tectus, re impudentior) sed etiam in tragoediis. quid est enim illud

quae mulier una

quid, inquam, est

usurpat duplex cubile?

quid

huius †ferei†[2]
hic cubile inire est ausus?

[1] *suspecta haec distinctione vindicavit SB (vide ed. Teubn.)*
[2] filiae *tempt. SB*

189 (IX.22)
CICERO TO PAPIRIUS PAETUS

Rome, 46–44 (?)

From Cicero to Paetus.[1]

I like your modesty!—or rather your freedom of language. But after all, this found favour with Zeno, a clever man, no getting away from it, though our Academy is mightily at loggerheads with him—but as I say, the Stoics hold it proper to call everything by its name. Their argument runs like this: There is no such thing as obscene or indecent language. For if there is anything shocking in obscenity, it lies either in the matter or in the word; there is no third possibility. Now it does not lie in the matter. Accordingly, there are accounts of the actual process, not only in Comedy (for example *The Demiurge:*[2] 'T'other day, as luck would have it . . .'—you know the solo,[3] you remember Roscius—'so she left me bare': the whole speech is guarded as to the words, but pretty shameless as to the matter) but in Tragedy too.[4] What else is this bit: 'When one woman' (mark it now) 'sleeps in two beds'? Or 'His daughter's (?) bed / This man dared enter?' Or 'Me, a vir-

---

[1] This exposition of the Stoic doctrine that 'the wise man will call a spade a spade' was provoked by the word *mentula* (cf. para. 2) in a letter from Paetus. That Cicero controverts or refutes the doctrine is a hallucination of certain annotators, though he does state (not very solemnly) a personal preference for 'Plato's modesty.' The whole thing is a *jeu d'esprit.*

[2] By Sex. Turpilius, second-century writer of Latin comedies.

[3] *Canticum* (lyric monologue).

[4] The sources of the following quotations are unknown.

quid est

> virginem me quondam invitam per vim violat
>   Iuppiter?

bene 'violat'; atqui idem significat, sed alterum nemo tullis-
2 set. vides igitur, cum eadem res sit, quia verba non sint,
nihil videri turpe. ergo in re non est.

Multo minus in verbis. si enim quod verbo significatur
id turpe non est, verbum, quod significat, turpe esse non
potest. 'anum' appellas alieno nomine; cur non suo potius?
si turpe est, ne alieno quidem; si non est, suo potius. cau-
dam antiqui 'penem' vocabant, ex quo est propter similitudinem 'penicillus'; at hodie penis est in obscenis. at vero
Piso ille Frugi in annalibus suis queritur adulescentis 'peni
deditos' esse. quod tu in epistula appellas suo nomine ille
tectius 'penem'; sed quia multi, factum est tam obscenum
quam id verbum quo tu usus es. quid quod vulgo dicitur
'cum nos te voluimus convenire'? num obscenum est?
memini in senatu disertum consularem ita eloqui: 'hanc
culpam maiorem an illam dicam?' potuit obscenius? 'non,'
inquis; 'non enim ita sensit.' non ergo in verbo est. docui
autem in re non esse; nusquam igitur est.

3   'Liberis dare operam' quam honeste dicitur; etiam
patres rogant filios. eius operae nomen non audent dicere.
Socraten fidibus docuit nobilissimus fidicen; is Connus

---

⁵ Meaning 'paintbrush.'   ⁶ *Mentula.*

⁷ *Cum nos* pronounced like *cunnos.*

⁸ Doubtless Cicero himself; cf. *Letters to Atticus* 44 (II.24).3,
consularem disertum.

gin all unwilling, Jupiter did rudely force.' 'Force' is very
good. And yet it means the same as the other word, which
nobody would have tolerated. You see therefore that, although the matter is the same, there is not thought to be
any indecency because the words are different. Therefore
it does not lie in the matter.

Much less does it lie in the words. For if that which is
signified by a word is not indecent, the word which signi-
fies it cannot be indecent either. You say 'seat,' using a
transferred word: why not use the proper one? If it's indecent, you should not use the first even; if not, you should
use the second. The ancients used to call a tail a penis—
hence 'penicillus'[5] from the similarity. But nowadays
'penis' is an obscene word. And yet Piso Frugi in his *Annals* complains of young men being 'devoted to the penis.'
What you call by its proper name[6] in your letter he more
guardedly called 'penis'; but because many others did the
same, it became no less obscene a word than the one you
have employed. Again, 'When we[7] wanted to meet you' is
an ordinary enough phrase. Is it obscene? I remember an
eloquent Consular[8] once saying in the Senate 'Shall I call
this or that[9] the more reprehensible?' Most obscene, was it
not? no, you say, for he didn't intend it so. Very well then,
obscenity does not lie in the word; and I have shown that it
does not lie in the matter. Therefore it lies nowhere.

'Provide for the continuation of your family.' What a respectable phrase! Fathers even ask their sons to do it. But
they dare not utter the word for this 'provision.' Socrates
was taught the lute by a very celebrated player whose

[9] *(Il)lam dicam* pronounced like *landicam.*

vocitatus est. num id obscenum putas? cum loquimur 'terni,' nihil flagiti dicimus; at cum 'bini,' obscenum est?
'Graecis quidem' inquies. nihil est ergo in verbo, quoniam
et ego Graece scio et tamen tibi dico 'bini,' idque tu facis
quasi ego Graece, non Latine, dixerim. 'ruta' et 'menta'
recte utrumque. volo mentam pusillam ita appellare ut
'rutulam': non licet. belle[3] 'tectoriola.' dic ergo etiam 'pavi-
menta' isto modo: non potes. viden igitur nihil esse nisi
ineptias, turpitudinem nec in verbo esse nec in re, itaque
nusquam esse?

4   Igitur in verbis honestis obscena ponimus. quid enim?
non honestum verbum est 'divisio'? at inest obscenum; cui
respondet 'intercapedo.' num haec ergo obscena sunt? nos
autem ridicule: si dicimus 'ille patrem strangulavit,' honorem non praefamur; sin de Aurelia aliquid aut Lollia,
honos praefandus est. et quidem iam etiam non[4] obscena
verba pro obscenis sunt. 'battuit,' inquit: impudenter;
'depsit': multo impudentius. atqui neutrum est obscenum.
stultorum plena sunt omnia. 'testes' verbum honestissimum in iudicio, alio loco non nimis. et[5] honesti 'colei
Lanuvini,' Cliternini non honesti. quid ⟨quod⟩[6] ipsa res
modo honesta, modo turpis? suppedit, flagitium est; iam
erit nudus in balneo, non reprehendes.

3 bella *(Or.)*
4 non etiam *(Lamb.)*
5 ad *(Wes.)*
6 *(SB)*

10 'Three each.'
11 'Two each'; *bini* phonetically = Greek *binei*.

name was Connus. Do you think that obscene? When we say 'terni'[10] there's nothing to shock; but when we say 'bini'[11] is it obscene? 'Yes,' you say, 'to a Greek.' Then there is nothing in the word, since I know Greek, and I still say to you 'bini,' and you behave as though I spoke in Greek instead of in Latin. Take 'ruta' and 'menta'; both all right. But if I want a word for 'little mint' corresponding to 'rutula,'[12] I can't have it. 'Tectoriola'[13] is a nice enough word. Try to make a diminutive from 'pavimentum' in the same way: you can't. Don't you see that it's all nonsense, that indecency does not exist either in word or matter, and therefore does not exist at all?

So we utter obscenities when we use respectable words. Take 'divisio.' A respectable word, wouldn't you say? But it contains an obscenity, just like 'intercapedo.' Are these words obscene? Our practice is really comical. If we say 'he throttled his father,' we don't apologize; but if we say something about Aurelia or Lollia,[14] an apology is due. Indeed even quite innocent words have come to count as obscene. 'Battuit,' somebody says: shameless! 'Depsit': much more so! Yet neither word is obscene. The world is full of fools. 'Testes' is a perfectly respectable word in a court of law, elsewhere not too respectable. Lanuvian bags are respectable, Cliternian not. Why even an action is sometimes respectable, sometimes indecent, is it not? It's shocking to break wind. Put the culprit naked in the bath, and you won't blame him.

---

[12] 'Little rue.' The corresponding diminutive from *menta* would be *mentula*.

[13] Diminutive of *tectorium,* 'wall plaster.'

[14] The notorious wives of Catiline and A. Gabinius.

Habes scholam Stoicam: ὁ σοφὸς εὐθυρρημονήσει.
quam multa ex uno verbo tuo! te adversus me omnia audere gratum est; ego servo et servabo (sic enim adsuevi)
Platonis verecundiam. itaque tectis verbis ea ad te scripsi
quae apertissimis agunt Stoici. sed illi etiam crepitus aiunt
aeque liberos ac ructus esse oportere. honorem igitur Kalendis Martiis.

Tu me diliges et valebis.

190 (IX.16)

Scr., ut vid., in Tusculano med. m. Quint. an. 46

CICERO PAETO S.

1   Delectarunt me tuae litterae, in quibus primum amavi
amorem tuum, qui te ad scribendum incitavit verentem ne
Silius suo nuntio aliquid mihi sollicitudinis attulisset; de
quo et tu mihi antea scripseras bis quidem eodem exemplo, facile ut intellegerem te esse commotum, et ego tibi
accurate rescripseram, ut, quo modo in tali re atque tempore, aut liberarem te ista cura aut certe levarem.

2   Sed quoniam proximis quoque litteris ostendis quantae
tibi curae sit ea res, sic, mi Paete, habeto, quicquid arte
fieri pot⟨u⟩erit (non enim iam satis est consilio pugnare,

---

[15] The date of the Matronalia, the festival of married women,
on which husbands and lovers gave presents to their ladies.

[1] Probably the ex-governor of Bithynia; possibly a former of-
ficer of Caesar, T. Sil(l)ius. His report seems to have concerned
some sharp saying of Cicero which had been passed on to Caesar.
Paetus was afraid it might give offence.

So there you have a Stoic lecture: 'The Sage will call a spade a spade.' What a multitude of words out of one of yours, to be sure! I like you to have no inhibitions when you are addressing me. For myself, I adhere (and shall so continue, since it is my habit) to the modesty of Plato. That is why I have written to you in guarded language on a theme which the Stoics handle with complete freedom. But they also say that we ought to break wind and belch with equal unconstraint. So let us respect the Kalends of March![15]

Remember me kindly and keep well.

190 (IX.16)
CICERO TO PAPIRIUS PAETUS

Tusculum (?), mid July 46

Cicero to Paetus greetings.

Your letter gave me great pleasure. In the first place I was touched by the affection which prompted you to write, because you were afraid that Silius'[1] report had caused me some anxiety. You had written to me previously on the subject, sending two copies of your letter separately, so that I could well see how much it disturbed you; and I had replied in detail in such a way as to remove your concern, or at any rate to relieve it, so far as possible in such a case and at such a time.

But since your latest letter also shows how deeply you are taking this matter to heart, let me assure you, my dear Paetus, that whatever art could do (we cannot nowadays rely on the weapon of good judgement, a degree of artifice

artificium quoddam excogitandum est)—sed tamen, quicquid elaborari aut effici potuerit ad istorum benevolentiam conciliandam et colligendam, summo studio me
consecutum esse, nec frustra, ut arbitror; sic enim color,
sic observor ab omnibus iis qui a Caesare diliguntur ut ab
iis me amari putem. tametsi[1] non facile diiudicatur amor
verus et fictus, nisi aliquod incidit eius modi tempus ut
quasi aurum igni sic benevolentia fidelis periculo aliquo
perspici possit; cetera sunt signa communia. sed ego uno
utor argumento quam ob rem me ex animo vereque arbitrer diligi, quia et nostra fortuna ea est et illorum ut simu-
landi causa non sit.

3   De illo autem quem penes est omnis potestas, nihil
video quod timeam, nisi quod omnia sunt incerta cum a
iure discessum est nec praestari quicquam potest quale
futurum sit quod positum est in alterius voluntate, ne
dicam libidine. sed tamen eius ipsius nulla re a me offensus
est animus. est enim adhibita in ea re ipsa summa a nobis
moderatio. ut enim olim arbitrabar esse meum libere
loqui, cuius opera esset in civitate libertas, sic ea nunc
amissa nihil loqui quod offendat aut illius aut eorum qui ab
illo diliguntur voluntatem. effugere autem si velim non
nullorum acute aut facete dictorum opinionem, fama inge-
4   ni mihi est abicienda; quod, si id possem, non recusarem.
sed tamen ipse Caesar habet peracre iudicium et, ut Servius, frater tuus, quem litteratissimum fuisse iudico, facile

---

[1] nam etsi *(Camerarius)*

---

[2] The leading Caesarians.
[3] Or 'cousin,' Ser. Claudius; cf. *Letters to Atticus* 20 (I.20).7.

and ingenuity is called for)—anyhow, all that pains could effect towards gaining and garnering the good will of these gentry[2] has been achieved by me, no effort spared; and I do not think I have wasted my endeavours. The courtesies and attentions I receive from all who stand high with Caesar are such that I believe they have an affection for me. Admittedly it is no easy matter to distinguish the genuine article from the sham, unless a situation happens to arise in which the gold of loyal attachment is discerned in the fire of danger—all other signs being common to both. But one circumstance goes far to prove to my own mind that their regard for me is sincere and genuine: my position and theirs being what they respectively are, these people have no motive to dissemble.

As for the All-Powerful, I see no reason why I should be apprehensive, unless it be that all becomes uncertain when the path of legality has been forsaken, and that there is no guaranteeing the future of what depends on someone else's wishes, not to say whims. However, I have done nothing to offend Caesar's personal sensibilities. In that very particular I have been extremely careful to regulate my conduct. Time was when I thought that free speech became me, for was not the existence of freedom in the community my doing? Now that freedom is lost, I think it no less becomes me to say nothing offensive to his sentiments or those of the people he likes. But if I were to disclaim the authorship of certain pungent or amusing remarks, I should have to renounce my reputation as a wit. Well, I should not object to the latter, if the former lay within my power. But Caesar himself is a keenly discriminating connoisseur. Your brother[3] Servius, in my judgement a man of outstanding literary culture, could easily pronounce that

diceret 'hic versus Plauti non est, hic est,' quod tritas auris
haberet notandis generibus poetarum et consuetudine le-
gendi, sic audio Caesarem, cum volumina iam confecerit
apophthegmatorum, si quid[2] adferatur ad eum pro meo
quod meum non sit, reicere solere. quod eo nunc magis
facit quia vivunt mecum fere cottidie illius familiares; inci-
dunt autem in sermone vario multa quae fortasse illis, cum
dixi, nec illitterata nec insulsa esse videantur. haec ad illum
cum reliquis actis perferuntur; ita enim ipse mandavit. sic
fit ut, si quid praeterea de me audiat, non audiendum
putet.

Quam ob rem Oenomao tuo nihil utor; etsi posuisti loco
5 versus Accianos. sed quae est invidia aut quid mihi nunc
invideri potest? verum fac esse[3] omnia: sic video philoso-
phis placuisse iis qui mihi soli videntur vim virtutis tenere,
nihil esse sapientis praestare nisi culpam. qua mihi videor
dupliciter carere, et quod ea senserim quae rectissima fuerunt et qui‹a›,[4] cum viderem praesidi non satis esse ad ea
obtinenda, viribus certandum cum valentioribus non puta-
rim. ergo in officio boni civis certe non sum reprehenden-
dus. reliquum est ne quid stulte, ne quid temere dicam aut
faciam contra potentis. id quoque puto esse sapientis.

---

2 quod *(SB)*   3 posse *Wes.*   4 *(Vict.)*

---

4 According to Suetonius' biography (56.7) Caesar made a collection of witticisms as a boy or young man; along with other of his
juvenilia Augustus forbade it to be published.

5 Paetus had cited lines from Accius' tragedy *Oenomaus,* to
the effect that *invidia* (envy, jealous ill will) made no more impression on a strong mind than waves upon a rock (see next
paragraph). Cicero remarks that he does not in fact have to fear

Plautus did not write one line or did write another, because his taste has been refined by observation of the styles of poets and by constantly reading their work. In the same way I hear that, having in his day compiled volumes of *bons mots*,[4] Caesar will reject any specimen offered him as mine which is not authentic. He does this all the more now because his intimates are in my company almost every day. Talk of this and that produces many casual remarks which perhaps strike these people when I say them as not deficient in polish and point. They are conveyed to him with the rest of the day's news, according to his express instructions. Thus it is that if he hears anything about me from some other source he does not think it worth his attention.

So I don't need your Oenomaus;[5] not but what your Accian lines come apropos. But where is the envy? What is there about me nowadays to inspire such a sentiment? However, suppose there were all manner of things: I find that those philosophers who alone to my mind grasp the essence of virtue hold that the wise man is answerable for nothing save guilt. But of that I conceive myself doubly free, both in that my sentiments were thoroughly sound and because, when I saw that the strength to assert them was lacking, I did not think it right to struggle against superior force. Therefore I certainly cannot be said to have failed in the duty of a good citizen. All that remains is not to act or speak foolishly or rashly against the powers that be. That too I reckon part of wisdom. For the rest, what this or

invidia, and would rather apply the simile to Fortune. The quotation was clearly intended to encourage Cicero, not to warn him. It should not be identified with the only surviving fragment of the play, in which there happens to be mention of a rock.

201

cetera vero, quid quisque me dixisse dicat, aut quo modo
ille accipiat, aut qua fide mecum vivant ii qui me adsidue
colunt et observant, praestare non possum.

6 Ita fit ut et consiliorum superiorum conscientia et praesentis temporis moderatione me consoler et illam Acci
similitudinem non modo iam ad invidiam sed ad Fortunam
transferam, quam existimo levem et imbecillam ab animo
firmo et gravi tamquam fluctum a saxo frangi oportere.
etenim, cum plena sint monumenta Graecorum quem ad
modum sapientissimi viri regna tulerint vel Athenis vel
Syracusis, cum servientibus suis civitatibus fuerint ipsi
quodam modo liberi, ego me non putem tueri meum statum sic posse ut neque offendam animum cuiusquam nec
frangam dignitatem meam?

7 Nunc venio ad iocationes tuas, quoniam tu secundum
'Oenomaum' Acci non, ut olim solebat, Atellanam sed,
ut nunc fit, mimum introduxisti. quem tu mihi Po‹m›pi-
lium,[5] quem denarium narras, quam tyrotarichi patinam?
facilitate mea ista ferebantur antea; nunc mutata res est.
Hirtium ego et Dolabellam dicendi discipulos habeo, ce-
nandi magistros; puto enim te audisse, si forte ad vos
omnia perferuntur, illos apud me declamitare, me apud

5 popillium (ς, *Demmel*)

6 Socrates at Athens under the Thirty, Plato at Syracuse under
the two Dionysii.   7 The former were both more witty and
more indecent than the latter.

8 M. Demmel's correction *Pompilium* for *popillium* is most
attractive. In his work on Grammarians (8) Suetonius tells us that
M. Pompilius Andronicus was a devoted Epicurean, that he spent
his later life at Cumae, and that he was poor and needy. Each of

that person says I have said, how *he* takes such reports, how trustworthy are these associates of mine who pay me such assiduous attention and courtesy—for all this I cannot answer.

So I comfort myself with the consciousness of my motives in the past and the regulation of my conduct in the present, and I may apply that simile of Accius' to Fortune instead of merely to envy; fickle and feeble as she is, I hold that she must break against a firm, constant mind like a wave against a rock. The records of Greece are full of instances of how men of the highest wisdom bore despotic regimes, whether at Athens or Syracuse,[6] and managed amidst the servitude of their communities to keep in some sort their personal liberty. Am I to suppose myself incapable of preserving my position while neither offending any man nor impairing my dignity?

Now I come to your jests, seeing that you have followed up Accius' *Oenomaus* with a mime à la mode instead of the old-fashioned Atellane farce.[7] What's this about Pompilius[8] and a denarius[9] and a plate of salt fish au gratin?[10] In days gone by I used to put up with that kind of thing, being an easygoing fellow, but times are changed. Hirtius and Dolabella are my pupils in oratory, but my masters in gastronomy. I expect you have heard, if all news travels to Naples, that they practise declaiming at my house, and

these three details helps to qualify him as a prospective guest at Paetus' dinner table.

[9] Paetus would naturally mention price in telling Cicero what kind of meal he might expect.

[10] A poor man's dish which Paetus particularly liked; cf. *Letters to Atticus* 370 (XIV.16).1.

illos cenitare. tu autem quod mihi bonam copiam eiures
nihil est. tum enim cum rem habebas quaesticulus[6] te
faciebat attentiorem; nunc <cur>,[7] cum tam aequo animo
bona perdas, non eo sis consilio ut, cum me hospitio recipias, aestimationem te aliquam putes accipere? etiam[8]

8 haec levior est plaga ab amico quam a debitore. nec tamen
eas cenas quaero ut magnae reliquiae fiant; quod erit,
magnificum sit et lautum. memini te mihi Phameae cenam
narrare. temperius fiat, cetera eodem modo. quod si perse-
veras me ad Matris tui[9] cenam revocare, feram id quoque.
volo enim videre animum qui mihi audeat ista quae scribis
apponere aut etiam polypum miniati[10] Iovis similem. mihi
crede, non audebis. ante meum adventum fama ad te de
mea nova lautitia veniet; eam tu extimesces. neque est
quod in promulside spei ponas aliquid, quam totam sustuli; solebam enim antea debilitari oleis et lucanicis tuis.

9 Sed quid haec loquimur? liceat modo isto venire. tu
vero (volo enim abstergere animi tui metum) ad tyrotari-
chum antiquum redi. ego tibi unum sumptum adferam,
quod balneum calfacias oportebit; cetera more nostro.
superiora illa lusimus.

6 -culis *(Man.)*   7 *(SB)*
8 et tamen *Or.:* etenim *C.F.Hermann*
9 matris tu(a)e *(Dieterich)*   10 miniani *(Lamb.)*

11 By Caesar's legislation creditors were obliged to take their
debtors' property in settlement at valuations based on prewar
prices.
12 'The grander the dinner party at Rome the earlier it began'
(Tyrrell–Purser).
13 Celebrated Athenian (or Theban) plain-liver of uncertain

I practise dining at theirs. As for making me an affidavit
of insolvency, you'd be wasting your time. When you had
money, a profitable little deal would make you all the
closer. But now, when you are losing your pile so philosophically, why not take the view that when you entertain
me you are being served with a valuation?[11] Such a knock
actually hurts less coming from a friend than from a
debtor. Not that I am demanding the sort of banquet that
produces a great quantity of leftovers; but what there is
must be sumptuous and elegant. I remember your reciting
Phamea's dinner to me. Yours may start earlier,[12] but the
rest should be in the same style. However, if you insist on
bringing me back to your friend Matris'[13] bill of fare, all
right, I'll put up with that too. I should like to see anybody
with the courage to dare to serve me with the things you
mention, or even with octopus the colour of vermilioned
Jupiter![14] No, no, you'll never dare! The report of my styl-
ish new ways will reach you before I arrive, and make you
shake in your shoes. And don't go building hopes on the
hors d'oeuvres. I have done away with that entirely. I used
to half-ruin my appetite with your olives and sausages in
the old days!

But what am I saying? I only wish I may be able to come
down! As for yourself, let me dispel your alarm; go back to
your old salt fish au gratin. My visit shall put you to no expense except that you will have to heat a bath. All else shall
be as usual between you and me. I was only joking.

date, who ate nothing but figs and drank nothing but water. Author of hymns.

[14] I.e., probably, in a red sauce. In ancient times the clay image
of Jupiter was given a new coat of vermilion paint on festal days.

10   De villa Seliciana et curasti diligenter et scripsisti face-
tissime. itaque puto me praetermissurum; salis enim satis
est, salinorum[11] parum.

191 (IX.18)

Scr. in Tusculano paulo ante VII *Kal. Sext. an.* 46

CICERO S. D. PAETO

1   Cum essem otiosus in Tusculano propterea quod discipulos obviam miseram, ut eadem me quam maxime conci-
liarent familiari suo, accepi tuas litteras plenissimas suavi-
tatis; ex quibus intellexi probari tibi meum consilium,[1]
quod, ut Dionysius tyrannus, cum Syracusis pulsus esset,
Corinthi dicitur ludum aperuisse, sic ego sublatis iudiciis,
2   amisso regno forensi ludum quasi habere coeperim. quid
quaeris? me quoque delectat consilium. multa enim con-
sequor: primum, id quod maxime nunc opus est, munio me
ad haec tempora. id cuius modi sit nescio; tantum video,
nullius adhuc consilium me huic anteponere, nisi forte
mori melius fuit. in lectulo, fateor, sed non accidit; in acie

---

[11] sann⟨i⟩onum MDV: sanniorum H *(SB)*
[1] consilio *(Ern.)*

---

[15] I.e., if the conjecture *salinorum* is right, silver ('siller,'
money), salt cellars being normally made of that metal. 'Salt' here
has a double meaning, 'wit' (of which Paetus provided a suf-
ficiency in his letter) and (of a villa) 'elegance' (Paetus having presumably praised the villa as having 'plenty of salt').

Thank you for taking so much trouble and writing so amusingly about Selicius' country house. So I think I'll pass it by. I have plenty of salt, but not enough salt cellars![15]

191 (IX.18)
CICERO TO PAPIRIUS PAETUS

Tusculum, shortly before 26 July 46

Cicero to Paetus greetings.

While I was at a loose end at Tusculum, having sent my pupils to meet their friend[1] with the idea that they should at the same time put me in the best possible odour with him, I received your most charming letter. It appears then that my plan meets with your approbation: like Dionysius the tyrant,[2] who is said to have opened a school at Corinth after his expulsion from Syracuse, I have set up as a schoolmaster, as it were, now that the courts are abolished and my forensic kingdom lost. Well, I too am pleased with my plan, which brings me many advantages. To begin with, I gain some protection against the hazards of these times, which is what is most needed just now. What that amounts to I don't know; all I can see is that nobody else has yet produced a plan which I consider superior to mine—unless perhaps it would have been better to die. Better to die in one's bed, I admit it; but that did not happen. At the battle

---

[1] I.e. Hirtius and Dolabella to meet Caesar on his return from Africa. When he says he sent them Cicero is probably joking—they would naturally go anyway.

[2] Dionysius II of Syracuse; cf. *Letters to Atticus* 176 (IX.9).1.

non fui. ceteri quidem, Pompeius, Lentulus tuus, Scipio, Afranius foede perierunt. at Cato praeclare. iam istuc quidem cum volemus licebit; demus modo operam ne tam necesse nobis sit quam illi fuit, id quod agimus. ergo hoc primum.

3   Sequitur illud: ipse melior fio, primum valetudine, quam intermissis exercitationibus amiseram; deinde ipsa illa, si qua fuit in me, facultas orationis, nisi me ad has exercitationes rettulissem, exaruisset. extremum illud est, quod tu nescio an primum putes: pluris iam pavones confeci quam tu pullos columbinos. tu istic te Hateriano iure delectas, ego me hic Hirtiano. veni igitur, si vir es, et disce a m⟨e⟩[2] προλεγομένας quas quaeris; etsi sus Miner-

4 vam. sed, quo modo video, si[3] aestimationes tuas vendere non potes neque ollam denariorum implere, Romam tibi remig⟨r⟩andum est; satius est hic cruditate quam istic fame. video te bona perdidisse; spero idem istuc familiaris tuos. actum igitur de te est nisi provides. potes mulo isto, quem tibi reliquum dicis esse, quoniam cantherium comedisti, Romam pervehi. sella tibi erit in ludo, tamquam hypodidascalo, proxima; eam pulvinus sequetur.

    [2] *(Bengel)*
    [3] sed . . . si *dist.* SB, *Demmel*

---

    [3] L. Lentulus Crus, Consul in 49.
    [4] Literally 'Haterian law,' Haterius being presumably a jurist. There is a play on two senses of *ius,* 'law' and 'sauce.'

I was not present. The others—Pompey, your friend Lentulus,[3] Scipio, Afranius—came to miserable ends. But Cato's, you say, was splendid. Well, that will be open to me any time I choose. I have only to see that it does not become so much a matter of necessity for me as it was for him. I am doing just that. This then to begin with.

Next, I benefit directly, first in health, which I lost when I gave up my exercises; and then my oratorical faculty, if I had any, would have dried up had I not gone back to these exercises. There is a final point, which *you* might perhaps put first: I have already polished off more peacocks than you young pigeons. While you enjoy Haterius' legal gravity[4] in Naples, I regale myself with Hirtius' gravy here. Be a man then, and come along! Let me teach you the principia you want to learn—though it will be a case of teaching my grandmother.[5] But, as I see the situation, if you can't sell your valuations[6] or fill a pot with silver,[7] you have got to move back to Rome. Better die of stomach-ache here than starvation down there. I see you have lost your money, and I expect it is just the same with your friends. So if you don't look ahead, it's all up with you. You can get up on that mule, which you say you still have left after spending your gelding on food, and ride to Rome. There will be a chair for you in school as assistant master next to mine, and a cushion will follow.

[5] Literally 'of the pig teaching Minerva,' a proverbial saying. The pig was regarded as the most stupid of animals.

[6] I.e. properties compulsorily accepted in lieu of debts.

[7] I.e. 'if you don't have enough money to fill a pot with silver coins *(denarii).*'

192 (VII.33)

Scr. Romae ex. m. Quint., ut vid., an. 46

M. CICERO S. D. VOLUMNIO

1   Quod declamationibus nostris cares, damni nihil facis.
quod Hirtio invideres nisi eum amares, non erat causa invi-
dendi, nisi forte ipsius eloquentiae magis quam quod me
audiret invideres. nos enim plane, mi suavissime Volumni,
aut nihil sumus aut nobis quidem ipsis displicemus gregali-
bus illis quibus te plaudente vigebamus amissis, ut etiam,
si quando aliquid dignum nostro nomine emisimus, inge-
miscamus quod haec 'pinnigero, non armigero in corpore
tela exerceantur,' ut ait Philoctetes apud Accium, 'abiecta
gloria.'

2   Sed tamen omnia mihi erunt, si tu veneris, hilariora.
quamquam venis, ut ipse intellegis, in maximarum quasi
concursum occupationum. quas ⟨s⟩i, ut volumus, explica-
rimus,[1] ego vero multam salutem et foro dicam et curiae
vivamque tecum multum et cum communibus nostris
amatoribus. nam et Cassius tuus et Dolabella noster, vel
potius uterque noster, studiis iisdem tenentur et meis ae-
quissimis utuntur auribus. opus est huc limatulo et polito
tuo iudicio et illis interioribus litteris tuis[2] quibus saepe ve-
recundiorem me in loquendo facis. mihi enim iudicatum
est, si modo hoc Caesar aut patietur aut volet, deponere

[1] exceper- (*SB*: expedier- *Madvig*)
[2] meis *(Ern.)*

---

[1] In a play of that name.

192 (VII.33)
CICERO TO VOLUMNIUS EUTRAPELUS

Rome, end of July (?) 46

From Cicero to Volumnius greetings.

In missing my declamations you lose nothing at all. As for your envying Hirtius if you were not so fond of him, you had no cause for such a feeling, unless perhaps you envied him his own oratorical gifts rather than the privilege of listening to me. As for myself, my charming friend, I am simply nothing; or if not that, I am disgusted with my own performance, now that I have lost my old stablemates who made me my paces—to your applause. If ever I do strike out anything worthy of my reputation, I groan to think that

On feathered, not on armoured forms I ply
These shafts, my glory humbled,

as Philoctetes[1] says in Accius.

None the less, my whole horizon will brighten if you come. But, as you realize yourself, you are coming into a rush of pressing affairs. If I dispose of these satisfactorily, I shall bid a long farewell to Forum and Senate House, and shall pass much of my time with you and our common admirers. Your friend Cassius and our friend Dolabella (I should rather say 'our' in both cases) are devoted to the same pursuits and find in me a very well-disposed audience. We need your delicately filed and polished critical judgement and that recherché learning of yours before which I often check my own exuberant tongue. For my part I am quite determined, if only Caesar either permits or welcomes my resolution, to lay aside the role in which

illam iam personam in qua me saepe illi ipsi probavi ac me totum in litteras abdere tecumque et cum ceteris earum studiosis honestissimo otio perfrui.

Tu vellem ne veritus esses ne pro libris[3] legerem tuas litteras si mihi, quem ad modum scribis, longiores forte misisses; ac velim posthac sic statuas, tuas mihi litteras longissimas quasque gratissimas fore.

193 (IX.20)

Scr. Romae in. m. Sext. an. 46

CICERO PAETO

1   Dupliciter delectatus sum tuis litteris, et quod ipse risi et quod te intellexi iam posse ridere. me autem a te ut scurram velitem malis oneratum esse non moleste tuli; illud doleo, in ista loca venire me, ut constitueram, non potuisse. habuisses enim non hospitem sed contubernalem. at quem virum! non eum quem tu es solitus promulside conficere. integram famem ad ovum adfero; itaque usque ad assum vitulinum opera perducitur. illa mea quae solebas antea laudare ('o hominem facilem! o hospitem non

3 pluribus *(SB: alii alia)*

---

[2] I.e. as too long to be read at one sitting (see my Commentary). The reading is conjectural.

[1] Paetus had apparently called Cicero *scurra veles* ('skirmisher jester'), perhaps because he had begun the fight. The verb *velitari* is used elsewhere of verbal skirmishing.

[2] Untranslatable pun on *malis* (with a short *a*) meaning 'abuse'

he himself has often approved me and to bury myself in literary work, enjoying an honourable retirement in your company and that of other devotees of letters.

I wish you had not been afraid that I might read your letters like books,[2] if (as you say) they should happen to be on the lengthy side. In future do please depend upon it that the longer the letters you write the better I shall like them.

193 (IX.20)
CICERO TO PAPIRIUS PAETUS

Rome, early August 46

From Cicero to Paetus.

I was doubly delighted with your letter—laughed myself, and saw that you are now capable of laughing. As a light-armed buffoon,[1] I did not object to your pelting me with insults.[2] What does vex me is that I have not been able to get down to your part of the world as I had determined. You would have found me a comrade[3] in arms rather than a guest. And what a warrior! Not the man you used to lay low with your hors d'oeuvres. I bring an appetite unimpaired to the eggs,[4] and so carry on the good work down to the roast veal. 'What an accommodating fellow!' you used to

and *malis* (with a long *a*) meaning 'apples' (which might be thrown at a buffoon).   [3] Literally 'tent mate.' The military metaphor continues, but the word may imply a longer stay than would be normal for a guest.   [4] Here regarded as beginning the main meal, as opposed to the hors d'oeuvres. The roast veal would be the last course, followed by dessert *(mensae secundae).*

CICERO'S LETTERS TO FRIENDS

gravem!') abierunt. nam[1] omnem nostram de re publica curam, cogitationem de dicenda in senatu sententia, commentationem causarum abiecimus, in Epicuri nos, adversari nostri, castra coiecimus, nec tamen ad hanc insolentiam sed ad illam tuam lautitiam, veterem dico, cum in sumptum habebas; etsi numquam plura praedia habuisti.

2   Proinde te para. cum homine et edaci tibi res est et qui iam aliquid intellegat; ὀψιμαθεῖς autem homines scis quam insolentes sint. dediscendae tibi sunt sportellae et artolagyni tui. nos iam †ex† artis tantum habemus ut Verrium tuum et Camillum (qua munditia homines, qua elegantia!) vocare saepius audeamus. sed vide audaciam! etiam Hirtio cenam dedi, sine pavone tamen. in ea cena cocus meus praeter ius fervens nihil ‹non›[2] potuit imitari.

3   Haec igitur est nunc vita nostra: mane salutamus domi et bonos viros multos, sed tristis, et hos laetos victores, qui me quidem perofficiose et peramanter observant. ubi salutatio defluxit, litteris me involvo; aut scribo aut lego. veniunt etiam qui me audiunt quasi doctum hominem quia paulo sum quam ipsi doctior. inde corpori omne tempus datur. patriam eluxi iam et gravius et diutius quam ulla mater unicum filium.

[1] non (ς: *om. χ*)
[2] (*Or.*)

---

[5] Which Paetus had been forced to take from his debtors.

[6] Containing dates, as at Trimalchio's feast (Petronius, 40.3), or something of the kind. The meaning of the word translated 'scones' is doubtful.

say of me. 'What an easy man to entertain!' Not any more! I have dropped all my concern for public affairs, all preoccupation with what to say in the Senate, all study of briefs, and flung myself into the camp of my old adversary Epicurus. I don't aim at the excesses of Rome, however, but at *your* elegance—your former elegance, I mean, when you had money to spend (though, to be sure, you never owned more real estate[5] in your life).

So be prepared! You are dealing with a hearty eater, no longer wholly ignorant of what's what; and you know how opsimaths assert themselves. You had best forget about your little baskets[6] and your scones. I have acquired enough of the art by now to dare invite your friend Verrius and Camillus (the very acme of refinement and chic!) on several occasions. More, I even had the audacity to give a dinner to Hirtius (think of it!)—no peacock, though. At that meal nothing proved beyond my cook's powers of imitation except the hot sauce.

So this is the way I live nowadays. In the morning I receive callers—both honest men (numerous, but depressed) and these jubilant victors, who, I must say, are most obliging and friendly in their attentions to me. When the stream has ceased to flow, I absorb myself in literary work, writing or reading. Some of my visitors listen to me as a man of learning, because I know a little more than themselves. All the rest of the time is given to the claims of the body. As for my country, I have already mourned her longer and more deeply than any mother ever mourned her only son.

CICERO'S LETTERS TO FRIENDS

Sed cura, si me amas, ut valeas, ne ego te iacente bona tua comedim; statui enim tibi ne aegroto quidem parcere.

194 (IX.19)

Scr. Romae med. m. Sext. an. 46

CICERO S. D. PAETO

1   Tamen a malitia non discedis? tenu‹i›culo apparatu significas Balbum fuisse contentum. hoc videris dicere, cum reges tam sint continentes, multo magis consularis esse oportere. nescis me ab illo omnia expiscatum. recta enim a porta domum meam venisse ‹scito›;[1] neque hoc admiror quod non suam potius sed illud, quod non ad suam. ego autem tribus primis verbis 'quid noster Paetus?'

2   at ille adiurans nusquam se umquam libentius. hoc si verbis adsecutus es, auris ad te adferam non minus elegantis; sin autem obsonio, peto a te ne pluris esse balbos quam disertos putes. me cottidie aliud ex alio impedit; sed si me expediero, ut in ista loca venire possim, non committam ut te sero a me certiorem factum putes.

---

[1] *(Sjögren)*

---

[1] *Rex* is often applied to a rich and powerful personage, but has special reference here to Balbus' relations with the despot Caesar; cf. *Letters to Atticus* 259 (XII.12).1.

But if you are my friend, take care of your health, or I shall be consuming your substance while you lie flat on your back. For I have made up my mind not to spare you, well or sick.

194 (IX.19)
CICERO TO PAPIRIUS PAETUS

Rome, mid August 46

From Cicero to Paetus.

Still up to your tricks? You intimate that Balbus was satisfied with a modest little spread. I suppose you imply that when kings[1] are so temperate, Consulars should be much more so. What you don't know is that I fished the whole story out of him—he came straight from the city gate, let me tell you, to my house (I'm not surprised that he didn't rather go to his own, but I *should* have expected him to go to his sweetheart).[2] My first four words were: 'What of old Paetus?' And *he* said he'd be hanged if he had ever had a better time. If you have achieved this by talk, you will find me no less discriminating a listener. But if the credit goes to your cuisine, I must ask you not to rate balbutients[3] above orators. Every day one thing after another holds me up. But if I get clear and can pay a visit to your part of the world, I shall take very good care not to let you think I have given you insufficient notice.[4]

[2] Play on *suam (domum),* 'to his house,' and *ad suam,* 'to his mistress.'   [3] *Balbus* = 'stammerer.'

[4] And so provide an excuse for meagre entertainment.

195 (IX.17)

Scr. Romae in. m. Sept., ut vid., an. 46

CICERO PAETO

1   Ne[1] tu homo ridiculus es qui, cum Balbus noster apud
te fuerit, ex me quaeras quid de istis municipiis et agris futurum putem. quasi aut ego quicquam sciam quod iste
nesciat aut, si quid aliquando scio, non ex isto soleam scire!
immo vero, si me amas, tu fac ut sciam quid de nobis futurum sit. habuisti enim in tua potestate ex quo vel ex sobrio
vel certe ex ebrio scire posses. sed ego ista, mi Paete, non
quaero; primum quia de lucro prope iam quadriennium
vivimus, si aut hoc lucrum est aut haec vita, superstitem rei
publicae vivere; deinde quod scire quoque mihi videor
quid futurum sit. fiet enim quodcumque volent qui valebunt; valebunt autem semper arma. satis igitur nobis esse
debet quicquid conceditur. hoc si qui pati non potuit, mori
debuit.

2   Veientem quidem agrum et Capenatem metiuntur. hoc
non longe abest a Tusculano; nihil tamen timeo. fruor dum
licet, opto ut semper liceat; si id minus contigerit, tamen,
quoniam ego vir fortis idemque philosophus vivere pul-
cherrimum duxi, non possum eum non diligere cuius
beneficio id consecutus sum. qui si cupiat esse rem publicam qualem fortasse et ille vult et omnes optare debemus,

---

[1] non (*Gron.* *)

---

[1] Paetus was afraid that land belonging to municipalities or
private individuals might be confiscated by Caesar for distribu-
tion to his veterans.

195 (IX.17)
CICERO TO PAPIRIUS PAETUS

Rome, early (?) September 46

Cicero to Paetus.

You really are a comedian! After a visit from our friend Balbus you ask *me* what I think is going to happen about these towns and lands![1] As though I know anything that he doesn't know! Or as though, if ever I *do* know anything, I don't get my information from him! On the contrary, if you are a friend of mine, you tell me what is going to happen to us! After all, you had him in your power, you could have pumped him, drunk if not sober. But as for me, my dear Paetus, I am not inquisitive about such matters. For almost four years past the fact that we are still alive is a bonus to which we are not entitled—that is, if to survive freedom can be called a bonus or a life. Moreover, I fancy I know the answer too: what will happen will be whatever those who have the power want to happen. And power will always lie with armed force. So we ought to be content with whatever is allowed us. Anybody unable to put up with life on these terms should have taken leave of it.

They *are* surveying land at Veii and Capena. That is not so far from Tusculum. But I have no fears. I enjoy while I am able. I pray I may always be able. But if my prayer is not granted, well, as a man of courage and a philosopher, I thought life a very fine thing. Therefore I cannot but have a regard for the man to whose favour I owe it. Even if he were to will that the state be such as he perhaps desires and as all of us ought to pray for, there is nothing he can do. He

quid faciat tamen non habet; ita se cum multis colligavit.

3   Sed longius progredior; scribo enim ad te. hoc tamen scito, non modo me, qui consiliis non intersum, sed ne ipsum quidem principem scire quid futurum sit; nos enim illi servimus, ipse temporibus. ita nec ille quid tempora postulatura sint nec nos quid ille cogitet scire possumus.

4   Haec tibi antea non rescripsi, non quo cessator esse solerem, praesertim in litteris, sed, cum explorati nihil haberem, nec tibi sollicitudinem ex dubitatione mea nec spem adfirmatione adferre volui. illud tamen adscribam, quod est verissimum, me his temporibus adhuc de isto periculo nihil audisse. tu tamen pro tua sapientia debebis optare optima, cogitare difficillima, ferre quaecumque erunt.

196 (IX.15)

Scr. Romae fort. m. interc. priore an. 46

CICERO PAETO S.

1   Duabus tuis epistulis respondebo: uni quam quadriduo ante acceperam a Zetho, alteri quam attulerat Phileros tabellarius.

Ex prioribus tuis litteris intellexi pergratam tibi esse curam meam valetudinis tuae, quam tibi perspectam esse gaudeo; sed mihi crede, non perinde ut est reapse ex litteris perspicere potuisti. nam cum a satis multis (non enim

has too many associates to whom he has tied himself.

But I am going further than I meant—after all, I am writing to *you*. However, you may take my word for it that not only I, who am not in his counsels, but the great man himself does not know what will happen. We are his slaves, he is the slave of circumstances. So he cannot know what circumstances will demand, and we cannot know what he has in his mind.

If I have not replied sooner, it is not because I am habitually lazy, particularly where writing is concerned, but, having nothing solid to go on, I was reluctant to cause you anxiety by expressing a doubt or to raise your hopes by a positive statement. I will only add the bare truth, that so far I have heard nothing in recent times about the danger you fear. But you are a man of sense, and as such you should pray for the best, contemplate the worst, and bear whatever happens.

196 (IX.15)
CICERO TO PAPIRIUS PAETUS

Rome, first (?) intercalary month 46

Cicero to Paetus greetings.

I am replying to two letters of yours. I received one of them four days ago by Zethus, the other was brought by your courier Phileros.

Your earlier letter had made it plain to me that my concern for your health was very welcome to you. I am glad you appreciated it, but, believe me, you could not appreciate it as it really is from a letter. I find myself the object of attention and regard from a fair number of persons (I

possum aliter dicere) et coli me videam et diligi, nemo est
illorum omnium mihi te iucundior. nam quod me amas,
quod id et tam pridem et constanter facis, est id quidem
magnum atque haud scio an maximum, sed tibi commune
cum multis; quod tu ipse tam amandus es tamque dulcis
tamque in omni genere iucundus, id est proprie tuum.

2 accedunt non Attici sed salsiores quam illi Atticorum
Romani veteres atque urbani sales. ego autem (existimes
licet quidlibet) mirifice capior facetiis, maxime nostrati-
bus, praesertim cum eas videam primum oblitas Latio,
tum cum in urbem nostram est infusa peregrinitas, nunc
vero etiam bracatis et Transalpinis nationibus, ut nullum
veteris leporis vestigium appareat. itaque te cum video,
omnis mihi Granios, omnis Lucilios, vere ut dicam, Cras-
sos quoque et Laelios videre videor. moriar si praeter te
quemquam reliquum habeo in quo possim imaginem anti-
quae et vernaculae festivitatis agnoscere. ad hos lepores
cum amor erga me tantus accedat, miraris me tanta pertur-
batione valetudinis tuae tam graviter exanimatum fuisse?

3 Quod autem altera epistula purgas te non dissuasorem
mihi emptionis Neapolitanae fuisse sed auctorem commorationis[1] urbanae, neque ego aliter accepi ⟨et⟩[2] intellexi tamen idem quod his intellego litteris, non existimasse te
mihi licere, id quod ego arbitrabar, res has non omnino
quidem sed magnam partem relinquere. Catulum mihi
narras et illa tempora. quid simile? ne mi quidem ipsi tunc

---

[1] moderat- *(Rut.)*   [2] *(Nipperdey)*

---

[1] The sharp-tongued auctioneer of Puteoli; cf. *Letters to Atticus* 28 (II.8).1.   [2] L. Crassus, the orator. He and Laelius were men of high birth and official rank.

cannot say otherwise), but none of them all is more agreeable to me than you. That you love me, and have done so steadily and long, is certainly important, perhaps the most important thing of all; but in this you are by no means alone. What is singular to yourself is that *you* are so lovable, such pleasant company, so agreeable in every way. And then there is the salt of your wit—not Attic, but genuine old Roman, saltier than the Athenian variety. For my part, make what you will of it, I am marvellously fond of pleasantries, our native brand most of all, especially in view of its present decline; for adulterated as it had already become by Latium after the influx of the foreign element into our city, it is now with the accession of the trousered tribes from over the Alps so overwhelmed (?) that no trace of the old gay charm is any more to be found. So when I see you, I imagine I have Granius,[1] Lucilius, and their like—indeed, to say the truth, Crassus[2] and Laelius and *their* like—all before my eyes. Confound me if I have anyone left but you in whom I can recognize the image of the good old home-bred humour! When these charms of wit are combined with so hearty an affection for myself, do you wonder that your serious illness threw me into such a panic?

In your second letter you excuse yourself. You say you were not dissuading me from buying a place in Naples, but encouraging me to spend my time in Rome. That was what I took you to mean; but I also understood (as I understand from this later letter) that you thought I do not have the right to abandon metropolitan life, as I conceive myself entitled to do, not altogether indeed, but to a great extent. You talk to me of Catulus and those days. Where is the resemblance? At that time I myself did not care to be absent

223

placebat diutius abesse ab rei publicae custodia; sedeba-
mus enim in puppi et clavum tenebamus. nunc autem vix
4 est in sentina locus. an minus multa senatus consulta futura putas si ego sim Neapoli? Romae cum sum et urgeo
forum senatus consulta scribuntur apud amatorem tuum,
familiarem meum; et quidem, cum in mentem venit,
ponor ad scribendum et ante audio senatus consultum in
Armeniam et Syriam esse perlatum, quod in meam sententiam factum esse dicatur, quam omnino mentionem ullam
de ea re esse factam. atque hoc nolim me iocari putes. nam
mihi scito iam a regibus ultimis adlatas esse litteras quibus
mihi gratias agant quod se mea sententia reges appellave-
rim, quos ego non modo reges appellatos sed omnino natos
nesciebam.

5 　　Quid ergo est? tamen, quam diu hic erit noster hic
praefectus moribus, parebo auctoritati tuae. cum vero
aberit, ad fungos me tuos conferam. domum si habebo,
in denos dies singulos sumptuariae legis dies conferam;
sin autem minus invenero quod placeat, decrevi habitare
apud te; scio enim me nihil tibi gratius facere posse. domum Sullanam desperabam iam, ut tibi proxime scripsi,
sed tamen non abieci. tu velim, ut scribis, cum fabris eam
perspicias. si enim nihil est in parietibus aut in tecto viti,
cetera mihi probabuntur.

---

3 Doubtless Cornelius Balbus.

4 Caesar was so appointed for three years by the Senate after
his victory in Africa.

5 Caesar's.

too long from watching over the commonwealth. I was sitting in the poop, you see, with the helm in my hands. But now I have scarcely so much as a place in the hold. Do you suppose there will be any the fewer senatorial decrees if I am in Naples? When I am in Rome, up and down the Forum, decrees are drawn up at the residence of your admirer, my very good friend.[3] What is more, when it happens to occur to him, I am put down as present at drafting, and I hear of some decree, allegedly passed on my motion, reaching Armenia and Syria before I know that there has been so much as a mention of the matter concerned. You must not think I am joking. Let me tell you that letters have been brought to me before today from monarchs at the other end of the earth, thanking me for my motion to give them the royal title, when I for my part was unaware of their very existence, let alone of their elevation to royalty.

Very well then. Despite the foregoing, as long as our new Prefect of Morals[4] remains in Rome, I shall defer to your advice: But when he is gone, I'll betake myself to your mushrooms. If I have a house, I shall make the daily maximum under the sumptuary law[5] last ten days. But if I don't find anything to my taste, I've decided to make my home with you—I know I could do nothing that would please you more! I am now giving up hope of Sulla's house,[6] as I said in my last letter, but still I have not quite abandoned it. Would you please inspect the place with the builders, as you say? If there is nothing wrong with the walls or roof, I shall find no fault with the rest.

[6] This may have belonged to P. Sulla, who lived in Naples after his conviction in 66, or to the Dictator's son Faustus, killed in Africa.

197 (IX.26)

Scr. Romae med. m. interc. post., ut vid., an. 46

CICERO PAETO S. D.

1   Accubueram hora nona cum ad te harum exemplum in
codicillis exaravi. dices 'ubi?' apud Volumnium Eutrapelum, et quidem supra me Atticus, infra Verrius, familiares
tui. miraris tam exhilaratam esse servitutem nostram? quid
ergo faciam? te consulo, qui philosophum audis. angar,
excruciem me? quid adsequar? deinde, quem ad finem?
'vivas' inquis 'in litteris.' an quicquam me aliud agere censes aut posse m⟨e⟩[1] vivere nisi in litteris viverem? sed est
earum etiam non satietas sed quidam modus; a quibus cum
discessi, etsi minimum mihi est in cena, quod tu unum
ζήτημα Dioni philosopho posuisti, tamen quid potius faciam prius quam me dormitum conferam non reperio.

2   Audi reliqua. infra Eutrapelum Cytheris accubuit. 'in
eo igitur' inquis 'convivio Cicero ille'

> quem aspectabant, cuius ob os Grai ora obvertebant
> sua?

non mehercule suspicatus sum illam adfore. sed tamen
ne Aristippus quidem ille Socraticus erubuit cum esset
obiectum habere eum Laida. 'habeo' inquit, 'non habeor a

[1] possem (*Man.**)

---

[1] I.e. intercalated; see Appendix.
[2] See Glossary.
[3] Otherwise unknown; but see below.

197 (IX.26)
CICERO TO PAPIRIUS PAETUS

Rome, shortly before 17 November (true[1] calendar) (?) 46

From Cicero to Paetus greetings.

I am scribbling the lines of which you are reading a copy on my tablets[2] after taking my place at dinner at two-thirty of the afternoon. If you wish to know where, my host is Volumnius Eutrapelus. Your friends Atticus and Verrius are on either side of me. Does it surprise you that we have become such a merry lot of slaves? Well, what am I to do? I ask *you*, since you are going to philosophy lectures. Am I to torture and torment myself? What should I gain? And how long should I keep it up? You may advise me to spend my life in literary work. Surely you realize that this *is* my only occupation, that if I did not spend my life in that way I could not live at all. But even literary work has, I won't say its saturation point, but its due limit. When I leave it, little as I care about dinner (the one problem *you* put to philosopher Dio),[3] I really do not see anything better to do with the time before I go to bed.

Well, to the rest of my tale. Cytheris lay down next Eutrapelus. 'So?' I hear you say, '*Cicero* at such a party,

> He the admired, upon whose countenance
> The Greeks all turned their eyes?[4]

I assure you I had no idea *she* would be there. But after all, even Aristippus the Socratic did not blush when someone twitted him with keeping Lais as his mistress. 'Lais is my mistress,' said he, 'but I'm my own master' (it's better in

---

[4] Source unknown.

Laide' (Graece hoc melius; tu, si voles, interpretabere).
me vero nihil istorum ne iuvenem quidem movit umquam,
ne nunc senem. convivio delector; ibi loquor quod in solum, ut dicitur, et gemitum [et]² in risus maximos transfe-
3 ro. an tu id melius qui etiam [in] philosophum irriseris,
cum ille si quis quid quaereret dixisset, cenam te quaerere
a mane dixeris? ille baro te putabat quaesiturum unum
caelum esset an innumerabilia. quid ad te? at hercule cena
num quid ad te, ibi³ praesertim?
4   Sic igitur vivitur. cottidie aliquid legitur aut scribitur.
dein, ne amicis nihil tribuamus, epulamur una non modo
non contra legem, si ulla nunc lex est, sed etiam intra
legem, et quidem aliquanto. qua re nihil est quod adventum nostrum extimescas. non multi cibi hospitem accipies,
multi ioci.

198 (IX.23)

Scr. in Cumano XIII *Kal. Dec., ut vid., an. 46*
CICERO PAETO
    Heri veni in Cumanum, cras ad te fortasse; sed cum
certum sciam, faciam te paulo ante certiorem. etsi M. Cae-

---

² *(Man.)*   ³ tibi *(Man.)*

---

⁵ The Latin means literally 'I possess Lais but am not possessed by her.' In the Greek *ekhomai* has a double sense, 'I am
possessed by' and 'I cling to.'
⁶ The lecturer asked *'num quid quis quaerit?'* ('any questions?'). Paetus replied *'cenam quaero,'* 'I'm looking for a dinner.'

the Greek;[5] make your own rendering, if you care to). As for me, even when I was young I was never attracted by anything of that sort, much less now that I'm old. It's the party I enjoy. I talk about whatever comes uppermost, as they say, and transform sighs into shouts of laughter. Do you manage matters better, actually making mock of a philosopher? When he put his question whether anybody had anything to ask, you called out 'Who's going to ask me to dinner? Been wondering all day.'[6] The poor dunderhead[7] thought you would be enquiring whether there is one sky or an infinite number. What business is that of yours? But, confound it, is a dinner any business of yours, especially one in *this* house?[8]

Well, so life passes. Every day a bit of reading, or a bit of writing. Then, since something is due to my friends, I dine with them. We don't go beyond the law, if there is such a thing nowadays, we even stop short of it, and that by a considerable margin. So you don't have to dread my arrival. You'll receive a guest with a small appetite for food, but a large one for frolic.

198 (IX.23)
CICERO TO PAPIRIUS PAETUS

Cumae, 22 November (true calendar) 46

From Cicero to Paetus.

I arrived at Cumae yesterday and shall perhaps be with you tomorrow. But when I know for certain, I shall send

---

[7] Cicero was fond of so referring to Epicurean philosophers because of their professed hostility to culture; cf. Letter 63, n. 4.

[8] The house of such a person as Eutrapelus.

parius, cum mihi in silva Gallinaria obviam venisset quae-
sissemque quid ageres, dixit te in lecto esse quod ex pedibus laborares. tuli scilicet moleste, ut debui, sed tamen
constitui ad te venire, ut et viderem te et viserem et cena-
rem etiam; non enim arbitror cocum etiam te arthriticum
habere. exspecta igitur hospitem cum minime edacem tum
inimicum cenis sumptuosis.

199 (VII.4)

Scr. in Cumano XIV *vel* XIII *Kal. Dec. an. 46*

M. CICERO S. D. M. MARIO

A. d. XIIII[1] Kal. in Cumanum veni cum Libone tuo, vel
nostro potius. in Pompeianum statim cogito, sed faciam
ante te certiorem. te cum semper valere cupio tum certe
dum hic sumus; vides enim quanto post una futuri simus.
qua re, si quod constitutum cum podagra habes, fac ut in
alium diem differas. cura igitur ut valeas, et me hoc biduo
aut triduo exspecta.

200 (VII.28)

Scr. Romae m. Sext., ut vid., an. 46

M. CICERO S. D. CURIO

1   Memini cum mihi desipere videbare quod cum istis
potius viveres quam nobiscum. erat enim multo domici-

[1] VIII (*Schiche*)

you word a little beforehand. To be sure, when M. Caeparius met me in Poultry Wood[1] and I asked after you, he told me you were in bed with the gout in your feet. I was properly sorry of course, but decided to come all the same—to see you, visit you, and even dine, for I don't suppose your cook is a fellow sufferer. Expect a guest then—a small eater and a foe to sumptuous banquets.

199 (VII.4)
CICERO TO M. MARIUS

Cumae, 21 or 22 November (true calendar) 46

From M. Cicero to M. Marius greetings.

On 21 November I arrived at my place near Cumae with your, or rather our, friend Libo. I mean to go on to Pompeii straight away, but shall send you word in advance. I always wish you to keep well, but particularly during my visit; for you see what a long time it is since we were last in one another's company. So if you have an appointment with the gout, please put it off for another day. Take care of yourself then, and expect me in two or three days' time.

200 (VII.28)
CICERO TO MANIUS CURIUS

Rome, August (?) 46

From M. Cicero to Curius greetings.

I remember the time when I thought you were out of your mind to prefer life with your friends over there to life

---

[1] Silva Gallinaria, a pine forest on the coast north of Cumae.

lium huius urbis, cum quidem haec urbs, aptius humanita-
ti et suavitati tuae quam tota Peloponnesus, nedum Patrae.
nunc contra et vidisse mihi multum ⟨tum⟩[1] videris cum
prope desperatis his rebus te in Graeciam contulisti et hoc
tempore non solum sapiens qui hinc absis sed etiam beatus. quamquam quis qui aliquid sapiat nunc esse beatus
potest?

2   Sed quod tu, cui licebat, pedibus es consecutus, ut ibi
esses 'ubi nec Pelopidarum' (nosti cetera), nos idem prope
modum consequimur alia ratione. cum enim salutationi
nos dedimus amicorum, quae fit hoc etiam frequentius
quam solebat quod quasi avem albam videntur bene sen-
tientem civem videre, abdo me in bibliothecam. itaque
opera efficio tanta quanta fortasse tu senties; intellexi enim
ex tuo sermone quodam, cum meam maestitiam et desperationem accusares domi tuae, dicere te ex meis libris animum meum desiderare.

3   Sed mehercule et tum rem publicam lugebam, quae
non solum ⟨a suis erga me⟩[2] sed etiam a meis erga se
beneficiis erat mihi ⟨vita mea⟩[3] carior, et hoc tempore,
quamquam me non ratio solum consolatur, quae plurimum debet valere, sed etiam dies, quae stultis quoque me-

[1] *(SB)*   [2] *add. SB* (a suis R, a me G, suis erga me ⸠)
[3] *(Wes.)*

---

[1] From an unknown Latin play: 'Where I may never hear the
name or deeds or fame of the sons of Pelops.' The 'sons of Pelops'
will represent the people now dominant in Rome.

[2] Literally 'a white bird.' A white crow stood for something impossible or at any rate extremely rare; but the idea of rarity is not
in Cicero's phrase, though implicit in the context.

with us. When Rome was Rome, it would have been a much more suitable residence for a person of your culture and social gifts than the whole Peloponnesus, let alone Patrae. Today, on the contrary, I applaud your foresight then in betaking yourself to Greece when affairs here were in well-nigh hopeless case; and at the present time I think you not only sensible to be away from here but happy too— though I don't know how a man of any sense *can* be happy at the present time.

However, what you have done, and were free to do, by locomotion, i.e. to live 'where nevermore of Pelops' line ...' (you know how it goes on),[1] I am achieving more or less in a different way. After receiving my friends' morning calls, which are in even greater numbers than of yore because they seem to see a loyal citizen as a bird of good omen,[2] I bury myself in my library. And so I produce books—of their importance you will perhaps judge; for from a conversation you had with me at your house, when you were taking me to task for my gloom and despondency, I understood you to say that you wondered what had become of the spirit you saw in my writings.

But the truth is that I mourned in those days for the commonwealth, which for benefits conferred as well as received was dearer to me than my life, and that now, though solaced not only by reflection, which ought to be man's most efficacious comforter, but by time, which is wont to bring healing even to fools, I still grieve to see our common

deri solet, tamen doleo ita rem communem esse dilapsam
ut ne spes quidem melius aliquando fore relinquatur. nec
vero nunc quidem culpa in eo est in cuius potestate omnia
sunt, nisi forte id ipsum esse non debuit; sed alia casu, alia
etiam [in] nostra culpa sic acciderunt ut de praeteritis non
sit querendum. reliquam spem nullam video. qua re ad
prima redeo: sapienter haec reliquisti si consilio, feliciter
si casu.

201 (V.13)

Scr., ut arbitror, Romae aestate vel autumno an. 46

M. CICERO S. D. L. LUCCEIO Q. F.

1   Quamquam ipsa consolatio litterarum tuarum mihi
gratissima est (declarat enim summam benevolentiam
coniunctam pari prudentia), tamen illum fructum ex iis
litteris vel maximum cepi, quod te praeclare res humanas
contemnentem et optime contra Fortunam paratum arma-
tumque cognovi; quam quidem laudem sapientiae statuo
esse maximam, non aliunde pendere nec extrinsecus aut
2   bene aut male vivendi suspensas habere rationes. quae
cogitatio, cum mihi non omnino excidisset (etenim penitus
insederat), vi tamen tempestatum et concursu calamita-
tum erat aliquantum labefactata atque convulsa; cui te
opitulari et video et id fecisse etiam proximis litteris multumque profecisse sentio. itaque hoc saepius dicendum
tibique non significandum solum sed etiam declarandum

---

[1] See my Commentary.

heritage so fallen to pieces that we are not even left the hope of better things in days to come. Nor does the fault now at any rate lie with our all-powerful governor (unless in the sense that there ought not to be any such person). No, events have so fallen out, part by chance but part also by our own fault, that recrimination is idle. I see no hope remaining. So, to go back to my starting point, if calculation made you leave Rome, you are a sensible man; if chance, a lucky one.

201 (V.13)
CICERO TO LUCCEIUS

Rome, summer or autumn 46 (?)[1]

From M. Cicero to L. Lucceius, son of Quintus, greetings.

The consolation you offer in your letter is in itself most welcome, showing, as it does, the most sincere good will combined in equal measure with good sense. But the feature of your letter from which I have especially derived benefit was its revelation of your splendid disregard for human vicissitudes and your admirable readiness and equipment to meet the blows of Fortune. This I hold to be the highest glory of wisdom, to depend upon oneself alone, and not to let externals govern one's ideas of the good life and the bad. This conception had not altogether fallen out of my mind, where indeed it had taken deep root, but the storm of calamities bursting all around had in some degree weakened it and shaken its hold. I perceive that you aim to lend it support, and in your latest letter too I am conscious that you have done so effectively and helped me a great deal. So I feel bound to say again and again, and not merely

arbitror, nihil mihi esse potuisse tuis litteris gratius.

3   Ad consolandum autem cum illa valent quae eleganter
copioseque collegisti tum nihil plus quam quod firmitudi-
nem gravitatemque animi tui perspexi; quam non imitari
turpissimum existimo. atque[1] hoc etiam fortiorem me puto
quam te ipsum, praeceptorem fortitudinis, quod tu mihi
videris spem non nullam habere haec aliquando futura
meliora; casus enim gladiatorii similitudinesque eae, tum
rationes in ea disputatione a te collectae vetabant me rei
publicae penitus diffidere. itaque alterum minus mirum,
fortiorem te esse cum aliquid speres; alterum mirum,
spe ulla teneri. quid est enim non ita adfectum ut id non
deletum exstinctumque esse fateare? circumspice omnia
membra rei publicae, quae notissima sunt tibi; nullum re-
peries profecto quod non fractum debilitatumve sit. quae
persequerer si aut melius ea viderem quam tu vides aut
commemorare possem sine dolore, quamquam tuis moni-
tis praeceptisque omnis est abiciendus dolor.

4   Ergo et domestica feremus ut censes et publica paulo
etiam fortius fortasse quam tu ipse qui praecipis. te enim
aliqua spes consolatur, ut scribis, nos erimus etiam in omnium[2] desperatione fortes, ut tu tamen idem et hortaris
et praecipis. das enim mihi iucundas recordationes con-
scientiae nostrae rerumque earum quas te in primis auctore gessimus. praestitimus enim patriae non minus certe
quam debuimus, plus profecto quam est ab animo cuius-
5   quam aut consilio hominis postulatum. ignosces mihi de

---

[1] itaque *(Ferrarius)**
[2] omnibus *(Man.)*

---

[2] Terentia, Quintus, and Tullia (Dolabella) may all be in mind.

to intimate but to declare to you, that nothing could have been more welcome to me than your letter.

The arguments which you have so gracefully and copiously brought to bear have indeed their consolatory effect; but nothing is more effective than my perception of *your* steadfastness and imperturbability of spirit. I should be deeply ashamed if I did not imitate it. And I account myself even braver than you, my instructor in fortitude, in that *you* appear to cherish a hope that things will one day improve; the chances of gladiator fights and your other similitudes and the arguments you assemble in discussing the topic tell me not to despair utterly of the commonwealth. No wonder then that you should be braver than I, since you have some hope; the wonder is that any hope remains to you. Can you say of any part that its decline does not amount to total annihilation? Survey all the members of the body politic, with which you are well acquainted: I am sure you will find none that is not shattered or enfeebled. I should pursue the theme, if I saw all this more plainly than you see it, or could recall it without distress—though that is an emotion which according to your counsels and precepts must be utterly cast aside.

Therefore I shall bear domestic troubles[2] as you recommend, and public calamities a little more bravely, it may be, than my mentor himself. For you are comforted, so you say, by a measure of hope; whereas I shall be brave even in total despair, as, notwithstanding your hope, you enjoin and instruct me, offering me the agreeable recollections of my conscience and of those achievements which you were foremost to encourage. For I have done some service to my country; certainly no less than I owed her, and more, I suppose, than has ever before been demanded of a man's

237

me ipso aliquid praedicanti; quarum enim tu rerum cogitatione nos levari³ aegritudine voluisti earum etiam commemoratione lenimur.

Itaque, ut mones, quantum potero, me ab omnibus molestiis et angoribus abducam transferamque animum ad ea quibus secundae res ornantur, adversae adiuvantur, tecumque et ero tantum quantum patietur utriusque aetas et valetudo et, si esse una minus poterimus quam volemus, animorum tamen coniunctione iisdemque studiis ita fruemur ut numquam non una esse videamur.

202 (IV.3)

Scr. Romae parte pr. m. Sept., ut vid., vel fort. antea an. 46
M. CICERO S. D. SER. SULPICIO

1   Vehementer te esse sollicitum et in communibus miseriis praecipuo quodam dolore angi multi ad nos cottidie deferunt. quod quamquam minime miror et meum quodam modo agnosco, doleo tamen te sapientia praeditum prope singulari non tuis bonis delectari potius quam alienis malis laborare. me quidem, etsi nemini concedo qui maiorem ex pernicie et peste rei publicae molestiam traxerit, tamen multa iam consolantur maximeque conscientia consiliorum meorum. multo enim ante tamquam ex aliqua specula prospexi tempestatem futuram, neque id solum

³ levare *(Man.)*

---

1 Now governor of Achaea by Caesar's appointment.

spirit and brain. You will forgive me for claiming something on my own behalf. You hope that the thought of these things will relieve my sore heart; in the mention of them also there is balm.

Therefore I shall follow your counsel. As far as I can, I shall withdraw myself from all that troubles and torments, transferring my mind to those pursuits by which prosperity is embellished and adversity aided. I shall be with you as much as the age and health of both of us allow. And if we cannot be together as much as we should wish, we shall so enjoy our unity of heart and our common studies that we shall never seem to be apart.

202 (IV.3)

CICERO TO SERVIUS SULPICIUS RUFUS

Rome, first half of September or perhaps earlier, 46

From M. Cicero to Ser. Sulpicius[1] greetings.

Every day I hear reports from many informants that you are deeply troubled in mind, suffering a distress somehow over and above the general portion of afflictions. I am not at all surprised, and I might almost say that I recognize my own condition in yours. And yet I am sorry that a man so almost uniquely wise as you should not rather take satisfaction in the good things that are his than grieve over the ills of others. For myself, I will not allow that any man has been harder hit than I by the dire disaster that has overtaken the commonwealth. None the less, I now have much to console me, above all the knowledge of my past policies. Long before the storm broke, I saw it brewing as from a high tower—and that not simply by my own vision but far

mea sponte sed multo etiam magis monente et denun-
tiante te. etsi enim afui magnam partem consulatus tui,
tamen et absens cognoscebam quae esset tua in hoc pesti-
fero bello cavendo et praedicendo sententia et ipse adfui
primis temporibus tui consulatus, cum accuratissime mo-
nuisti senatum collectis omnibus bellis civilibus ut et illa
timerent quae meminissent et scirent, cum superiores
nullo tali exemplo antea in re publica cognito tam crudeles
fuissent, quicumque postea rem publicam oppressisset
armis multo intolerabiliorem futurum. nam quod exemplo
fit id etiam iure fieri putant, sed aliquid atque adeo multa
addunt et adferunt de suo.

2   Qua re meminisse debes eos qui auctoritatem et consilium tuum non sint secuti sua stultitia occidisse, cum tua
prudentia salvi esse potuissent. Dices 'quid me ista res
consolatur in tantis tenebris et quasi parietinis rei publicae?' est omnino vix consolabilis dolor. tanta est omnium
rerum amissio et desperatio reciperandi. sed tamen et
Caesar ipse ita de te iudicat et omnes cives sic existimant,
quasi lumen aliquod exstinctis ceteris elucere sanctitatem
et prudentiam et dignitatem tuam. haec tibi ad levandas
molestias magna esse debent. quod autem a tuis abes, id eo
levius ferendum est quod eodem tempore a multis et
magnis molestiis abes. quas ad te omnis perscriberem nisi
vererer ne ea cognosceres absens quae quia non vides mihi
videris melior⟨e⟩ esse condicione quam nos qui videmus.

3   Hactenus existimo nostram consolationem recte adhi-

more by the aid of your admonitions and warnings. I was away, it is true, during a great part of your Consulship, but in my absence I was informed of the line you took, how you tried to guard against this disastrous war and foretold it; and I was myself on the spot in the early months of your term of office, when you gave the Senate the fullest warning. I remember how you rehearsed all the civil wars of former days, and told your audience both to fear the calamities they remembered and to be sure that, as the men of the past, with no such precedents in our history to follow, had perpetrated these atrocities, any subsequent armed oppressor of the commonwealth would be far worse to endure. People think they have a right to do what others have done, but they also put in some contribution, say rather a large contribution, of their own.

So you must bear in mind that those who refused to follow your lead and listen to your advice have perished by their own folly when they might have been saved by your wisdom. You will ask what consolation that thought brings you in these dark days, when our country lies in ruins. Indeed it is a sorrow almost beyond comfort—the utter loss of all, and the despair of recovery. Yet in the judgement of Caesar himself and the estimation of all our countrymen your integrity, wisdom, and high standing shine like a lamp when all other lights are extinguished. These things should count much towards alleviating your troubles. As for absence from your family and friends, it should be the easier to bear because you are also away from many severe vexations. I should tell you about them all, if I were not reluctant to have you learn in absence what you do not see, and are on that account happier, I think, than we who do.

I judge my words of consolation well placed in so far as

bitam esse quoad certior ab homine amicissimo fieres iis
de rebus quibus levari possent molestiae tuae. reliqua sunt
in te ipso neque mihi ignota nec minima solacia, aut, ⟨ut⟩[1]
quidem ego sentio, multo maxima. quae ego experiens
cottidie sic probo ut ea mihi salutem adferre videantur. te
autem ab initio aetatis memoria teneo summe omnium
doctrinarum studiosum fuisse omniaque quae a sapientissimis[2] ad bene vivendum tradita essent summo studio
curaque didicisse. quae quidem vel optimis rebus et usui
et delectationi esse possent; his vero temporibus habemus
aliud nihil in quo acquiescamus. nihil faciam insolenter
neque te tali vel scientia vel natura praeditum hortabor ut
ad eas te referas artis quibus a primis temporibus aetatis
4   studium tuum dedisti. tantum dicam, quod te spero appro-
baturum, me, postea quam illi arti cui studueram nihil esse
loci neque in curia neque in foro viderim,[3] omnem meam
curam atque operam ad philosophiam contulisse. tuae
scientiae excellenti ac singulari non multo plus quam
nostrae relictum est loci. qua re non equidem te moneo,
sed mihi ita persuasi, te quoque in isdem versari rebus,
quae etiam si minus prodessent, animum tamen a sollicitu-
dine abducerent.

    Servius quidem tuus in omnibus ingenuis artibus in
primisque in hac in qua ego me scripsi acquiescere ita
versatur ut excellat. a me vero sic diligitur ut tibi uni concedam, praeterea nemini, mihique ab eo gratia refertur. in
quo ille existimat, quod facile appareat, cum me colat et
observet, tibi quoque in eo se facere gratissimum.

[1] (SB)
[2] -mis ⟨viris⟩ Mart.
[3] viderem (Man.)

they tell you, from a true friend, of considerations which may serve to lighten your troubles. All other sources of comfort lie in yourself. I know them, and they are not small; or rather to my way of thinking, they are by far the greatest of all. I experience them every day and value them so highly as to see my salvation in them. I well remember how keen a student *you* have been from childhood in every branch of letters, how eagerly and attentively you learned all that the wisest of mankind have handed down to show us how to live. These studies could be useful and delightful in the height of prosperity; but in times like these we have nothing else to ease our hearts. I will not presume. I will not urge a man of your attainments and disposition to have recourse to the pursuits to which you have given your energies from your earliest years. I shall only say something I think you will approve: seeing that there is no further place in Senate House or Forum for the craft which I have studied, I have devoted all my time and attention to philosophy. Little more scope is left for your branch of knowledge,[2] in which you have attained such outstanding distinction, than for mine.[3] So, not to offer you counsel, I feel sure that you are engaged in the same pursuits as myself. Even if they do little good, they distract the mind from its anxiety.

Your son Servius engages and excels in all the pursuits of a gentleman, especially in the one in which I have told you my heart finds ease. In my regard for him I yield to you and to nobody else; and he requites me. He thinks, as is plain to see, that in paying attention and respect to me he is doing what best pleases you.

[2] Jurisprudence.
[3] Oratory.

203 (IV.4)

Scr. Romae c. med. m. Oct., ut vid., an. 46

M. CICERO S.D. SER. SULPICIO

1   Accipio excusationem tuam qua usus es cur saepius ad
me litteras uno exemplo dedisses, sed accipio ex ea parte
quatenus aut neglegentia aut improbitate eorum qui epistulas accipiant fieri scribis ne ad nos perferantur; illam partem excusationis qua te scribis orationis paupertate (sic
enim appellas) isdem verbis epistulas saepius mittere nec
nosco nec probo. et ego ipse, quem tu per iocum (sic enim
accipio) divitias orationis habere dicis, me non esse verborum admodum inopem agnosco (εἰρωνεύεσθαι enim non
necesse est), sed tamen idem (nec hoc εἰρωνευόμενος)
facile cedo tuorum scriptorum subtilitati et elegantiae.

2   Consilium tuum quo te usum scribis hoc Achaicum negotium non recusavisse, cum semper probavissem, tum
multo magis probavi lectis tuis proximis litteris. omnes
enim causae quas commemoras iustissimae sunt tuaque et
auctoritate et prudentia dignissimae. quod aliter cecidisse
rem existimas atque opinatus sis, id tibi nullo modo adsen-
tior. sed quia tanta perturbatio et confusio est rerum, ita
perculsa et prostrata foedissimo bello iacent omnia ut is
cuique locus ubi ipse sit et[1] sibi quisque miserrimus esse
videatur, propterea et tui consili paenitet te et nos qui
domi sumus tibi beati videmur, at contra nobis non tu qui-

---

[1] ut *(Gron.)*

---

[1] I.e. virtually identical. The letters would not be actual dupli-
cates.

203 (IV.4)

CICERO TO SERVIUS SULPICIUS RUFUS

Rome, ca. mid October (?) 46

From M. Cicero to Ser. Sulpicius greetings.

I accept the excuse you make for often sending me identical[1] letters, but I accept that part of it only in which you say that letters are not always delivered to me because of the negligence or dishonesty of those who take charge of them. The other part, in which you write that you often send identically phrased letters because of your 'verbal poverty,' I neither recognize nor approve. I myself, whom you jestingly (so I suppose) credit with verbal riches, acknowledge that I am not altogether unprovided with words (no need for false modesty!); but also, and with no false modesty, I readily yield the palm to the spareness and elegance of your compositions.

I had all along approved the considerations which led you, as you say, not to refuse this job in Achaea, but my approval was notably confirmed after reading your most recent letter. All the reasons which you advance are thoroughly valid, eminently worthy of your reputation and wisdom. I do not at all agree with your judgement that the matter has turned out otherwise than you had supposed. But in the general perturbation and chaos, when all lies overthrown and prostrate in the wake of a hideous war, each man reckons his own whereabouts as the worst of places and himself as the most wretched of beings. That is why you regret your decision and why we at home seem happy to you; whereas to us *you* seem, not indeed trouble-

dem vacuus molestiis, sed prae nobis beatus. atque hoc
ipso melior est tua quam nostra condicio quod tu quid do-
leat scribere audes, nos ne id quidem tuto possumus; nec
id victoris vitio, quo nihil moderatius, sed ipsius victoriae,
quae civilibus bellis semper est insolens.

3   Uno te vicimus quod de Marcelli, collegae tui, salute
paulo ante quam tu cognovimus, etiam ⟨h⟩ercle quod
quem ad modum ea res ageretur vidimus. nam sic fac existimes, post has miserias, id est postquam armis disceptari
coeptum sit de iure publico, nihil esse actum aliud cum
dignitate. nam et ipse Caesar, accusata acerbitate Marcelli
(sic enim appellabat) laudataque honorificentissime et ae-
quitate tua et prudentia, repente praeter spem dixit se
senatui roganti de Marcello ne ominis quidem causa nega-
turum. fecerat autem hoc senatus, ut, cum a L. Pisone
mentio esset facta de Marcello et C.[2] Marcellus se ad Caesaris pedes abiecisset, cunctus consurgeret et ad Caesarem
supplex accederet. noli quaerere: ita mihi pulcher hic dies
visus est ut speciem aliquam viderer videre quasi revivis-
centis rei publicae.

4   Itaque, cum omnes ante me rogati gratias Caesari egissent praeter Volcacium (is enim, si eo loco esset, negavit
se facturum fuisse), ego rogatus mutavi meum consilium;
nam statueram, non mehercule inertia sed desiderio pristinae dignitatis, in perpetuum tacere. fregit hoc meum
consilium et Caesaris magnitudo animi et senatus offi-

---

[2] cum *(Baiter)*

---

[2] These would concern private or provincial matters which
might safely be put on paper.

free, but happy by comparison with ourselves. And your state is better than ours in this very respect, that you dare to put your discontents[2] on paper, whereas we cannot even do that without risk. It is the fault, not of the victor, who is as moderate as could be, but of the victory itself. In civil war victory is always insolent.

On one point we have had the advantage of you. We learned of your colleague Marcellus' restitution a little sooner than you, and I will add furthermore that we saw *how* the matter was handled. For I do assure you that since the start of these calamities, that is, since force of arms first came to be arbiter of constitutional right, no other piece of public business has been transacted with dignity. Caesar himself, after complaining of Marcellus' acerbity (that was the word he used) and lauding your fair-mindedness and wisdom in the most complimentary terms, suddenly and unexpectedly declared that, if only for the omen's sake, he would not say no to the Senate's petition on Marcellus' behalf. This was after the House had risen in a body and approached Caesar in supplication, which they did when L. Piso had made mention of Marcellus in his speech and C. Marcellus had fallen at Caesar's feet. Take my word, it seemed to me a fine day's work; I thought I saw some semblance of reviving constitutional freedom.

Accordingly, after all those called upon to speak ahead of me had expressed thanks to Caesar except Volcacius (*he* said he would not have done it in Caesar's place), my name was called; and I changed my resolution. I had determined to hold my peace forever, not, let me say, from sluggishness, but because I remembered the station that used to be mine and is mine no longer. This resolution of mine was overborne by Caesar's magnanimity and the Senate's solic-

247

cium; itaque pluribus verbis egi Caesari gratias, meque
metuo ne etiam in ceteris rebus honesto otio privarim,
quod erat unum solacium in malis. sed tamen, quoniam
effugi eius offensionem, qui fortasse arbitraretur me hanc
rem publicam non putare si perpetuo tacerem, modice hoc
faciam aut etiam intra modum, ut et illius voluntati et meis
studiis serviam. nam etsi a prima aetate me omnis ars et
doctrina liberalis et maxime philosophia delectavit, tamen
hoc studium cottidie ingravescit, credo, et aetatis maturi-
tate ad prudentiam et iis temporum vitiis ut nulla res alia
5 levare animum molestiis possit. a quo studio te abduci
negotiis intellego ex tuis litteris, sed tamen aliquid iam
noctes te adiuvabunt.

Servius tuus, vel potius noster, summa me observantia
colit; cuius ego cum omni probitate summaque virtute tum
studiis doctrinaque delector. is mecum saepe de tua man-
sione aut decessione communicat. adhuc in hac sum sententia, nihil ut faciamus nisi quod maxime Caesar velle
videatur. res sunt eius modi ut, si Romae sis, nihil[3] praeter
tuos delectare possit. de reliquis nihil melius ipso est;
ceteri et cetera eius modi ut, si alterum utrum necesse sit,
audire ea malis quam videre. hoc nostrum consilium nobis
minime iucundum est, qui te videre cupimus; sed consuli-
mus tibi.

Vale.

[3] nihil <te> *Man.*

---

[3] The speech is extant *(Pro Marcello).*

itude. So I expressed gratitude to Caesar at considerable length,[3] and I am afraid I may have thus forfeited in other contexts the decent retirement which was my only consolation in adversity. However, now that I have escaped his displeasure (he might have thought I did not regard the present regime as constitutional if I never broke silence), I shall do this in moderation, or rather on the near side of moderation, so as to meet his wishes on the one hand and the claims of my literary pursuits on the other. From my childhood I have taken pleasure in every liberal art and branch of knowledge, most of all in philosophy; but my devotion to this study grows upon me every day. I suppose I have reached an age ripe for wisdom; and the evils of the times are such that nothing else can relieve one's mind of its burdens. I see from your letter that business is distracting you from this pursuit, but the lengthening nights will soon be some help.

Your boy, Servius, our boy rather, is most attentive to me. His sterling worth and high character, and more particularly his devotion to literary studies, are my delight. He often confers with me about the question of your staying on or coming home. So far I take the view that we should do nothing but what appears most in accord with Caesar's wishes. The state of affairs is such that, if you were in Rome, nothing could give you pleasure except your family and friends. That aside, the best feature in the scene is himself. Other persons and things are such as one would prefer to learn of by report than see, if it were necessary to do one or the other. This advice of mine is by no means agreeable to *me*—I am anxious to see you, but counsel for your good.

Good-bye.

CICERO'S LETTERS TO FRIENDS

204 (XII.17)

Scr. Romae med. m. Sept. an. 46

CICERO S. D. CORNIFICIO COLLEGAE[1]

1   Grata mihi vehementer est memoria nostri tua quam significasti litteris; quam ut conserves, non quo de tua constantia dubitem sed quia mos est ita rogandi, rogo.

    Ex Syria nobis tumultuosiora quaedam nuntiata sunt,[2] quae, quia tibi sunt propiora quam nobis, tua me causa magis movent quam mea. Romae summum otium est, sed ita ut malis salubre aliquod et honestum negotium; quod spero fore. video id curae esse Caesari.

2   Me <s>cito, dum tu absis, quasi occasionem quandam et licentiam nactum scribere audacius, et cetera quidem fortasse quae etiam tu concederes, sed proxime scripsi de optimo genere dicendi;[3] in quo saepe suspicatus sum te a iudicio nostro, sic scilicet ut doctum hominem ab non indocto, paulum dissidere. huic tu libro maxime velim ex animo, si minus, gratiae causa suffragere. dicam tuis ut eum, si velint, describant ad teque mittant. puto enim, etiam si rem minus probabis, tamen in ista solitudine quicquid a me profectum sit iucundum tibi fore.

3   Quod mihi existimationem tuam dignitatemque commendas, facis tu quidem omnium more, sed velim sic

---

[1] Now governing Cilicia; he is a colleague as Augur.

[2] First news of the soldiers' mutiny headed by Caecilius Bassus seems to have reached Rome shortly before Cicero wrote.

[3] Known as *The Orator;* the title was decided later.

250

204 (XII.17)
CICERO TO CORNIFICIUS

Rome, mid September 46

From Cicero to his colleague Cornificius[1] greetings.

I am truly gratified by your remembrance of me, which you signify in your letter. Let me ask you to keep it in being. I do so, not as doubting your constancy, but as a common form.

Reports of disturbances have reached us from Syria.[2] As you are nearer their source than we, I am more concerned on your account than on my own. Rome is profoundly quiet. One would prefer some action, of a wholesome and honourable sort. I hope there will be such—Caesar evidently has it in mind.

You may be interested to learn that, profiting by your absence, I have taken the opportunity and licence, so to speak, to write more adventurously. Most of the results, it is true, might pass muster even with you. But my latest work is a treatise on the best style of oratory,[3] a subject on which I have often suspected that you are not altogether at one with my judgement—a case, naturally, of an expert differing from one not wholly without claim to that description. I hope you will befriend the book because you really like it; but if not that, then for my sake. I shall ask your people to copy it if they please, and send it to you. For I fancy that, even if the contents do not quite meet with your approval, any product of my pen will be agreeable to you in your present isolation.

In commending your reputation and consequence to my care you follow the general form of courtesy; but I hope you will believe not only that I set great store by the mutual

existimes, me, cum amori quem inter nos mutuum esse
intellegam plurimum tribuam, tum de summo ingenio et
de studiis tuis optimis et de spe amplissimae dignitatis ita
iudicare ut neminem tibi anteponam, comparem paucos.

205 (XII.18)

Scr. Romae ex. m. Sept. vel in. Oct. an. 46

CICERO S. D. CORNIFICIO COLLEGAE

1   Quod extremum fuit in ea epistula quam a te proxime
accepi ad id primum respondebo; animum adverti enim
hoc vos magnos oratores facere non numquam. epistulas
requiris meas; ego autem numquam, cum mihi denuntia-
tum esset a tuis ire aliquem, non dedi.

Quod mihi videor ex tuis litteris intellegere, te nihil
commissurum esse temere nec ante quam scisses quo iste
nescio qui Caecilius Bassus erumperet quicquam certi
constituturum, id ego et speraram prudentia tua fretus
et ut confiderem fecerunt tuae gratissimae mihi litterae;
idque ut facias quam saepissime, ut et quid tu agas et quid
agatur scire possim et etiam quid acturus sis, valde te rogo.

Etsi periniquo patiebar animo te a me digredi, tamen
eo tempore me consolabar quod et in summum otium te
ire arbitrabar et ab impendentibus magnis negotiis disce-
2   dere. utrumque contra accidit; istic enim bellum est exor-
tum, hic pax consecuta, sed tamen eius modi pax in qua, si

affection which I am conscious exists between us but also that in the brilliance of your talents, your devotion to culture, and the prospect of a splendid political future you stand second to none in my estimation and comparable to few.

205 (XII.18)
CICERO TO CORNIFICIUS

Rome, September (end) or October (beginning) 46

From Cicero to his colleague Cornificius greetings.

The latest point in the letter I most recently received from you is the one which I shall answer first (I have observed that you great orators do this now and then). You complain that you don't hear from me. The fact is that I have never failed to send a letter when notified by your people that someone was going.

I think I may gather from your letter that you will take no hasty step and make no definite decision until you know the upshot of this Caecilius Bassus fellow. That is what I had expected, counting upon your good sense, and your most welcome letter has confirmed it. I would particularly ask you to write as often as you can, so that I know what you are doing and what is going on, also your further intentions.

Although I was sorry indeed to say good-bye to you, I consoled myself at the time with the belief that all was completely quiet where you were going, and that on the other hand you were leaving the threat of serious trouble behind you. In both respects the opposite has happened. War has broken out there, peace has ensued here. But it is

adesses, multa te non delectarent, ea tamen quae ne ipsum
Caesarem quidem delectant. bellorum enim civilium ii
semper exitus sunt ut non ea solum fiant quae velit victor
sed etiam ut iis mos gerendus sit quibus adiutoribus sit
parta victoria. equidem sic iam obdurui ut ludis Caesaris
nostri animo aequissimo viderem T. Plancum, audirem
Laberi et Publi<l>i poemata. nihil mihi tam deesse scito
quam quicum haec familiariter docteque rideam. is tu eris
si quam primum veneris; quod ut facias non mea solum sed
etiam tua interesse arbitror.

206 (XII.19)

Scr. Romae c. m. Dec. an. 46

CICERO CORNIFICIO S.

1   Libentissime legi tuas litteras, in quibus iucundissimum mihi fuit quod cognovi meas tibi redditas esse. non
enim dubitabam quin eas libenter lecturus esses; verebar
ut redderentur.

    Bellum quod est in Syria Syriamque provinciam tibi tri-
butam esse a Caesare ex tuis litteris cognovi. eam[1] rem tibi
volo bene et feliciter evenire; quod ita fore confido fretus
2 et industria et prudentia tua. sed de Parthici belli suspi-

---

[1] ea(n)dem *(Lamb.)*

---

[1] The *ludi Victoriae Caesaris,* instituted in honour of Caesar's
victory at Thapsus.   [2] Bursa, restored by Caesar from exile.
[3] Cicero had to sit through the mimes lest his absence should
offend the Dictator.

a peace in which many things would displease you if you were on the spot—things, however, which do not please Caesar either. This is what always happens at the end of a civil war. It is not just a matter of the victor's wishes coming into effect; he also has to humour the people with whose assistance the victory has been gained. For my part, I have grown so thick a skin that at our friend Caesar's show[1] I saw T. Plancus[2] and heard Laberius' and Publilius' verses with perfect composure.[3] Let me tell you that what I lack most is someone with whom to laugh at all this in an intimate, sophisticated way. You shall be the one, if you come back as soon as possible. I think it is to your own interest that you should do so as well as to mine.

206 (XII.19)
CICERO TO CORNIFICIUS

Rome, ca. December 46

From Cicero to Cornificius greetings.

I was delighted to read your letter. What pleased me most was to know that mine had been delivered. I did not doubt that you would be glad to read it, but I was uneasy about its safe delivery.

Your letter tells me that the present war in Syria and the province itself have been entrusted to you by Caesar. I wish you good luck and success in that responsibility; and I feel sure you will have it, counting as I do on your diligence and good sense. But what you say about the possibility of a war with Parthia has alarmed me not a little, for I could

cione quod scribis sane me commovit. quid enim copia-
rum haberes cum ipse coniectura consequi poteram tum
ex tuis litteris cognovi. itaque opto ne se illa gens moveat
hoc tempore, dum ad te legiones eae perducantur quas
audio duci. quod si paris copias ad confligendum non habebis, non te fugiet uti consilio M. Bibuli, qui se oppido
munitissimo et copiosissimo tam diu tenuit quam diu in
provincia Parthi fuerunt.

3   Sed haec ‹tu›[2] melius ex re et ex tempore constitues.
mihi quidem usque[3] curae erit quid agas dum quid egeris
sciero. litteras ad te numquam habui cui darem quin dede-
rim; a te ut idem facias peto, in primisque ut ita ad tuos
scribas ut me tuum sciant esse.

207 (XV.21)

Scr. Romae fort. in. m. Dec. an. 46

M. CICERO S. D. C. TREBONIO

1   Et epistulam tuam legi libenter et librum libentissime;
sed tamen in ea voluptate hunc accepi dolorem quod, cum
incendisses cupiditatem meam consuetudinis augendae
nostrae (nam ad amorem quidem nihil poterat accedere),
tum discedis a nobis meque tanto desiderio adficis ut
unam mihi consolationem relinquas, fore ut utriusque nostrum absentis desiderium crebris et longis epistulis lenia-

---

    [2] *(Wes.)**   [3] usque ‹eo› *Cobet*

---

   [1] Antioch.

guess for myself the size of your forces, and now learn it from your letter. So I pray that nation makes no move for the time being, before the legions which I hear are being brought to your support actually reach you. If you do not have troops enough to engage on equal terms, I trust you won't fail to follow M. Bibulus' tactics, who shut himself inside an extremely well-fortified and well-provisioned town[1] so long as the Parthians remained in the province.

But you will be better able to decide this in the light of the situation at the time. I shall be wondering anxiously what you are doing, until I know what you have done. I have taken every opportunity of sending you a letter and request you to do the same. Above all please write to your people in such a way as to let them know that I am one of their number.

207 (XV.21)
CICERO TO TREBONIUS

Rome, beginning of December 46 (?)

From M. Cicero to C. Trebonius[1] greetings.

It was a pleasure to read your letter, and a great pleasure to read your book. But there was a touch of pain too, for, having inflamed my eagerness to increase our intercourse (our *affection* admitted of no addition), you then go away. Missing you as sorely as I do, you leave me only one consolation—that long, frequent letters will mitigate the sense of loss we both feel in each other's absence. I can

---

[1] On his way to Spain, where Caesar's last campaign against the resurgent republicans was about to begin.

tur. quod ego non modo de me tibi spondere possum sed
de te etiam mihi. nullam enim apud me reliquisti dubita-
2 tionem quantum me amares. nam ut illa omittam quae
civitate teste fecisti, cum mecum inimicitias communica-
visti, cum me contionibus tuis defendisti, cum quaestor in
mea atque in publica causa consulum partis suscepisti,
cum tribuno plebis quaestor non paruisti, cui tuus praesertim collega pareret; ut haec recentia, quae meminero semper, obliviscar, quae tua sollicitudo de me in armis, quae
laetitia in reditu, quae cura, qui dolor cum ad te curae et
dolores mei perferrentur, Brundisium denique te ad me
venturum fuisse nisi subito in Hispaniam missus esses—
ut haec igitur omittam, quae mihi tanti aestimanda sunt
quanti vitam aestimo et salutem meam: liber iste quem
mihi misisti quantam habet declarationem amoris tui! primum quod tibi facetum videtur quicquid ego dixi, quod
alii fortasse non item; deinde quod illa, sive faceta sunt sive
sic, fiunt narrante te venustissima, quin etiam ante quam
3 ad me veniatur risus omnis paene consumitur. quod si in iis
scribendis nihil aliud nisi, quod necesse fuit, de uno me
tam diu cogitavisses, ferreus essem si te non amarem; cum
vero ea quae scriptura persecutus es sine summo amore
cogitare non potueris, non possum existimare plus quemquam a se ipso quam me a te amari. cui quidem ego amori
utinam ceteris rebus possem, amore certe respondebo,
quo tamen ipso tibi confido futurum satis.

---

2 Clodius. We are not otherwise informed of Trebonius' activities as City Quaestor (apparently in 60, or perhaps 58). His
colleague is not identified, but the Tribune was probably one
C. Herennius, who was promoting efforts to make Clodius a
plebeian.

vouch to you for my part, and to myself for yours too; for you have left me in no doubt how much you care for me. Suppose I put out of account what you did in full public view, when you made my enemy[2] yours, defended me in your speeches, as Quaestor took upon yourself the duty of the Consuls on my behalf and the public's, and as Quaestor refused to obey the orders of a Tribune, even though your colleague obeyed them. Suppose I forgot matters of recent date, which I shall always remember—your concern for me at the war, your gladness at my return, your anxiety and distress when you were told of *my* anxieties and distress, your intention to visit me at Brundisium had you not suddenly been ordered to Spain: leaving all this aside (and I must needs value it as highly as I value my existence as a man and a citizen), this book[3] you have sent me, what a declaration of your affection! To begin with, you find wit in every saying of mine—another perhaps would not; and then, these things, whether witty or only so-so, become irresistible when you are their raconteur. In fact the laugh is nearly all over before *I* come on the scene. I should have a heart of stone not to love you simply for thinking so long about me and me only, as in writing these pieces you necessarily did. But you could not have thought what you have put down on paper without the most sincere affection. So I cannot suppose that anybody loves himself more than you love me. I wish I could repay your affection in all other ways, but at least I shall repay it with my own; and, after all, I feel sure that this by itself will be all the return you desire.

[3] A collection, as appears, of Ciceronian witticisms, each in its anecdotal setting.

4   Nunc ad epistulam venio; cui copiose et suaviter scrip-
tae nihil est quod multa respondeam. primum enim ego
illas Calvo litteras misi non plus quam has quas nunc legis
existimans exituras; aliter enim scribimus quod eos solos
quibus mittimus, aliter quod multos lecturos putamus.
deinde ingenium eius maioribus[1] extuli laudibus quam tu
id vere potuisse fieri putas primum quod ita iudicabam.
acute movebatur, genus quoddam sequebatur in quo iudicio lapsus, quo valebat, tamen adsequebatur quod pro-
barat;[2] multae erant et reconditae litterae. vis non erat; ad
eam igitur adhortabar. in excitando autem et in acuendo
plurimum valet si laudes eum quem cohortere. habes de
Calvo iudicium et consilium meum; consilium, quod hor-
tandi causa laudavi, iudicium, quod de ingenio eius valde
existimavi bene.

5   Reliquum est tuam profectionem amore prosequar,
reditum spe exspectem, absentem memoria colam, omne
desiderium litteris mittendis accipiendisque leniam. tu velim tua in me studia et officia multum tecum recordere.
quae cum tibi liceat, mihi nefas sit oblivisci, non modo
virum bonum me existimabis verum etiam te a me amari
plurimum iudicabis.

        Vale.

[1] melior- *(Ern.)*
[2] probaret *(Nipperdey)*

I come now to your charming and communicative letter, to which there is no necessity for me to reply at great length. First, I sent that letter to Calvus[4] not thinking that it would get into circulation any more than the one you are reading at this moment. Now our way of writing when we think we shall be read only by our addressee is not the same as when we write for a multitude of eyes. Secondly, if I praised his talent more generously than in your opinion the truth could warrant, it was first and foremost because such was really my opinion. Calvus' intellect was keen and quick; he followed a style in which, though he failed in judgement (a strong point with him), he none the less succeeded in the manner of his choice; his reading was wide and recondite. But he lacked force, and I was urging him to make good the deficiency. Now in trying to rouse a man and spur him on, it works wonders if you mingle some praise with your admonitions. So that's what I think of Calvus, and why I wrote as I did. I praised in order to exhort; and I did think very highly of his talent.

It remains for me to let my affection follow you on your way, to look forward hopefully to your return, to remember you faithfully in your absence, and to mitigate all sense of loss by sending and receiving letters. I hope you will often think of all you have done for me and tried to do. *You* are at liberty to forget it, but for me to forget would be a sin. So you will not only rate me an honourable man but conclude that I have a deep affection for you.

Good-bye.

---

[4] The poet and orator, C. Licinius Macer Calvus, now dead.

208 (XV.20)

Scr. Romae non multo post superiorem

M. CICERO S. D. C. TREBONIO

1   'Oratorem' meum (sic enim inscripsi) Sabino tuo commendavi. natio me hominis impulit ut ei recte putarem,
nisi forte candidatorum licentia hic quoque usus hoc subito cognomen arripuit; etsi modestus eius vultus sermoque
constans habere quiddam a Curibus videbatur. sed de
Sabino satis.

2   Tu, mi Treboni, quoniam ad amorem meum aliquantum olei[1] discedens addidisti, quo tolerabilius feramus
igniculum desideri tui crebris nos litteris appellato, atque
ita si idem fiet a nobis. quamquam duae causae sunt cur tu
frequentior in isto officio esse debeas quam nos: primum
quod olim solebant qui Romae erant ad provincialis amicos de re publica scribere, nunc tu nobis scribas oportet
(res enim publica istic est); deinde quod nos aliis officiis
tibi absenti satis facere possumus, tu nobis nisi litteris non
video qua re alia satis facere possis.

3   Sed cetera scribes ad nos postea. nunc haec prima
cupio cognoscere, iter tuum cuius modi sit, ubi Brutum
nostrum videris, quam diu simul fueris; deinde, cum pro-

---

[1] olim *(Koch)*

---

[1] The *cognomen* Sabinus suggested Sabine origin, and Sabine
country was traditionally the home of the old-time virtues. Or had
Sabinus merely assumed his *cognomen,* like certain candidates for
office (possibly an allusion to C. Calvisius Sabinus)? Probably,

208 (XV.20)
CICERO TO TREBONIUS

Rome, shortly after the foregoing

From M. Cicero to C. Trebonius greetings.

I have entrusted my *Orator,* as I have entitled it, to your friend Sabinus. His race gave me the notion that he would make a trustworthy messenger—unless he has taken a leaf out of the candidates' book, and laid hold of the name incontinent![1] But his modest face and his firm, even way of talking seemed to have something of Cures.[2] But that's enough of Sabinus.

My dear Trebonius, when you left Rome you poured some oil on the flame of my affection; and so, to make it easier for me to bear the smart of missing you, salute me with letters in plenty, on the understanding that the same shall be forthcoming on my side. To be sure, you ought to be more assiduous in this office than I for two reasons: firstly, because, whereas in the old days people in Rome used to write to their friends in the provinces about politics, it is now for you to write to me, for the body politic is over there with you; secondly, because I can give you your due by other services while you are away, but I do not see how you can give me mine except by writing letters.

You will be writing me the rest of your news later on, but now I want first of all to know what sort of a journey you are having, where you saw our friend Brutus,[3] and how long you spent with him. Then, when you are further on

however, he was a freedman of Trebonius or even a slave. Cicero is facetious.   [2] Ancient chief town of the Sabines.

[3] Now governing Cisalpine Gaul.

cesseris longius, de bellicis rebus, de toto negotio, ut existimare possimus quo statu simus. ego tantum me scire putabo quantum ex tuis litteris habebo cognitum.

Cura ut valeas meque ames amore illo tuo singulari.

209 (VII.23)

Scr. Romae post m. interc. post. an. 46

CICERO S. D. M. FABIO GALLO

1   Tantum quod ex Arpinati veneram cum mihi a te litterae redditae sunt ab eodemque accepi Aviani litteras, in quibus hoc inerat liberalissimum, nomina se facturum cum venisset qua ego vellem die. fac, quaeso, qui ego sum esse te: estne aut tui pudoris aut nostri primum rogare de die, deinde plus annua postulare? sed essent, mi Galle, omnia facilia si et ea mercatus esses quae ego desiderabam et ad eam summam quam volueram. ac tamen ista ipsa quae te emisse scribis non solum rata mihi erunt sed etiam grata. plane enim intellego te non modo studio sed etiam amore usum quae te delectarint, hominem, ut ego semper iudicavi, in omni iudicio elegantissimum, quae me digna putaris, coemisse. sed velim maneat Damasippus in sententia; prorsus enim ex istis emptionibus nullam desidero.
2   tu autem, ignarus instituti mei, quanti ego genus omnino

---

1 Doubtless the sculptor, C. Avianius Evander; cf. Letter 314. Gallus had bought some statues from him on Cicero's behalf.

2 L. Licinius Crassus Damasippus, probably the bankrupt art connoisseur of Horace, *Satires* 2.3. He had offered to take the purchases off Cicero's hands.

your way, tell me about military matters and the whole situation, so that I can make an estimate of how we stand. I shall consider I know just as much as I learn from your letters.

Take care of your health and the affection which you so generously bestow on me.

209 (VII.23)
CICERO TO M. FABIUS GALLUS

Rome, beginning of December (true calendar) 46

From Cicero to M. Fabius Gallus greetings.

I had just got in from Arpinum when I was handed a letter from you. By the same bearer I received a letter from Avianius,[1] containing a very handsome offer to debit me after he arrives from any date I please. Now pray put yourself in my shoes. Can you reconcile it with your sense of decency or with mine to ask for credit in the first place, and in the second for more than a year's credit? But everything would be straightforward, my dear Gallus, if you had bought what I needed and within the price I had wished to pay. Not but what I shall stand by these purchases you say you have made, indeed I am grateful. I fully understand that you acted out of good will, affection indeed, in buying the pieces which pleased you (I have always regarded you as a very fine judge in any matter of taste), and which you considered worthy of me. But I hope Damasippus[2] doesn't change his mind, for, frankly, I don't need any of these purchases of yours. Not being acquainted with my regular practice, you have taken these four or five pieces at a price

signorum omnium non aestimo tanti ista quattuor aut quinque sumpsisti. Bacchas istas cum Musis Metelli comparas. quid simile? primum ipsas ego Musas numquam tanti putassem atque id fecissem Musis omnibus approbantibus, sed tamen erat aptum bibliothecae studiisque nostris congruens; Bacchis vero ubi est apud me locus? at pulchellae sunt. novi optime et saepe vidi. nominatim tibi signa mihi nota mandassem si probassem. ea enim signa ego emere soleo quae ad similitudinem gymnasiorum exornent mihi in palaestra locum. Martis vero signum quo mihi pacis auctori? gaudeo nullum Saturni signum fuisse; haec enim duo signa putarem mihi aes alienum attulisse. Mercuri mallem aliquod fuisset; felicius,[1] puto, cum Avianio transigere possemus.

3   Quod tibi destinaras trapezophorum, si te delectat, habebis; sin autem sententiam mutasti, ego habe<b>o scilicet. ista quidem summa ne ego multo libentius emerim deversorium Tarracinae, ne semper hospiti molestus sim. omnino liberti mei video esse culpam, cui plane res certas mandaram, itemque Iuni, quem puto tibi notum esse, Aviani familiarem. exhedria quaedam mihi nova sunt instituta in porticula Tusculani. ea volebam tabellis ornare. etenim, si quid generis istius modi me delectat, pictura delectat. sed tamen si ista mihi sunt habenda, certiorem

---

[1] facilius *Vict.*

---

[3] Probably Metellus Scipio.

[4] Probably in his house on the Palatine; cf. *Letters to Atticus* 24 (II.4).7.

[5] The god of gain. In astrology Saturn and Mars generally bring the opposite.

I should consider excessive for all the statuary in creation. You compare these Bacchantes with Metellus'[3] Muses. Where's the likeness? To begin with, I should never have reckoned the Muses themselves worth such a sum—and all Nine would have approved my judgement! Still, that would have made a suitable acquisition for a library, and one appropriate to my interests. But where am I going to put Bacchantes? Pretty little things, you may say. I know them well, I've seen them often. I should have given you a specific commission about statues which I know, if I had cared for them. My habit is to buy pieces which I can use to decorate a place in my palaestra,[4] in imitation of lecture halls. But a statue of Mars! What can I, as an advocate of peace, do with that? I'm glad there was none of Saturn—I should have thought those two between them had brought me debt! I had sooner have had one of Mercury[5]—we might fare better in our transactions with Avianius!

As for that table rest which you had earmarked for yourself, if you like it, you shall have it; but if you have altered your mind, I'll keep it of course. For the sum you have spent I should really have much preferred to buy a lodge at Tarracina,[6] so as not to be continually imposing on hospitality. To be sure, I realize that my freedman is to blame (I had given him quite definite commissions), and Junius too—I think you know him, Avianius' friend. I am making some new alcoves in the little gallery of my house at Tusculum, and I wanted some pictures for their decoration—indeed, if anything in this way appeals to me, it is painting. However, if I have to keep these things of

[6] Cicero had recently visited his Campanian villas and will have stayed at Tarracina en route; perhaps Gallus was his host.

velim me facias ubi sint, quando arcessantur, quo genere
vecturae. si enim Damasippus in sententia non manebit,
aliquem Pseudodamasippum vel cum iactura reperiemus.

4   Quod ad me de domo scribis iterum, iam id ego proficiscens mandaram meae Tulliae; ea enim ipsa hora acceperam tuas litteras. egeram etiam cum tuo Nicia, quod is
utitur, ut scis, familiariter Crasso.[2] ut redii autem, prius-
quam tuas legi has proximas litteras, quaesivi de mea Tullia
quid egisset. per Liciniam se egisse dicebat (sed opinor
Crassum[3] uti non ita multum sorore); eam porro negare se
audere, cum vir abesset (est enim profectus in Hispaniam
Dexius), illo et absente et insciente migrare. est mihi
gratissimum tanti a te aestimatam consuetudinem vitae
victusque nostri primum ut eam domum sumeres ut non
modo prope me sed plane mecum habitare posses, deinde
ut migrare tanto opere festines. sed ne vivam si tibi concedo ut eius rei tu cupidior sis quam ego sum. itaque omnia
experiar. video enim quid mea intersit, quid utriusque
nostrum. si quid egero, faciam ut scias. tu et ad omnia
rescribes et quando te exspectem facies me, si tibi videtur,
certiorem.

[2] cassio (*Man.*)
[3] cassium (*Man.*)

yours, please let me know where they are, and when they are sent for, and by what mode of transport. If Damasippus changes his mind, I shall find some Damasippus *manqué*, even if it means taking a loss.

You write again about the house. I had already given directions on this head to my girl Tullia as I was leaving— I got your letter that same hour. I had also taken it up with your friend Nicias, since he is on familiar terms with Crassus,[7] as you know. On my return, before I read this last letter of yours, I asked Tullia how she had got on. She said she had gone to work through Licinia (I have an impression, though, that Crassus does not have a great deal to do with his sister), and that Licinia in her turn said that while her husband was away (Dexius has left for Spain) she did not venture to move house in his absence and without his knowledge. I take it very kindly that you set so much store on our friendly day-to-day intercourse that you took a house so as to live not only in my neighbourhood but in my actual company, and that you are in such a hurry to move. But on my life I won't admit that you are any more eager for that arrangement than myself. So I shall try every way, conscious as I am of what it means to me and to both of us. If I have any success, I'll let you know. Write back on all points and inform me, if you will, when I am to expect you.

[7] If the manuscript readings *Cassio* and *Cassium* are sound, this would be C. Cassius' brother Lucius; and Licinia was his half-sister. But the change is very probable. Crassus will be the 'Triumvir's' surviving son, M. Licinius Crassus.

210 (VII.26)

Scr. in Tusculano c. XI Kal. m. interc. post. an. 46

CICERO S. D. GALLO

1   Cum decimum iam diem graviter ex intestinis laborarem neque iis qui mea opera uti volebant me probarem
non valere quia febrim non haberem, fugi in Tusculanum,
cum quidem biduum ita ieiunus fuissem ut ne aquam quidem gustarem. itaque confectus languore et fame magis
tuum officium desideravi quam a te requiri putavi meum.
ego autem cum omnis morbos reformido tum ⟨eum in⟩
quo¹ Epicurum tuum Stoici male accipiunt quia dicat
στραγγουρικὰ καὶ δυσεντερικὰ πάθη sibi molesta esse;
quorum alterum morbum edacitatis esse putant, alterum
etiam turpioris intemperantiae. sane δυσεντερίαν perti-
mueram; sed visa est mihi vel loci mutatio vel animi etiam
relaxatio vel ipsa fortasse iam senescentis morbi remissio
profuisse.

2   Ac tamen, ne mirere unde hoc acciderit quo modove
commiserim, lex sumptuaria, quae videtur λιτότητα attulisse, ea mihi fraudi fuit. nam dum volunt isti lauti terra
nata, quae lege excepta sunt, in honorem adducere, fungos, helvellas, herbas omnis ita condiunt ut nihil possit esse
suavius. in eas cum incidissem in cena augurali apud Len-
tulum, tanta me διάρροια adripuit ut hodie primum videatur coepisse consistere. ita ego, qui me ostreis et murenis
facile abstinebam, a beta et a malva deceptus sum. posthac

---

¹ quod *(Lamb.)*

---

¹ Caesar's.   ² P. Lentulus Spinther the younger.

210 (VII.26)
CICERO TO M. FABIUS GALLUS

Tusculum, ca. 17 October (true calendar) 46

From Cicero to Gallus greetings.

For ten days my stomach had been seriously out of order, but as I did not have a fever I could not convince the folk who wanted my services that I was really sick. So I took refuge here at Tusculum, after two days of strict fasting—not so much as a drop of water! Famished and exhausted, I was craving your good offices rather than expecting you to demand mine. I am terrified of all forms of illness, but especially of the one over which your master Epicurus gets a rough handling from the Stoics—for complaining of trouble with his bladder and his bowels, the latter being according to them a consequence of overeating and the former of an even more discreditable indulgence! Well, I was really afraid of dysentery. However, I think I am better for the change, or maybe the mental relaxation; or perhaps the malady is simply wearing itself into abatement.

But in case you wonder how this happened or what I did to deserve it, the Sumptuary Law,[1] supposed to have brought plain living, has been my downfall. Our *bons vivants,* in their efforts to bring into fashion products of the soil exempted under the statute, make the most appetizing dishes out of fungi, potherbs, and grasses of all sorts. Happening on some of these at an augural dinner at Lentulus'[2] house, I was seized with a violent diarrhea, which has only today begun (I think) to check its flow. So: oysters and eels I used to resist well enough, but here I lie, caught in the toils of Mesdames Beet and Mallow! Well, I

igitur erimus cautiores. tu tamen, cum audisses ab Anicio (vidit enim me nauseantem), non modo mittendi causam iustam habuisti sed etiam visendi.

Ego hic cogito commorari quoad me reficiam. nam et viris et corpus amisi; sed si morbum depulero, facile, ut spero, illa revocabo.

211 (XIII.68)

Scr. Romae c. Kal. Oct. an. 46

M. TULLIUS CICERO P. SERVILIO ISAURICO PRO COS.
1   COLLEGAE S.P.

Gratae mihi vehementer tuae litterae fuerunt, ex quibus cognovi cursus navigationum tuarum; significabas enim memoriam tuam nostrae necessitudinis, qua mihi nihil poterat esse iucundius. quod reliquum est, multo etiam erit gratius si ad me de re publica, id est de statu provinciae, de institutis tuis, familiariter scribes. quae quamquam ex multis pro tua claritate audiam, tamen libentissime ex tuis litteris cognoscam.

2   Ego ad te de re publica summa quid sentiam non saepe scribam propter periculum eius modi litterarum; quid agatur autem scribam saepius. sperare tamen videor Caesari, collegae nostro, fore curae et esse ut habeamus aliquam rem publicam; cuius consiliis magni referebat te interesse. sed si tibi utilius est, id est gloriosius, Asiae praeesse et istam partem rei publicae male adfectam tueri, mihi

---

1 To his province of Asia.
2 As Augur.

shall be more careful in future. As for you, you heard of it from Anicius (he saw me in the qualms), and that should have been reason enough for a visit, let alone a letter.

I intend to stay here until I have convalesced, having lost strength and weight. But I expect I shall recover both easily enough, once I have thrown off the attack.

211 (XIII.68)
CICERO TO SERVILIUS ISAURICUS

Rome, ca. 1 October (?) 46

M. Tullius Cicero to P. Servilius Isauricus, Proconsul and colleague, best greetings.

I am extremely grateful for your letter giving the stages of your voyaging;[1] it showed that you have not forgotten our friendly relations, and nothing could be more agreeable to me than that. For the future, I shall be much more grateful even if you will write to me as friend to friend on public matters, that is to say the state of the province and the rules you institute. I shall hear all this from many informants (your light does not shine under a bushel), but I should like most of all to learn about it from your letters.

On my side, I shall not often be giving you my views on high politics because of the risk attached to such letters, but I shall write fairly often about what is going on. In spite of all, I think I see a hope that our colleague[2] Caesar will try, and is already trying, to get us some sort of a constitutional system. It would have been very desirable that you should have been present and party to his plans. But if it is more to your advantage, to your honour that is to say, to govern Asia and care for a part of our state interests that

quoque idem quod tibi et laudi tuae profuturum est opta-
3   tius debet esse.

Ego quae ad tuam dignitatem pertinere arbitrabor
summo studio diligentiaque curabo in primisque tuebor
omni observantia clarissimum virum, patrem tuum; quod
et pro vetustate necessitudinis et pro beneficiis vestris et
pro dignitate ipsius facere debeo.

212 (XIII.77)

Scr. Romae c. ex. m. Oct. an. 46

1   M. CICERO S. D. P. SULPICIO IMP.

Cum his temporibus non sane in senatum ventitarem,
tamen, ut tuas litteras legi, non existimavi me salvo iure
nostrae veteris amicitiae multorumque inter nos officiorum facere posse ut honori tuo deessem. itaque adfui sup-
plicationemque tibi libenter decrevi nec reliquo tempore
ullo aut rei aut existimationi aut dignitati tuae deero. atque
hoc ut tui necessarii sciant, hoc me animo erga te esse,
velim facias eos per litteras certiores, ut, si quid tibi opus
2   sit, ne dubitent mihi iure suo denuntiare.

M.[1] Bolanum, virum bonum et fortem et omnibus
rebus ornatum meumque veterem amicum, tibi magno
opere commendo. pergratum mihi feceris si curaris ut is
intellegat hanc commendationem sibi magno adiumento

---

[1] *hinc novam ep. inc. Beaujeu*

---

[1] Now governor of Illyricum. Any relationship to the jurist Ser.
Sulpicius Rufus is uncertain.

has suffered so severely, I too am bound to prefer what will benefit you and your reputation.

Whatever may seem to me to concern your public standing shall receive my most active care. In particular, I shall pay every respect and attention to your illustrious father, as is my duty in view of our old friendship, the kindness I have received from you both, and his own eminence.

212 (XIII.77)
CICERO TO P. SULPICIUS RUFUS[1]

Rome, ca. end of October 46

From M. Cicero to P. Sulpicius, Imperator, greetings.

Though I do not go to the Senate very often nowadays, I felt after reading your letter that I should be failing in my obligations to our old friendship and the many good offices we have rendered one another if I was not present when the honour was conferred upon you. So present I was, and happy to vote for your Supplication. Nor shall a time ever come when I shall not play my part in furthering your interest or your reputation or your dignity. I should be glad if you would so inform your friends, so that they know of my disposition towards you and feel entitled to call upon me without hesitation if you should stand in need of any service.

M. Bolanus is an honourable, gallant, in every way respectable gentleman, and an old friend of mine. I recommend him to you warmly. You will oblige me very much if you let him realize that this recommendation has been of

fuisse, ipsumque virum optimum gratissimumque cognosces. promitto tibi te ex eius amicitia magnam voluptatem
3 esse capturum.

   Praeterea a te peto in maiorem modum pro nostra amicitia et pro tuo perpetuo in me studio ut in hac re etiam elabores: Dionysius, servus meus, qui meam bibliothecen multorum nummorum tractavit, cum multos libros surripuisset nec se impune laturum putaret, aufugit. is est in provincia tua. eum et M. Bolanus, familiaris ⟨meus⟩,[2] et multi alii Naronae viderunt, sed cum se a me manu missum esse diceret, crediderunt. hunc tu si mihi restituendum curaris, non possum dicere quam mihi gratum futurum sit. res ipsa parva, sed animi mei dolor magnus est. ubi sit et quid fieri possit Bolanus te docebit. ego, si hominem per te receiperaro, summo me a te beneficio adfectum arbitrabor.

213 (XV.18)

Scr. Romae ex. m. Dec. an. 46

1 M. CICERO S. D. C. CASSIO
   Longior epistula fuisset nisi eo ipso tempore petita esset a me cum iam iretur ad te, longior autem si φλύαρον aliquem habuissem;[1] nam σπουδάζειν sine periculo vix possumus. 'ridere igitur' inquies 'possumus?' non mehercule facillime; verum tamen aliam aberrationem a molestiis nullam habemus. 'ubi igitur' inquies 'philosophia?' tua

[2] *(Man.)*
[1] -isset *(Lamb.)*

great assistance to him, and you will find himself an excellent, most appreciative person. I can promise you that his friendship will bring you no small gratification.

There is another matter in which I would earnestly request you to put yourself to some trouble, in virtue of our friendship and your unfailing readiness to serve me. My library, worth a considerable sum, was in the charge of a slave of mine called Dionysius.[2] Having pilfered a large number of books and anticipating a day of reckoning, he ran away. He's now in your province. Many people, including my friend M. Bolanus, saw him at Narona, but believed his story that I had given him his freedom. If you see to it that he is returned to me, I cannot tell you how much it will oblige me. In itself it is no great matter, but I am intensely vexed. Bolanus will tell you where he is and what can be done. If I recover the fellow thanks to you, I shall regard you as having done me a very great favour.

213 (XV.18)
CICERO TO CASSIUS

Rome, late December 46

From M. Cicero to C. Cassius[1] greetings.

This letter would have been longer, if I had not been asked for it just as your post was leaving—longer, anyhow, if I had had any bavardage to hand, since writing *au sérieux* is hardly possible without risk. Is joking possible then, you will ask. Well, it certainly isn't very easy, but we have no other means of diversion from our troubles. Where then is

---

[2] Cf. Letter 255.2.   [1] Now in Brundisium.

quidem in culina, mea molesta est; pudet enim servire.
itaque facio me alias res agere ne convicium Platonis au-
2 diam.

De Hispania nihil adhuc certi, nihil omnino novi. te
abesse mea causa moleste fero, tua gaudeo. sed flagitat tabellarius. valebis igitur meque, ut a puero fecisti, amabis.

214 (XV.17)

Scr. Romae in. an. 45

1 M. CICERO C. CASSIO S.

Praeposteros habes tabellarios, etsi me quidem non of-
fendunt; sed tamen, cum a me discedunt, flagitant litteras,
cum ad me veniunt, nullas adferunt. atque id ipsum facerent commodius si mihi aliquid spati ad scribendum darent; sed petasati veniunt, comites ad portam exspectare
dicunt. ergo ignosces: alteras iam habebis has brevis; sed
exspecta πάντα περὶ πάντων. etsi quid ego me tibi purgo,
cum tui ad me inanes veniant, ad te cum epistulis revertan-
2 tur?

Nos hic, ut tamen ad te scribam aliquid, P. Sullam patrem mortuum habebamus. alii a latronibus, alii cruditate
dicebant. populus non curabat; combustum enim esse
constabat. hoc tu pro tua sapientia feres aequo animo;
quamquam πρόσωπον πόλεως amisimus. Caesarem pu-

---

2 Cassius had joined the Epicureans, whose master had written 'the beginning and root of all good is the pleasure of the belly.'

3 The founder of the Academic school to which Cicero
belonged.

philosophy? Yours[2] is in the kitchen, mine is a scold—to be a slave makes me ashamed of myself. So I make believe to be otherwise occupied, so as not to have Plato's[3] reproaches in my ears.

Of Spain nothing certain yet, no news at all in fact. I am sorry for my own sake that you are away but glad for yours. But the courier is getting impatient. So keep well and fond of me, as you have been from a boy.

214 (XV.17)
CICERO TO CASSIUS

Rome, January (beginning) 45

M. Cicero to C. Cassius greetings.

Your couriers are a queer set—not that I mind; but when they go away they demand a letter, while when they arrive they bring none. Even so, it would be more convenient if they gave me a little time to write, but they arrive with their travelling caps on and say their party is waiting for them at the city gate. So you must forgive me. You are going to get a second short letter. But you may look forward to full amends. Though I can't think why *I* am apologizing to *you,* when your people come to my house empty-handed and go back to you with letters.

Here in Rome (just to write you something after all) we have a death to talk about—P. Sulla senior. Some say it was bandits, others overeating. The public doesn't care which, as there's no doubt that he's ashes. You will bear the news like the philosopher you are. Still, the town has lost a *personnage.* They think Caesar will take it hard—he'll be

CICERO'S LETTERS TO FRIENDS

tabant moleste laturum verentem ne hasta refrixisset.
Mindius Marcellus et Attius pigmentarius valde gaudebat
3 se adversarium perdidisse.

De Hispania novi nihil, sed exspectatio valde magna;
rumores tristiores sed ἀδέσποτοι. Pansa noster paludatus
a. d. III Kal. Ian. ⟨ita⟩[1] profectus est ut quivis intellegere
posset, id quod tu nuper dubitare coepisti, τὸ καλὸν δι’
αὑτὸ αἱρετὸν esse. nam quod multos miseriis levavit et
quod se in his malis hominem praebuit, mirabilis eum viro-
4 rum bonorum benevolentia prosecuta est.

Tu quod adhuc Brundisi moratus es valde probo et gaudeo, et mehercule puto te sapienter facturum si ἀκενό-
σπουδος fueris; nobis quidem qui te amamus erit gratum.
et amabo te, cum dabis posthac aliquid domum litterarum,
mei memineris. ego numquam quemquam ad te, cum
sciam, sine meis litteris ire patiar.

Vale.

215 (XV.16)

Scr. Romae c. IV Id. Ian. an. 45

1 M. CICERO S. D. C. CASSIO
Puto te iam suppudere quem[1] haec tertia iam epistula
ante oppressit quam tu scidam aut litteram. sed non urgeo;
longiores enim ⟨ex⟩spectabo, vel potius exigam. ego, si

[1] *(Mend.)*
[1] cum *(Gron.)*

---

[1] Sales of confiscated property.

afraid the public auctions[1] may go with less of a swing. Mindius Marcellus[2] and Attius the perfumer are delighted to have shed a competitor.

From Spain nothing new, but keen expectancy of news. Rumours tending to gloom, but nobody to vouch for them. Our friend Pansa left Rome[3] in uniform on 30 December, an unmistakable illustration of what you have latterly begun to question—that Good is to be chosen *per se.* He has given a helping hand to many persons in distress and behaved like a human being in these bad times; accordingly he went off in astonishingly good odour with honest men.

So you are still at Brundisium. I heartily approve and rejoice. Upon my word, I think you will do wisely to avoid worry to no purpose. We who care for you will be glad if you do. And in future, when you send a line home, be a good fellow and remember me. I shall never knowingly let anybody go to you without a letter from me.

Good-bye.

215 (XV.16)
CICERO TO CASSIUS

Rome, ca. 10 January 45

From M. Cicero to C. Cassius greetings.

I think you must be a trifle ashamed of yourself now. Here comes a third letter down upon you before you have produced so much as a sheet or a line! However, I am not pressing you. I shall expect a longer letter, or rather I shall

---

[2] Later a naval commander in the service of his friend and fellow townsman Octavian. Nothing is known of Attius.

[3] We do not know where he was going.

semper haberem cui darem, vel ternas in hora darem. fit
enim nescio qui[2] ut quasi coram adesse videare cum scribo
aliquid ad te, neque id κατ' εἰδ<ώλ>ων[3] φαντασίας ut dicunt tui amici novi, qui putant etiam διανοητικὰς φαντασίας spectris Catianis excitari. nam, ne te fugiat, Catius
Insuber Ἐπικούρειος, qui nuper est mortuus, quae ille
Gargettius et iam ante Democritus εἴδωλα, hic spectra no-
minat. his autem spectris etiam si oculi possent feriri, quod
<pup>ulis[4] ipsa incurrunt, animus qui possit ego non vi-
deo; doceas tu me oportebit cum salvus veneris. in meane
potestate ut sit spectrum tuum, ut, simul ac mihi collibi-
tum sit de te cogitare, illud occurrat?[5] neque solum de te,
qui mihi haeres in medullis, sed si insulam Britanniam
coepero cogitare, eius εἴδωλον mihi advolabit ad pectus?

Sed haec posterius; tempto enim te quo animo accipias.
si enim stomachabere et moleste feres, plura dicemus
postulabimusque ex qua αἱρέσει 'vi hominibus armatis'
deiectus sis in eam restituare. in hoc interdicto non solet
addi 'in hoc anno.' qua re, si iam biennium aut triennium
est cum virtuti nuntium remisisti delenitus illecebris
voluptatis, in integro res nobis erit.

² quid *(Ern.)*   ³ *(Vict.)*
⁴ velis *(SB, qui etiam* illis *coni.)*   ⁵ *dist. SB*

---

¹ Epicurus belonged to the Attic district (deme) of Gargettus.
² Greek *eidōla. Spectrum* in classical Latin occurs only in this
letter and Cassius' reply. Perhaps Catius coined it (from *specio,*
'look at'). On the theory of visual perception through images see
Letters to Atticus 23 (II.3).2.   ³ What this was is uncertain.
Perhaps, like Brutus, Cassius had been an adherent of Antiochus
of Ascalon's Old Academy, which was close to Stoicism.

require one. As for me, if I always had a bearer, I should dispatch them three an hour. I don't know how it is, but when I write something to you, I seem to see you here in front of me. I am not speaking according to the doctrine of appearances of images, to use the terminology of your new friends, who think that even mental appearances are aroused by Catius' *spectres*. For, in case you have not noticed it, what he of Gargettus,[1] and Democritus before him, called 'images'[2] are termed 'spectres' by the late lamented Catius, Insubrian and Epicurean. Now even granting that those spectres could strike the eyes, because they run upon the pupils of their own accord, I for one don't see how they can strike the mind—you will have to teach me when you are safely home again. Are we really to suppose that your spectre is in my control, so that as soon as I take a fancy to think about you, up it comes? And not only you, who are in my heart all the time, but if I start thinking about the island of Britain, will its image fly into my brain?

But of all this later on. I am just testing your reactions. If you are nettled and upset, I shall continue and file a claim for your restitution to the philosophical persuasion[3] from which you have been ousted 'by violence, by force of arms.'[4] In this formula they don't usually add 'during the current year,' so that if it is now two or three years since you were seduced by the wiles of Miss Pleasure into serving notice of divorce on Lady Virtue,[5] my action will still lie.

[4] Cf. Letter 36.2. It seems to be implied that Cassius' conversion was in some way due to the Civil War.

[5] See Letter 22, n. 2.

Quamquam quicum loquor? cum uno fortissimo viro, qui, postea quam forum attigisti, nihil fecisti nisi plenissimum amplissimae dignitatis. in ista ipsa αἱρέσει metuo ne plus nervorum sit quam ego putaram[6] si modo eam tu probas.

'Qui ‹i›d[7] tibi in mentem venit?' inquies. quia nihil habebam aliud quod scriberem. de re publica enim nihil scribere possum. nec enim quod sentio libet scribere.

216 (XV.19)

Scr. Brundisii med. m. Ian. an. 45

1   C. CASSIUS S. D. M. CICERONI
    S. v. b.
    Non mehercule in hac mea peregrinatione quicquam libentius facio quam scribo ad te; videor enim cum praesente loqui et iocari. nec tamen hoc usu venit propter spectra Cati‹a›na; pro quo tibi proxima epistula tot rusticos
2   Stoicos regeram ut Catium Athenis natum esse dicas.
    Pansam nostrum secunda voluntate hominum paludatum ex urbe exisse cum ipsius causa gaudeo tum mehercule etiam omnium nostrum. spero enim homines intellecturos quanto sit omnibus odio crudelitas et quanto amori probitas et clementia, atque ea quae maxime mali petant et concupiscant ad bonos pervenire. difficile est enim per-

---

[6] -rim *(Wes.)*   [7] quid *(Scheller)*

---

[1] *To kalon;* cf. *Letters to Atticus* 134 (VII.11).1. Capitals here indicate Greek terms.

But to whom am I talking? Why, to the most gallant gentleman alive, whose every action since entering public life has been in the fullest accord with his exalted standing. I am afraid that even this system of yours must have more spunk in it than I had supposed, that is if you are really an adherent.

'How on earth did he come to think of that?' you will be wondering. Why, because I have nothing else to write about. Of politics I can write nothing, for I do not care to write what I feel.

216 (XV.19)
CASSIUS TO CICERO

Brundisium, mid January 45

From C. Cassius to M. Cicero greetings.

I trust you are well.

You may be sure that nothing I do in this sojourn of mine abroad is done more willingly than writing to you. It is as though I was chatting and joking with you in the flesh. That does not, however, come about because of Catius' spectres—in return for him I'll throw so many clodhopping Stoics back at you in my next letter that you'll declare Catius Athenian born!

I am glad that our friend Pansa left Rome in uniform amid general good will, both for his own sake and, let me add, for all our sakes. For I trust people will realize how intense and universal is hatred for cruelty and love for worth and clemency, and that they will see how the prizes most sought and coveted by the wicked come to the good. It is hard to persuade men that Good[1] is to be chosen *per se;*

suadere hominibus τὸ καλὸν δι' αὐτὸ αἱρετὸν esse; ἡδονὴν vero et ἀτ‹αρ›αξίαν[1] virtute, iustitia, τῷ καλῷ parari
et verum et probabile est. ipse enim Epicurus, a quo
omnes Catii et Amafinii, mali verborum interpretes, pro-
3 ficiscuntur, dicit 'οὐκ ἔστιν ἡδέως ἄνευ τοῦ καλῶς καὶ
δικαίως ζῆν.' itaque et Pansa, qui ἡδονὴν sequitur, virtutem retinet et ii qui a vobis φιλήδονοι vocantur sunt
φιλόκαλοι et φιλοδίκαιοι omnisque virtutes et colunt et
retinent. itaque Sulla, cuius iudicium probare debemus,
cum dissentire philosophos videret, non quaesiit quid bonum esset ‹s›ed[2] omnia bona coemit. cuius ego mortem
forti mehercules animo tuli. nec tamen Caesar diutius nos
eum desiderare patietur (nam habet damnatos quos pro
illo nobis restituat) nec ipse sectorem desiderabit cum
4 filium viderit.

Nunc, ut ad rem publicam redeam, quid in Hispaniis
geratur rescribe. peream nisi sollicitus sum; ac malo veterem et clementem dominum habere quam novum et cru-
delem experiri. scis Gnaeum[3] quam sit fatuus, scis quo
modo crudelitatem virtutem putet, scis quam se semper a
nobis derisum putet; vereor ne nos rustice gladio velit
ἀντιμυκτηρίσαι. quid fiat, si me diligis, rescribe. hui,
quam velim scire utrum ista sollicito animo an soluto legas!
sciam enim eodem tempore quid me facere oporteat.

Ne longior sim, vale. me, ut facis, ama. si Caesar vicit,
celeriter me exspecta.

[1] (Vict.) [2] et (Lamb.)
[3] Cn. (Bertotti: Gnaeus ꝯ)

but that Pleasure and Peace of Mind are won by virtue, justice, and Good is both true and easily argued. Epicurus himself, from whom all these sorry translators of terms, Catius, Amafinius, etc., derive, says: 'To live pleasurably is not possible without living rightly and justly.' Thus it is that Pansa, whose goal is Pleasure, retains Virtue; and those whom you and your friends call Pleasure-lovers are Good-lovers and Justice-lovers, practising and retaining all the virtues. And so Sulla[2] (whose judgement[3] we must respect) saw that the philosophers were at loggerheads: instead of trying to discover *what* was good, he went and bought up all the goods he could find! Indeed I have borne his death with fortitude. However, Caesar will not let us miss him long—he has other victims of justice to offer us in his place. Nor will *he* miss Sulla's activity in the auction rooms—he will only have to look at Sulla junior.

Now to get back to public affairs, let me know in your reply how things are going in Spain. I'm devilish worried, and I'd rather have the old easygoing master than try a cruel new one. You know what a fool Gnaeus[4] is, how he takes cruelty for courage, how he thinks we always made fun of him. I'm afraid he may answer our persiflage with his sword, hobbledehoy fashion. If you love me, tell me what is going on. Ah, how I should like to know your frame of mind as you read this! Anxious or easy? I should know by the same token what I ought to do.

Not to be too prolix, good-bye. Go on caring for me. If Caesar has won, expect me quickly back.

[2] Cf. Letter 214.2.   [3] Perhaps in allusion to Sulla's conviction on charges of electoral malpractice in 66.

[4] Pompey's elder son.

217 (IX.10)

Scr. Romae in. an. 45

M. CICERO S. D. P. DOLABELLAE

1   Non sum ausus Salvio nostro nihil ad te litterarum dare; nec mehercule habebam quid scriberem nisi te a me mirabiliter amari, de quo etiam nihil scribente me te non dubitare certo scio. omnino mihi magis litterae sunt exspectandae a te quam a me tibi; nihil enim Romae geritur quod te putem scire curare, nisi forte scire vis me inter Niciam nostrum et Vidium iudicem esse. profert alter, opinor, duobus versiculis expensum Niciae, alter Aristarchus hos ὀβελίζει; ego tamquam criticus antiquus iudicaturus sum utrum sint τοῦ ποιητοῦ an παρεμβεβλημένοι.

2   Puto ⟨te⟩[1] nunc dicere 'oblitusne es igitur fungorum illorum quos apud Niciam et ingentium †cularum[2] cum sophia septimae†?' quid ergo? tu adeo mihi excussam severitatem veterem putas ut ne in foro quidem reliquiae pristinae frontis appareant? sed tamen suavissimum συμβιωτὴν nostrum praestabo integellum, nec committam ut, si ego eum condemnaro, tu restituas, ne ⟨non⟩[3] habeat Bursa Plancus apud quem litteras discat.

3   Sed quid ago? cum mihi sit incertum tranquillone sis

[1] *(Man.)*
[2] coc(h)learum ⸋: *alii alia*
[3] *(Sedgwick)*

---

[1] Now with Caesar in Spain.
[2] Probably Caesar's freedman, not Atticus' slave.
[3] Several words are corrupt in the manuscripts.

217 (IX.10)
CICERO TO DOLABELLA

Rome, beginning of 45

From M. Cicero to P. Dolabella[1] greetings.

I dare not let our friend Salvius[2] leave without giving him something in the way of a letter to you, though upon my word I have nothing to write except that I am marvellously fond of you; and of that I am sure you are convinced without my writing a word. In point of fact I have better cause to expect to hear from you than you from me. Nothing is afoot in Rome which I judge you would care to know, unless perhaps you wish to know that I am appointed arbiter between our friend Nicias and Vidius. The latter, I believe, is producing a couple of lines registering a payment to Nicias, who on his side Aristarchus-like obelizes these same. My job is to decide like a critic of old whether they are the poet's own or interpolated.

I expect you may ask now whether I have forgotten those mushrooms at Nicias' and the jumbo snails(?) with * * *.[3] Come now, do you suppose that my old austerity has been so thoroughly shaken off that even in a court of law there isn't a remnant to be seen of my former grave demeanour? Never mind, I shall give our charming little mate back as good as new. I shan't be so foolish as to find against him only for you to rehabilitate him for fear Bursa Plancus be left without a school master.[4]

But, here I go rambling on and on, when I don't know

[4] Cicero playfully writes as though Nicias was facing a criminal charge and would go into exile if he lost the case. Nicias was a scholar, the obnoxious Bursa an ignoramus.

animo an ut in bello in aliqua maiuscula cura negotiove
versere, labor longius. cum igitur mihi erit exploratum te
libenter esse risurum, scribam ad te pluribus. te tamen hoc
scire volo, vehementer populum sollicitum fuisse de P.
Sullae morte ante quam certum scierit. nunc quaerere
desierunt quo modo perierit; satis putant se scire quod
sciunt. ego ceteroqui animo aequo fero. unum vereor, ne
hasta Caesaris refrixerit.

218 (VI.18)

Scr. Romae c. Kal. Febr. an. 45

CICERO LEPTAE

1   Simul accepi a Seleuco tuo litteras, statim quaesivi e
Balbo per codicillos quid esset in lege. rescripsit eos qui
facerent praeconium vetari esse in decurionibus; qui
fecissent, non vetari. qua re bono animo sint et tui et mei
familiares. neque enim erat ferendum, cum qui hodie
haruspicinam facerent in senatu‹m›[1] Romae legerentur,
eos qui aliquando praeconium fecissent in municipiis
decuriones esse non licere.

[1] *(Lamb.)*

---

[1] Evidently a new law of Caesar, drafted (presumably by Balbus) but not yet promulgated. The provision respecting auctioneers may have been taken over from earlier legislation.

[2] Their trade was not highly regarded, perhaps because they made money out of the distress of others—debtors forced to sell their property.

whether your mind is at ease or whether you are anxiously employed on some substantial bit of military business. So when I am assured of finding you in a mood to laugh, I shall write more at length. However, I want you to know that there was much public concern about P. Sulla's death before it was known for certain. Now they have stopped wondering *how* he met his end. What they know is all they want to know. I bear the event philosophically, apart from one misgiving—I'm afraid Caesar's auctions may go with less of a swing.

218 (VI.18)
CICERO TO Q. LEPTA

Rome, ca. 1 February 45

From Cicero to Lepta.

As soon as your letter came to hand by your man Seleucus, I at once sent a note to Balbus enquiring what the law[1] had to say. He replied that practising auctioneers[2] are debarred from membership of a town council, but that the bar does not apply to persons who have practised in the past. So your friends and mine can set their minds at rest. It would have been intolerable, after all, if persons who had once practised as auctioneers were not allowed to sit on their town councils, while currently practising inspectors of entrails[3] were appointed to the Roman Senate.

[3] *Haruspices* practised the Etruscan system of divination from the entrails of sacrificial animals.

2   De Hispaniis novi nihil. magnum tamen exercitum Pompeium habere constat. nam Caesar ipse ad ⟨s⟩uos[2] misit exemplum Paciaeci litterarum in quo erat illas XI esse legiones. scripserat etiam Messalla Q. Salasso P. Curtium, fratrem eius, iussu Pompei inspectante exercitu interfectum, quod consensisset cum Hispanis quibusdam, si in oppidum nescio quod Pompeius rei frumentariae causa venisset, eum comprehendere ad Caesaremque deducere.

3   De tuo negotio, quod sponsor es pro Pompeio, si Galba, consponsor tuus, redierit, homo in re familiari non parum diligens, non desinam cum illo communicare, si quid expediri possit; quod videbatur mihi ille confidere.

4   'Oratorem' meum tanto opere a te probari vehementer gaudeo. mihi quidem sic persuadeo, me quicquid habuerim iudici de dicendo in illum librum contulisse. qui si est talis qualem tibi videri scribis, ego quoque aliquid sum. sin aliter, non recuso quin quantum de illo libro tantundem de mei iudici fama detrahatur. Leptam nostrum cupio delectari iam talibus scriptis. etsi abest maturitas aetatis, tamen personare auris eius huiusmodi vocibus non est inutile.

5   Me Romae tenuit omnino Tulliae meae partus. sed cum ea, quem ad modum spero, satis firma sit, teneor tamen dum a Dolabellae procuratoribus exigam primam pensionem. et mehercule non tam sum peregrinator iam quam

---

2 *(Bengel)*

---

4 M. Valerius Messalla Rufus, Consul in 53.

5 Q. Curtius Salassus was a Prefect under Antony in 41. He was burned alive by the people of Aradus in Syria.

6 Lepta's son.

No news of Spain. But it is generally accepted that Pompey has a large army, as Caesar himself sent his people a copy of a letter of Paciaecus' stating the number of legions as eleven. Messalla[4] too has written to Q. Salassus[5] that his brother, P. Curtius, has been executed in front of the army by Pompey's orders on a charge of conspiring with certain Spaniards to seize Pompey, when he entered some town or other to obtain supplies, and hand him over to Caesar.

As regards your own affair (your standing surety for Pompey), when your co-surety Galba (a gentleman who cannot be accused of carelessness where his finances are concerned) gets back, I shall be in constant touch with him to see if a solution can be found. He seemed confident that it could.

I am greatly pleased that you think so well of my *Orator*. I do flatter myself that I have put into that book whatever judgement I may possess on the subject of public speaking. If it is as you say you find it, then I too amount to something. If not, I am content that my reputation for sound judgement and the book shall suffer in exactly the same proportion. I hope our little boy[6] has already developed a taste for such compositions. Though he has still to grow up, there is something to be said for letting his ears buzz with utterances of this kind.

My Tullia's confinement has kept me in Rome. But even now that she has, as I hope, fairly well regained her strength, I am still kept here waiting to extract the first instalment[7] out of Dolabella's agents. And in point of fact I am not the gadabout I used to be. My buildings and the

7 Of Tullia's dowry. She and Dolabella were now divorced.

solebam. aedificia mea me delectabant et otium: domus
est quae nulli mearum villarum cedat, otium omni deser-
tissima regione maius. itaque ne litterae quidem meae
impediuntur, in quibus sine ulla interpellatione versor. qua
re, ut arbitror, prius hic te nos quam istic tu nos videbis.

Lepta suavissimus ediscat Hesiodum et habeat in ore
'τῆς δ' ἀρετῆς ἱδρῶτα' et cetera.

219 (XVI.18)

Scr. Romae post m. Oct. an. 47

TULLIUS TIRONI S.

1   Quid igitur? non sic oportet? equidem censeo sic, ad-
dendum etiam 'suo.' sed, si placet, invidia vitetur; quam
quidem ego semper[1] contempsi.

Tibi διαφόρησιν gaudeo profuisse; si vero etiam Tusculanum, di boni, quanto mihi illud erit amabilius! sed
si me amas, quod quidem aut facis aut perbelle simulas,
quod tamen in modum procedit—sed, ut⟨ut⟩ est, indulge
valetudini tuae; cui quidem tu adhuc, dum mihi deservis,
servisti non satis. ea quid postulet non ignoras: πέψιν,
ἀκοπίαν, περίπατον σύμμετρον, τρῖψιν, εὐλυσίαν κοι-

[1] saepe (D)*

8 'The Gods set sweat in front of excellence,' from Hesiod's
Works and Days (289).
[1] Tiro seems to have suggested that the heading of Cicero's
previous letter, 'Tullius to Tiro greetings,' was too familiar. To all

freedom from distraction were what I used to enjoy. Well, I have a town house as pleasant as any of my country places, and greater freedom from distraction than anywhere in the wilds. So even my literary work is not hampered, and I employ myself in it without any interruptions. I fancy therefore that I shall see you here before you see me there.

Your charming boy should learn Hesiod by heart and never forget 'Sweat before excellence,' etc.[8]

219 (XVI.18)
CICERO TO TIRO

Rome, after October 47

From Tullius to Tiro greetings.

Well then! Isn't that as it should be? I think so, and should like to make it 'to his dear Tiro.'[1] However, let us beware of jealous malice, if you wish—the malice I have always despised.

I am glad your perspiration has done you good. If my place at Tusculum has done you good too, heavens, how much better I shall love it! But if you love me, and if you don't you make a very pretty pretence of it, which after all answers nicely—well, however that stands, humour your health. In your devotion to me you have not hitherto devoted yourself enough to that. You know what it requires—digestion, no fatigue, a short walk, massage,

other correspondents except his wife and brother Cicero uses his *cognomen.* Yet earlier letters to Tiro were similarly headed, and most of those after his manumission add *suo* ('his dear'). Perhaps the letter to which Tiro referred had to be shown to a third party.

λίας. fac bellus revertare, ⟨ut⟩² non modo te sed etiam Tusculanum nostrum plus amem.

2 Parhedrum excita ut hortum ipse conducat; sic holitorem ipsum commovebis. Helico nequissimus HS ∞ dabat, nullo aprico horto, nullo emissario, nulla maceria, nulla casa. iste nos tanta impensa derideat? calface hominem, ut ego Mothonem; itaque abutor coronis.

3 De Crabra quid agatur, etsi nunc quidem etiam nimium est aquae, tamen velim scire. horologium mittam et libros, si erit sudum. sed tu nullosne tecum libellos? an pangis aliquid Sophocleum? fac opus appareat.

A. Ligurius, Caesaris familiaris, mortuus est, bonus homo et nobis amicus. te quando exspectemus fac ut sciam. cura te diligenter.

Vale.

220 (XVI.20)

Scr. paulo post superiorem

TULLIUS TIRONI S.

Sollicitat, ita vivam, me tua, mi Tiro, valetudo. sed confido, si diligentiam quam instituisti adhibueris, cito te

² (*SB: post* nostrum *Or.*)

---

² Perhaps gardener at the house on the Palatine.

³ The Aqua Crabra, an aqueduct running into Rome, supplied water to the villa, for which Cicero paid.

proper evacuation. Mind you come back in good shape to make me love not only you but my house at Tusculum the more.

Prod Parhedrus to hire the garden himself. That will give the gardener a jolt. That rascal Helico used to pay HS1,000 when there was no sun trap, no drain, no wall, no shed. After all my expense is this fellow going to make fools of us? Give him a hot time, as I did Motho[2] and in consequence have more flowers than I can well use.

I should like to know what is happening about Crabra,[3] even though nowadays water is really too plentiful. I shall send the sundial and the books when the weather is clear. But have you no books with you? Or are you composing something Sophoclean? Mind you have results to show.[4]

Caesar's familiar A. Ligurius is dead, a good fellow and a friend of mine. Let me know when we are to expect you. Look after yourself carefully.

Good-bye.

220 (XVI.20)
CICERO TO TIRO

Rome, shortly after the foregoing

From Tullius to Tiro greetings.

On my life, my dear Tiro, I am anxious about your health. But I am sure that, if you continue to exercise the

[4] Probably a joke. The books were to be sent for Cicero's library at Tusculum. Tiro may be supposed to have kept reminding him to send them, so Cicero pretends to think that Tiro wanted them for his own reading.

firmum fore. libros compone; indicem cum Metrodoro
libebit, quoniam eius arbitratu vivendum est. cum holitore
ut videtur. tu potes Kalendis spectare gladiatores, postridie redire, et ita censeo; verum ut videbitur. cura te, si
me amas, diligenter.

Vale.

221 (VI.22)

Scr. Romae m. Mai., ut vid., an. 46

CICERO DOMITIO

1   Non ea res me deterruit quo minus, postea quam in Italiam venisti, litteras ad te mitterem quod tu ad me nullas
miseras, sed quia nec quid tibi pollicerer ipse egens rebus
omnibus nec quid suaderem, cum mihimet ipsi consilium
deesset, nec quid consolationis adferrem in tantis malis
reperiebam. haec quamquam nihilo meliora sunt nunc
[etiam][1] atque etiam multo desperatiora, tamen inanis esse
meas litteras quam nullas malui.

2   Ego si te intellegerem plus conatum esse suscipere rei
publicae causa muneris quam quantum praestare potuis-
ses, tamen, quibuscumque rebus possem, ad eam condicionem te vivendi quae daretur quaeque[2] esset hortarer.

[1] *(Lamb.)*
[2] quique (Ϛ: quaecumque *C.F.W.Mueller*)

---

[1] Not Cicero's library at Tusculum but those mentioned in the
previous letter.

same care, you will soon be strong again. Put the books[1] away. Do the catalogue when Metrodorus[2] likes, since you have to live under his ordinance. Deal with the gardener as you think best. You can see the gladiators on the Kalends and return the following day. That is my advice—but as you please. Look after yourself carefully if you care for me.

Good-bye.

221 (VI.22)
CICERO TO CN. DOMITIUS AHENOBARBUS

Rome, May (?) 46

From Cicero to Domitius.

I was not deterred from sending you a letter after your return to Italy by the fact that you had sent none to me. But I knew neither how to make you any promise, being myself in need of everything, nor how to advise you, when I was short of counsel myself, nor how to comfort you in the midst of such afflictions. The present situation in these respects is no better, it is far more hopeless even. However, I prefer to write an empty letter than not to write at all.

Even if I saw that you had tried to take upon yourself for the sake of the commonwealth a greater burden of duty than you would have been able to sustain,[1] I should still urge you in every way I could to accept life as it is on the conditions on which it is offered you. But you set a term

---

[2] Tiro's doctor.

[1] I.e. 'had gone to Africa in 48 to carry on the fight against Caesar.' Cicero's convoluted way of putting this shows that he felt himself on dangerous ground.

sed cum consili tui bene fortiterque suscepti eum tibi
finem statueris quem ipsa Fortuna terminum nostrarum
contentionum esse voluisset, oro obtestorque te pro vetere
nostra coniunctione ac necessitudine proque summa mea
in te benevolentia et tua in me pari te ut nobis, parenti,
coniugi, tuisque omnibus, quibus es fuistique semper carissimus, salvum conserves, incolumitati tuae tuorumque
qui ex te pendent consulas, quae didicisti quaeque ab adu-
lescentia pulcherrime a sapientissimis viris tradita memoria et scientia comprehendisti iis hoc tempore utare, quos
coniunctos summa benevolentia plurimisque officiis amisisti eorum desiderium, si non aequo animo, at forti feras.

3   Ego quid possim nescio, vel potius me parum posse
sentio. illud tamen tibi polliceor, me quaecumque saluti
dignitatique tuae conducere arbitrator tanto studio esse
facturum quanto semper tu et studio et officio in meis rebus fuisti. hanc meam voluntatem ad matrem tuam, opti-
mam feminam tuique amantissimam, detuli. si quid ad me
scripseris, ita faciam ut te velle intellexero. sin autem tu
minus scripseris, ego tamen omnia quae tibi utilia esse
arbitrator summo studio diligenterque curabo.
     Vale.

to the course you so well and gallantly undertook, the same that Fortune herself decreed as the final limit to our struggles.[2] Therefore I implore and conjure you in the name of our old association and friendship, and of the abundant good will I bear you and you equally bear me; preserve yourself for me, for your mother,[3] your wife, and all your family, to whom you are and have ever been most dear.[4] Think of your own safety and that of those near to you, who depend on you. Make use now of what you have learned, those admirable teachings handed down by the wisest of mankind which from youth up you have absorbed into your memory and knowledge. Bear the loss of persons bound to you by good will and good offices,[5] signal in measure and number, if not with equanimity, then at any rate with fortitude.

What *I* can do I do not know, or rather I am conscious that it is all too little. But I promise you to do whatever in my judgement conduces to your safety and dignity with the same devotion that *you* have always shown to practical effect in *my* affairs. This disposition of mine I have freely conveyed to that excellent lady your mother, who bears you so deep an affection. If you write to me, I shall execute your wishes as I understand them. But if you do not write, I shall none the less pay most zealous and particular heed to everything that seems to me for your advantage.

Good-bye.

[2] The defeat at Pharsalia.

[3] Cato's sister Porcia.

[4] Domitius seems to have been thinking of going to Spain to reenter the fight against Caesar.

[5] No word, strangely, of Domitius' father, killed at Pharsalia, or his uncle Cato.

222 (VI.10b)

Scr. Romae fort. in. m. Sept. an. 46

< M. CICERO TREBIANO S. >

1   Antea misissem ad te litteras si genus scribendi invenirem. tali enim tempore aut consolari amicorum est aut polliceri. consolatione non utebar quod ex multis audiebam quam fortiter sapienterque ferres iniuriam temporum quamque te vehementer consolaretur conscientia factorum et consiliorum tuorum. quod quidem si facis, magnum fructum studiorum optimorum capis, in quibus te semper scio esse versatum, idque ut facias etiam atque etiam te hortor.

2   Simul et illud tibi, homini peritissimo rerum et exemplorum et omnis vetustatis, ne ipse quidem rudis sed et in studio minus fortasse quam vellem et in rebus atque usu plus etiam quam vellem versatus spondeo, tibi istam acerbitatem et iniuriam non diuturnam fore. nam et ipse qui plurimum potest cottidie magis mihi delabi ad aequitatem et ad †rerum†[1] naturam videtur et ipsa causa ea est ut iam simul cum re publica, quae in perpetuum iacere non potest, necessario reviviscat atque recreetur; cottidieque aliquid fit lenius et liberalius quam timebamus. quae quoniam in temporum inclinationibus saepe parvis posita sunt, omnia momenta observabimus neque ullum praetermittemus tui iuvandi et levandi locum.

---

[1] veram < suam > *coni.* SB (*laudatis in comm. add. Plut.* Pelop. *31* Ἀλεξάνδρου . . . πάλιν εἰς τὴν αὑτοῦ φύσιν ἀναδραμόντος)

---

[1] This Pompeian exile is otherwise unknown.

222 (VI.10b)
CICERO TO TREBIANUS

Rome, beginning of September (?) 46

From M. Cicero to Trebianus[1] greetings.

I should have written sooner, if I had seen what type of letter to write. In circumstances like these the part of friends is either to offer comfort or to make promises. I have not been doing the former, because I heard from many quarters of the courage and good sense with which you bear the times' ill usage, and how efficacious a consolation you find in the consciousness of your past actions and motives. If you do this, you reap great profit from the noble studies in which I know you have always been engaged, and I earnestly urge you so to do.

Moreover you are very well versed in affairs and in all the lessons that history teaches, nor am I myself a novice in these matters, having engaged both in study, though less perhaps than I could wish, and in practical experience of affairs even more than I could wish. And I give you this pledge: the harsh ill usage you now suffer will not long continue. The personage whose power is greatest seems to me to be inclining ever more and more towards justice and his own natural disposition; and the cause itself is such that it must soon revive and be constituted once more, along with freedom, which cannot lie for ever in the dust. Each day brings some act of unexpected lenity or liberality. All this depends on shifts of circumstances which are often slight, and so I shall keep my eyes open for every movement and let no opportunity slip of helping and alleviating your condition.

3   Itaque illud alterum quod dixi litterarum genus cottidie mihi, ut spero, fiet proclivius, ut etiam polliceri possim. id re quam verbis faciam libentius. tu velim existimes
et pluris te amicos habere quam ⟨plerosque⟩[2] qui in isto
casu sint ac fuerint, quantum quidem ego intellegere potuerim, et me concedere eorum nemini. fortem fac animum habeas et magnum, quod est in uno te; quae sunt in
Fortuna temporibus regentur et consiliis nostris provide-
buntur.

223 (VI.10a)

Scr. Romae fort. m. Sept. an. 46

M. CICERO TREBIANO S.

1   Ego quanti te faciam semperque fecerim quantique me
a te fieri intellexerim sum mihi ipse testis. nam et consilium tuum, vel casus potius, diutius in armis civilibus com-
morandi semper mihi magno dolori fuit et hic eventus,
quod tardius quam est aequum et quam ego vellem recipe-
ras fortunam et dignitatem tuam, mihi non minori curae
est quam tibi semper fuerunt casus mei. itaque et Postu-
muleno et Sestio et saepissime Attico nostro proximeque
Theudae, liberto tuo, totum me patefeci et haec iis singulis
saepe dixi, quacumque re possem, me tibi et liberis tuis
satis facere cupere; idque tu ad tuos velim scribas, haec
quidem certe quae in potestate mea sunt, ut operam,
consilium, rem, fidem meam sibi ad omnis res paratam

[2] *(SB)*

304

So I hope the other type of letter which I mentioned will become easier for me every day, and that I shall also be in a position to make promises. That I shall do more gladly in deeds than in words. I would ask you to believe that (at least so far as I have been able to judge) you have more friends than most people who are, and have formerly been, in the same case as yourself; and that I yield to none of them. Keep a brave and lofty spirit—that depends on you alone. What depends on Fortune will be governed by circumstances, and our calculations will provide for it.

223 (VI.10a)
CICERO TO TREBIANUS

Rome, September (?) 46

From M. Cicero to Trebianus greetings.

How highly I regard you and always have, and how highly I have come to realize you regard me, I am my own witness. Your decision to continue fighting in the civil war, or rather the chance which led you to do so, was always a great distress to me; and the result, that the recovery of your position and status is taking longer than is right and than I should have wished, is a matter of no less concern to me than my misfortunes always were to you. Therefore I have freely opened my mind to Postumulenus, to Sestius, very often to our friend Atticus, and most recently to your freedman Theudas. I have told each one of them more than once that I am anxious to do my duty by you and your children in every way I can. I should like you to write to your people and tell them to regard my time, advice, money, and loyalty (these at least are under my own con-

2 putent. si auctoritate et gratia tantum possem quantum in
ea re publica de qua ita meritus sum posse deberem, tu
quoque is esses qui fuisti, cum omni gradu amplissimo
dignissimus tum certe ordinis tui facile princeps. sed quoniam eodem tempore eademque de causa nostrum uterque cecidit, tibi et illa polliceor quae supra scripsi, quae
sunt adhuc mea, et ea quae praeterea videor mihi ex aliqua
parte retinere tamquam ex reliquiis pristinae dignitatis.
neque enim ipse Caesar, ut multis rebus intellegere potui,
est alienus a nobis et omnes fere familiarissimi eius casu
devincti magnis meis veteribus officiis me diligenter observant et colunt. itaque, si qui mihi erit aditus de tuis fortunis, id est de tua incolumitate, in qua sunt omnia, agendi,
quod quidem cottidie magis ex eorum sermonibus addu-
cor ut sperem, agam per me ipse et moliar.

3 Singula persequi non est necesse; universum studium
meum et benevolentiam ad te defero. sed magni [mea]¹ interest hoc tuos omnis scire, quod tuis litteris fieri potest ut
intellegant, omnia Ciceronis patere Trebiano. hoc eo pertinet ut nihil existiment esse tam difficile quod non pro te
mihi susceptum iucundum sit futurum.

¹ (SB, *qui* nostra *etiam coni.*)

trol) as at their disposal for all purposes. If my public and private influence counted for what it should in a commonwealth to which I have done such service, you too would be what you were—most worthy of any rank, however exalted, and assuredly by far the most distinguished member of your own order.[1] But both of us have come down in the world at the same time and for the same reason. So I promise you the items I have just mentioned, which still belong to me, as well as those others which I fancy I retain in some degree as relics of my former status. Caesar himself, as I have had numerous opportunities to recognize, is not unfriendly to me; and almost all his most intimate associates happen to be bound to me by considerable services rendered in the past, and pay me assiduous attention and regard. If an opening occurs for me to make representations concerning your circumstances, I mean your status as a citizen, in which all else is included (and the way they talk makes me every day more hopeful of this), I shall make them personally and work hard.

There is no need to enter into details. My zeal and good will are yours in entirety. But it is very important that all your people should know (your letters can make it clear to them) that everything that is Cicero's is at Trebianus' disposal. The point is that they must think nothing too difficult for me to undertake with pleasure on your behalf.

[1] Equestrian.

224 (VI.11)

Scr. fort. in Tusculano med. m. Iun. an. 45

M. CICERO S. D. TREBIANO

1 Dolabellam antea tantum modo diligebam, obligatus ei nihil eram; nec enim acciderat mihi ⟨opera ut eius⟩[1] opus esset et ille mihi debebat quod non defueram eius periculis. nunc tanto sum devinctus eius beneficio, quod et antea in re et hoc tempore in salute tua cumulatissime mihi satis fecit, ut nemini plus debeam. qua in re tibi gratulor ita vehementer ut te quoque mihi gratulari quam gratias agere malim; alterum omnino non desidero, alterum vere facere poteris.

2 Quod reliquum est, quoniam tibi virtus et dignitas tua reditum ad tuos aperuit, est tuae sapientiae magnitudinisque animi quid amiseris oblivisci, quid reciperaris cogitare. vives cum tuis, vives nobiscum. plus acquisisti dignitatis quam amisisti rei familiaris; quae ipsa tum esset iucundior si ulla res esset publica.

Vestorius, noster familiaris, ad me scripsit te mihi maximas gratias agere. haec praedicatio tua mihi valde grata est eaque te uti facile patior cum apud alios tum mehercule apud Sironem, nostrum amicum. quae enim facimus ea prudentissimo cuique maxime probata esse volumus.

Te cupio videre quam primum.

---

[1] *(C.F.W.Mueller)*

---

[1] Cf. Letter 73, n. 5.

224 (VI.11)
CICERO TO TREBIANUS

Tusculum (?), mid June 45 (?)

From M. Cicero to Trebianus greetings.

My feelings towards Dolabella used to be merely of regard. I *owed* him nothing, for it had never so happened that I had need of his services, and he was indebted to me for standing by him in his ordeals.[1] But now, by his superlative response both previously in the matter of your estate and at the present time in that of your restoration, his kindness has placed me under so powerful an obligation that there is no man to whom I am more beholden. On this my hearty congratulations—and I would rather *you* congratulated me than thanked me. Thanks I do not at all crave, and congratulations you can offer in all sincerity.

For the rest, now that your high character and standing have cleared the way for your return to your family and friends, as a wise and high-minded man you must forget what you have lost and think of what you have recovered. You will live with your people and with me. You have gained more in respect than you have lost in possessions. And possessions themselves would be more enjoyable if there were a commonwealth.

Our friend Vestorius has written to me that you express the utmost gratitude to myself. Such acknowledgement on your part is very agreeable to me, and I am particularly willing that you make it among others to our friend Siro. One likes what one does to win approbation, and the approbation of our wisest is especially welcome.

I am looking forward to seeing you as soon as possible.

225 (IV.13)

Scr. Romae fort. m. Sext. an. 46

M. CICERO S. D. P. FIGULO

1   Quaerenti mihi iam diu quid ad te potissimum scriberem non modo certa res nulla sed ne genus quidem litterarum usitatum veniebat in mentem. unam enim partem et consuetudinem earum epistularum quibus secundis rebus uti solebamus tempus eripuerat, perfeceratque Fortuna ne quid tale scribere possem aut omnino cogitare. relinquebatur triste quoddam et miserum et his temporibus consentaneum genus litterarum. id quoque deficiebat me, in quo debebat esse aut promissio auxili alicuius aut consolatio doloris tui. quid pollicerer non erat; ipse enim pari fortuna adfectus aliorum opibus casus meos sustentabam, saepiusque mihi veniebat in mentem queri quod ita viverem quam gaudere quod viverem.

2   Quamquam enim nulla me ipsum privatim pepulit[1] insignis iniuria nec mihi quicquam tali tempore in mentem venit optare quod non ultro mihi Caesar detulerit, tamen †nihil† iis conficior curis ut ipsum[2] quod maneam in vita peccare me existimem. careo enim cum familiarissimis multis, quos aut mors eripuit nobis aut distraxit fuga, tum omnibus amicis quorum benevolentiam nobis conciliarat per me quondam te socio defensa res publica, versorque in eorum naufragiis et bonorum direptionibus nec audio solum, quod ipsum esset miserum, sed etiam id ipsum video, quo nihil est acerbius, eorum fortunas dissipari quibus nos

---

[1] perculit *Man.*
[2] <id> ipsum *noluit Or.*

225 (IV.13)
CICERO TO NIGIDIUS FIGULUS

Rome, August (?) 46

From M. Cicero to P. Figulus greetings.

I have been asking myself this long while past just what to write to you, but nothing comes to mind—not any particular thing to say, not even a *manner* of writing normally used in correspondence. Circumstances have taken away one element[1] customary in the letters we used to write in happier days. Fortune has made it impossible for me to write or even think in that vein. There remains a gloomy, doleful sort of letter-writing, suited to the times we live in. That too fails me. It should include either the pledge of some assistance or comfort for your distress. Now as for promises, I can make none, for I myself am in like case and support my misfortunes by others' means. I am more often inclined to complain of the life I lead than to be thankful for living at all.

True, I personally have suffered no conspicuous private injury, and I can think of nothing to wish for at such a time which Caesar has not spontaneously granted me. But my troubles are such that I feel guilty in continuing to live. I lack not only many personal intimates, snatched from me by death or scattered in exile, but all the friends whose good will I won when I defended the state with you at my side. I live among the wreckage of their fortunes, the plundering of their possessions. To hear of it would be sad enough, but I have actually before my eyes the heartrending spectacle of the dissipation of their estates—the men

[1] Jokes.

olim adiutoribus illud incendium exstinximus; et in qua
urbe modo gratia, auctoritate, gloria floruimus in ea nunc
his quidem omnibus caremus. obtinemus ipsius Caesaris
summam erga nos humanitatem, sed ea plus non potest
quam vis et mutatio omnium rerum atque temporum.

3   itaque orbus iis rebus omnibus quibus et natura me et voluntas et consuetudo adsuefecerat cum ceteris, ut quidem
videor, tum mihi ipse displiceo. natus enim ad agendum
semper aliquid dignum viro nunc non modo agendi rationem nullam habeo sed ne cogitandi quidem; et qui antea
aut obscuris hominibus aut etiam sontibus opitulari poteram nunc P. Nigidio, uni omnium doctissimo et sanctissi-
mo et maxima quondam gratia et mihi certe amicissimo, ne
benigne quidem polliceri possum.

4   Ergo hoc ereptum est litterarum genus. reliquum est ut
consoler et adferam rationes quibus te a molestiis coner
abducere. at ea quidem facultas vel tui vel alterius consolandi in te summa est, si umquam in ullo fuit. itaque eam
partem quae ab exquisita quadam ratione et doctrina pro-
ficiscitur non attingam; tibi totam relinquam. quid sit forti
et sapienti homine dignum, quid gravitas, quid altitudo
animi, quid acta tua vita, quid studia, quid artes quibus a
pueritia floruisti a te flagitent, tu videbis. ego quod intellegere et sentire, quia sum Romae et quia curo attendoque,
possum id tibi adfirmo, te in istis molestiis in quibus es hoc
tempore non diutius futurum, in iis autem in quibus etiam
nos sumus fortasse semper fore.

---

   [2] Catiline's conspiracy. Cicero is said to have relied much on
Nigidius' advice at that time.

who were my helpers when I put out that fire[2] in days gone by. In the city where not long ago I stood high in influence, respect, and fame, I now have none of these things. I do indeed enjoy the greatest consideration from Caesar himself, but that cannot counterbalance the violence, the total revolution of affairs and times. Bereft, therefore, as I am of everything to which I had been accustomed by nature, inclination, and habit, I cut a sorry figure in other men's eyes, so at least I fancy, and in my own. Born as I was for action, incessant action worthy of a man, I now have no way to employ my energies or even my thoughts. I, who once had it in my power to help the obscure and even the guilty, now find myself unable even to make a kindly promise to P. Nigidius, the most accomplished and the most virtuous man of our time, once so influential and assuredly so good a friend of mine.

This sort of letter-writing, therefore, is ruled out. It remains for me to offer you comfort and to try by reasoned argument to divert you from your troubles. But you have in the highest degree, if ever any man had, the faculty of consoling yourself or another. Therefore I shall not touch that side of the subject which starts from recondite philosophical theory. That I shall leave entirely to you. *You* will see what is worthy of a man of sense and courage, what is demanded of you by dignity, elevation of mind, your past, your studies, the pursuits in which you have distinguished yourself from childhood upwards. I merely assure you of what my understanding and intuition tell me, being in Rome and keeping a close eye on the course of events: that you will not have to bear your present troubles much longer, but that those that you share with us may be with you always.

Video‹r› mihi perspicere primum ipsius animum qui plurimum potest propensum ad salutem tuam. non scribo hoc temere. quo minus familiaris sum, hoc sum ad investigandum curiosior. quo facilius quibus est iratior respondere tristius possit, hoc est adhuc tardior ad te molestia liberandum. familiares vero eius, et ii quidem qui illi iucundissimi sunt, mirabiliter de te et loquuntur et sentiunt. accedit eodem vulgi voluntas, vel potius consensus omnium. etiam illa quae minimum nunc quidem potest sed possit ‹aliquando aliquid›[3] necesse est, res publica, quascumque viris habebit, ab his ipsis ‹a› quibus tenetur de te propediem, mihi crede, impetrabit.

6   Redeo igitur ad id, ut iam tibi etiam pollicear aliquid, quod primo omiseram. nam et complectar eius familiarissimos, qui me admodum diligunt multumque mecum sunt, et in ipsius consuetudinem, quam adhuc meus pudor mihi clausit, insinuabo et certe omnis vias persequar quibus putabo ad id quod volumus perveniri posse. in hoc toto genere plura faciam quam scribere audeo. cetera, quae tibi a multis prompta esse certo scio, a me sunt paratissima. nihil in re familiari mea est quod ego meum malim esse quam tuum. hac de re et de hoc genere toto hoc scribo parcius quod te id quod ipse confido sperare malo, te esse usurum tuis.

7   Extremum illud est, ut te orem et obsecrem animo ut maximo sis nec ea solum memineris quae ab aliis magnis

---

[3] (SB: *alia alii*)

To begin with the personage whose word is law, I think I see his mind and that it is favourable to your cause. These are not idle words. The less I have of his intimacy, the more curious I am to probe. It is only because he wants to make it easier for himself to give discouraging answers to people with whom he is more seriously annoyed that he has so far been slow to release you from your unpleasant predicament. But his friends, especially those he likes best, speak and feel about you with remarkable warmth. To that we can add the popular sentiment, or rather the universal consensus. Even the Commonwealth, which counts for little enough at the moment but must count for something some day, will exert whatever power she may have to win your pardon from these very people in whose hands she lies, and, believe me, it will not be long.

So I will now go back on my tracks and make you a promise, which earlier in this letter I refrained from doing. I shall both cultivate his intimates, who have no small regard for me and are much in my company, and find a way into familiar intercourse with himself, from which a sense of shame on my part has deterred me hitherto. Assuredly I shall follow any path which I think likely to lead to our goal. In this whole sphere I shall do more than I venture to put on paper. Other kinds of service, I am sure, are at your disposal in many quarters; but from me they are most heartily at your command. Of my possessions there is none that I would not as soon were yours as mine. On this and all related points I say little only because I would rather have you expect to enjoy your own, as I am confident you will.

It only remains for me to beg and implore you to be of excellent courage and to remember not only the lessons you have learned from other great men but those of which

viris accepisti sed illa etiam quae ipse ingenio studioque
peperisti. quae si colliges, et sperabis omnia optime[4] et
quae accident, qualiacumque erunt, sapienter feres. sed
haec tu melius, vel optime omnium; ego quae pertinere ad
te intellegam studiossime omnia diligentissimeque curabo
tuorumque tristissimo meo tempore meritorum erga me
memoriam conservabo.

226 (VI.12)

Scr. Romae fort. in. m. Oct. an. 46

CICERO AMPIO S. P.

1   Gratulor tibi, mi Balbe, vereque gratulor; nec sum tam
stultus ut te usura falsi gaudi frui velim, deinde frangi repente atque ita cadere ut nulla res te ad aequitatem animi
possit postea extollere. egi tuam causam apertius quam
mea tempora ferebant. vincebatur enim fortuna ipsa debi-
litatae gratiae nostrae tui caritate et meo perpetuo erga te
amore culto a te diligentissime. omnia promissa, confirmata, certa et rata sunt quae ad reditum et ad salutem tuam
pertinent. vidi, cognovi, interfui.

2   Etenim omnis Caesaris familiaris satis opportune habeo implicatos consuetudine et benevolentia sic ut, cum
ab illo discesserint, me habeant proximum. hoc Pansa,
Hirtius, Balbus, Oppius, Matius, Postum[i]us[1] plane ita

---

[4] optima *Madvig*
[1] (*Or.*)

you are yourself the author, the products of your intellect and study. If you put them all together, you will be in the best of hope; and, come what may, good or bad, you will bear it with philosophy. But all this you know better than I, or rather better than any man. For my part I shall attend with all zeal and diligence to whatever I find to concern you, and shall treasure the memory of your kindness to me in the darkest days of my life.

226 (VI.12)
CICERO TO AMPIUS BALBUS

Rome, beginning of October (?) 46

From Cicero to Ampius best greetings.

I congratulate you, my dear Balbus, and in all sincerity. For I am not so foolish as to wish you temporary enjoyment of an illusory happiness, only to be dashed of a sudden and to fall so low that nothing later on could lift you into equanimity. I have pleaded your cause more openly than my present circumstances warranted, for I thought more of my fondness for you and the uninterrupted affection which you have been so sedulous to foster than of the debility which has overtaken my personal influence. All that concerns your return and restoration has been promised and confirmed, positively and definitely. I was present, observing and taking note.

The fact is, opportunely enough, that I have Caesar's intimates all linked to me in familiar intercourse and friendship, and stand with them second only to Caesar himself. Pansa, Hirtius, Balbus, Oppius, Matius, and Postumus carry their regard for me to really extraordinary

faciunt ut me unice diligant. quod si mihi per me efficien-
dum fuisset, non me paeniteret pro ratione temporum ita
esse molitum. sed nihil est a me inservitum temporis causa, veteres mihi necessitudines cum his omnibus intercedunt; quibuscum ego agere de te non destiti. principem
tamen habuimus Pansam, tui studiosissimum, mei cupi-
dum, qui valeret apud illum non minus auctoritate quam
gratia. Cimber autem ⟨T⟩illius mihi plane satis fecit. valent tamen apud Caesarem non tam ambitiosae rogationes
quam necessariae; quam quia Cimber habebat, plus valuit
quam pro ullo alio valere potuisset.

3   Diploma statim non est datum quod mirifica est impro-
bitas in quibusdam, qui tulissent acerbius veniam tibi dari
quam illi appellant tubam belli civilis multaque ita dicunt
quasi non gaudeant id bellum incidisse. qua re visum est
occultius agendum neque ullo modo divulgandum de te
iam esse perfectum. sed id erit perbrevi, nec dubito quin
legente te has litteras confecta iam res futura sit. Pansa
quidem mihi, gravis homo et certus, non solum confirma-
vit verum etiam recepit perceleriter se ablaturum diploma. mihi tamen placuit haec ad te perscribi. minus enim te
firmum sermo Eppuleiae tuae lacrimaeque Ampiae decla-
rabant quam significant tuae litterae; atque illae arbitra-
bantur cum a te abessent ipsae multo in graviore te cura
futurum. qua re[2] magno opere ⟨e re⟩[3] putavi angoris et

2 quam
3 (Gul.)

1 Ampius' wife and (probably) daughter. Apparently they had
been with him but had recently returned to Italy.

318

lengths. If I had had to bring this about by my own exertions, I should not regret my trouble, considering the times we live in. But I have done nothing in the way of time serving. With all of them I have friendships of long standing; and I have pleaded with them incessantly on your behalf. But my principal reliance has been on Pansa, who is most zealous for your welfare and anxious to please myself; for he has influence with Caesar founded on respect no less than personal liking. And I am very pleased with Cimber Tillius. When all is said, petitions founded on obligation carry more weight with Caesar than those of self-interest; and because Cimber had such an obligation, he carried more weight than he would have carried on behalf of any other person.

A passport was not granted straight away because of the unconscionable rascality of certain people, who would have resented the granting of a pardon to the Trumpet of the Civil War, as they call you, and who talk at large as though they were not glad enough that the war took place. It therefore seemed best to proceed discreetly and on no account to let it be generally known that your case had already been settled. But it will go through very soon; indeed I have no doubt that by the time you read these lines the thing will have been done. Pansa, a responsible and reliable person, assured me, in fact guaranteed, that he would procure the passport in no time. Nevertheless I thought I should tell you all this, for the way your dear Eppuleia spoke and Ampia's[1] tears make it evident that you are not in such stout heart as your letters suggest. Moreover, they think your trouble of mind will grow much worse now that they are no longer with you. So I considered it highly desirable to relieve your anxiety and distress by giving you the

doloris tui levandi causa pro certis ad te ea quae essent certa perscribi.

4   Scis me antea sic solitum esse scribere ad te magis ut consolarer fortem virum atque sapientem quam ut exploratam spem salutis ostenderem, nisi eam quam ab ipsa re publica, cum hic ardor restinctus esset, sperari oportere censerem. recordare tuas litteras, quibus et magnum animum mihi semper ostendisti et ad omnis casus ferendos constantem ac paratum. quod ego non mirabar, cum recordarer te et a primis temporibus aetatis in re publica esse versatum et tuos magistratus in ipsa discrimina incidisse salutis fortunarumque communium et in hoc ipsum bellum esse ingressum non solum ut victor beatus sed etiam
5   [ut], si ita accidisset, victus ut sapiens esses. deinde, cum studium tuum consumas in virorum fortium factis memoriae prodendis, considerare debes nihil tibi esse committendum quam ob rem eorum quos laudas te non simillimum praebeas.

Sed haec oratio magis esset apta ad illa tempora quae iam effugisti. nunc vero tantum te para ad haec nobiscum ferenda; quibus ego si quam medicinam invenirem, tibi quoque eandem traderem. sed est unum perfugium doctrina ac litterae, quibus semper usi sumus; quae secundis rebus delectationem modo habere videbantur, nunc vero etiam salutem.

Sed ut ad initium revertar, cave dubites quin omnia de salute ac reditu tuo perfecta sint.

facts fully and definitely, since definite they are.

You know that in my earlier letters I have sought to console you as a brave, sensible man rather than hold out any assurance of restoration, apart from what I thought should be hoped for from the commonwealth itself, once this conflagration has been extinguished. Remember your own letters, in which you have always shown me a lofty spirit, steadfast and ready for whatever might betide. That gave me no surprise, recalling as I did that you have been engaged in public affairs from your youth upwards, that your periods of office have coincided with the very crises of our national fortunes and existence,[2] and that you embarked on this very war prepared for the role not only of happy winner but, should it so fall out, of philosophic loser. Since, furthermore, you devote your literary activity to recording the deeds of brave men for posterity, it behoves you to consider it your duty not to present yourself as in any way dissimilar to the objects of your eulogies.

Such words, however, would be more appropriate to a state of things which you have already left behind you. As matters now stand, you have only to prepare yourself to bear conditions here along with us. If I knew any remedy for them, I should pass it on to you. But the one refuge is learning and literary work, which we have always pursued. Merely a source of pleasure in good times, it now appears as our lifeline.

But to return to my starting point: have no doubt that all is settled for your restoration and return.

---

[2] Ampius was Tribune in Cicero's Consulship (63) and Praetor in Caesar's (59).

227 (VI.13)

Scr. Romae fort. m. Sept. an. 46

CICERO LIGARIO

1   Etsi tali tuo tempore me aut consolandi aut iuvandi tui causa scribere ad te aliquid pro nostra amicitia oportebat, tamen adhuc id non feceram, quia neque lenire videbar oratione neque levare posse dolorem tuum. postea vero quam magnam spem habere coepi fore ut te brevi tempore incolumem haberemus, facere non potui quin tibi et sententiam et voluntatem declararem meam.

2   Primum igitur scribam quod intellego et perspicio, non fore in te Caesarem ⟨diutius⟩[1] duriorem. nam et res eum cottidie et dies et opinio hominum et, ut mihi videtur, etiam sua natura mitiorem facit; idque cum de reliquis sentio tum de te etiam audio ex familiarissimis eius. quibus ego ex eo tempore quo primum ex Africa nuntius venit supplicare una cum fratribus tuis non destiti; quorum quidem et virtute et pietate et amor⟨e⟩ in te singulari[s] et adsidua et perpetua cura salutis tuae tantum proficit⟨ur⟩ ut

3   nihil sit quod non ipsum Caesarem tributurum existimem. sed si tardius fit quam volumus, magnis occupationibus eius a quo omnia petuntur aditus ad eum difficiliores fuerunt; et simul Africanae causae iratior diutius velle videtur eos habere sollicitos a quibus se putat diuturnioribus esse molestiis conflictatum. sed hoc ipsum intellegimus eum

---

[1] (SB*)

---

[1] Of the battle of Thapsus (6 April); or possibly of Ligarius' subsequent capture at Hadrumetum.

227 (VI.13)
CICERO TO Q. LIGARIUS

Rome, September (?) 46

From Cicero to Ligarius.

In your present circumstances I owed it to our friendship to write to you something that might bring comfort or help, but hitherto I have not done so, because I did not see how my words could assuage or alleviate your distress. But now that I have begun to entertain high hopes that we shall soon have you back in your rightful place, I feel I must make clear to you both my opinion and my disposition.

First then, let me say that, in my understanding and perception, Caesar will not be over hard on you for long. Circumstances, time, public opinion, and, I think, his own nature make him more lenient every day. This I feel where others are concerned, and as regards yourself I also hear it from his most intimate friends. Ever since the news[1] arrived from Africa, I have never stopped pleading with them in conjunction with your brothers. Their high character, family feeling, conspicuous affection for you, and assiduous, unflagging concern for your rehabilitation are producing an effect; so much so that I believe there is nothing which Caesar himself will not concede. But if it goes more slowly than we wish, the heavy pressure of business upon him as the recipient of all petitions has made access to him more difficult, and at the same time he was especially irritated by the resistance in Africa, and seems inclined to prolong the anxieties of those who he feels caused himself protracted difficulty and annoyance. But in this too I understand that every day makes him more toler-

cottidie remissius et placatius ferre. qua re mihi crede et
memoriae manda me tibi id adfirmasse, te in istis molestiis
diutius non futurum.

4   Quoniam quid sentirem exposui, quid velim tua causa
re potius declarabo quam oratione. etsi, ⟨si⟩[2] tantum possem quantum in ea re publica de qua ita sum meritus ut tu
existimas posse debebam, ne tu quidem in istis ⟨in⟩com-
modis esses; eadem enim causa opes meas fregit quae
tuam salutem in discrimen adduxit. sed tamen, quicquid
imago veteris meae dignitatis, quicquid reliquiae gratiae
valebunt, studium, consilium, opera, gratia, ⟨res⟩,[3] fides
mea nullo loco deerit tuis optimis fratribus.

5   Tu fac habeas fortem animum, quem semper habuisti:
primum ob eas causas quas scripsi, deinde quod ea ⟨de⟩ re
publica semper voluisti atque sensisti ut non modo nunc[4]
secunda sperare debeas sed etiam si omnia adversa essent
tamen conscientia et factorum et consiliorum tuorum
quaecumque acciderent fortissimo et maximo animo ferre
deberes.

228 (VI.14)

Scr. Romae ex. m. Nov. an. 46

CICERO LIGARIO

1   Me scito omnem meum laborem, omnem operam, curam, studium in tua salute consumere. nam cum te semper

2 *(SB)*
3 *(Wes.)*
4 cum *(Man.)*

ant and forgiving. So trust me, and make a mental note of my assurance that you will not long remain in your present disagreeable position.

Having told you what I think, I shall make plain my friendly disposition towards you by deed rather than word, though if I had as much say as I ought to have in a state which I have served as you rate my services, you too would not be in this unpleasant situation. The same cause that has brought your civic existence into peril has dissolved the power I used to have. Nevertheless, whatever the shadow of my old prestige and the residue of my influence may count for, my zeal, advice, time, influence, money, and loyalty shall be at the disposal of your excellent brothers in all things.

You have always had a stout heart. Keep it now, partly for the reasons I have given and partly because of the political aims and sentiments you have always held. In view of these, not only ought you to hope for a favourable outcome now but, even if everything were against you, the consciousness of your past acts and motives should strengthen you to bear whatever may betide with fortitude and magnanimity.

228 (VI.14)
CICERO TO Q. LIGARIUS

Rome, end of November 46

From Cicero to Ligarius.

Be assured that I am devoting all my effort, all my time, attention, and energy to your restitution. I have always had the greatest regard for you, and the conspicuous family

maxime dilexi tum fratrum tuorum, quos aeque atque te
summa benevolentia sum complexus, singularis pietas
amorque fraternus nullum me patitur offici erga te stu-
dique munus aut tempus praetermittere. sed quae faciam
fecerimque pro te ex illorum te litteris quam ex meis malo
cognoscere. quid autem sperem, aut confidam et exploratum habeam, de salute tua, id tibi a me declarari volo.

Nam si quisquam est timidus in magnis periculosisque
rebus semperque magis adversos rerum exitus metuens
quam sperans secundos, is ego sum et, si hoc vitium est, eo
2 me non carere confiteor. ego idem tamen, cum a. d. v Kal.
intercalaris priores rogatu fratrum tuorum venissem mane
ad Caesarem atque omnem adeundi et conveniendi illius
indignitatem et molestiam pertulissem, cum fratres et pro-
pinqui tui iacerent ad pedes et ego essem locutus quae
causa, quae tuum tempus postulabat, non solum ex oratione Caesaris, quae sane mollis et liberalis fuit, sed etiam
ex oculis et vultu, ex multis praeterea signis, quae facilius
perspicere potui quam scribere, hac opinione discessi ut
mihi tua salus dubia non esset.

3 Quam ob rem fac animo magno fortique sis et, si tur-
bidissima sapienter ferebas, tranquilliora laete feras. ego
tamen tuis rebus sic adero ut difficillimis neque Caesari solum sed etiam amicis eius omnibus, quos mihi amicissimos
esse cognovi, pro te, sicut adhuc feci, libentissime suppli-
cabo.

Vale.

loyalty and fraternal affection shown by your brothers, whose friendship I have embraced no less warmly than your own, do not permit me to omit any act or occasion of service and good will towards you. But what I am doing, and have done, on your behalf I prefer you to learn from their letters rather than from mine. My hope, or rather my confident assurance, of your restoration is what I want personally to make clear to you.

If any man tends to be apprehensive in affairs of moment and danger, always fearing the worst rather than hoping for the best, I am that man. If this is a failing, I confess that I am not immune from it. But I tell you this: on 26 November, at your brothers' request, I paid Caesar a morning visit. I had to put up with all the humiliating and wearisome preliminaries of obtaining admission and interview. Your brothers and relations knelt at his feet, while I spoke in terms appropriate to your case and circumstances. When I took my leave, it was with the persuasion, not only from Caesar's words, gentle and gracious as these were, but from the look in his eyes and many other indications more easily perceived than described, that there was no doubt about your reinstatement.

So keep a brave and lofty spirit. If you have been taking the foulest weather with philosophy, take the fairer with good cheer. Despite what I have told you, I shall lend my support to your cause as though it was one of the utmost difficulty, and shall continue to plead for you most gladly, not only with Caesar himself but with all his friends, whom I have found very friendly to me.

Good-bye.

229 (IV.8)

Scr. Romae m. Sext. an. 46

M. CICERO S. D. M. MARCELLO

1   Neque monere te audeo, praestanti prudentia virum,
nec confirmare, maximi animi hominem unumque fortissi-
mum, consolari vero nullo modo. nam si ea quae acciderunt ita fers ut audio, gratulari magis virtuti debeo quam
consolari dolorem tuum; sin te tanta mala rei publicae
frangunt, non ita abundo ingenio ut te consoler, cum ipse
me non possim. reliquum est igitur ut tibi me in omni re
eum praebeam praestemque et[1] ad omnia quae tui velint
ita sim praesto ut me non solum omnia †debere tua causa
sed causa†[2] quoque etiam quae non possim putem.

2   Illud tamen vel tu[3] me monuisse vel censuisse puta vel
propter benevolentiam tacere non potuisse, ut, quod ego
facio, tu quoque animum inducas, si sit aliqua res publica,
in ea te esse oportere iudicio hominum reque principem,
necessitate cedentem tempori; sin autem nulla sit, hunc
tamen aptissimum esse etiam ad exsulandum locum. si
enim libertatem sequimur, qui locus hoc dominatu vacat?
sin qualemcumque locum, quae est domestica sede iucundior? sed, mihi crede, etiam is qui omnia tenet favet inge-

[1] ut *(Lamb.)*
[2] *vide comm.*
[3] vultu *(Crat.)*

229 (IV.8)
CICERO TO M. MARCELLUS

Rome, August 46

From M. Cicero to M. Marcellus greetings.

I do not venture to offer advice to a man of your exemplary sagacity, or encouragement to the noblest and bravest of souls; and certainly I must not attempt consolation. If you are bearing all that has befallen as I am told you are, I ought rather to congratulate you on your manly spirit than to comfort your distress. If, on the other hand, you are bowed by the weight of the public calamities, I cannot boast such ingenuity as to find comfort for you when I can find none for myself. All that remains then is for me to proffer and render my services to you in all things and to be at the disposal of your family in any way they may desire, holding myself bound to do on your behalf not only whatever I can but what I cannot as well.

One thing though I will say, and you may take it as a piece of advice or as an expression of opinion, or you may suppose that the good will I have for you made it impossible for me to keep silence: I hope you will come round to the view I take in my own case, that if there is to be some form of commonwealth, you ought to be in it, as one of its leaders in virtue of public opinion and reality, but of necessity yielding to the conditions of the time; whereas if there is no commonwealth, Rome is still a better place than any other, even for passing one's exile. After all, if liberty is our object, where does this ruler's writ not run? But if we are merely looking for a place to live, what is more pleasant than hearth and home? But believe me, even he in whom all power resides is well disposed towards talent; and as for

329

niis, nobilitatem vero et dignitates hominum, quantum ei res et ipsius causa concedit, amplectitur.

Sed plura quam statueram. redeo e‹r›go ad unum illud, me tuum esse; fore cum tuis, si modo erunt tui; si minus, me certe in omnibus rebus satis nostrae coniunctioni amorique facturum.

Vale.

230 (IV.7)

Scr. Romae fort. m. Sept. an. 46

M. CICERO S. D. M. MARCELLO

1 Etsi eo te adhuc consilio usum intellego ut id reprehendere non audeam, non quin ab eo ipse dissentiam sed quod ea te sapientia esse iudicem ut meum consilium non anteponam tuo, tamen et amicitiae nostrae vetustas et tua summa erga me benevolentia, quae mihi iam a pueritia tua cognita est, me hortata est ut ea scriberem ad te quae et saluti tuae conducere arbitrarer et non aliena esse ducerem a dignitate.

2 Ego eum te esse qui horum malorum initia multo ante videris, consulatum magnificentissime atque optime gesseris, praeclare memini. sed idem etiam illa vidi, neque te consilium civilis belli ita gerendi nec copias Cn. Pompei nec genus exercitus probare semperque summe diffidere; qua in sententia me quoque fuisse memoria tenere te arbitror. itaque neque tu multum interfuisti rebus gerendis et

birth and rank, he cherishes them so far as circumstances and his own political position allow.

But I am saying more than I had intended. Let me return then to the single point, that I am at your service. I shall stand with those near to you, if near they really are. Otherwise, I shall at any rate do no less in all things than is due to our friendship and mutual affection.

Good-bye.

230 (IV.7)
CICERO TO M. MARCELLUS

Rome, September (?) 46

From M. Cicero to M. Marcellus greetings.

Your policy hitherto, as I understand it, is one with which I do not venture to find fault—not that I do not disagree with it, but because I think too highly of your wisdom to prefer my opinion to yours. However, the length of our friendship and your notable kindness towards me, of which I have had evidence ever since you were a boy, urge me to write to you in terms which I believe to be conducive to your welfare and judge not incompatible with your honour.

I very well remember that I am addressing a man who saw the seeds of these calamities long beforehand; nor do I forget your fine and splendid record as Consul. But this is not all. I also saw your dissatisfaction, the utter lack of confidence you always felt in the way the civil war was conducted, in Cn. Pompeius' forces, in the type of army he led. I think you remember that I held the same views. Accordingly, you took little part in the conduct of operations,

331

ego id semper egi ne interessem. non enim iis rebus pugnabamus quibus valere poteramus, consilio, auctoritate, causa, quae erant in nobis superiora, sed lacertis et viribus, quibus pares non eramus. victi sumus igitur; aut, si vinci dignitas non potest, fracti certe et abiecti. in quo tuum consilium nemo potest non maxime laudare, quod cum spe vincendi simul abiecisti certandi etiam cupiditatem ostendistique sapientem et bonum civem initia belli civilis invitum suscipere, extrema libenter non persequi. qui non idem consilium quod tu secuti sunt, eos video in duo genera esse distractos; aut enim renovare bellum conati sunt, ii qui se in Africam contulerunt, aut, quem ad modum nos, victori sese[1] crediderunt. medium quoddam tuum consilium fuit, qui hoc fortasse humilis animi duceres, illud pertinacis.

3

Fateor a plerisque, vel dicam ab omnibus, sapiens tuum consilium, a multis etiam magni ac fortis animi iudicatum. sed habet ista ratio, ut mihi quidem videtur, quendam modum, praesertim cum nihil tibi deesse arbitrer ad tuas fortunas omnis obtinendas praeter voluntatem. sic enim intellexi, nihil aliud esse quod dubitationem adferret ei penes quem est potestas nisi quod vereretur ne tu illud beneficium omnino non putares. de quo quid sentiam nihil attinet dicere, cum appareat ipse quid fecerim. sed tamen, si iam ita constituisses ut abesse perpetuo malles quam ea quae nolles videre, tamen id cogitare deberes, ubicumque esses, te fore in eius ipsius quem fugeres potestate. qui si

4

[1] victores esse *(Vict.)*

and I was always careful to take none. We were not fighting with the weapons with which we might have prevailed—policy, prestige, cause. In these lay our superiority, but we fought with brute force, in which we were outmatched. So we were vanquished, or, if moral standing cannot be vanquished, at any rate broken and cast down. Your reaction to that outcome cannot fail of high and universal acclaim. With the hope of victory you discarded the desire of combat, and showed that a wise man and a patriot will join with reluctance in the opening stages of a civil war, but willingly decline to pursue it to the end. Those who followed a different plan from yours manifestly split into two categories. Some, those who betook themselves to Africa, tried to resuscitate the war; others, like myself, committed themselves to the victor. You chose a middle way; you thought the former course savoured of obstinacy, the latter perhaps of pusillanimity.

I allow that your plan is generally, or shall I say universally, judged wise, and that many think it high-minded and courageous as well. But there is a limit, so at least it seems to me, to your present line of conduct; especially as I believe there is nothing except lack of will to hinder you from the enjoyment of all that is yours. For it is my understanding that the personage in whose hands power lies would not be hesitating but for one reason, a fear that you might not regard the concession as a favour at all. My own opinion on this subject it is needless to state, since my action is manifest. None the less, even suppose you had determined to prefer perpetual absence to the sight of what you did not wish to see, you ought still to have reflected that, wherever you were, you would be in the power of the very man whose presence you avoided. Assume it were the case that

facile passurus esset te carentem patria et fortunis tuis
quiete et libere vivere, cogitandum tibi tamen esset Romaene et domi tuae, cuicuimodi[2] res esset, an Mytilenis
aut Rhodi malles vivere. sed cum ita late pateat eius potestas quem veremur ut terrarum orbem complexa sit, nonne
mavis sine periculo tuae domi esse quam cum periculo
alienae? equidem, etiam si oppetenda mors esset, domi
atque in patria mallem quam in externis atque alienis locis.

Hoc idem omnes qui te diligunt sentiunt; quorum est
magna pro tuis maximis clarissimisque virtutibus multi-
5 tudo. habemus etiam rationem rei familiaris tuae, quam
dissipari nolumus. nam etsi nullam potes[3] accipere iniuriam quae futura perpetua sit, propterea quod neque is
qui tenet rem publicam patietur neque ipsa res publica,
tamen impetum praedonum in tuas fortunas fieri nolo. ii
autem qui essent auderem scribere nisi te intellegere
confiderem.

6 Hic te unius sollicitudines, unius etiam multae et ad-
siduae lacrimae, C. Marcelli, fratris optimi, deprecantur.
nos cura et dolore proximi sumus, precibus tardiores quod
ius adeundi, cum ipsi deprecatione eguerimus, non habemus, gratia tantum possumus quantum victi. sed tamen
consilio ‹et›[4] studio Marcello non desumus; a tuis reliquis
non adhibemur. ad omnia parati sumus.

2 cuiusm- *(Lamb.)*
3 potest *(Vict.)*
4 *(Kayser)*

he would be content to let you live a quiet, independent life far from your country and all that is yours, you would still have to ask yourself whether you would rather live in Rome, in your own house, under whatever conditions, than in Mytilene or Rhodes. But the power of him we fear is worldwide. Do you not prefer safety at your own hearth to danger at a stranger's? For my part, I would rather face death, if need were, at home in my country than as a stranger in a foreign land.

This view is shared by all who care for you—a mighty throng, to match your great and splendid qualities. We are also thinking of your private fortune, which we do not want to see dissipated. True, you can suffer no damage of a permanent sort, because neither the ruler of the commonwealth nor the commonwealth itself will tolerate that. All the same, I do not wish to see the pirates make an onslaught on your estate. I should not baulk at naming them if I were not confident that you know whom I mean.[1]

Here your best of cousins, C. Marcellus, intercedes for you as none other, with anxious thought, yes, and constant flow of tears. I stand next in solicitude and distress, but in supplication I am less forward because, having needed intercession myself, I do not have the right of approach, and my influence is that of a member of a vanquished party. But my counsel and zeal are at Marcellus' disposal. Your other relatives do not call me in. I am ready to do anything.

[1] We do not know. M. Marcellus himself complains of the disloyalty of his family and friends, apart from his cousin (Letter 232.1).

231 (IV.9)

Scr. Romae paulo post superiorem

M. CICERO S. D. M. MARCELLO

1   Etsi perpaucis ante diebus dederam Q. Mucio litteras
ad te pluribus verbis scriptas quibus declaraveram quo te
animo censerem esse oportere et quid tibi faciendum arbitrarer, tamen, cum Theophilus, libertus tuus, proficisceretur, cuius ego fidem erga te benevolentiamque perspexeram, sine meis litteris eum ad te venire nolui.

Isdem igitur de rebus[1] etiam atque etiam hortor quibus
superioribus litteris hortatus sum, ut in ea re publica quaecumque est quam primum velis esse. multa videbis fortasse quae nolis, non plura tamen quam audis cottidie. non
est porro tuum uno sensu solum oculorum moveri, cum
idem illud auribus percipias, quod[2] etiam maius videri solet, minus laborare.

2   At tibi ipsi dicendum erit aliquid quod non sentias aut
faciendum quod non probes. primum tempori cedere, id
est necessitati parere, semper sapientis est habitum. deinde non habet, ut nunc quidem est, id viti res. dicere fortasse quae sentias non licet, tacere plane licet. omnia enim
delata ad unum sunt. is utitur consilio ne suorum quidem,
sed suo. quod non multo secus fieret si is rem publicam
teneret quem secuti sumus. an qui in bello, cum omnium
nostrum coniunctum esset periculum, suo et certorum

---

[1] te rationibus *Or.*
[2] quo (*coni. Watt:* quo ⟨quicquid est⟩ *coni. SB*)

---

[1] Pompey.

231 (IV.9)
CICERO TO M. MARCELLUS

Rome, shortly after the foregoing

From M. Cicero to M. Marcellus greetings.

It is only a very few days since I gave Q. Mucius a letter for you of considerable length in which I made clear how I thought you ought to feel and what I thought you ought to do. But since your freedman Theophilus is setting out, whose loyalty and good will towards you I have plainly seen, I did not wish him to go to you without a letter from me.

So once again, I urge you on the same points as in my previous letter, to choose without delay to live in whatever commonwealth we have. You will perhaps see much that you do not like, but no more than you *hear* every day. And it is not worthy of you to be affected by one sense only, that of sight, and to be less troubled when you perceive the very same thing with your ears, although what is so perceived is apt to seem even bigger than it really is.

Perhaps you are afraid of having yourself to say things you do not mean, or do things you disapprove. Well, in the first place, to yield to the pressures of the time, that is, to obey necessity, has always been considered a wise man's part. In the second, this particular evil, at present anyway, is not in the case. One is not free, it may be, to say what one thinks, but one is quite free to keep silence. All power has been handed over to one man; and he follows no counsel, not even that of his friends, except his own. It would not be very different if *our* leader[1] ruled the commonwealth. In the war, when all of us were united in danger, he followed his own judgement and that of certain persons by

337

hominum minime prudentium consilio uteretur, eum
magis communem censemus in victoria futurum fuisse
quam incertis in rebus fuisset? et qui nec te consule tuum
sapientissimum consilium secutus esset nec fratre tuo
consulatum ex auctoritate tua gerente vobis auctoribus uti
voluerit, nunc omnia tenentem nostras sententias deside-
raturum censes fuisse?

3   Omnia sunt misera in bellis civilibus, quae maiores
nostri ne semel quidem, nostra aetas saepe iam sensit, sed
miserius nihil quam ipsa victoria; quae etiam si ad meliores
venit, tamen eos ipsos ferociores impotentioresque reddit,
ut, etiam si natura tales non sint, necessitate esse cogantur.
multa enim victori eorum arbitrio per quos vicit etiam
invito facienda sunt. an tu non videbas mecum simul quam
illa crudelis esset futura victoria? igitur tunc quoque care-
res patria ne quae nolles videres? 'non' inquies; 'ego enim
ipse tenerem opes et dignitatem meam.' at erat tuae virtutis in minimis tuas res ponere, de re publica vehementius
laborare.

Deinde qui finis istius consili est? nam adhuc et factum
tuum probatur et ut in tali re etiam fortuna laudatur: factum, quod et initium belli necessario secutus sis et extrema
sapienter persequi nolueris; fortuna, quod honesto otio
tenueris et statum et famam dignitatis tuae. nunc vero nec
locus tibi ullus dulcior esse debet patria nec eam diligere
minus debes quod deformior est, sed misereri potius nec
eam multis claris viris orbatam privare etiam aspectu tuo.

no means conspicuous for their good sense. Are we to suppose that he would have been more democratically minded in victory than he was when the issue hung in the balance? When you were Consul he did not follow your admirable advice; and when your cousin administered the office under your guidance, he would not make you his counsellors. If he were now supreme, do you suppose he would feel any need of our opinions?

In civil war, never once experienced by our forbears but often by our own generation, all things are sad, but none sadder than victory itself. Even if it goes to the better party, it makes them more fierce and violent; though they may not be so by nature, they are forced to it willy-nilly. For the victor has often to act even against his inclination at the behest of those to whom he owes his victory. Did you not see as I did how cruel that other victory would have proved? Would you *then* have kept away from your country for fear of seeing what you would not have liked? 'No,' you will say, 'for I myself should have retained my wealth and status.' Surely to a man of your moral stature his own affairs count as trifles, his stronger concern is for the commonwealth.

And then, where does this policy of yours end? So far your conduct is approved, and even your fortune is held to be good in the circumstances: the first, because you joined in the opening of the civil war of necessity and wisely declined to persevere to the end; the second, because you have retained your high standing and reputation in honourable retirement. But now no place should have more charms for you than your country, and you must not love her the less because her beauty is marred. You ought rather to pity her, and not deprive her of the sight of you also, bereft as she is of many illustrious children.

4   Denique, si fuit magni animi non esse supplicem victori, vide ne superbi sit aspernari eiusdem liberalitatem, et, ‹si› sapientis est carere patria, duri non desiderare, et, si re publica non possis frui, stulti sit[3] nolle privata.

    Caput illud est, ut, si ista vita tibi commodior esse videatur, cogitandum tamen sit ne tutior non sit. magna gladiorum est licentia, sed in externis locis minor etiam ad facinus verecundia.

    Mihi salus tua tantae curae est ut Marcello, fratri tuo, aut par aut certe proximus sim. tuum est consulere temporibus et incolumitati et vitae et fortunis tuis.

232 (IV.11)

Scr. Mytilenis m. Nov. an. 46

MARCELLUS CICERONI S.

1   Plurimum valuisse apud me tuam semper auctoritatem cum in omni re tum in hoc maxime negotio potes existimare. cum mihi C. Marcellus, frater amantissimus mei, non solum consilium daret sed precibus quoque me obsecraret, non prius mihi persuadere potuit quam tuis est effectum litteris ut uterer vestro potissimum consilio.

    Res quem ad modum sit acta vestrae litterae mihi declarant. gratulatio tua etsi est mihi probatissima quod ab

---

[3] stultum est *(SB)*

Furthermore, if refusal to supplicate the victor was nobility of spirit, are you sure it is not pride to spurn his generosity? If it is wisdom to keep away from your country, is it not insensibility not to miss her? If you may not be able to enjoy public life, is it not foolish to refuse to enjoy your private fortune?

The capital point is this: if you feel the life you are leading suits you better, you must still consider whether it is equally secure. Swords are loose in their scabbards nowadays; but abroad there are fewer scruples to check a deed of violence.

In my concern for your welfare I can claim to rival, or at any rate to approach, your cousin Marcellus. It is for you to take thought for your present circumstances, your status as a citizen, your life, and your estate.

232 (IV.11)
M. MARCELLUS TO CICERO

Mytilene, November 46

From Marcellus to Cicero greetings.

That your advice has always weighed heavily with me you can judge from all previous experience, but the matter in hand is a notable example. My cousin C. Marcellus, who is dearly fond of me, not only advised, but begged and implored me; yet he could not persuade me until your letter determined me to follow your joint judgement rather than any other.

The letters I have had from you both tell me how the affair went through. I cordially accept your congratulations because of the friendly spirit in which they are offered; but

optimo fit animo, tamen hoc mihi multo iucundius est et
gratius quod in summa paucitate amicorum, propinquo-
rum ac necessariorum qui vere meae saluti faverent te
cupidissimum mei singularemque mihi benevolentiam
2   praestitisse cognovi. reliqua sunt eius modi quibus ego,
quoniam haec erant tempora, facile et aequo animo care-
bam. hoc vero eius modi esse statuo ut sine talium virorum
et amicorum benevolentia neque in adversa neque in secunda fortuna quisquam vivere possit. itaque in hoc ego
mihi gratulor. tu vero ut intellegas homini amicissimo te
tribuisse officium re tibi praestabo.

    Vale.

233 (IV.10)

Scr. Romae fort. m. Dec. an. 46

CICERO MARCELLO S.

1   Etsi nihil erat novi quod ad te scriberem magisque litteras tuas iam exspectare incipiebam, vel te potius ipsum,
tamen, cum Theophilus proficisceretur, non potui nihil ei
litterarum dare. cura igitur ut quam primum venias. venies
enim, mihi crede, exspectatus, neque solum nobis, id est
tuis, sed prorsus omnibus. venit enim mihi in mentem
2   subvereri interdum ne te delectet tarda decessio. quod si
nullum haberes sensum nisi oculorum, prorsus tibi ignos-
cerem si quosdam nolles videre; sed cum leviora non multo essent quae audirentur quam quae viderentur, suspica-
rer autem multum interesse rei familiaris tuae te quam

I am far more pleased and grateful to find that, when so very few of my friends and relatives and connections sincerely wished for my restoration, you have shown such conspicuous affection and good will towards me. As for the rest, it is such that, given the times, I was quite well content to do without it. But *this* is another matter; without the good will of such men and such friends as you, nobody, in my judgement, can truly live, whether in good fortune or bad. So herein I do congratulate myself; and I shall not fail to give you substantial proof that the man to whom you have rendered your service is your very sincere friend.

Good-bye.

233 (IV.10)
CICERO TO M. MARCELLUS

Rome, December 46 (?)

From Cicero to Marcellus greetings.

I have no news to give you, and was in fact beginning to expect a letter from you, or rather you yourself in person; but since Theophilus is leaving, I could not let him go without something in the way of a letter. Be sure then to come as soon as you can. Your coming, believe me, is eagerly awaited, not only by us your friends but by every man in Rome. I am sometimes visited by a sneaking apprehension that you are disposed to take your time about your homecoming. If your eyes were your only organ of perception, I should quite forgive you for preferring to avoid the sight of certain individuals. But things heard are not much less vexatious than things seen, and I suspect that your early arrival will be much to the advantage of your private estate;

primum venire idque[1] in omnis partis valeret, putavi ea de
re te esse admonendum. sed quoniam quid[2] mihi placeret
ostendi, reliqua tu pro tua prudentia considerabis. me
tamen velim quod ad tempus te exspectemus certiorem
facias.

234 (VI.6)

Scr. Romae fort. m. Oct. an. 46

1 M. CICERO S. D. A. CAECINAE
   Vereor ne desideres officium meum, quod tibi pro
nostra et meritorum multorum et studiorum parium[1] coniunctione deesse non debet—sed tamen vereor ne litterarum a me officium requiras. quas tibi et iam pridem et
saepe misissem nisi cottidie melius exspectans gratulatio-
nem quam confirmationem animi tui complecti litteris
maluissem. nunc, ut spero, brevi gratulabimur; itaque in
2 aliud tempus id argumentum epistulae differo.
   His autem litteris animum tuum, quem minime imbecillum esse et audio et spero, etsi non sapientissimi, at amicissimi hominis auctoritate confirmandum etiam atque
etiam puto, nec iis quidem verbis quibus te consoler ut
adflictum et iam omni spe salutis orbatum sed ut eum de
cuius incolumitate non plus dubitem quam te memini dubitare de mea. nam cum me ex re publica expulissent ii qui
illam cadere posse stante me non putarunt, memini me ex

---

[1] atque *(Man.)*
[2] quod *(Ern.)*
[1] partum *(Vict.)*

and the same applies from all other points of view. So I have thought it right to say a word in season. But having made my opinion plain, I leave the rest to your wise consideration. I should, however, be grateful if you would let me know when we may expect you.

234 (VI.6)
CICERO TO A. CAECINA

Rome, October (?) 46

From M. Cicero to A. Caecina[1] greetings.

I fear you may think me negligent, which I have no business to be towards a friend to whom I am bound by many obligations and by pursuits in common; still, I fear you find me a neglectful correspondent. I should have written long ago and often but that, as my hopes rose higher day by day, I wanted to send you a letter of congratulation rather than one of moral encouragement. As matters stand, I hope to congratulate you soon, and so I defer that theme to another occasion.

In this letter I think I should use yet again the influence I command with you, not indeed as one much wiser than the ordinary but as a most sincere friend, to fortify your spirit; though, from what I hear and hope, it is very far from feeble. I shall not console you as a man undone beyond all hope of recovery, but as one of whose rehabilitation I feel no more doubt than I remember you used to feel of mine. For I recall that, after my expulsion from the commonwealth by those who believed it could not fall so long

[1] Now in Sicily, awaiting Caesar's permission to return to Italy.

multis hospitibus qui ad me ex Asia, in qua tu eras, vene-
3 rant audire te de glorioso et celeri reditu meo confirmare.
si te ratio quaedam Etruscae[2] disciplinae, quam a patre,
nobilissimo atque optimo viro, acceperas, non fefellit, ne
nos quidem nostra divinatio fallet, quam[3] cum sapientissi-
morum virorum moni[men]tis[4] atque praeceptis plurimo-
que, ut tu scis, doctrinae studio tum magno etiam usu
4 tractandae rei publicae magnaque nostrorum temporum
varietate consecuti sumus. cui quidem divinationi hoc plus
confidimus quod ea nos nihil in his tam obscuris rebus
tamque perturbatis umquam omnino fefellit. dicerem
quae ante futura dixissem ni vererer ne ex eventis fingere
viderer. sed tamen plurimi sunt testes me et initio ne con-
iungeret se cum Caesare monuisse Pompeium et postea ne
seiungeret. coniunctione frangi senatus opes, diiunctione
civile bellum excitari videbam. atque utebar familiarissime
Caesare, Pompeium faciebam plurimi; sed erat meum
consilium cum fidele Pompeio tum salutare utrique.
5   Quae praeterea providerim praetereo; nolo enim hunc
de me optime meritum existimare ea me suasisse Pompeio
quibus ille si paruisset esset hic quidem clarus in toga et
princeps, sed tantas opes quantas nunc habet non haberet.
eundum in Hispaniam censui; quod si fecisset, civile bel-

---

2 iratuscae (ϛ: mira Tusc(a)e R, *Baiter*)
3 nam
4 (*Kayser*)

---

2 But was Caesar likely to see the letter?
3 Perhaps in January 49, immediately before war broke out.
Earlier Cicero had been against Pompey going to Spain; cf. *Letters to Atticus* 104 (V.11).3.

as I stood upright, many travellers coming to me from Asia, where you were at the time, told me how confidently you predicted my speedy and glorious return. Now if *you* had a system which did not mislead you, based on certain lore of Etruria as imparted to you by your noble and excellent father, no more shall I be led astray by my prophetic skill. I gained it not only from the admonitions and precepts of sages and by assiduous theoretical study, as you know, but also by my long experience as a statesman and the remarkable vicissitudes of my career. My reliance upon it is the more secure because in all these dark and perplexed transactions it has never once deceived me. I would give you examples of my predictions, were I not afraid of being thought to have manufactured them *ex post facto.* However, there are witnesses in abundance to attest that I originally advised Pompey against allying himself with Caesar, and later against dissolving the alliance. I saw that the alliance broke the power of the Senate, whereas its dissolution spelt civil war. I was on the closest terms with Caesar, and held Pompey in the greatest regard; but my advice was loyal to Pompey and salutary to both.

Of my other previsions I say nothing, because I would not have our present ruler, who has been very good to me, think that I gave counsels to Pompey which, had Pompey heeded them, would have meant that he himself would indeed be enjoying a position of distinction and leadership in civil life, but would not be holding so much power as is now his.[2] I recommended that Pompey should go to Spain.[3] Had he done so, there would have been no civil war. I did

lum nullum omnino fuisset. rationem haberi absentis non
tam pugnavi ut liceret quam ut, quoniam ipso consule
pugnante populus iusserat, haberetur. causa orta belli est:
quid ego praetermisi aut monitorum aut querelarum, cum
6   vel iniquissimam pacem iustissimo bello anteferrem? victa
est auctoritas mea, non tam a Pompeio (nam is movebatur)
quam ab iis qui duce Pompeio freti peropportunam et rebus domesticis et cupiditatibus suis illius belli victoriam
fore putabant. susceptum bellum est quiescente me, de-
pulsum ex Italia manente me quoad potui. sed valuit apud
me plus pudor meus quam timor; veritus sum deesse Pompei saluti, cum ille aliquando non defuisset meae. itaque
vel officio vel fama bonorum vel pudore victus ut in fabulis
Amphiaraus sic ego

> prudens et sciens
> ad pestem ante oculos positam

sum profectus. quo in bello nihil adversi accidit non prae-
dicente me.

7   Qua re, quoniam, ut augures et astrologi solent, ego
quoque augur publicus ex meis superioribus praedictis
constitui apud te auctoritatem auguri et divinationis meae,
debebit habere fidem nostra praedictio. non igitur ex alitis

---

4 In 52 the ten Tribunes had carried a law allowing Caesar
to stand for the Consulship *in absentia*. Pompey backed it and
Cicero assisted; *Letters to Atticus* 124 (VII.1).4.

5 The flight of the two Tribunes, Antony and Q. Cassius, to
Caesar's camp on 7 January 49.

6 In the legend of the Seven against Thebes the seer Amphiaraus was persuaded by his wife Eriphyle to join the Argive expe-

not so much contend that Caesar should be granted permission to stand for office in his absence as that his candidature should in fact be admitted, seeing that at Pompey's own urging during his Consulship the People had so ordered.[4] A pretext[5] for war arose. Did I leave anything undone in the way of warning or protest in advocating the most inequitable peace as preferable to the most righteous of wars? My advice was overborne, not so much by Pompey, on whom it made an impression, as by persons who in reliance on Pompey's generalship conceived that victory in such a war would be highly opportune for their personal affairs and ambitions. When hostilities were joined I remained passive, and I stayed in Italy as long as I was able after they had been shifted elsewhere. But sensibility prevailed with me over fear. I was ashamed to fail Pompey in his hour of need, when he in time gone by had not failed me. Duty then, or my reputation with the honest men, or sensibility carried the day. Like Amphiaraus[6] in the plays I set out

> witting full well,
to bane right plain to see.

And no reverse befell us in that war which I did not predict.

Well then, since after the manner of augurs and astrologers I have established with you, as a public Augur, the credit of my augural and divinatory claims on the basis of my past predictions, my prophecy will be entitled to respect. I do not make it from the flight of one kind of

dition though he knew it would end in disaster. The quotation that follows may be from Accius' tragedy *Eriphyle*.

involatu nec e cantu sinistro oscinis, ut in nostra disciplina
est, nec ex tripudiis solistimis aut soniviis tibi auguror, sed
habeo alia signa quae observem; quae etsi non sunt cer-
8 tiora illis, minus tamen habent vel obscuritatis vel erroris.
notantur autem mihi ad divinandum signa duplici quadam
via; quarum alteram duco e Caesare ipso, alteram e temporum civilium natura atque ratione.

    In Caesare haec sunt: mitis clemensque natura, qualis
exprimitur praeclaro illo libro 'Querelarum' tuarum. accedit quod mirifice ingeniis excellentibus, quale est tuum,
delectatur. praeterea cedit multorum iustis et officio in-
censis, non inanibus aut ambitiosis voluntatibus; in quo
vehementer eum consentiens Etruria movebit. cur haec
9 igitur adhuc parum profecerunt? quia non putat se sustinere causas posse multorum si tibi, cui iustius videtur
irasci posse, concesserit. 'quae est igitur' inquies 'spes ab
irato?' eodem ⟨de⟩[5] fonte se hausturum intelleget laudes
suas a quo sit leviter aspersus. postremo homo valde est
acutus et multum providens. intellegit te, hominem in
parte Italiae minime contemnenda facile omnium nobilis-
simum et in communi re publica cuivis summorum tuae
aetatis vel ingenio vel gratia vel fama populi Romani pa-
rem, non posse prohiberi re publica diutius. nolet hoc temporis potius esse aliquando beneficium quam iam suum.

[5] *(R. Klotz)*

---

  [7] Omens taken from food dropping from the mouths of the
sacred chickens.
  [8] Caecina had written a 'very libellous' (so Suetonius, *Julius*
75.5) book against Caesar during the war. Later he tried to make

ominous bird or the left-hand cry of another, as our system prescribes, nor yet from *tripudia solistima* or *sonivia*.[7] I have other signs to watch—no surer, perhaps, but less difficult to perceive and less readily mistaken. For the purpose of my divining the signs are observed in two categories, one deriving from Caesar's personality, the other from the general nature of political conditions.

In Caesar we find a mild and merciful disposition, as portrayed in your excellent volume of *Remonstrances*.[8] Moreover, he is remarkably partial to outstanding talents like your own. He also defers to a widespread sentiment, when it is just and inspired by principle, not frivolous or self-interested; and in that connection he will be powerfully impressed by the united voice of Etruria. Why then have these factors hitherto failed of their due effect? Because he reckons he will be unable to resist a multitude of claims if once he gives way to you, with whom he is supposed to have more right to be angry. You will ask what in that case we have to hope for from an angry arbiter. This: he will realize that he is going to draw his praises from the fountain that sprinkled him with cold water. Finally, he is a very clever, farsighted man. He realizes that a man like you, of birth easily the highest in your part of Italy, which is a very far from contemptible part, and in our common body politic equal to any of the best of your generation in talent, influence, and public reputation, cannot be barred from the commonwealth in the long run. He will not wish you to owe your eventual restoration to time rather than to himself straight away.

amends by a book of Remonstrances *(querelarum),* extolling Caesar's merciful disposition.

10   Dixi de Caesare. nunc dicam de temporum rerumque
natura. nemo est tam inimicus ei causae quam Pompeius
animatus melius quam paratus susceperat qui nos malos
civis dicere aut homines improbos audeat. in quo admirari
soleo gravitatem et iustitiam et sapientiam Caesaris. numquam nisi honorificentissime Pompeium appellat. at in
eius persona multa fecit asperius. armorum ista et victoriae sunt facta, non Caesaris. at nos quem ad modum est
complexus! Cassium sibi legavit, Brutum Galliae praefe-
cit, Sulpicium Graeciae; Marcellum, cui maxime suscense-
bat, cum summa illius dignitate restituit. quo igitur haec
11   spectant? rerum hoc natura et civilium temporum non patietur nec manens nec muta⟨ta⟩[6] ratio feret, primum ut
non in causa pari eadem sit et condicio et fortuna omnium,
deinde ut in eam civitatem boni viri et boni cives nulla
ignominia notati non revertantur in quam tot nefariorum
scelerum condemnati reverterunt.
12   Habes augurium meum; quo, si quid addubitarem, non
potius uterer quam illa consolatione qua facile fortem virum sustentarem, te, si explorata victoria arma sumpsisses
pro re publica (ita enim tum putabas), non nimis esse lau-
dandum; sin propter incertos exitus eventusque bellorum
posse accidere ut vinceremur putasses, non debere te ad
secundam fortunam bene paratum fuisse, adversam ferre
nullo modo posse. disputarem etiam quanto solacio tibi

6 *(Man.)*

Having spoken of Caesar, I pass to the nature of things and circumstances. Nobody is so unfriendly to the cause which Pompey espoused with more spirit than forethought as to dare to call us bad citizens or scoundrels. In this connection I often admire Caesar's responsibility, fairness, and good sense. He never mentions Pompey's name except in the most respectful terms. It may be said that he has committed many acts of harshness towards Pompey, but these were the work of war and victory, not of Caesar personally. And think how he has taken us into his favour: Cassius made his Legate, Brutus appointed to Cisalpine Gaul, Sulpicius to Greece, Marcellus, against whom he was especially incensed, restored in a fashion most honourable to Marcellus himself. All this I mention to show that it would be intolerable to the nature of things and political circumstances and incompatible with existing policy or any change of policy (a) that all men engaged in the same cause should not receive the same treatment and lot, and (b) that honest men and good citizens, to whom no stigma of disgrace has been attached, should not return to a community which has readmitted so many found guilty of heinous crimes.

There then is my augury. If I felt any uncertainty about it, I should not employ it in preference to a different consolation, which I might easily offer a brave man to sustain his spirits. If you took up arms for the commonwealth (as you then thought) in full assurance of victory, your conduct would not be so very praiseworthy; but if you recognized the possibility of our defeat, the issues and events of warfare being uncertain, you ought not to have been fully prepared for good fortune but quite unable to bear bad. I should also speak of the comfort you should find in your

conscientia tui facti, quantae delectationi in rebus adversis litterae esse deberent; commemorarem non solum veterum sed horum etiam recentium vel ducum vel comitum tuorum gravissimos casus; etiam externos multos claros viros nominarem (levat enim dolorem communis quasi legis et humanae condicionis recordatio); exponerem etiam quem ad modum hic et quanta in turba quantaque in confusione rerum omnium viveremus (necesse est enim minore desiderio perdita re publica carere quam bona). sed hoc genere nihil opus est. incolumem te cito, ut spero, vel potius ut perspicio, videbimus.

13

Interea tibi absenti et huic qui adest imagini animi et corporis tui, constantissimo atque optimo filio tuo, studium, officium, operam, laborem meum iam pridem et pollicitus sum et detuli, nunc hoc amplius quod me amicissime cottidie magis Caesar amplectitur, familiares quidem eius sicuti neminem. apud quem quicquid valebo vel auctoritate vel gratia, valebo tibi. tu cura ut cum firmitudine te animi tum etiam spe optima sustentes.

235 (VI.8)

Scr. Romae m. Dec. an. 46

CICERO CAECINAE

1   Cum esset mecum Largus, homo tui studiosus, locutus Kalendas Ianuarias tibi praefinitas esse, quod omnibus re-

conscience, and the pleasure in adversity which literary work should provide. I should recall the melancholy fates not only of men long dead but of your own late leaders and comrades. I should cite many celebrated names from the history of foreign peoples; for a reminder of the common law, so to speak, and the condition of humanity makes sorrow weigh less heavily. I should also set forth our mode of life here, where all is turmoil and confusion. After all, one cannot but miss a ruined commonwealth less keenly than a sound one. But nothing in this style is called for. As I hope, or rather as I perceive, we shall shortly see you restored to your rights.

Meanwhile, I long ago promised you in your absence and that present mental and physical image of you, your steadfast and excellent son, my support and friendly offices, my time and trouble; and they have been at your disposal. I do so now in larger measure, because Caesar's attitude towards me is every day more expressive of the warmest friendship, while his intimates pay me a quite unparalleled regard. Whatever influence I come to have with him, whether public or private, it shall be for your behoof. Do you keep up your spirits, not only in fortitude of mind but in the brightest of hope.

235 (VI.8)
CICERO TO A. CAECINA

Rome, December 46

From Cicero to Caecina.

Largus, who is much concerned for your welfare, told me when we met that the Kalends of January had been

bus perspexeram quae Balbus et Oppius absente Caesare
egissent ea solere illi rata esse, egi vehementer cum iis ut
hoc mihi darent, tibi in Sicilia, quoad vellemus, esse uti
liceret. qui mihi consuessent aut libenter polliceri, si quid
esset eius modi quod eorum animos non offenderet, aut
etiam negare et adferre rationem cur negarent, huic meae
rogationi, ⟨vel efflagitationi⟩[1] potius, non continuo re-
sponderunt. eodem die tamen ad me reverterunt, mihi hoc
dederunt ut esses in Sicilia quoad velles; se praestaturos
nihil ex eo te offensionis habiturum.

2   Quoniam quid tibi permittatur cognosti, quid mihi placeat puto te scire oportere. actis his rebus litterae a te mihi
redditae sunt quibus a me consilium petis quid sim tibi
auctor, in Siciliane subsidas[2] an ut[3] ad reliquias Asiaticae
negotiationis proficiscare. haec tua deliberatio non mihi
convenire visa est cum oratione Largi. ille enim mecum,
quasi tibi non liceret in Sicilia diutius commorari, ita locutus erat; tu autem, quasi concessum sit, ita deliberas. sed
ego, sive hoc sive illud est, in Sicilia censeo commorandum. propinquitas locorum vel ad impetrandum adiuvat
crebris litteris et nuntiis vel ad reditus celeritatem re aut
impetrata, quod spero, aut aliqua ratione confecta. quam
ob rem censeo magno opere commorandum.

3   T. Furfano Postumo, familiari meo, legatisque eius,
item meis familiaribus, diligentissime te commendabo
cum venerint. erant enim omnes Mutinae. viri sunt optimi

---

1 (Wes., aut flag- *iam Schütz*)
2 ⟨ut⟩ subsidas *Wes.*
3 *del.* ⌐

fixed as the limit of your stay. Having observed in all sorts of contexts that Caesar is in the habit of confirming arrangements made by Balbus and Oppius in his absence, I made strong representations to them that as a favour to myself you should be allowed to stay in Sicily as long as we wished. Usually I find they readily promise me anything that does not fall foul of their own ideas, or else they say no and give their reason. But to this request of mine, or rather urgent demand, they made no immediate reply. However, later the same day they came back, and gave me their assurance that you shall stay in Sicily as long as you like, personally guaranteeing that you will incur no disfavour thereby.

Now that you know what you *may* do, I think I ought to tell you what in my view you ought to do. After the aforesaid transactions I received a letter from you in which you ask my advice; do I think you should stay where you are in Sicily or set off to see to what remains of your business in Asia? This deliberation on your part did not seem to me consistent with what Largus had said. He had spoken to me as though it was not open to you to stay in Sicily indefinitely, whereas you pose your question as though you had permission. But whichever is right, for my part I think you should remain in Sicily. Its proximity allows frequent interchange of letters and messengers, and is thus an advantage in the process of gaining your pardon. It will also enable you to come back quickly when that goes through, as I hope it will, or the business is settled in some other way. Therefore I strongly advise you to remain.

I shall particularly recommend you to my friend T. Furfanus Postumus and to his Legates, who are also friends of mine, when they return—they are all at Mutina.

et tui similium studiosi et mei necessarii. quae mihi venient in mentem quae ad te pertinere arbitrabor ea mea sponte faciam; si quid ignorabo, de eo admonitus omnium studia vincam. ego, etsi coram de te cum Furfano ita loquar ut tibi litteris meis ad eum nihil opus sit, tamen, quoniam tuis placuit te habere meas litteras quas ei redderes, morem iis gessi. earum litterarum exemplum infra scriptum est.

236 (VI.9)

Superiori adiuncta

M. CICERO FURFANO PRO COS. S.

1   Cum A. Caecina tanta mihi familiaritas consuetudoque semper fuit ut nulla maior esse possit. nam et patre eius, claro homine et forti viro, plurimum sum us‹us›[1] et hunc a puero, quod et spem magnam mihi adferebat summae probitatis summaeque eloquentiae et vivebat mecum coniunctissime non solum officiis amicitiae sed etiam studiis communibus, sic semper dilexi nullo ut cum homine coniunctius viverem.

2   Nihil attinet me plura scribere. quam mihi necesse sit eius salutem et fortunas, quibuscumque rebus possim, tueri vides. reliquum est ut, cum cognorim plurimis[2] rebus quid tu et de bonorum fortuna et de rei publicae calamita-

[1] sumus *(Buecheler)*
[2] pluribus *(Watt)*

They are excellent people, with a regard for men like your-self and closely attached to me. Anything that occurs to me in furtherance of your interests I shall do without prompt-ing. Certain points may lie outside my knowledge; once my attention is drawn to such, I shall press harder than any-body. I shall speak of you personally to Furfanus in a way which will make it needless for you to have a letter ad-dressed to him from myself; but since your people thought it desirable that you should have a letter of mine to present to him, I have complied with their wish. I append a copy of the letter.

236 (VI.9)
CICERO TO FURFANUS POSTUMUS

Copy attached to the above

From M. Cicero to Furfanus, Proconsul, greetings.

My familiar friendship with A. Caecina has always been of the most intimate. I had a great deal to do with his father, a gallant and distinguished gentleman, and have en-tertained a warm regard for Caecina himself ever since he was a boy, both for the high promise I saw in him of excep-tional character and oratorical ability and from the closest association in common pursuits as well as the usual offices of friendship. There is no man with whom I have lived on closer terms.

There can be no need for me to write at greater length. You see how compelling an obligation I have to make every effort on behalf of his welfare in person and estate. It re-mains to say that, aware as I am from many indications of your sentiments concerning the plight of honest men and

tibus sentias, nihil a te petam nisi ut ad eam voluntatem
quam tua sponte erga Caecinam habiturus es tantus cumulus accedat commendatione mea quanti me a te fieri intellego. hoc mihi gratius facere nihil potes.

Vale.

237 (VI.7)

Scr. in Sicilia m. Dec. an. 46 vel in. an. 45

CAECINA CICERONI P. S.

1   Quod tibi non tam celeriter liber est redditus, ignosce
timori nostro et miserere temporis. filius, ut audio, per-
timuit, neque iniuria, si liber exisset (quoniam non tam
interest quo animo scribatur quam quo accipiatur), ne ea
res inepte mihi noceret, cum praesertim adhuc stili poenas
dem. qua quidem in re singulari sum fato. nam cum men-
dum scripturae litura tollatur, stultitia fama multetur,
meus error exsilio corrigitur, cuius summa criminis est
2   quod armatus adversario male dixi. nemo nostrum est, ut
opinor, quin vota Victoriae suae fecerit, nemo quin, etiam
cum de alia re immolaret, tamen eo quidem ipso tempore
ut quam primum Caesar superaretur optarit. hoc si non
cogitat, omnibus rebus felix est; si scit et persuasus est,

---

1 Not the book of Remonstrances, which Cicero had already
seen and praised, but a new production. From what follows it
appears to have contained praise of Cicero, though less lavish
than its author would have wished, and criticism of others. Since

the misfortunes of the commonwealth, I shall only ask you to let my recommendation go to increase in a measure proportionate to the regard I know you have for me the good will which you will bear Caecina spontaneously. You can render me no greater service.

Good-bye.

237 (VI.7)
A. CAECINA TO CICERO

Sicily, December 46 or early January 45

From Caecina to Cicero greetings.

As regards the delay in forwarding the book[1] to you, do please forgive our nervousness and sympathize with our situation. I hear that my son was afraid, and not unreasonably so, that if the book got out, this might do me stupid damage, seeing that it is the reader's attitude rather than the writer's that counts. And after all, I am still suffering for my pen.[2] Mine is a strange fate. A *lapsus calami* is removed by an erasure, folly is punished by talk; whereas my mistake is corrected by exile! And the sum total of my offence is that as a fighting soldier I said nasty things about the enemy! None of us, I dare say, but made his vows to Victory—*his* victory—and, even when offering a sacrifice to the Gods in some other connection, used at the same time to pray for Caesar's speedy defeat. If he does not think of this, he's a happy man all round! If he knows and is per-

Caecina was a noted orator, it may have been on the subject of eloquence.

[2] I.e. the attack on Caesar written during the war.

quid irascitur ei qui aliquid scripsit contra suam voluntatem cum ignorit omnibus qui multa deos venerati sint
contra eius salutem?

3   Sed ut eodem revertar, causa haec fuit timoris: scripsi
de te parce me dius fidius et timide, non revocans me ipse
sed paene refugiens. genus autem hoc scripturae non
modo liberum sed incitatum atque elatum esse debere
quis ignorat? solutum existimatur esse alteri male dicere,
tamen cavendum est ne in petulantiam incidas; impeditum
se ipsum laudare, ne vitium adrogantiae subsequatur;
solum vero liberum alterum laudare, de quo quicquid de-
trahas necesse est aut infirmitati aut invidiae adsignetur. ac
nescio an tibi gratius opportuniusque acciderit; nam quod
praeclare facere non poteram primum erat non attingere,
secundum beneficium[1] quam parcissime facere. sed tamen ego quidem me sustinui; multa minui, multa sustuli,
complura ne posui quidem. quem ad modum igitur scala-
rum gradus si alios tollas, alios incidas, non nullos male
haerentis relinquas, ruinae periculum struas, non ascen-
sum pares, sic tot malis tum vinctum, tum fractum studium scribendi quid dignum auribus aut probabile potest
adferre?

4   Cum vero ad ipsius Caesaris nomen veni, toto corpore
contremesco, non poenae metu sed illius iudici. totum
enim Caesarem non novi. quem putas animum esse ubi secum loquitur? 'hoc probabit, hoc verbum suspiciosum est.
quid si hoc muto? at vereor ne peius sit.' age vero, laudo

---

[1] ben- *del. Lamb*

[3] Inhibited presumably by fear of offending Caesar.
[4] Eulogy of another person.

suaded of it, why is he angry with somebody for writing something to his displeasure, when he has pardoned all the folk who often prayed heaven for his destruction?

But to resume, the reason for our nervousness was this: I have written about yourself, sparingly and gingerly enough upon my word,[3] not only keeping myself in check but almost running the other way. Now we all know that this type of composition[4] calls for freedom, indeed for excitement and enthusiasm. Attack upon another person is held to be licensed; all the same one has to be on one's guard against degenerating into bullying. Praise of self is held to be fraught with embarrassment—the vice of arrogance is at its heels. Only praise of others is regarded as completely uninhibited, for any stinting is ascribed to fickleness or jealousy. But perhaps it was more agreeable and convenient to you so. What I could not do supremely well it would have been best to leave alone, but the second-best kindness was to do it very sparingly. Anyhow, restrain myself I did. Much I toned down, deleted much else, and there was a good deal that never got on paper. Think of a ladder. If you take away some of the rungs, and hack into others, and leave others loose, you will be setting a booby trap, not constructing a means of ascent. So with my literary endeavour. Clogged and fractured by so many adversities, how can it produce anything fit to hear or worthy of approval?

Coming to the name of Caesar himself, I tremble from head to foot for fear, not of punishment, but of his critical opinion. Of Caesar I know personally nothing at all. Imagine my feelings when I take counsel with myself: 'He'll like that. But this word might be misconstrued. Well then, suppose I change it—but I'm afraid I may make matters

aliquem: num offendo? cum porro reprehendam,[2] quid si
non vult? armati stilum persequitur; victi et nondum resti-
tuti quid faciet? auges etiam tu mihi timorem, qui in 'Ora-
tore' tuo caves tibi per Brutum et ad excusationem socium
quaeris. ubi hoc omnium patronus facit, quid me, veterem
tuum, nunc omnium clientem, sentire oportet? in hac igitur calumnia timoris et caecae suspicionis tormento, cum
plurima ad alieni sensus coniecturam, non ad suum iudicium scribantur, quam difficile sit evadere, si minus expertus es, quod te ad omnia summum atque excellens ingenium armavit, nos sentimus. sed tamen ego filio dixeram
librum tibi legeret et auferret, aut ea condicione daret si
reciperes te correcturum, hoc est, si totum alium faceres.

5   De Asiatico itinere, quamquam summa necessitas pre-
mebat, ut imperasti feci.

Te pro me quid horter? vides tempus venisse quo necesse sit de nobis constitui. nihil est, mi Cicero, quod
filium meum exspectes. adulescens est; omnia excogitare
vel studio vel aetate vel metu non potest. totum negotium
tu sustineas oportet; in te mihi omnis spes est. tu pro tua
prudentia quibus rebus gaudeat, quibus capiatur Caesar,
tenes; a te omnia proficiscantur et per te ad exitum perducantur necesse est. apud ipsum multum, ad eius omnis
6   plurimum potes. unum tibi si persuaseris, non hoc esse tui

2 offendam *(Wes.)*

---

5 In allusion to Cicero's statement in the *Orator* (35) that his
eulogy of Cato was written at Brutus' instigation.

6 Probably a reference to Cicero's (extant) speech on behalf of
the writer's father.

worse.' Now then, I praise so-and-so: am I giving offence?
Again, when I criticize, suppose he doesn't like it. He per-
secutes a fighting man for his pen; what will he do to a
beaten enemy, still under sentence of banishment? You
yourself add to my apprehension, when I see you in your
Orator making Brutus your shield and casting about apolo-
getically for a partner.[5] When every man's advocate behaves so, what am *I* to feel, your old client[6] and now every
man's? Armed against all contingencies by superlative ge-
nius, you may not know by experience how difficult it is to
make a tolerable showing in such a torment of self-induced
anxiety and groping surmise, writing for most of the time
not as one's judgement directs but with a view to the probable effect on another person's mind. I feel it. However, I
did tell my son to read the volume to you and then take
it away, or else to give it to you on condition that you undertook to correct it, that is, to make a totally different book of
it.

Concerning the trip to Asia, despite the urgent and
compelling character of my business, I have done as you
commanded.

I do not need to urge you on my own behalf. You see
that the time has arrived when a decision on my case must
be made. There is no call, my dear Cicero, for you to wait
for my son. He is a young man. Eagerness, youth, and anxiety make it impossible for him to think everything out. *You*
must carry the whole affair. My entire hope lies in you.
In your sagacity you know the kind of thing that gives
Caesar pleasure and wins him over. The whole campaign
must start with you and be conducted by you to the finish.
You have much influence with himself, and more with his
whole circle. If only you make up your mind that it is not

365

muneris, si quid rogatus fueris, ut facias (quamquam id magnum et amplum est), sed totum tuum esse onus, perficies; nisi forte aut in miseria nimis stulte aut in amicitia nimis impudenter tibi onus impono. sed utrique rei excusationem tuae vitae consuetudo dat. nam quod ita consuesti pro amicis laborare, non iam sic sperant abs te sed etiam sic imperant tibi familiares.

Quod ad librum attinet quem tibi filius dabit, peto a te ne exeat, aut ita corrigas ne mihi noceat.

238 (XIII.66)

Scr. Romae fort. m. Ian. an. 45

M. CICERO P. SERVILIO S.

1   A. Caecinam, maxime proprium clientem familiae vestrae, non commendarem tibi, cum scirem qua fide in tuos, qua clementia in calamitosos soleres esse, nisi me et patris eius, quo sum familiarissime usus, memoria et huius fortuna ita moveret ut hominis omnibus mecum studiis officiisque coniunctissimi movere debebat. a te hoc omni contentione peto, sic ut maiore cura, maiore animi labore petere non possim, ut ad ea quae tua sponte sine cuiusquam commendatione faceres in hominem tantum et talem calamitosum aliquem adferant cumulum meae litterae, quo studiosius eum quibuscumque rebus possis iuves.

only your business to do what is asked of you (though that is a great deal in all conscience), but that the whole load is yours to bear, you will succeed. Or do I act like a fool in my present sorry state, or presume too far upon friendship, when I saddle you so? But your habit of conduct offers an excuse for both. You are so indefatigable on your friends' behalf that they have come not merely to hope for your help as I do, but to demand it as I am doing.

As for the book which my son will give you, let me beg of you not to let it get into circulation, or else to revise it in such a way that it can do me no damage.

238 (XIII.66)
CICERO TO SERVILIUS ISAURICUS

Rome, January 45 (?)

From M. Cicero to P. Servilius greetings.

Since A. Caecina is a particularly attached client of your family, and since I know how loyal you are to those connected with you and how merciful to the unfortunate, I should not be recommending him to you, were it not that the memory of his father, who was on very close terms with me, and his own adversity affects me as it ought in the case of a person with whom I have the most intimate and comprehensive ties of common pursuits and good offices. May I request you with all urgency—I could ask nothing with more earnestness and concern of mind—to let my letter add a little extra to what you would have done of your own accord, without anybody's recommendation, for so eminent and worthy a person in distress, hoping that on this account you will assist him all the more actively in any way you can?

2   Quod si Romae fuisses, etiam salutem A. Caecinae
essemus, ut opinio mea fert, per te consecuti; de qua
tamen magnam spem habemus freti clementia collegae
tui. nunc, quoniam tuam iustitiam secutus tutissimum sibi
portum provinciam istam duxit esse, etiam atque etiam te
rogo atque oro ut eum et in reliqui⟨i⟩s veteris negotiationis colligendis iuves et ceteris rebus tegas atque tueare.
hoc mihi gratius facere nihil potes.

239 (VI.5)

Scr. Romae fort. m. Ian. an. 45

M. CICERO S. D. A. CAECINAE

1   Quotienscumque filium tuum vidi (video autem fere
cottidie) polliceor ei studium quidem meum et operam
sine ulla exceptione aut laboris aut occupationis aut temporis, gratiam autem atque auctoritatem cum hac exceptione, quantum valeam quantumque possim.

Liber tuus et lectus est et legitur a me diligenter et cus-
toditur diligentissime. res et fortunae tuae mihi maximae
curae sunt. quae quidem cottidie faciliores mihi et meliores videntur multisque video magnae esse curae; quorum
de studio et de sua spe filium ad te perscripsisse certo scio.

2   Iis autem de rebus quas coniectura consequi possumus
non mihi sumo ut plus ipse prospiciam quam te videre
atque intellegere mihi persuaserim. sed tamen, quia fieri

---

[1] Caesar, as Consul in 48.
[1] But dated by Beaujeu, rightly as I now think, to end of August 46. The book referred to will then be the Remonstrances.

If you had been in Rome, my opinion is that we should actually have obtained A. Caecina's pardon through your intercession. However, I have high hopes of this, founded on the merciful disposition of your colleague.[1] As matters stand, since in his reliance on your sense of justice he has chosen your province as his securest haven, I would entreat you once again to assist him in gathering together the remnants of his old business, and to give him in other ways the benefit of your shield and support. You can do nothing to oblige me more.

239 (VI.5)
CICERO TO A. CAECINA

Rome, January 45 (?)[1]

From M. Cicero to A. Caecina greetings.

Whenever I see your son, and I see him practically every day, I promise him my zeal and service, without reservation as to work or pressure of business or time; my personal and public influence I promise with the reservation 'so far as it extends, so far as I can.'

I have read, and am reading, your book carefully, and am keeping it most carefully in custody. Your affairs and fortunes are the object of my closest solicitude. They look to me to be in daily process of easement and amelioration; and I notice that many people have them much at heart. I am sure your son has written to you in detail of the support given by these persons and of his own hopes.

As for what lies in the sphere of conjecture, I do not pretend myself to see more ahead than I take to be apparent to your vision and understanding. But since it may be

potest ut tu ea perturbatiore animo cogites, puto esse meum quid sentiam exponere. ea natura rerum est et is temporum cursus ut non possit ista aut tibi aut ceteris fortuna esse diuturna neque haerere in tam bona causa et in 3 tam bonis civibus tam acerba iniuria. quo adde[1] eam spem quam extra ordinem de te ipso habemus, non solum propter dignitatem et fortunam[2] tuam (haec enim ornamenta sunt tibi etiam cum aliis communia) ‹sed, quae›[3] accedunt tua praecipua, propter eximium ingenium summamque virtutem, cui mehercules hic cuius in potestate sumus multum tribuit. itaque ne punctum quidem temporis in ista fortuna fuisses nisi eo ipso bono tuo quo delectatur se violatum putasset: quod ipsum lenitur cottidie, significaturque nobis ab iis qui simul cum eo vivunt tibi hanc ipsam opinionem ingeni apud illum plurimum profuturam.

4   Quapropter primum fac animo forti atque magno sis— ita enim natus, ita educatus, ita doctus es, ita etiam cognitus ut tibi id faciendum sit; deinde spem quoque habeas firmissimam propter eas causas quas scripsi. a me vero tibi omnia liberisque tuis paratissima esse confidas velim. id enim et vetustas nostri amoris et mea consuetudo in meos et tua multa erga me officia postulant.

[1] qua re ad *(Beaujeu)*
[2] virtutem *(SB)*
[3] *(SB)*

that you consider the prospects under a greater mental stress, I think I ought to set out my impressions. The nature of things and the trend of events make it impossible that this plight in which you and others find yourselves should be of long duration. So cruel an injustice to good citizens in a good cause cannot last. The hope we entertain in all such cases is reinforced by that which applies peculiarly to yourself: not only on account of your standing and wealth, distinctions you possess in common with others, but what is additional and special to yourself, your outstanding talents and qualities, attributes of much importance, I do assure you, in the eyes of the personage in whose power we lie. You would not have been a moment in your present predicament if he had not thought himself injured by the very gift[2] of yours that pleases him. But his resentment grows milder every day, and his associates intimate to me that your literary reputation will in fact count with him heavily in your favour.

First, then, you must keep a stout heart and a lofty spirit. One born, educated, taught, and I may add, proved, as you have been can do no less. Second, you must be confidently hopeful, for the reasons I have given. Please rest assured that I am most ready to assist you and your children in every way. I owe it to our longstanding affection, and my habits of behaviour to my friends, and your many services to me.

[2] Skill as a writer.

240 (IV.14)

Scr. Romae c. ex. an. 46

M. CICERO S. D. CN. PLANCIO

1   Binas a te accepi litteras Corcyrae datas, quarum alteris
mihi gratulabare quod audisses me meam pristinam dignitatem obtinere, alteris dicebas te velle quae egissem bene
et feliciter evenire.

Ego autem, si dignitas est bene de re publica sentire
et bonis viris probare quod sentias, obtineo dignitatem
meam; sin autem in eo dignitas est si quod sentias aut re
efficere possis aut denique libera oratione defendere, ne
vestigium quidem ullum est reliquum nobis dignitatis agi-
turque praeclare si nosmet ipsos regere possumus ut ea
quae partim iam adsunt, partim impendent, moderate feramus; quod est difficile in eius modi bello cuius exitus ex
altera parte caedem ostentet, ex altera servitutem. quo in
2   periculo non nihil me consolatur cum recordor haec me
tum vidisse cum secundas etiam res nostras, non modo ad-
versas, pertimescebam videbamque quanto periculo de
iure publico disceptaretur armis; quibus si ii vicissent ad
quos ego pacis spe, non belli cupiditate, adductus accesse-
ram, tamen intellegebam et iratorum hominum et cupidorum et insolentium quam crudelis esset futura victoria, sin
autem victi essent, quantus interitus esset futurus civium
partim amplissimorum, partim etiam optimorum; qui me

---

1 Cicero had divorced Terentia and married his young ward
Publilia, only to divorce her a few months later. There is reason to
believe that her family had Caesarian affiliations (cf. para. 3).

240 (IV.14)

CICERO TO CN. PLANCIUS

Rome, ca. end of 46

From M. Cicero to Cn. Plancius greetings.

I have received two letters from you, dispatched at Corcyra. In one you felicitate me on hearing that I maintain my former standing. In the other you wish me good fortune and prosperity in the step I have taken.[1]

Well, if 'standing' means to feel as a loyal citizen and to have one's sentiments approved by honest men, then I do maintain my standing. But if it consists in the power to implement one's feelings, or even to speak freely in their defence, not a vestige of standing is left us. We have good cause for satisfaction if we can discipline our own selves to bear calmly evils both present and imminent. That is no easy matter in a war which threatens to end in massacre from one side or in slavery from the other.[2] In this peril I take some comfort in recollecting that I foresaw these consequences in the days when I feared our party's success as well as its disaster, and perceived the deadly danger involved in settling a constitutional issue by force of arms. If such force brought victory to those with whom I had associated myself, not desiring war but hoping for peace, I saw none the less the cruelty with which angry, greedy, and unbridled men would exploit it. On the other hand, I realized what their defeat would cost in the lives of our countrymen, some of the highest and some of the best too, men

---

[2] Caesar was now fighting his last campaign against the republicans in Spain. Their victory would mean massacre, Caesar's would mean slavery.

haec praedicentem atque optime consulentem saluti suae
malebant nimium timidum quam satis prudentem existimari.

3   Quod autem mihi de eo quod egerim gratularis, te ita
velle certo scio. sed ego tam misero tempore nihil novi
consili cepissem nisi in reditu meo nihilo meliores res do-
mesticas quam rem publicam offendissem. quibus enim
pro meis immortalibus beneficiis carissima mea salus et
meae fortunae esse debebant, cum propter eorum scelus
nihil mihi intra meos parietes tutum, nihil insidiis vacuum
viderem, novarum me necessitudinum fidelitate contra
veterum perfidiam muniendum putavi.

4   Sed de nostris rebus satis, vel etiam nimium multa. de
tuis velim ut eo sis animo quo debes esse, id est ut ne quid
tibi praecipue timendum putes. si enim status erit aliquis
civitatis, quicumque erit, te omnium periculorum video
expertem fore; nam alteros tibi iam placatos esse intellego,
alteros numquam iratos fuisse. de mea autem in te voluntate sic velim iudices, me, quibuscumque rebus opus esse
intellegam, quamquam videam qui sim hoc tempore et
quid possim, opera tamen et consilio, studio quidem certe,
rei, famae, saluti tuae praesto futurum. tu velim et quid
agas et quid acturum te putes facias me quam diligentissime certiorem.

who, when I declared these views and advised in their own best interests, preferred to have me considered unduly timid than reasonably far-sighted.

As for your felicitations on the step I have taken, I am sure your good wishes are sincere. But I should not have taken any new decision at so sad a time, if on my return I had not found my household affairs in as sorry a state as the country's. In my own house I knew no security, had no refuge from intrigue, because of the villainy of those to whom my welfare and estate should have been most precious in view of the signal kindnesses I had showered upon them. Therefore I thought it advisable to fortify myself by the loyalty of new connections against the treachery of old ones.

But there's enough or perhaps too much about *my* affairs. As for yours, I would have you think as you should, that is, you must not suppose that you have anything specially to fear. If there is to be a settlement of the community, of whatever nature, you will clearly be free of all hazards. One party is now appeased, as I gather, and the other you have never offended. As for my own disposition towards you, I should like you to feel assured of my support for your estate, reputation, and civil rights in all matters where it seems required. I am well aware of my present position and capabilities, but I can promise my service and advice, and certainly my zeal. I hope you will keep me informed as fully as possible of your activities and plans.

Good-bye.

241 (IV.15)

Scr. Romae post. parte m. Ian. 45

‹M. CICERO S. D. CN. PLANCIO›

1   Accepi perbrevis tuas litteras, quibus id quod scire
cupiebam cognoscere non potui, cognovi autem id quod
mihi dubium non fuit; nam quam fortiter ferres communis
miserias non intellexi, quam me amares facile perspexi.
sed hoc scieram; illud si scissem, ad id meas litteras accom-
modavissem.

2   Sed tamen, etsi antea scripsi quae existimavi scribi
oportere, tamen hoc ‹te›[1] tempore breviter commonen-
dum putavi ne quo periculo te proprio existimares esse. in
magno omnes, sed tamen in communi sumus. qua re non
debes aut propriam fortunam et[2] praecipuam postulare
aut communem recusare. quapropter eo animo simus inter nos quo semper fuimus; quod de te sperare, de me
praestare possum.

242 (VI.1)

Scr. Romae c. fin. an. 46.

M. CICERO S. D. A. TORQUATO

1   Etsi ea perturbatio est omnium rerum ut suae quem-
que fortunae maxime paeniteat nemoque sit quin ubivis
quam ibi ubi sit[1] esse malit, tamen mihi dubium non est

[1] *(hic Wes., alii alibi)*   [2] aut *(Man.)*
[1] est *(Wes.)*

241 (IV.15)
CICERO TO CN. PLANCIUS

Rome, latter January 45

From M. Cicero to Cn. Plancius greetings.

A very brief letter from you has come to hand. I was unable to learn from it what I wanted to know; I did learn what I have never doubted. That is to say, it does not tell me with what courage you are facing the common lot of affliction, but your affection for me is plain to see. The latter, however, I knew. If I knew the former, I should frame my letter accordingly.

Nevertheless, although I have previously written what I thought proper to write, I feel I should now briefly advise you that you ought not to regard yourself as in any peculiar danger. All of us are in great danger, but we share it in common. So you must not demand a special privileged lot, or reject the common one. Therefore let us feel towards one another as we have always felt. I hope you do, and can answer for myself.

242 (VI.1)
CICERO TO A. TORQUATUS

Rome, ca. end of 46

From M. Cicero to A. Torquatus[1] greetings.

In the present state of universal upheaval each one of us thinks his own lot the hardest and would rather be anywhere but where he is. Even so, I have no doubt that to be

---

[1] In Athens.

quin hoc tempore bono viro Romae esse miserrimum sit.
nam etsi, quocumque in loco quisquis est, idem est ei
sensus et eadem acerbitas ex interitu rerum et publicarum
et suarum, tamen oculi augent dolorem, qui ea quae ceteri
audiunt intueri cogunt nec avertere a miseriis cogitationem sinunt. qua re, etsi multarum rerum desiderio te angi
necesse est, tamen illo dolore quo maxime te confici audio,
quod Romae non sis, animum tuum libera. etsi enim cum
magna molestia tuos tuaque desideras, tamen illa quidem
quae requiris suum statum tenent nec melius si tu adesses
tenerent nec sunt ullo in proprio periculo; nec debes tu,
cum de tuis cogitas, aut praecipuam aliquam fortunam
postulare aut communem recusare.

2   De te autem ipso, Torquate, est tuum sic agitare animo
ut non adhibeas in consilium cogitationum tuarum desperationem aut timorem. nec enim is qui in te adhuc iniustior
quam tua dignitas postulabat fuit non magna signa dedit
animi erga te mitigati nec tamen is ipse a quo salus petitur
habet explicatam aut exploratam rationem salutis suae;
cumque omnium bellorum exitus incerti sint, ab altera victoria tibi periculum nullum esse perspicio, quod quidem
‹se›iunctum sit ab omnium interitu, ab altera te ipsum
numquam timuisse certo scio.

3   Reliquum est ut te id ipsum quod ego quasi consolationis loco pono maxime excruciet, commune periculum rei
publicae. cuius tanti mali, quamvis docti viri multa dicant,
tamen vereor ne consolatio nulla possit vera reperiri praeter illam quae tanta est quantum in cuiusque animo robo-

---

2 Caesar.

3 The republicans, whose cause had revived in Spain.

in Rome is the worst of all for an honest man at the present time. True, wherever a man may be, his feelings are the same; public and private ruin fills him with the same bitterness. But the eyes add to the pain, forcing us to look at what others only hear and forbidding us to turn our thoughts away from our sorrows. So although you must be suffering from the absence of much that you miss, do free your spirit from the distress which I hear weighs upon you most heavily—that you are not in Rome. Painfully as you miss your people and possessions, the objects of your regret continue in their usual state, and would be in no better if you were here. They are in no special danger, and in thinking of what is yours you ought not to claim a privileged lot or reject the common one.

As for yourself, dear sir, when you revolve the situation, it would ill become you to take despair or fear into your mental council chamber. The individual[2] who has been less fair to you hitherto than your personal eminence made incumbent has given no small indications of a softening in his attitude towards you. Yet he himself, from whom men beg their lives, has no plain assurance for his own. Bearing in mind that no war has a certain issue, I perceive that you have nothing to fear from the victory of the one side, apart that is from involvement in a universal destruction; from that of the other[3] I am sure that you yourself have never apprehended any danger.

There remains the possibility that what I am placing almost in the light of a consolation may constitute your chief torment—the general danger to the commonwealth. For so vast an evil I fear that, much as philosophers have to say on the subject, no true consolation is to be discovered, excepting one; and the efficacy of that one is in proportion to

ris est atque nervorum: si enim bene sentire recteque facere satis est ad bene beateque vivendum, vereor ne eum
qui se optimorum consiliorum conscientia sustentare possit miserum esse nefas sit dicere. nec enim nos arbitror victoriae praemiis ductos patriam olim et liberos et fortunas
reliquisse, sed quoddam nobis officium iustum et pium et
debitum rei publicae nostraeque dignitati videbamur sequi,[2] nec, cum id faciebamus, tam eramus amentes ut

4 explorata nobis esset victoria. qua re, si id evenit quod
ingredientibus nobis in causam propositum fuit accidere
posse, non debemus ita cadere animis quasi aliquid eveneˉ
rit quod fieri posse numquam putarimus. simus igitur ea
mente quam ratio et veritas praescribit, ut nihil in vita
nobis praestandum praeter culpam putemus, eaque cum
careamus, omnia humana placate et moderate feramus.
atque haec eo pertinet oratio ut perditis rebus omnibus tamen ipsa virtus se sustentare posse videatur. sed si est spes
aliqua ‹d›e[3] rebus communibus, ea tu, quicumque status
est futurus, carere non debes.

5   Atque haec mihi scribenti veniebat in mentem me esse
eum cuius tu desperationem accusare solitus esses quem-
que auctoritate tua cunctantem et diffidentem excitare.
quo quidem tempore non ego causam nostram sed consilium improbabam. sero enim nos iis armis adversari videbam quae multo ante confirmata per nosmet ipsos erant,
dolebamque pilis et gladiis, non consiliis neque auctorita-
tibus nostris de iure publico disceptari. neque ego, ea quae
facta sunt fore cum dicebam, divinabam futura, sed quod
et fieri posse et exitiosum fore si evenisset videbam, id

[2] videatur sed qui (Man.)
[3] (Wes.)

each individual's spiritual strength and energy. If an honest heart and rectitude of conduct suffice for the good and happy life, I ask myself whether it be not blasphemy to speak of a man who can rest upon an excellent political conscience as unfortunate: After all, I do not suppose it was for the prizes of victory that we left country, children, and estate years ago. We thought we were fulfilling a valid and sacred duty to the commonwealth and to our own public characters, and in thus acting we were not so deluded as to take victory for granted. So if what we knew *might* happen when we first embarked upon the struggle has come to pass, we ought not to let it deject us, as though a thing had come about which we never reckoned within the bounds of possibility. Let us then follow the dictates of truth and reason, not holding ourselves answerable for anything for which we are not to blame, and, so long as we are blameless, bearing all the chances of mortality with sober composure. The purport of what I am saying is that, when all is lost, virtue must still be thought capable of resting upon its own support. But if there is some hope for our communal affairs, you must have your share in it, whatever the nature of the settlement is to be.

As I write, it crosses my mind that it was you who used to challenge *my* despair, and whose admonitions roused me from hesitation and despondency. It was not our cause with which I found fault in those days, but the conduct of it. I saw that it was too late for us to oppose the military power which we ourselves had long ago made strong, and I was sorry that constitutional questions should be decided by spears and swords rather than by our counsels and characters. When I foretold what has come about, I had no prophetic vision; perceiving what *could* happen, and would be

ne accideret timebam, praesertim cum, si mihi alterum
utrum de eventu atque exitu rerum promittendum esset,
id futurum quod evenit exploratius possem promittere. iis
enim rebus praestabamus quae non prodeunt in aciem,
usu autem armorum et militum robore inferiores eramus.
sed tu illum animum nunc adhibe, quaeso, quo me tum
esse oportere censebas.

6   Haec eo scripsi quod mihi Philargyrus tuus omnia de te
requirenti fidelissimo animo, ut mihi quidem visus est,
narravit te interdum sollicitum solere esse vehementius.
quod facere non debes nec dubitare quin aut aliqua re
publica sis is futurus qui esse debes aut perdita non adflic-
tiore condicione quam ceteri. hoc vero tempus, quo ex-
animati omnes et suspensi sumus, hoc moderatiore animo
ferre debes quod et in urbe ea es ubi nata et alta est ratio ac
moderatio vitae et habes Ser. Sulpicium, quem semper
unice dilexisti; qui te profecto et benevolentia et sapientia
consolatur. cuius si essemus et auctoritatem et consilium
secuti, togati potius potentiam quam armati victoriam sub-
issemus.

7   Sed haec longiora fortasse fuerunt quam necesse fuit;
illa quae maiora sunt brevius exponam. ego habeo cui plus
quam tibi debeam neminem; quibus tantum debebam
quantum tu intellegis, eos huius mihi belli casus eripuit.
qui sim autem hoc tempore intellego. sed quia nemo est
tam adflictus qui⟨n⟩,[4] si nihil aliud studeat nisi id quod

4 *(Vict.)*

---

4 More strictly, 'a civilian.'
5 Pompey, Lentulus Spinther, Milo.

disastrous if it did, I feared it, especially since, if I had been obliged to predict the final outcome one way or the other, I could have predicted that which actually occurred with greater confidence. For while we were superior in matters extraneous to the battlefield, we were weaker in military experience and in the calibre of our troops. Well, pray now yourself take the courage which you used then to think I ought to display.

I write in this strain because your man Philargyrus told me (in reply to my searching enquiries about you and, as it seemed to me, in a spirit of thorough loyalty) that you were subject to fits of rather severe depression. This ought not to happen. You ought not to doubt that either you will take your proper place in the commonwealth, if there is one, or, if that is lost, your state will be no more unhappy than anyone else's. You have two special reasons for self-control just now, when all of us are holding our breath in suspense: the city where you are residing is the mother and nurse of reason and restraint applied to the conduct of life; and you have Ser. Sulpicius, for whom you have always had a unique regard, at your side. I am sure his good will and wisdom are a comfort to you. If we had followed his weighty advice, we should have succumbed to the power of a citizen[4] rather than to the sword of a conqueror.

But perhaps all this has been more prolix than was necessary. Let me put what is of greater moment more succinctly. I have nobody to whom I owe more than to yourself. There were others[5] to whom I owed much, you know how much; but the chances of this war have swept them away. Of my position at this time I am well aware. But nobody is in so sorry a case but that he can do yeoman service, if he applies himself wholeheartedly to the matter in

agit, possit navare aliquid et efficere, omne meum consilium, operam, studium certe velim existimes tibi tuisque
liberis esse debitum.

243 (VI.3)

Scr. Romae non multo post superiorem

M. CICERO S. D. A. TORQUATO

1   Superioribus litteris benevolentia magis adductus
quam quo res ita postularet fui longior. neque enim confir-
matione nostra egebat virtus tua neque erat ea mea causa
atque fortuna ut, cui ipsi omnia deessent, alterum con-
2 firmarem. hoc autem[1] tempore brevior esse debeo. sive
enim nihil tum opus fuit tam multis verbis, nihilo magis
nunc opus est; sive tum opus fuit, illud satis est, praesertim
cum accesserit nihil novi. nam etsi cottidie aliquid audi-
mus earum rerum quas ad te perferri existimo, summa tamen eadem est et idem exitus; quem ego tam video animo
quam ea quae oculis cernimus, nec vero quicquam video
quod non idem te videre certo sciam.[2] nam etsi quem exitum acies habitura sit divinare nemo potest, tamen et belli
exitum video et, si id minus, hoc quidem certe, cum sit necesse alterum utrum vincere, qualis futura sit vel haec vel
3 illa victoria. idque cum optime perspexi ‹tum›[3] tale video,
nihil ut mali videatur futurum si id vel ante acciderit quod
vel maximum ad timorem proponitur. ita enim vivere ut
tum sit vivendum miserrimum est; mori autem nemo sa-

1 item *(Rut.)*   2 scio *(Rut.)*   3 *(Wes.)*

hand. I hope you will believe that anything I can give in advice, time, and devotion at least is yours and your children's by right.

243 (VI.3)
CICERO TO A. TORQUATUS

Rome, soon after the foregoing

From M. Cicero to A. Torquatus greetings.

In my earlier letter I wrote at considerable length, more out of friendly feeling than because the case required it. Your manly spirit needed no fortifying by me; and in my present necessitous predicament I am poorly qualified to fortify another. Now too I should be brief. If so many words were unnecessary then, they are no more necessary today; if they were needed then, what I wrote is sufficient, particularly as no new development has supervened. Every day, to be sure, we hear some part of the events which I imagine are reaching your ears, but the sum total remains the same, as does the final outcome. I see it in my mind as plain as what we see with our eyes, but I am sure I see nothing which is not equally visible to you. The outcome of the battle nobody can divine, but I see the outcome of the war; or if not that, at any rate I see what the victory of either side will mean—and, after all, one or the other must win. Perceiving this very plainly, I find the picture such that, if what is presented as the ultimate terror[1] comes to pass even sooner, it will be no misfortune. For to live what would then be life is misery indeed; whereas no

[1] Death.

piens miserum duxit, ne beato quidem. sed in ea es urbe in
qua haec, vel plura et ornatiora, parietes ipsi loqui posse
videantur.

4   Ego tibi hoc confirmo, etsi levis est consolatio ex miseriis aliorum, nihilo te nunc maiore in discrimine esse quam
quemvis ‹aut eorum qui in armis permanserint›[4] aut eorum qui discesserint. alteri dimicant, alteri victorem ti-
ment. sed haec consolatio levis est; illa gravior, qua te ut‹i›
spero, ego certe utor: nec enim dum ero angar ulla re, cum
omni vacem culpa, et si non ero, sensu omnino carebo. sed
rursus γλαῦκ᾽εἰς Ἀθήνας qui ad te haec.

      Mihi tu, tui, tua omnia maximae curae sunt et, dum
vivam, erunt.

      Vale.

244 (VI.4)

Scr. Romae non multo post superiorem

M. CICERO S. D. A. TORQUATO

1   Novi quod ad te scriberem nihil erat et tamen, si quid
esset, sciebam te a tuis certiorem fieri solere. de futuris autem rebus etsi semper difficile est dicere, tamen interdum
coniectura possis propius accedere cum est res eius modi
cuius exitus provideri possit. nunc tantum videmur intellegere, non diuturnum bellum; etsi id ipsum non nullis

      [4] *(SB)*

wise man ever counted it misery to die, even for the happy. But you are in a city where one fancies the very walls can say these things, only more, and more eloquently.

One thing I can tell you confidently, though it is a poor comfort that is founded on the miseries of others: you are in no greater danger now than any one of those who fought on or of those who gave up. The former are fighting, the latter fear the victor. But that is a poor comfort. There is a better one, of which I hope you avail yourself, as I certainly do. While I exist, nothing will give me pain, since I have nothing with which to reproach myself; and if I cease to exist, I shall feel nothing at all. But here I go again, sending an owl to Athens![2]

You and your family and your possessions are all the objects of my closest care, and shall be while I live.

Good-bye.

244 (VI.4)
CICERO TO A. TORQUATUS

Rome, soon after the foregoing

From M. Cicero to A. Torquatus greetings.

I have no news to tell you and anyhow, if there were any, I know your own people keep you informed. Of things to come it is always difficult to speak, but sometimes a guess can land near the mark, when the nature of the matter makes it possible to foresee the outcome. Now so much only seems clear, that the war will not last long—though

---

[2] See Letter 176, n. 4. Here the saying has additional point, in that Torquatus *was* in Athens.

videtur secus. equidem, cum haec scribebam, aliquid iam
actum putabam; [non quo][1] sed quid, difficilis erat coniectura. nam cum omnis belli Mars communis et cum semper
incerti exitus proeliorum sunt, tum hoc tempore ita magnae utrimque copiae, ita paratae ad depugnandum esse
dicuntur ut, utercumque vicerit, non sit mirum futurum.
illa in dies singulos magis magisque opinio hominum con-
firmatur, etiam si inter causas armorum aliquantum intersit, tamen inter victorias non multum interfuturum. alteros prope modum iam sumus experti, de altero nemo est
quin cogitet quam[2] sit metuendus iratus victor armatus.

2   Hoc loco si videor augere dolorem tuum quem consolando levare debe<b>am, fateor me communium malorum
consolationem nullam invenire praeter illam, quae tamen,
si possis eam suscipere, maxima est quaque ego cottidie
magis utor, conscientiam rectae voluntatis maximam consolationem esse rerum incommodarum nec esse ullum
magnum malum praeter culpam. a qua quoniam tantum
absumus ut etiam optime senserimus eventusque magis
nostri consili quam consilium reprehendatur et quoniam
praestitimus quod debuimus, moderate quod evenit feramus. sed hoc mihi tamen non sumo ut te consoler de communibus miseriis, quae[3] ad consolandum maioris ingeni et
ad ferendum singularis virtutis indigent; illud cuivis facile
est docere, cur praecipue tu dolere nihil debeas. eius enim
qui tardior in te levando fuit quam fore putaremus non est

---

[1] *(Schütz)*   [2] cum *(Man.)*   [3] quae <et> *Man.*

---

[1] The Caesarians.
[2] Cn. Pompeius the younger.
[3] Caesar.

even that is not everybody's opinion. At the time of writing I think something decisive has already taken place, but *what*—that is hard to guess. In every war the God of Battles fights in both ranks, and the outcome of a battle is always in doubt. But at the present time the forces on both sides are said to be so large and so ready to fight to the death that whichever of the two wins it will be no matter for surprise. One general conviction gains ground with every passing day: that even though there may be a certain amount to choose between the causes for which they are in arms, the victory of either side will amount to much about the same. One set[1] we have by now pretty well experienced. As for the rival leader,[2] the formidable figure of an angry conqueror sword in hand is in everybody's mind.

Here I may seem to be adding to your distress, which I ought to console and alleviate. I must admit that I find no consolation for our common calamities, save one; but that one, if we can make it ours, is sovereign, and I myself have recourse to it more and more every day. I mean that the consciousness of honest intentions is a sovereign consolation in adversity, and that there is no great calamity apart from guilt. We are free of that. On the contrary our hearts have always been in the right place, and the issue of our course of action is deplored rather than the course itself. Having done our duty, let us bear the event without too much repining. However, I do not take it upon myself to console you for the common afflictions. They are such that consolation demands a greater intellect than mine, endurance an exceptional courage. But anyone may easily show why you ought not specially to distress yourself. A certain personage[3] has been slower to come to your relief than we might have expected, but I have no doubts about his

389

mihi dubia de tua salute sententia, de illis autem non arbitror te expectare quid sentiam.

3   Reliquum est ut te angat quod absis a tuis tam diu, res molesta, praesertim ab iis pueris quibus nihil potest esse festivius; sed, ut ad te scripsi antea, tempus est huius modi ut suam quisque condicionem miserrimam putet et, ubi quisque sit, ibi esse minime velit. equidem nos qui Romae sumus miserrimos esse duco, non solum quod in malis omnibus acerbius est videre quam audire sed etiam quod ad omnis casus subitorum periculorum magis obiecti sumus quam [et] si abessemus.

    Etsi me ipsum consolatorem tuum non tantum litterae, quibus semper studui, quantum longinquitas temporis mi-
4 tigavit. quanto fuerim dolore meministi. in quo prima illa consolatio est, vidisse me plus quam ceteros cum cupiebam quamvis iniqua condicione pacem. quod etsi casu, non divinatione mea, factum est, tamen in hac inani prudentiae laude delector. deinde, quod mihi ad consolationem commune tecum est, si iam vocer ad exitum vitae, non ab ea re publica avellar qua carendum esse doleam, praesertim cum id sine ullo sensu futurum sit. adiuvat ⟨et⟩iam[4] aetas et acta iam vita, quae cum cursu suo bene confecto delectat[5] tum vetat in eo vim timere quo nos iam natura ipsa paene perduxerit. postremo is vir vel etiam ii viri hoc bello occiderunt ut impudentia videatur eandem fortunam, si res cogat, recusare. equidem mihi omnia propono, nec ullum est tantum malum quod non putem impendere. sed cum plus in metuendo mali sit quam in ipso illo quod

---

4 *(Man.)*   5 delectatur *(Wes.)*

---

4 The republicans.   5 Pompey.

purpose concerning your rehabilitation. As for the others,[4] I do not suppose you are waiting for me to express my opinon.

There remains the pain you feel at so long an absence from your friends and family—a loss indeed, especially those quite delightful boys. But as I wrote to you earlier, the times are such that every man thinks his own lot the hardest and would least wish to be where he actually is. For my part I rate us who are in Rome as most to be pitied, not merely because in all calamities it is more bitter to see than to hear but also because we are more exposed to every sudden, dangerous accident than if we were elsewhere.

Yet I, your comforter, have felt my grief assuaged not so much by the books to which I have always been devoted as by the passing of time. You remember how sorely distressed I was. My first consolation is that I saw further than others in desiring peace, on terms however unfavourable. That was chance, not any prophetic gift of mine; and yet this empty credit I get for foresight gives me pleasure. And then, a comforting reflection which you and I have in common, if I were to be called upon to meet life's end, I should not be torn away from a commonwealth which I should grieve to lose, especially as the condition will be entirely unconscious. My age helps too, and the life that is now behind me. There is satisfaction in the thought of a race well run; and I must not be afraid of violence at a juncture which I have now almost reached in the course of nature. Finally, when I think of the great man,[5] I might even say men, who perished in this war, I should feel shameless if I rebelled against a like fate, should it be forced upon me. To be sure I set all manner of contingencies before my mind; no catastrophe so terrible that I do not envisage it as immi-

timetur, desino, praesertim cum id impendeat in quo non
modo dolor nullus verum finis etiam doloris futurus sit.

Sed haec satis multa, vel plura potius quam necesse
fuit; facit autem non loquacitas mea sed benevolentia longiores epistulas.

5   Servium discessisse Athenis moleste tuli. non enim dubito quin magnae tibi levationi solitus sit esse cottidianus
congressus et sermo cum familiarissimi hominis tum optimi et prudentissimi viri. tu velim te, ut debes et soles, tua
virtute sustentes. ego quae te velle quaeque ad te et ad
tuos pertinere arbitrabor omnia studiose diligenterque
curabo. quae cum faciam, benevolentiam tuam erga me
imitabor, merita non adsequar.

Vale.

245 (VI.2)

Scr., ut vid., in Attici Nomentano m. Apr. an. 45

M. CICERO S. D. A. TORQUATO

1   Peto a te ne me putes oblivione tui rarius ad te scribere
quam solebam, sed aut gravitate valetudinis, qua tamen
iam paulum videor levari, aut quod absim ab urbe, ut qui
ad te proficisca⟨n⟩tur scire non possim. qua re velim ita
statutum habeas, me tui memoriam cum summa benevolentia tenere tuasque omnis res non minori mihi curae
quam meas esse.

2   Quod maiore in varietate versata est adhuc tua causa

nent. But since fearing hurts us more than the actuality of what we fear, I desist. Besides, the impending doom will be painless, indeed it will be the end of pain.

However, I have written enough in this strain, or rather more than was necessary. But it is my friendly concern, not loquacity, that make my letters long.

I was sorry to hear of Servius' departure from Athens, for I don't doubt that you found daily meetings and talks with so close a friend and so excellent and wise a man a great solace. Let me hope that you fall back upon your own strength of mind, as is your duty and your wont. I shall give zealous and sedulous attention to anything I think to be your wish, or of concern to you and yours. In so doing I shall emulate your good will towards me, but shall not equal your deserts.

Good-bye.

245 (VI.2)
CICERO TO A. TORQUATUS

Atticus' villa near Nomentum, April 45 (?)

From M. Cicero to A. Torquatus greetings.

I beg you not to suppose that, if my letters come less frequently than of yore, it is because I have forgotten you. The cause lies in my poor health, though now I think it has a little improved, and my absence from Rome, which prevents me hearing of travellers to your whereabouts. So I want you to be sure once for all that I keep you in mind with the most friendly feelings and pay as much attention to all your affairs as to my own.

Considering the bad times we live in, you ought not, be-

quam homines aut volebant aut opinabantur, mihi crede,
non est pro malis temporum quod moleste feras. necesse
est enim aut armis urgeri rem publicam sempiternis aut iis
positis recreari aliquando aut funditus interire. si arma
valebunt, nec eos a quibus reciperis vereri debes nec eos
quos adiuvisti; si armis aut condicione positis aut defatiga-
tione abiectis aut victoria detractis civitas respiraverit, et
dignitate tua frui tibi et fortunis licebit; sin omnino interierint omnia fueritque is exitus quem vir prudentissimus, M.
Antonius, iam tum timebat cum tantum instare malorum
suspicabatur, misera est illa quidem consolatio, tali praesertim civi et viro, sed tamen necessaria, nihil esse praecipue cuiquam dolendum in eo quod accidat universis.

3   Quae vis insit in his paucis verbis (plura enim commit-
tenda epistulae non erant) si attendes, quod facis profecto
etiam sine meis litteris, intelleges te aliquid habere quod
speres, nihil quod aut hoc aut aliquo rei publicae statu timeas; omnia si interierint, cum superstitem te esse rei publicae ne si liceat quidem velis, ferendam esse fortunam,
praesertim quae absit a culpa. sed haec hactenus.

Tu velim scribas ad me quid agas et ubi futurus sis ut
aut quo scribam aut quo veniam scire possim.

lieve me, to take it hard that your case has hitherto gone through more ups and downs than was generally hoped or expected. There are three possible futures for the commonwealth: oppression in endless armed conflict, eventual revival when arms are laid aside, and complete annihilation. If arms are to prevail, you should not fear the side which is pardoning you, nor yet that which you assisted. If arms are laid aside on terms, or cast away in exhaustion, or withdrawn in victory, and the state breathes once more, you will be free to enjoy your rank and fortune. If, however, the sum of things goes down to destruction, the end feared long ago by a very wise man, M. Antonius,[1] when he surmised the vast calamities to come, well then, you have the consolation (a sad one indeed, especially for a man and a citizen like yourself, but necessary) that in what happens to all the individual has no special reason for distress.

If you will carefully consider the significance implicit in these few words (more it would not have been wise to commit to a letter), you will realize, as I am sure you do without any letter of mine, that you have something to hope and nothing, in this or any other state of the commonwealth, to be afraid of; and that if all goes to ruin, you must bear what Fortune sends, especially as your conscience is clear. For you would not wish to survive the commonwealth, even if that were possible. But I have written enough on this topic.

Please write and tell me of your doings and your future whereabouts, so that I may know where to write or where to go.

[1] The orator.

246 (VI.21)

Scr. Romae m. Ian. an. 45 (?)

CICERO TORANIO

1   Etsi cum haec ad te scribebam aut appropinquare exitus huius calamitosissimi belli aut iam aliquid actum et confectum videbatur, tamen cottidie commemorabam te unum in tanto exercitu mihi fuisse adsensorem et me tibi, solosque nos vidisse quantum esset in eo bello mali in quo spe pacis exclusa ipsa victoria futura esset acerbissima, quae aut interitum adlatura esset, si victus esses, aut, si vicisses, servitutem. itaque ego, quem tum fortes illi viri et sapientes, Domitii et Lentuli, timidum esse dicebant (eram plane; timebam enim ne evenirent ea quae acciderunt), idem nunc nihil timeo et ad omnem eventum paratus sum. cum aliquid videbatur caveri posse, tum id neglegi dolebam. nunc vero eversis omnibus rebus, cum consilio profici nihil possit, una ratio videtur quicquid evenerit ferre moderate, praesertim cum omnium rerum mors sit extremum et mihi sim conscius me ⟨et⟩,[1] quoad licuerit, dignitati rei publicae consuluisse et hac ⟨a⟩missa salutem retinere voluisse.

2   Haec scripsi, non ut de me ipse dicerem, sed ut tu, qui coniunctissima fuisti mecum et sententia et voluntate, eadem cogitares. magna enim consolatio est cum recordare,

---

[1] *(Lamb.)*

---

[1] C. Toranius had probably been Quaestor in 73 and Plebeian Aedile in 64, the latter as colleague of C. Octavius, who left him guardian to his son, the future Augustus. He was now in Corcyra.

246 (VI.21)
CICERO TO TORANIUS

Rome, January 45 (?)

From Cicero to Toranius.[1]

As I write these lines to you, it looks as though the final issue of this most disastrous of wars is approaching; or it may be that a decisive action has already taken place. But every day I recall how you and I alone in that great army shared each other's views, and saw, as no one else did, with what an infinity of evil that war was charged. All hope of peace being excluded, even victory was bound to prove a most bitter experience, fraught with destruction to the vanquished and slavery to the victors. In those days such paragons of courage and wisdom as Domitius and Lentulus[2] used to call me timid—and so indeed I was; I was afraid that what has happened would come to pass. But today I have no fears, and am ready for any outcome. When it still seemed possible to make some provisions against the future, I was sorry to see the chance neglected. But now that all is topsy-turvy and nothing can be achieved by policy, resignation to whatever may betide appears the only rational course; especially as death is the end of all, and my conscience tells me that I took thought for the dignity of the commonwealth so long as I could and, when that was lost, was fain to save its existence.

I have written thus, not in order to talk about myself, but to put the same thoughts into your mind, since your view and aims were very close to mine. It is a great consolation to remember that one has meant well and honestly,

---

[2] Lentulus Crus, Consul in 49.

etiam si secus acciderit, te tamen recte vereque sensisse. atque utinam liceat aliquando aliquo rei publicae statu nos frui inter nosque conferre sollicitudines nostras, quas contulimus[2] tum cum timidi putabamur quia dicebamus ea futura quae facta sunt.

3   De tuis rebus nihil esse quod timeas praeter universae rei publicae interitum tibi confirmo. de me autem sic velim iudices, quantum ego possim me tibi, saluti tuae liberisque tuis summo cum studio praesto semper futurum.

    Vale.

247 (VI.20)

Scr. in Tusculano c. fin. m. Quint. an. 45, ut vid.

CICERO TORANIO S.

1   Dederam triduo ante pueris Cn. Planci litteras ad te. eo nunc ero brevior teque, ut antea consolabar, hoc tempore monebo. nihil puto tibi esse utilius quam ibidem opperiri quoad scire possis quid tibi agendum sit. nam praeter navigationis longae et hiemalis et minime portuosae periculum, quod vitaveris, ne illud quidem non quan‹ti›vis,[1] subito, cum certi aliquid audieris, te istim posse proficisci. nihil est praeterea cur adven‹ien›tibus te offerre gestias. multa praeterea metuo, quae cum Cilone nostro communicavi. quid multa? loco opportuniore in his malis nullo

2

2 pert- *(SB)*
1 quamvis *(Vict.)*

_____

1 Caesar and his party returning from Spain.

even though things have fallen out awry. I only hope we may one day enjoy some form of settled constitution and talk over our anxieties, as we did in the days when we were thought timid because we said that what has come would come.

As for your affairs, I assure you that you have nothing to fear apart from the destruction of the whole common-wealth. As for me, I hope you will determine that, so far as I can, I shall ever stand by you devotedly, and by the cause of your restoration, and by your children.

Good-bye.

247 (VI.20)
CICERO TO TORANIUS

Tusculum, ca. end of July 45 (?)

From Cicero to Toranius.

Three days ago I gave a letter for you to Cn. Plancius' boys so I shall now write more briefly; and whereas in my earlier letter I offered you comfort, I am now going to offer advice. I think you have no better course than to wait where you are until you can decide what to do. Besides the risk in a long, stormy voyage along a coast very poorly pro-vided with harbours, which you will thus avoid, there is the infinitely important consideration that, when you do hear something definite, you can set out straight away from your present place of residence. Also there is no reason why you should be all agog to put yourself in their way as they[1] approach. And I have many other apprehensions, of which I have told our friend Cilo. In short, you could have found no more convenient place to stay in these distressing

esse potuisti ex quo te, quocumque opus erit, facillime et
expeditissime conferas. quod si recipiet ille se ad tempus,
aderis; sin, quoniam multa accidere possunt, aliqua res
eum vel impediet vel morabitur, tu ibi eris ubi omnia scire
possis. hoc mihi prorsus valde placet.

3   De reliquo, ut te saepe per litteras hortatus sum, ita velim tibi persuadeas, te in hac causa nihil habere quod tibi
timendum sit praeter communem casum civitatis. qui etsi
est gravissimus, tamen ita viximus et id aetatis iam sumus
ut omnia quae non nostra culpa nobis accidant fortiter
ferre debeamus.

Hic tui omnes valent summaque pietate te desiderant
et diligunt et colunt. tu cura ut valeas et te istim ne temere
commoveas.

248 (IV.5)

Scr. Athenis c. med. m. Mart. an. 45

SERVIUS CICERONI S.

1   Postea quam mihi renuntiatum est de obitu Tulliae,
filiae tuae, sane quam pro eo ac debui graviter molesteque
tuli communemque eam calamitatem existimavi, qui, si
istic adfuissem, neque tibi defuissem coramque meum
dolorem tibi declarassem; etsi genus hoc consolationis
mi<se>rum[1] atque acerbum est propterea quia per quos ea
confieri debet, propinquos ac familiaris, ii ipsi pari moles-

[1] *(Crat.)*

circumstances; for it is one you can leave and go wherever may be advisable with the maximum of ease and expedition. If *he* returns on time, you will be close at hand; whereas if something hampers or delays him (many things can happen), you will be where you can get all the news. This really does seem to me best.

For the rest, as I have often borne in upon you in my letters, I hope you will make up your mind that you have nothing to fear in your present situation over and above the general fate of the community. That, no doubt, is a very hard one, but considering the character of our lives and the age we have now reached, we ought to bear with fortitude anything that happens to us for which we are not responsible.

All your family here are well. They miss you and love you and cherish you with the fondest affection. See you keep fit and do not move from where you are without good reason.

248 (IV.5)

SERVIUS SULPICIUS RUFUS TO CICERO

Athens, mid March 45

From Servius to Cicero greetings.

When the report reached me of the death of your daughter Tullia, I was indeed duly and deeply and grievously sorry, and I felt that the blow had struck us both. Had I been in Rome, I should have been with you and shown you my grief in person. And yet that is a melancholy and bitter sort of comfort. Those who should offer it, relations and friends, are themselves no less afflicted. They cannot

tia adficiuntur neque sine lacrimis multis id conari possunt, uti magis ipsi videantur aliorum consolatione indi-
gere quam aliis posse suum officium praestare. tamen,
quae in praesentia in mentem mihi venerunt, decrevi brevi
ad te perscribere, non quo ea te fugere existimem sed
quod forsitan dolore impeditus minus ea perspicias.

2   Quid est quod tanto opere te commoveat tuus dolor in-
testinus? cogita quem ad modum adhuc Fortuna nobiscum egerit; ea nobis erepta esse quae hominibus non minus quam liberi cara esse debent, patriam, honestatem,
dignitatem, honores omnis. hoc uno incommodo addito
quid ad dolorem adiungi potuit? aut qui non in illis rebus
exercitatus animus callere iam debet atque omnia minoris
existimare?

3   At[2] illius vicem, credo, doles. quotiens in eam cogitationem necesse est et tu veneris et nos saepe incidimus, hisce
temporibus non pessime cum iis esse actum quibus sine
dolore licitum est mortem cum vita commutare! quid
autem fuit quod illam hoc tempore ad vivendum magno
opere invitare posset? quae res, quae spes, quod animi
solacium? ut cum aliquo adulescente primario coniuncta
aetatem gereret? licitum est tibi, credo, pro tua dignitate
ex hac iuventute generum deligere cuius fidei liberos tuos
te tuto committere putares. an ut ea liberos ex sese pareret
quos cum florentis videret laetaretur, qui rem a parente
traditam per se tenere possent, honores ordinatim petituri
essent, in re publica, in amicorum negotiis libertate sua
‹us›uri?[3] quid horum fuit quod non prius quam datum est
ademptum sit? at vero malum est liberos amittere. malum,

2 an (*Man.*)
3 uti (*Gul.*)

make the attempt without many tears, and rather seem themselves to stand in need of comfort *from* others than to be capable of doing their friendly office *for* others. None the less, I have resolved to set briefly before you the reflections that come to my mind in this hour, not that I suppose you are unaware of them, but perhaps your grief makes them harder for you to perceive.

What reason is there why your domestic sorrow should affect you so sorely? Think how Fortune has dealt with us up to now. All that man should hold no less dear than children—country, dignity, standing, distinctions—has been snatched away from us. Could this one further mishap add appreciably to your grief? How should not any heart practised in such experience have grown less sensitive and count all else as of relatively little consequence?

But I suppose you grieve for her sake. How often must you have thought, and how often has it occurred to me, that in this day and age they are not most to be pitied who have been granted a painless exchange of life for death! What was there after all to make life so sweet a prospect for her at this time? What did she have or hope? What comfort for her spirit? The thought perhaps of spending her life wedded to some young man of distinction? Do you suppose it was possible for you to choose from this modern generation a son-in-law suitable to your standing to whose protection you could feel safe in confiding your child? Or the thought of bearing children herself, whose bloom would cheer her eyes, sons who could maintain their patrimony, would seek public office in due course, and act in public affairs and in their friends' concerns like free men? Was not all this taken away before it was granted? The loss of children is a calamity, sure enough—except that it is a

403

nisi hoc peius est,[4] haec sufferre et perpeti.

4   Quae res mihi non mediocrem consolationem attulit
volo tibi commemorare, si forte eadem res tibi dolorem
minuere possit. ex Asia rediens cum ab Aegina Megaram
versus navigarem, coepi regiones circumcirca prospicere.
post me erat Aegina, ante me Megara, dextra Piraeus, si-
nistra Corinthus, quae oppida quodam tempore florentis-
sima fuerunt, nunc prostrata et diruta ante oculos iacent.
coepi egomet mecum sic cogitare: 'hem! nos homunculi
indignamur si quis nostrum interiit aut occisus est, quorum vita brevior esse debet, cum uno loco tot oppidum
cadavera proiecta iacent? visne tu te, Servi, cohibere et
meminisse hominem te esse natum?' crede mihi, cogitatione ea non mediocriter sum confirmatus. hoc idem, si
tibi videtur, fac ante oculos tibi proponas. modo ‹autem›[5]
uno tempore tot viri clarissimi interierunt, de imperio populi Romani tanta deminutio facta est, omnes provinciae
conquassatae sunt: in unius mulierculae animula si iactura
facta est, tanto opere commoveris? quae si hoc tempore
non diem suum obisset, paucis post annis tamen ei mo-
5   riendum fuit, quoniam homo nata fuerat. etiam tu ab hisce
rebus animum ac cogitationem tuam avoca atque ea potius
reminiscere quae digna tua persona sunt: illam, quam diu
ei opus fuerit, vixisse, una cum re publica fuisse,[6] te, patrem suum, praetorem, consulem, augurem vidisse, adu-
lescentibus primariis nuptam fuisse, omnibus bonis prope
perfunctam esse, cum res publica occideret, vita exces-

---

[4] sit (*Wes.*)   [5] (*SB*)   [6] floruisse *v. l. ap. Lamb.*

---

[1] If Sulpicius had suffered a bereavement we do not know
what it was.

worse calamity to bear our present lot and endure.

I want to tell you of something which has brought me no slight comfort,[1] in the hope that perhaps it may have some power to lighten your sorrow too. As I was on my way back from Asia,[2] sailing from Aegina towards Megara, I began to gaze at the landscape around me. There behind me was Aegina, in front of me Megara, to the right Piraeus, to the left Corinth; once flourishing towns, now lying low in ruins before one's eyes. I began to think to myself: 'Ah! How can we manikins wax indignant if one of us dies or is killed, ephemeral creatures as we are, when the corpses of so many towns lie abandoned in a single spot? Check yourself, Servius, and remember that you were born a mortal man.' That thought, I do assure you, strengthened me not a little.[3] If you please, picture the same spectacle to yourself. Not long ago so many great men died at one time, the Roman Empire was so gravely impaired, all its provinces shaken to pieces; can you be so greatly moved by the loss of one poor little woman's frail spirit? If her end had not come now, she must none the less have died in a few years' time, for she was mortal. You too must take your mind and thoughts away from such things, and dwell instead on recollections worthy of the character you hold. Tell yourself that she lived as long as it was well for her to live, and that she and freedom existed together. She saw you, her father, Praetor, Consul, and Augur. She was married to young men of distinction. Almost all that life can give, she en-

---

[2] I.e. from Samos. Sulpicius will have been returning to Rome in the autumn of 47.   [3] Byron refers to this passage in *Childe Harold* (IV.44), as does Sterne, *Tristram Shandy*, V, 3, who probably got it from Burton's *Anatomy of Melancholy*.

sisse. quid est quod tu aut illa cum Fortuna hoc nomine
queri possitis?

Denique noli te oblivisci Ciceronem esse et eum qui
aliis consueris praecipere et dare consilium, neque imitare
malos medicos, qui in alienis morbis profitentur tenere se
medicinae scientiam, ipsi se curare non possunt, sed potius quae aliis tute praecipere soles ea tute tibi subiace

6 atque apud animum propone. nullus dolor est quem non
longinquitas temporis minuat ac molliat. hoc te exspectare
tempus tibi turpe est ac non ei rei sapientia tua te occur-
rere. quod si qui etiam inferis sensus est, qui illius in te
amor fuit pietasque in omnis suos, hoc certe illa te facere
non vult. da hoc illi mortuae, da ceteris amicis ac familiaribus, qui tuo dolore maerent, da patriae, ut, si qua in re
opus sit, opera et consilio tuo uti possit. denique, quoniam
in eam fortunam devenimus ut etiam huic rei nobis serviendum sit, noli committere ut quisquam te putet non
tam filiam quam rei publicae tempora et aliorum victoriam
lugere.

Plura me ad te de hac re scribere pudet, ne videar prudentiae tuae diffidere. qua re, si hoc unum proposuero,
finem faciam scribendi: vidimus aliquotiens secundam
pulcherrime te ferre fortunam magnamque ex ea re te laudem apisci; fac aliquando intellegamus adversam quoque
te aeque ferre posse neque id maius quam debeat tibi onus
videri, ne ex omnibus virtutibus haec una tibi videatur
deesse.

joyed; and she left life when freedom died. How can you or she quarrel with Fortune on this account?

And then, do not forget that you are Cicero, a man accustomed to give rules and advice to others. Do not be like a bad physician, who professes medical knowledge to his patients but does not know how to treat himself. Rather lay to your heart and place before your mind the precepts you are wont to offer others. There is no grief that is not lessened or softened by the passage of time. For you to wait for this time to pass, instead of anticipating the result by your own good sense, does you discredit. And if consciousness remains to those below, loving you as she did, dutifully fond as she was of all her family, she assuredly does not wish you to act so. Listen then for her dead sake, for the sake of others, your well-wishers and friends who are sad for your grief, and for your country's sake, so that if need arise she may have the benefit of your service and counsel. And then, since in the pass to which we have come we must not disregard even *this* aspect, do not let anyone suppose that it is not so much a daughter you are mourning as the public predicament and the victory of others.

I am ashamed to write at greater length to you on this matter, lest I seem to doubt your good sense, and so I shall end my letter with one final observation. We have seen more than once how nobly you sustain prosperity, and how great the glory you gain thereby. Let us recognize at last that you are no less able to bear adversity, and that you count it no heavier load than you should, lest of all fine qualities you may seem to lack this only.[4]

---

[4] Livy wrote of Cicero that he bore none of his misfortunes like a man except death.

Quod ad me attinet, cum te tranquilliorem animo esse cognoro, de iis rebus quae hic geruntur quemadmodumque se provincia habeat certiorem faciam.

Vale.

249 (IV.6)

Scr. in Attici Nomentano med. m. Apr. an. 45

M. CICERO S.D. SER. SULPICIO

1   Ego vero, Servi, vellem, ut scribis, in meo gravissimo casu adfuisses. quantum enim praesens me adiuvare potueris et consolando et prope aeque dolendo facile ex eo intellego quod litteris lectis aliquantum acquievi. nam et ea scripsisti quae levare luctum possent et in me consolando non mediocrem ipse animi dolorem adhibuisti. Servius tamen tuus omnibus officiis quae illi tempori tribui potuerunt declaravit et quanti ipse me faceret et quam suum talem erga me animum tibi gratum putaret fore. cuius officia iucundiora scilicet saepe mihi fuerunt, numquam tamen gratiora.

Me autem non oratio tua solum et societas paene aegritudinis sed etiam auctoritas consolatur; turpe enim esse existimo me non ita ferre casum meum ut tu tali sapientia praeditus ferendum putas. sed opprimor interdum et vix resisto dolori, quod ea me solacia deficiunt quae ceteris, quorum mihi exempla propono, simili in fortuna non defuerunt. nam et Q. Maximus, qui filium consularem, cla-

---

[1] Q. Fabius Maximus 'Cunctator.'

As for me, I shall inform you of what is going on here and of the state of the province when I hear that your mood is calmer.

Good-bye.

249 (IV.6)

CICERO TO SERVIUS SULPICIUS RUFUS

Atticus' villa near Nomentum, mid April 45

From M. Cicero to Ser. Sulpicius greetings.

Yes, my friend, I wish you had been with me, as you say, in my most grievous affliction. How much your presence would have helped me by consolation and by sorrow well-nigh equal to my own I readily recognize from the measure of easement I felt when I read your letter. You have written the words that could alleviate mourning and your own no small distress has given you the means of comforting mine. But your son Servius has shown by every friendly attention that could be rendered at such a time how much he thinks of me and how welcome he believes such a disposition on his part will be to you. I have often felt more pleasure in his attentions than I feel now (as you may imagine), but they were never more highly appreciated.

Not only am I comforted by your words and (I might almost say) your fellowship in sorrow, but by your counsel as well. I feel it discreditable in me not to bear my bereavement as so wise a man as you considers it should be borne. But sometimes I am overwhelmed, and scarcely offer any resistance to grief, because I have no such solaces as others in similar plight, whose examples I set before my mind, did not lack. Q. Maximus[1] lost a son of consular rank, high

409

rum virum et magnis rebus gestis, amisit, et L. Paullus, qui
duo septem diebus, et vester Galus et M. Cato, qui summo
ingenio, summa virtute filium perdidit, iis temporibus fuerunt ut eorum luctum ipsorum dignitas consolaretur, ea
2 quam ex re publica consequebantur. mihi autem, amissis
ornamentis iis quae ipse commemoras quaeque eram
maximis laboribus adeptus, unum manebat illud solacium
quod ereptum est. non amicorum negotiis, non rei publicae procuratione impediebantur cogitationes meae, nihil
in foro agere libebat, aspicere curiam non poteram, existimabam, id quod erat, omnis me et industriae meae fructus
et fortunae perdidisse. sed cum cogitarem haec mihi tecum et cum quibusdam esse communia et cum frangerem
iam ipse me cogeremque illa ferre toleranter, habebam
quo confugerem, ubi conquiescerem, cuius in sermone et
suavitate omnis curas doloresque deponerem.

Nunc autem hoc tam gravi vulnere etiam illa quae con-
sanuisse videbantur recrudescunt. non enim, ut tum me a
re publica maestum domus excipiebat quae levaret, sic
nunc domo maerens ad rem publicam confugere possum
ut in eius bonis acquiescam. itaque et domo absum et foro,
quod nec eum dolorem quem e re publica capio domus
iam consolari potest nec domesticum res publica.

3 Quo magis te exspecto teque videre quam primum
cupio. maior mihi <le>vatio [mihi][1] adferri[2] nulla potest
quam coniunctio consuetudinis sermonumque nostrorum;

[1] vatio mihi *(Man.)*
[2] adferre *(Crat.)*

---

[2] L. Aemilius Paullus, victor of Pydna.
[3] C. Sulpicius Galus was Consul in 166.

reputation, and splendid record. L. Paullus[2] lost two in a single week. Then there was Galus in your own family[3] and M. Cato,[4] who lost a son of the highest intellectual and moral qualities. But in those times their high standing derived from public life assuaged their mourning. I had already lost those distinctions which you yourself mention and which I had gained by dint of great exertions. The one comfort still left to me was that which has now been snatched away. Neither my friends' concerns nor the administration of the state detained my thoughts. I had no wish to appear in the courts, I could not endure the sight of the Senate House. I considered, as was the fact, that I had lost all the fruits of my work and success. However, I reflected that I shared this situation with yourself and certain others; I conquered my feelings and forced myself to bear it all patiently. But while I did so, I had a haven of refuge and repose, one in whose conversation and sweet ways I put aside all cares and sorrows.

Now this grievous blow has again inflamed the wounds I thought healed. When in the past I withdrew in sadness from public affairs, my home received and soothed me; but I cannot now take refuge from domestic grief in public life, to find relief in what it offers. And so I stay away from home and Forum alike, for neither public nor private life can any longer comfort the distress which each occasions me.

All the more then do I look forward to your return and desire to see you as soon as possible. Nothing can bring me greater comfort than our fellowship in daily life and talk.

---

[4] The Censor. Cicero had collected many such examples in his lost Consolation, addressed to himself.

quamquam sperabam tuum adventum (sic enim audiebam) appropinquare. ego autem cum multis de causis te
exopto quam primum videre tum etiam ut ante commen-
temur inter nos qua ratione nobis traducendum sit hoc
tempus, quod est totum ad unius voluntatem accommo-
dandum, et prudentis et liberalis et, ut perspexisse videor,
nec a me alieni et tibi amicissimi. quod cum ita sit, magnae
tamen est deliberationis quae ratio sit ineunda nobis non
agendi aliquid sed illius concessu et beneficio quiescendi.

Vale.

250 (IX.11)

Scr. in Attici Nomentano paulo post XII Kal. Mai. an. 45

CICERO DOLABELLAE S.

1   Vel meo ipsius interitu mallem litteras meas desidera-
res quam eo casu quo sum gravissime adflictus; quem ferrem certe moderatius si te haberem. nam et oratio tua
prudens et amor erga me singularis multum levaret. sed
quoniam brevi tempore, ut opinio nostra est, te sum visu-
rus, ita me adfectum offendes ut multum a te possim iuva-
ri; non quo ita sim fractus ut aut hominem me esse oblitus
sim aut Fortunae succumbendum putem, sed tamen hila-
ritas illa nostra et suavitas, quae te praeter ceteros delecta-
bat, erepta mihi omnis est; firmitatem tamen et constan-
tiam, si modo fuit aliquando in nobis, eandem cognosces
quam reliquisti.

However, from what I hear, I hope your arrival is imminent. One reason among many why I am anxious to see you as soon as may be is that I should like us to ponder together how we should best pass through this present time, all of which must be accommodated to the wishes of a single individual. He is a man of sense and generosity, and I think I have cause to believe him no enemy of mine and a very good friend of yours. Even so, what line we are to take needs careful consideration. I am not thinking of any positive action, but of retirement by his leave and favour.

Good-bye.

250 (IX.11)
CICERO TO DOLABELLA

Atticus' villa near Nomentum, shortly after 20 April 45

From Cicero to Dolabella greetings.

I would rather my failure to write had been due to my own death than to the grievous calamity which has come upon me. I should surely bear it less hard if I had you beside me. Your wise words and signal affection for me would be a great solace. However, I shall soon be seeing you, so we think here. You will find me in a state which offers plenty of scope for your assistance. Not that I am so far broken down as to forget my human lot or to think it right to sink under Fortune's blows. But the gaiety and charm which people saw in me, and you in particular used to find agreeable, is all swept away. My fortitude and resolution, however, if I ever possessed those qualities, you will recognize as no whit diminished.

2   Quod scribis proelia te mea causa sustinere, non tam id
laboro ut si qui mihi obtrectent a te refutentur quam intel-
legi cupio, quod certe intellegitur, me a te amari. quod ut
facias te etiam atque etiam rogo, ignoscasque brevitati litterarum mearum; nam et celeriter una futuros nos arbitror
et nondum satis sum confirmatus ad scribendum.

251 (V.14)

Scr. Romae c. VII Id. Mai. an. 45

L. LUCCEIUS Q. F. S. D. M. TULLIO M.F.

1   S. v. b.; e. v. sicut soleo, paululo tamen etiam deterius
quam soleo.

Te requisivi saepius ut viderem. Romae quia postea
non fuisti quam discesseras miratus sum, quod item nunc
miror. non habeo certum quae te res hinc maxime retrahat.
si solitudine delectare, cum scribas et aliquid agas eorum
quorum consuesti, gaudeo neque reprehendo tuum consilium. nam nihil isto potest esse iucundius non modo
miseris his temporibus et luctuosis sed etiam tranquillis et
optatis, praesertim vel animo defatigato tuo, qui nunc
requiem quaerat ex magnis occupationibus, vel erudito,
qui semper aliquid ex se promat quod alios delectet, ipsum
laudibus illustret.

---

1 Against his nephew, the younger Q. Cicero, now also with
Caesar's forces in Spain. Reports of his evil tongue had arrived
from other quarters; cf. *Letters to Atticus* 346 (XIII.37).2.

1 The studious avoidance of elision (confluence of final and
initial vowels) in this letter was first brought to light by C. T. H. R.

You tell me that you have to fight my battles.[1] I am less concerned that you should rebut my detractors than anxious that your affection for me should be recognized, as it surely is. Let me earnestly request you to act accordingly, and to forgive the brevity of this letter. I expect we shall shortly be together, and I have not yet sufficiently regained my strength for writing.

251 (V.14)
LUCCEIUS TO CICERO

Rome, ca. 9 May 45

From L. Lucceius, son of Quintus, to M. Tullius, son of Marcus, greetings.[1]

I hope you are well, as I am—that is, I am in my usual state of health, but just a little worse even than usual.

I have often asked after your whereabouts in the hope of seeing you. I was surprised that you have not been in Rome[2] since you left, and it still surprises me. What chiefly draws you away I am not sure. If you enjoy solitude while writing or engaged in one of your usual occupations, I am glad and make no criticism of your plan. Nothing can be more agreeable even in calm, prosperous times, let alone in these dark days of mourning, especially as yours is a weary mind, needing rest now from the heavy pressure of affairs, and a well-instructed one, ever creating something to delight others and shed lustre on yourself.

Ehrhard (*Mnemosyne* 38 (1985): 152f.; see also 40 (1987): 42f.), but the reason for it is a mystery. From his reply Cicero, like later readers, appears to have been unaware of it.

[2] I.e. even for a short visit.

2   Sin autem †sicut† hinc[1] discesseras,[2] lacrimis ac tris-
titiae te tradidisti, doleo quia doles et angere, non possum
te non, si concedis quod sentimus ut liberius dicamus, accusare. quid enim? tu solus aperta non videbis, qui propter
acumen occultissima perspicis? tu non intelleges te querelis cottidianis nihil proficere? non intelleges duplicari sollicitudines quas elevare tua te prudentia postulat?

3   Quod si non possumus aliquid proficere suadendo, gratia contendimus et rogando, si quid nostra causa vis, ut istis
te molestiis laxes et ad convictum nostrum redeas ⟨et⟩ ad
consuetudinem vel nostram communem vel tuam solius ac
propriam. cupio non obtundere te, si non delectare nostro
studio, cupio deterrere ne permaneas in incepto. †cum†[3]
duae res istae contrariae me conturbant, ex quibus aut in
altera mihi velim, si potes, obtemperes aut in altera non
offendas.

      Vale.

252 (V.15)

Scr. Asturae reddita ep. superiore

M. CICERO S. D. L. LUCCEIO Q. F.

1   Omnis amor tuus ex omnibus partibus se ostendit in iis
litteris quas a te proxime accepi, non ille quidem mihi
ignotus sed tamen gratus et optatus; dicerem 'iucundus'
nisi id verbum in omne tempus perdidissem, neque ob
eam unam causam quam tu suspicaris et in qua me lenissi-

---

[1] sicut hinc ⟨ante quam⟩ *coni. SB:* ut h- *Watt*
[2] dicas seras   [3] *del. Hunt: alii alia*

If, on the other hand, as before you left, you have abandoned yourself to tears and sorrow, I grieve in your grievous pain; but, if you allow me to speak my mind plainly, I cannot help taking you to task. For consider: Will you, whose intelligence pierces the darkest abstrusities, alone be blind to the obvious? Will you not understand that you gain nothing by constant complaining, that you double the cares which your good sense enjoins you to make lighter?

If advice can be of no avail, then I ask as a personal favour and beg of you, if you have any regard for me, to loose yourself from the bonds of your distresses and come back to live with us and to your normal way of life, both that which you share with the rest of us and that which is personal and peculiar to yourself. I am anxious not to importune you, if you find my concern irksome; and I am anxious to turn you from perseverance in this course. These two conflicting desires confuse me. As to the latter, I hope you will comply with my request, if you can; or else, as to the former, I hope you will take no offence.

Good-bye.

252 (V.15)
CICERO TO LUCCEIUS

Astura, in reply to the foregoing

From M. Cicero to L. Lucceius, son of Quintus, greetings.

All your affection stands revealed from every angle in the letter I have lately received from you, an affection not unknown to me indeed, but none the less welcome and wished for; I should say 'pleasant,' had I not lost that word forever. The reason is not only the one which you suspect,

mis et amantissimis verbis utens re graviter accusas, sed
quod illius tanti vulneris quae remedia esse debebant

2 ea nulla sunt. quid enim? ad amicosne confugiam? quam
multi sunt? habuimus enim fere communis; quorum alii
occiderunt, alii nescio quo pacto obduruerunt. tecum vivere possem equidem et maxime vellem. vetustas, amor,
consuetudo, studia paria—quod vinclum, quaeso, deest[1]
nostrae coniunctioni[s]? possumusne igitur esse una? nec
mehercule intellego quid impediat; sed certe adhuc non
fuimus, cum essemus vicini in Tusculano, in Puteolano.
nam quid dicam in urbe, in qua, cum forum commune sit,
vicinitas non requiritur?

3 Sed casu nescio quo in ea tempora nostra aetas incidit
ut, cum maxime florere nos oporteret, tum vivere etiam
puderet. quod enim esse poterat mihi perfugium spoliato
et domesticis et forensibus ornamentis atque solaciis? litterae, credo. quibus utor adsidue; quid enim aliud facere
possum? sed nescio quo modo ipsae illae excludere me a
portu et perfugio videntur et quasi exprobrare quod in ea
vita maneam in qua nihil insit nisi propagatio miserrimi
temporis.

4 Hic tu me abesse urbe miraris, in qua domus nihil delectare possit, summum sit odium temporum, hominum,
fori, curiae? itaque sic litteris utor, in quibus consumo
omne tempus, non ut ab iis medicinam perpetuam sed ut

5 exiguam oblivionem doloris petam. quod si id egissemus
ego atque tu quod ne in mentem quidem nobis veniebat
propter cottidianos metus ⟨et⟩[2] omne tempus una fuissemus, neque me valetudo tua offenderet neque te maeror
meus. quod, quantum fieri poterit, consequamur. quid

[1] quas idest *(Rost)*   [2] *(SB)*

and for which, in terms of the most loving gentleness, you take me in effect severely to task; it is also that the remedies appropriate to my grievous wound no longer exist. For consider: Am I to have recourse to my friends? How many do I have? You know, for most of them were yours too. Some have perished, others have somehow grown less feeling. With you, it is true, I could live, and should greatly so desire. Old acquaintance, affection, habit, community of pursuits—what tie, pray, is wanting to our attachment? Can we then be together? Upon my word, I do not know what hinders us. Yet the fact is that hitherto we have not been so, neighbours though we were at Tusculum and Puteoli—of Rome I say nothing, for where the Forum is common ground there is no need to live next door.

But by some malign chance my lot has fallen in times when, at what should be the crown of my career, life itself seems a dishonour. Bereft of embellishment and solace indoors and out, what refuge could I find? Literature, to be sure. I go to it constantly; what else am I to do? And yet it too seems somehow to bar my way to haven and refuge, and almost to reproach me for lingering in a life that has nothing to offer save the protraction of sad days.

In these circumstances are you surprised that I stay away from Rome, where my home can afford me no pleasure, while I am mortally weary of times and men, of Forum and Senate House? So I go to literature, on which I spend all my time, not looking for a lasting cure but only for brief forgetfulness of pain. But if you and I had done what continual alarms prevented us even thinking of, and had been always together, your health would be no burden to me nor my mourning to you. Let us, as far as may be,

enim est utrique nostrum aptius? propediem te igitur videbo.

253 (IV.12)

Scr. Athenis prid. Kal. Iun. an. 45

SERVIUS CICERONI S.P.

1   Etsi scio non iucundissimum me nuntium vobis adlaturum, tamen, quoniam casus et natura in nobis[1] dominatur, visum est faciendum, quoquo modo res se haberet, vos certiores facere.[2]

A. d. x Kal. Iun., cum ab Epidauro Piraeum navi advectus essem, ibi ‹M.› Marcellum, collegam nostrum, conveni eumque diem ibi consumpsi ut cum eo essem. postero die ‹cu›m ab eo digressus essem eo consilio ut ab Athenis in Boeotiam irem reliquamque iuris dictionem absolverem, ille, ut aiebat, supra Mal‹e›as[3] in Italiam versus navi-
2 gaturus erat. post diem tertium eius diei, cum ab Athenis proficisci in animo haberem, circiter hora decima noctis P. Postumius, familiaris eius, ad me venit et mihi nuntiavit M. Marcellum, collegam nostrum, post cenae tempus a P. Magio Cilone, familiare eius, pugione percussum esse et duo vulnera accepisse, unum in stomacho, alterum in capite secundum aurem; sperari[4] tamen eum vivere posse. Magium se ipsum interfecisse postea; se a Marcello ad me missum esse qui haec nuntiaret et rogaret uti medicos ei mitterem. itaque medicos coegi et e vestigio eo sum pro-

---

[1] bonis (R: omnibus *Pricaeus*)   [2] ‹ut› facerem *Man.*
[3] maias *(Man.)*   [4] sperare *(Baiter)*

bring that to pass. Both of us will surely find our account in it. I shall see you soon then.

253 (IV.12)
SERVIUS SULPICIUS RUFUS TO CICERO

Athens, 31 May 45

From Servius to Cicero cordial greetings.

I know that my news will not be of the most agreeable[1] to you and other friends. But chance and nature are our masters. Stand the matter how it may, I feel it my duty to inform you.

On 23 May I took ship from Epidaurus to Piraeus, where I met my colleague M. Marcellus, and spent the day there to be with him. I took leave of him the following day, intending to travel from Athens to Boeotia and wind up what remained of my assizes. He proposed, as he told me, to sail round Cape Malea towards Italy. Two days later I was about to set out from Athens, when about three o'clock in the morning a friend of his, P. Postumius, arrived to tell me that my colleague[2] M. Marcellus had been attacked with a dagger by P. Magius Cilo, a friend of his, after dinner, and had received two wounds, one in the stomach and one in the head behind the ear. It was hoped, however, that there was a chance for his life. Magius had later committed suicide, and he himself had been sent to me by Marcellus to tell me what had occurred and ask me to send him doctors. Accordingly, I collected some doctors and set out

---

[1] An odd meiosis; but Sulpicius' writing is not of the most sensitive.   [2] As Consul in 51.

fectus prima luce. cum non longe a Piraeo abessem, puer
Acidini obviam mihi venit cum codicillis in quibus erat
scriptum paulo ante lucem Marcellum diem suum obisse.
ita vir clarissimus ab homine deterrimo acerbissima morte
est adfectus et cui inimici propter dignitatem pepercerant
inventus est amicus qui ei mortem offerret.

3   Ego tamen ad tabernaculum eius perrexi. inveni duos
libertos et pauculos servos; reliquos aiebant profugisse
metu perterritos, quod dominus eorum ante tabernaculum interfectus esset. coactus sum in eadem illa lectica qua
ipse delatus eram meisque lecticariis in urbem eum referre, ibique pro ea copia quae Athenis erat funus ei satis
amplum faciendum curavi. ab Atheniensibus locum sepul-
turae intra urbem ut darent impetrare non potui quod reli-
gione se impediri dicerent, neque tamen id antea cuiquam
concesserant. quod proximum fuit, uti in quo vellemus
gymnasio eum sepeliremus, nobis permiserunt. nos in
nobilissimo orbi terrarum gymnasio Academiae locum
delegimus ibique eum combussimus posteaque curavimus
ut eidem Athenienses in eodem loco monumentum ei
marmoreum faciendum locarent. ita quae nostra officia
fuerunt pro collegio et pro propinquitate et vivo et mortuo
omnia ei praestitimus.

Vale.

D. prid. Kal. Iun. Athenis.

straight away for Piraeus as day broke. I was not far away, when a boy of Acidinus' met me on the road with a note which stated that Marcellus had breathed his last shortly before dawn. So a very eminent man has been tragically murdered by a villain. He was spared by the respect of his enemies only to meet his death at the hand of a friend.

None the less I proceeded to his tent. I found two freedmen and a handful of slaves. They said the rest had fled in a panic, because their master had been killed in front of his tent. I had to bring him back to the city in the litter in which I myself had travelled, using my own bearers; and there I saw to his funeral, on as handsome a scale as the resources of Athens could provide. I could not induce the townspeople to grant him burial within the city precincts; they pleaded a religious bar, and it is a fact that they had never given such permission in the past. The next best thing they did allow, to bury him in a public hall, whichever I wished. So I chose a spot in the most celebrated hall in the world, the Academy. There we cremated him, and I later saw to it that the people of Athens should arrange for the erection of a monument to him in marble on the spot. So I have done all that in me lay for my colleague and kinsman, in life and in death.

Good-bye.

Dispatched 31 May, Athens.

254 (IX.8)

Scr. in Tusculano c. v Id. Quint. an. 45

CICERO VARRONI

1   Etsi munus flagitare, quamvis quis ostenderit, ne populus quidem solet nisi concitatus, tamen ego exspectatione
promissi tui moveor ut admoneam te, non ut flagitem. misi
autem ad te quattuor admonitores non nimis verecundos;
nosti enim profecto os huius[1] adulescentioris Academiae.
ex ea igitur media excitatos misi; qui metuo ne te forte
flagitent, ego autem mandavi ut rogarent. exspectabam
omnino iam diu meque sustinebam ne ad te prius ipse quid
scriberem quam aliquid accepissem, ut possem te remu-
nerari quam simillimo munere. sed cum tu tardius faceres,
id est, ut ego interpretor, diligentius, teneri non potui quin
coniunctionem studiorum amorisque nostri, quo possem
litterarum genere, declararem. feci igitur sermonem inter
nos habitum in Cumano, cum esset una Pomponius. tibi
dedi partis Antiochinas, quas a te probari intellexisse mihi
videbar, mihi sumpsi Philonis. puto fore ut, cum legeris,

---

[1] eius *(Lamb.)*

---

[1] This letter, of which Cicero wrote to Atticus (333 (XIII.25).3)
that he would never take so much trouble over anything again,
accompanied the presentation of the four Books of his dialogue
Academic Questions. Varro had a major role in the final version.

[2] *Munus* has the double meaning of 'present' and 'show'; cf.
Letter 47.

[3] Several years previously Varro had promised to dedicate his

254 (IX.8)
CICERO TO VARRO

Tusculum, ca. 11 July 45

From Cicero to Varro.[1]

To dun a man for a present, though promised, is in poor taste—even the crowd does not demand a show[2] unless stirred up to it. None the less my impatience for the fulfilment of your promise[3] impels me—not to dun, but to remind you. And I am sending you four monitors[4] not of the most bashful. I am sure you know how assertive this younger Academy[5] can be; well, the quartet I am sending you has been summoned from its headquarters. I am afraid they *may* dun you, but I have charged them to *request*. To be sure, I have been waiting quite a while and holding back, so as not to address a piece to you before I received one and thus repay you as nearly as possible in your own coin. But since you are proceeding rather slowly (and that is to say, as I interpret, carefully), I could not refrain from advertising the bond of common pursuits and affection between us by such a form of composition as lay within my powers. Accordingly, I have staged a conversation between us at Cumae, Pomponius also being present. I have assigned the exposition of Antiochus' tenets (being under the impression that you approve of them) to your role, that of Philo's to my own. I dare say you will be surprised when

work *On the Latin Language* to Cicero; cf. *Letters to Atticus* 320 (XIII.12).2.

[4] The four Books of the *Academic Questions*.

[5] The sceptical school of Arcesilas and Carneades. Elsewhere Cicero calls it the 'New Academy.'

mirere nos id locutos esse inter nos quod numquam locuti
2 sumus, sed nosti morem dialogorum. posthac autem, mi
Varro, quam plurima, si videtur, et [de]² nobis inter nos,
sero fortasse; sed superiorum temporum Fortuna rei publicae causam sustineat, haec ipsi praestare debemus. atque
utinam quietis temporibus atque aliquo, si non bono, at
saltem certo statu civitatis haec inter nos studia exercere
possemus! quamquam tum quidem vel aliae quaepiam
rationes honestas nobis et curas et actiones darent; nunc
autem quid est sine his cur vivere velimus? mihi vero cum
his ipsis vix, his autem detractis ne vix quidem. sed haec
coram et saepius.

Migrationem et emptionem feliciter evenire volo tu-
umque in ea re consilium probo. cura ut valeas.

255 (V.9)

Scr. in castris Naronae v Id. Quint. an. 45
VATINIUS IMP. CICERONI SUO S.
1   S. v. b.; e. e. ‹q.›¹ v.
Si tuam consuetudinem in patrociniis tuendis servas, P.
Vatinius cliens advenit qui pro se causam dicier vult. non,
puto, repudiabis in honore quem in periculo recepisti. ego
autem quem potius adoptem aut invocem quam illum quo

² (*SB, qui etiam* et nobiscum et *coni.*)
¹ (*SB*)

you read to find that you and I have discussed a subject which in fact we have never discussed; but you know the conventions of Dialogue. In future, my dear Varro, we shall have talks in plenty, if so minded, between ourselves and to please ourselves. Late in the day perhaps. But let the Fortune of the commonwealth answer for what is past; the present is our own responsibility. If only we could pursue these studies together in peaceful times and a settled, if not satisfactory, state of the community! And yet, if that were so, there would be other claims upon us, calling us to honourable responsibilities and tasks. As matters stand, why should we desire life without our studies? For my part, I have little enough desire for it even with them; take them away, and I should lack even that little. But all this we will talk over together and often.

All good luck to your change of residence and your new purchase. I think you are doing wisely. Take care of your health.

255 (V.9)

VATINIUS TO CICERO

Camp at Narona, 11 July 45

From Vatinius, Imperator, to his friend Cicero greetings.

I trust you are well, as I am and my army.

Do you keep up your practice of standing by old clients? If so, here comes one of them by the name of P. Vatinius, who wants an advocate to take his case! Surely you won't turn your back now he stands well in the world after taking him on when it was touch and go. As for me, whom should I choose and turn to but my old defender,

defendente vincere didici? an verear ne, qui potentissimo-
rum hominum conspirationem neglexerit pro mea salute,
is pro honore meo pusillorum ac malevolorum obtrectatio-
nes et invidias non prosternat atque obterat?

Qua re, si me, sicut soles, amas, suscipe meme totum
atque hoc, quicquid est, oneris ac muneris pro mea dignitate tibi tuendum ac sustinendum puta. scis meam fortunam nescio quo modo facile obtrectatores invenire, non
meo quidem mehercules merito; sed quanti id refert, si tamen fato nescio quo accidit? si qui forte fuerit qui nostrae
dignitati obesse velit, peto a te ut tuam consuetudinem et
liberalitatem in me absente defendendo mihi praestes.
litteras ad senatum de rebus nostris gestis, quo exemplo
miseram, infra tibi perscripsi.

2   Dicitur mihi tuus servus anagnostes fugitivus cum Var-
daeis esse. de quo tu mihi nihil mandasti, ego tamen terra
marique ut conquireretur praemandavi et profecto tibi
illum reperiam, nisi si in Dalmatiam aufugerit; et inde
tamen aliquando eruam.

Tu nos fac ames. Vale.

A. d. v Id.[2] Quint. ex castris Narona.

[2] l.d.v.l.d. (*Lamb.*)

who taught me how to win? When I think what a combination of powerful persons you disregarded to save my life, I can hardly doubt your readiness to smash and squash a set of petty backbiters with their spiteful tittle-tattle, when it's for an honour.[1]

Well then, if you love me as you usually do, let me put myself wholly in your hands. Look upon this load, such as it is, as yours to shoulder, a task you ought to perform for the sake of my standing. You know that somehow or other my career is apt to find tongues to carp at it—truly no fault of mine, but what difference does that make if the thing happens just the same, fated somehow? If anyone *does* show a disposition to stand in my light, may I ask you to defend me in my absence with no less than your usual generosity? I am appending the text of my dispatch to the Senate on my military operations for your perusal.

They tell me that a runaway slave[2] of yours, a reader, is with the Vardaei. You gave me no commission about him, but I have none the less issued instructions in advance that he be searched for by land and sea, and no doubt I shall find him for you, unless he has made off into Dalmatia—though even there I shall winkle him out sooner or later.

Don't forget me. Good-bye.

11 July, from camp at Narona.

[1] A Supplication for Vatinius' military successes in Illyricum.
[2] Cf. Letter 212.3.

256 (V.10c)[1]

Scr. Naronae parte priore m. Nov., ut vid., an. 45

<VATINIUS CICERONI SUO S.>

Caesar adhuc mi iniuriam facit. de meis supplicationibus et rebus gestis Dalmaticis adhuc non refert, quasi vero non iustissimi triumphi in Dalmatia res gesserim. nam si hoc exspectandum est, dum totum bellum conficiam, viginti oppida sunt Dalmatiae antiqua, quae ipsi sibi adsciverunt amplius sexaginta. haec nisi omnia expugno si mihi supplicationes non decernuntur, longe alia condicione ego sum ac ceteri imperatores.

257 (V.11)

Scr. Romae parte priore m. Dec., ut vid., an. 45

M. CICERO VATINIO IMP. S.

1   Grata tibi mea esse officia non miror; cognovi enim te gratissimum omnium idque numquam destiti praedicare. nec enim tu mihi habuisti modo gratiam verum etiam cumulatissime rettulisti. quam ob rem <in>[1] reliquis tuis rebus omnibus pari me studio erga te et eadem voluntate cognosces.

2   Quod mihi feminam primariam, Pompeiam, uxorem

1 *cum 259 coniungit* M *(SB)*
1 *(Mart.)*

256 (V.10c)
VATINIUS TO CICERO

Narona, early November 45 (?)

From Vatinius to his friend Cicero greetings

Caesar is treating me badly so far. He is still not putting the motion about my Supplications and my Dalmatian successes. One might think I had not done fully enough in Dalmatia to entitle me to a Triumph![1] Or am I supposed to wait until I have finished the whole war? Dalmatia has twenty towns of ancient foundation, more than sixty adopted later into the confederacy. If no Supplications are decreed me until I take them all, then I am on a very different footing from other generals.

257 (V.11)
CICERO TO VATINIUS

Rome, early December (?) 45

From M. Cicero to Vatinius, Imperator, greetings.

It is no surprise to me to find you appreciative of my good offices, for I know you of old as the most grateful of mankind, and I have never been behindhand in proclaiming it. You not only felt but showed your gratitude to me in deed, and in more than ample measure. Accordingly, in all your future concerns you shall find my devotion no less and my sentiments towards you unchanged.

As soon as I had read your letter, in which you com-

[1] Vatinius was finally granted a Triumph by the Triumvirs in 42.

tuam, commendas, cum Sura nostro statim tuis litteris lectis locutus sum ut ei meis verbis diceret ut, quicquid opus
esset, mihi denuntiaret; me omnia quae ea vellet summo
studio curaque facturum. itaque faciam eamque, si opus
esse videbitur, ipse conveniam. tu tamen ei velim scribas
ut nullam rem neque tam magnam neque tam parvam putet quae mihi aut difficilis aut parum me digna videatur.
omnia quae in tuis rebus agam et non laboriosa mihi et
honesta videbuntur.

3   De Dionysio, si me amas, confice. quamcumque ei
fidem dederis, praestabo; si vero improbus fuerit, ut est,
duces eum captivum in triumpho. Dalmatis di male faciant
qui tibi molesti sunt! sed, ut scribis, brevi capientur et
illustrabunt res tuas gestas; semper enim habiti sunt bel-
licosi.

258 (V.10b)

Scr. Naronae Non. Dec. an. 45

⟨VATINIUS CICERONI SUO S.⟩

    Ego post supplicationes mihi decretas in Dalmatiam
profectus sum. sex oppida vi oppugnando cepi, unum horum,[1] quod erat maximum, quater a me iam captum; quattuor enim turris et quattuor muros cepi et arcem eorum
totam. ex qua me nives, frigora, imbres detruserunt, in-
digneque, mi Cicero, oppidum captum et bellum confectum relinquere sum coactus. qua re te rogo, si opus erit, ad
Caesarem meam causam agas meque tibi in omnis partis

[1] hoc *(Goodyear)*

mend to me your excellent lady Pompeia, I had a word with our friend Sura and asked him to tell her from me to let me know of any service she might require, and to promise that I should give my most sedulous endeavours to perform her wishes. And so I shall, and, if need appears, I shall see her in person. But will you please write and tell her that she must not consider anything too big or too small? I shall find nothing too difficult and nothing beneath my attention. No part I take in your affairs will appear to me either troublesome or unbecoming.

Do please settle this affair of Dionysius. I shall honour any undertaking you make him. But if he behaves like the scoundrel he is, you shall lead him captive at your Triumph. Deuce take these Dalmatians, who are giving you so much trouble! But, as you say, they will soon be in the bag and will shed lustre on your successes, for they have always been accounted a warrior race.

258 (V.10b)
VATINIUS TO CICERO

Narona, 5 December 45

From Vatinius to his friend Cicero greetings.

After the Supplications in my honour were decreed, I set out for Dalmatia. I took six towns by storm: The single town of ∗, the biggest of the lot, was captured by me four times over, for I took four towers and four walls and their whole citadel, from which snow, frost, and rain dislodged me. Thus, my dear Cicero, I had to leave the town I had taken and the war I had won; it was too bad. Please plead my cause with Caesar, if need arises, and regard me as

defendendum putes, hoc existimans, neminem te tui
amantiorem habere.

Vale.

D. Non. Dec. Narona.

259 (V.10a)

Scr. Naronae m. Ian. an. 44

VATINIUS CICERONI SUO S.

1   S. v. b.; e. e. q. v.

De Dionysio tuo adhuc nihil extrico, et eo minus quod
me frigus Dalmaticum, quod illinc eiecit, etiam hic re-
frigeravit. sed tamen non desistam quin illum aliquando
eruam. sed tamen omnia mi dura imperas. De Catilio nescio quid ad me scripsisti deprecationis diligentissimae.
apage te cum nostro Sex. Servilio! nam mehercule ego
quoque illum amo. sed huiusce modi vos clientis, huius
modi causas recipitis? hominem unum omnium crudelissi-
mum, qui tot ingenuos, matresfamilias, civis Romanos occidit, abripuit, disperdidit, regiones vastavit? simius, non
semissis homo, contra me arma tulit et eum bello cepi.

2   Sed tamen, mi Cicero, quid facere possum? omnia
mehercule cupio quae tu mi imperas. meam animadver-
sionem et supplicium quo usurus eram in eum quem
cepissem remitto tibi et condono: quid illis respondere
possum qui sua bona direpta, navis expugnatas, fratres,

yours to defend on all fronts, believing that you have no more devoted friend than me.

Good-bye.

Dispatched Nones of December, from Narona.

259 (V.10a)
VATINIUS TO CICERO

Narona, January 44

From Vatinius to his friend Cicero greetings.

I trust you are well, as am I and my army.

So far I cannot fish anything out about your man Dionysius, especially as the Dalmatian cold, which drove me out from there, has frozen me up here too. But I shall not give up till sooner or later I winkle him out. But you are a hard taskmaster! You write me what reads like a very earnest intercession on behalf of Catilius. Get along with you, and our friend Sex. Servilius too! Upon my word, I think a lot of him, as you do. But is this the kind of client and case you people take on—a monster of savagery, who has murdered and kidnapped and ruined all those freeborn men and matrons and Roman citizens, and laid whole districts waste? This ape, this worthless ruffian, bore arms against me, and I took him prisoner of war.

But really, my dear Cicero, what can I do? Upon my word, I am anxious to obey your every command. My own right to inflict condign punishment upon him as my captive, which I was going to exercise, I forgo in deference to your request. But what am I to say to those who demand redress by process of law for the plunder of their property, the seizure of their ships, the slaughter of brothers, chil-

liberos, parentis occisos actione[1] expostulant? si mehercules Appi os haberem, in cuius locum suffectus sum,
tamen hoc sustinere non possem. quid ergo est? faciam
omnia sedulo quae te sciam velle. defenditur a Q. Volusio,
tuo discipulo, si forte ea res poterit adversarios fugare. in
eo maxima spes est.

3   Nos, si quid erit istic opus, defendes.

260 (VII.24)

Scr. in Tusculano XI *vel* X *Kal. Sept. an. 45*

M. CICERO S. D. M. FABIO GALLO

1   Amoris quidem tui, quoquo me verti, vestigia, vel
proxime de Tigellio; sensi enim ex litteris tuis valde te labo-
rasse. amo igitur voluntatem. sed pauca de re. Cipius, opinor, olim 'non omnibus dormio.' sic ego non omnibus, mi
Galle, servio. etsi quae est haec servitus? olim, cum reg-
nare existimabamur, non tam ab ullis quam hoc tempore
observor a familiarissimis Caesaris omnibus praeter istum.
id ego in lucris pono, non ferre hominem pestilentiorem

---

[1] actiones (*Rut.*)

---

[1] Literally 'into whose place I was elected.' Vatinius had
succeeded to the vacancy in the College of Augurs left by Ap.
Pulcher's death in 48.

[2] He may have taken lessons in declamation from Cicero, like
Hirtius and Dolabella.

[1] On this see *Letters to Atticus* 347 (XIII.49).

[2] The story (or an allusion to it) could be found in Lucilius.

dren, and parents? Upon my word, I could not face it out, not if I had the impudence of Appius, whose shoes I wear.[1] Well then, I shall spare no pains to meet your wishes, as I know them. He is defended by Q. Volusius, a pupil of yours[2]—perhaps that circumstance may rout the other side. There lies the best hope.

You will defend me in Rome, if need arises.

260 (VII.24)
CICERO TO M. FABIUS GALLUS

Tusculum, 22 or 23 August 45

From M. Cicero to M. Fabius Gallus greetings.

Everywhere I turn I come across traces of your affection, as most recently in the affair of Tigellius.[1] I could see from your letter that you have been very much concerned. So I thank you for the kind intention. But on the matter itself, one or two observations. Cipius I think it was who said on a certain occasion 'I am not asleep to everybody.'[2] Just so, my dear Gallus, I am not a slave to everybody. Though I don't know why I talk of slavery. In the old days, when I was supposed to be a monarch,[3] I was never so courted as I now am by Caesar's closest intimates, all except your friend. I consider myself so much the gainer, not to have to put up with the fellow—more pestilential than his native cli-

Cipius pretended to be asleep at dinner so that he could ignore his wife's misbehaviour. But when a slave tried to make off with some wine, he started up with the words quoted.

[3] Cf. *Letters to Atticus* 16 (I.6).10, where Clodius asks his mob 'How long shall we put up with this monarch?'

patria sua, eumque addictum iam tum puto esse Calvi Licini Hipponacteo praeconio.

2   At vide quid suscenseat. Phameae causam receperam, ipsius quidem causa; erat enim mihi sane familiaris. is ad me venit dixitque iudicem sibi operam dare constituisse eo ipso die quo de P. Sestio in consilium iri necesse erat. respondi nullo modo me facere posse; quem vellet alium diem si sumpsisset, me ei non defuturum. ille autem, qui sciret se nepotem bellum tibicinem habere et sat bonum cantorem,[1] discessit a me, ut mi videbatur, iratior. habes 'Sardos venalis, alium alio nequiorem.' cognosti meam causam et istius salaconis iniquitatem.

'Catonem' tuum mihi mitte; cupio enim legere. me adhuc non legisse turpe utrique nostrum est.

261 (VII.25)

Scr. in Tusculano c. IX Kal. Sept. an. 45

CICERO S. D. M. FABIO GALLO

1   Quod epistulam conscissam doles, noli laborare. salva

[1] unctorem *(Man.)**

---

[4] Sardinia was notoriously unhealthy.

[5] Calvus had composed a lampoon upon Tigellius after the manner and in the metre of the sixth-century Hipponax of Ephesus. The first line is preserved: 'Sardinian Tigellius for sale— stinking goods!'

[6] Sestius was accused of electoral corruption in 52.

[7] If *unctorem* (anointer) is right (so 'a tolerable hand with the

mate![4] I regard him as knocked down to the highest bidder all those years ago in Calvus Licinius' Hipponactean advertisement![5]

However, let me tell you about his grievance. I had taken on Phamea's case, for his own sake—he was quite a friend of mine. He came and told me that the judge had fixed a day for the hearing, being the very day that the jury had to consider their verdict in P. Sestius' case.[6] I replied that I could not possibly manage it; if he picked any other day he liked, I should not fail him. However, conscious of having a nephew, a pretty performer on the flute and a tolerable singer,[7] he took his leave, in something of a huff, I thought. So there you are: 'Sardinians for sale, each worse than t'other.'[8] You now know my side, and can see how unreasonable this beggar on horseback is being.

Send me your 'Cato'[9]—I am anxious to read it. It's a disgrace to us both that I have not read it already.

261 (VII.25)
CICERO TO M. FABIUS GALLUS

Tusculum, ca. 24 August 45

From Cicero to M. Fabius Gallus greetings.

Don't distress yourself about the letter which you are so

oil can') there may be a reference to athletes' training, but I now prefer Manutius' conjecture *cantorem* (singer).

[8] A proverb quoted elsewhere and variously interpreted.

[9] After Cato's death in April 46 there was a brisk output of pamphlets for and against his character and record. Cicero's had appeared about a year previously.

est; domo petes cum libebit. quod autem me mones, valde
gratum est idque ut semper facias rogo. videris enim mihi
vereri ne, si istum ‹ludibrio›[1] habuerimus, rideamus γέ-
λωτα σαρδάνιον.

Sed heus tu, manum de tabula! magister adest citius
quam putaramus. vereor ne in catomum Catoni‹a›nos.[2]

2   Mi Galle, cave putes quicquam melius quam epistulae
tuae partem ab eo loco, 'cetera labuntur.' secreto hoc audi,
tecum habeto, ne Apellae quidem, liberto tuo, dixeris.
praeter duo nos loquitur isto modo nemo; bene malene
videro, sed, quicquid est, nostrum est. urge igitur nec
transversum unguem, quod aiunt, a stilo; is enim est dicendi opifex. atque equidem aliquantum iam etiam noctis
adsumo.

262 (VI.19)

Scr. Asturae c. v *Kal. Sept. an. 45*

CICERO LEPTAE

1   Maculam officio functum esse gaudeo. eius Falernum

---

[1] *(Streicher: alii alia)*   [2] *(Corr.)*

---

[1] I.e. a copy. The letter was probably Letter 260.

[2] The Greek phrase *sardonion gelan,* 'to laugh scornfully' or
'bitterly' ('the wrong side of one's mouth'), was variously explained
in antiquity. Cicero of course alludes to the Sardinian origin of
Tigellius.   [3] Literally 'hands off the tablet.' When the schoolmaster comes in the boys must stop writing their exercise. The
schoolmaster here is Caesar.

sorry you tore up. I have it safe at home.[1] You can ask for it any time you like. As for your word of warning, I'm very grateful, and hope you will always so favour me. Apparently you are afraid that, if we make mock of your friend, we may come to laugh—*sard*onically![2]

Attention now! No more writing![3] Here comes the beak, sooner than expected! It's the cat for Catonians, I fear.

My dear Gallus, that part of your letter from 'all goes downhill' onwards—depend upon it, its the best thing ever. This for your private ear, keep it to yourself—not a word to your freedman Apella even. Nobody but us two talks in this style—good or bad; that's another question; but whatever it is, it's ours. So press on and don't budge a nail's breadth, as they say, from your pen. The pen makes the author! For my own part, I work o'nights nowadays as well as in the daytime.

262 (VI.19)
CICERO TO LEPTA

Astura, ca. 28 August 45

From Cicero to Lepta.

Glad to hear that Macula[1] has behaved as he should. I

---

[1] Probably a relative of Lepta who had died leaving him money; cf. the beginning of *Letters to Atticus* 65 (III.20). Lepta seems to have suggested that Cicero might like to acquire part of the estate, a small property in the Falernian district eastward of Sinuessa, as a lodge for use on his journeys up and down the Appian Way; cf. Letter 339.

mihi semper idoneum visum est deversorio, si modo tecti satis est ad comitatum nostrum recipiendum. ceteroqui mihi locus non displicet. nec ea re Petrinum tuum deseram; nam et villa et amoenitas illa commorationis est, non deversori.

2   De curatione aliqua munerum regiorum cum Oppio locutus sum; nam Balbum, postea quam tu es profectus, non vidi. tantis pedum doloribus adficitur ut se conveniri nolit. omnino de tota re, ut mihi videris, sapientius faceres si non curares. quod enim eo labore adsequi vis nullo modo adsequere. tanta est enim intimorum multitudo ut ex iis aliquis potius effluat quam novo sit aditus, praesertim qui nihil adferat praeter operam, in qua ille se dedisse beneficium putabit, si modo ⟨id⟩ ipsum sciet, non accepisse. sed tamen aliquid videbimus in quo sit species. aliter quidem non modo non appetendum sed etiam fugiendum puto.

Ego me Asturae diutius arbitror commoraturum quoad ille ⟨qua⟩[1] quandoque veniat.

Vale.

[1] (SB)

always thought his Falernian place suitable for a lodge, provided there is enough shelter for my entourage. In other respects I don't dislike the place. But I shall not on that account give up your Petrine establishment—the house and amenities generally are for residence, not just a lodge.

I have spoken to Oppius about a Curatorship of the royal shows[2] (Balbus I have not seen since you left; the gout in his feet is so bad that he doesn't want visitors). To be sure, I think you would be wiser to forget the whole thing. You will stand no chance of gaining the object for which you put yourself to such drudgery. He[3] has so many intimates that there is more likelihood of one dropping out than of any opening for a newcomer, especially one who has nothing to contribute except his services; and as for them, he will think he has conferred a favour (if he so much as knows of it) rather than received one. However, we'll try to find something that looks good; otherwise I think that, far from seeking such employment, you should steer clear of it.

I think I shall stay at Astura until I learn his route and time of arrival.

Good-bye.

[2] Cf. *Letters to Atticus* 338 (XIII.46).2. 'Royal,' of course, is a hostile reference to Caesar, called *rex* in *Letters to Atticus* 346 (XIII.37).2.

[3] Caesar.

263 (IX.12)

Scr. in villa sua aliqua fort. m. Dec. an. 45

CICERO DOLABELLAE

1   Gratulor Baiis nostris si quidem, ut scribis, salubres repente factae sunt; nisi forte te amant et tibi adsentantur et tam diu dum tu ades sunt oblitae sui. quod quidem si ita est, minime miror caelum etiam et terras vim suam, si tibi ita conveniat, dimittere.

2   Oratiunculam pro Deiotaro, quam requirebas, habebam mecum, quod non putaram. itaque eam tibi misi. quam velim sic legas ut causam tenuem et inopem nec scriptione magno opere dignam. sed ego hospiti veteri et amico munusculum mittere volui, levidense crasso filo, cuius modi ipsius solent esse munera.

Tu velim animo sapienti fortique sis, ut tua moderatio et gravitas aliorum infamet iniuriam.

264 (VII.29)

Scr. Patris IV *Kal. Nov. an. 45*

CURIUS M. CICERONI SUUS[1] S.

1   S. v. b.

[1] (*SB**, *qui etiam* SUO ‹VEL POTIUS SUUS› *coni.*)

[1] Oddly enough, this most celebrated of Roman resorts was considered unhealthy, as confirmed by Symmachus, *Letters* 7.24. The suggestion in my Commentary is therefore cancelled.

263 (IX.12)
CICERO TO DOLABELLA

A villa, December 45 (?)

From Cicero to Dolabella.

I congratulate our Baiae if, as you say, it has suddenly become a healthy spot.[1] But perhaps it is out of fondness and flattery towards yourself; perhaps the place has forgotten its nature so long as you are there. If that is the explanation, I am not in the least surprised that even air and soil put aside their natural properties for your benefit.

Contrary to what I thought, I find I have with me the little speech in defence of Deiotarus[2] which you were asking for, and so I am sending it to you. Please bear in mind, when you read it, that the case was a meagre, paltry affair, hardly worth writing up. But I wanted to send my old friend and host a little present—on the light, coarse-spun side, as his own presents are apt to be.

I wish you good sense and courage, so that your moderation and responsibility will bring shame on the misconduct of others.

264 (VII.29)
MANIUS CURIUS TO CICERO

Patrae, 29 October 45

From his friend Curius to M. Cicero greetings.

I trust you are well.

---

[2] Accused of an attempt on Caesar's life. Cicero's defence survives.

Sum enim χρήσει μὲν tuus, κτήσει δὲ Attici nostri.
ergo fructus est tuus, mancipium illius; quod quidem si
inter senes comptionalis[2] venale proscripserit, egerit non
multum. at illa nostra praedicatio quanti est, nos quod
simus, quod habeamus, quod homines existimemur, id
omne abs te habere! qua re, Cicero mi, persevera constanter nos conservare et Sulpici successori nos de meliore
nota commenda, quo facilius tuis praeceptis obtemperare
possimus teque ad ver libentes videre et nostra refigere
deportareque tuto possimus.

2   Sed, amice magne, noli hanc epistulam Attico ostend-
dere. sine eum errare et putare me virum bonum esse nec
solere duo parietes de eadem fidelia dealbare.

Ergo, patrone mi, bene vale Tironemque meum saluta
nostris verbis.

Data a.d. IIII Kal. Nov.

265 (VII.30)

Scr. Romae in. an. 44

CICERO CURIO S. D.

1   Ego vero iam te nec hortor nec rogo ut domum redeas;
quin hinc ipse evolare cupio et aliquo pervenire

ubi nec Pelopidarum nomen nec facta audiam.

incredibile est quam turpiter mihi facere videar qui his re-

---

2 coempt- *Vict.*

---

1 On *senes comptionales* see my Commentary.

I say '*his* friend,' for I am yours in usufruct, though I belong to our good Atticus by right of ownership. You have the enjoyment, and he the title. If he puts the goods up for sale as a job lot,[1] he won't get much by it. But *I* advertise that everything I am and have, my entire place in society, comes from you. That's worth something! So, Cicero mine, carry on your good work. Keep me in good shape, and give me a first-class recommendation to Sulpicius' successor,[2] thus making it easier for me to obey your precepts, and see you gladly come spring, and pull up stakes here, and take my all safely home.

Only, exalted friend, please don't show Atticus this letter. Leave him in his delusion. Let him go on thinking me a man of honour, not one to cover two walls from the same pot of whitewash.

And so, patron mine, a very good day to you. Give my regards to my good friend Tiro.

Dispatched 29 October.

265 (VII.30)
CICERO TO MANIUS CURIUS

Rome, beginning of 44

From Cicero to Curius greetings.

Not so. I no longer urge you or ask you to come home. On the contrary, I am anxious to take wing myself and go to some place 'where nevermore of Pelops' line I'll hear the name or deeds.'[1] You cannot imagine the sense of personal

---

[2] As governor of Achaea. His name was Acilius (Letter 266).
[1] See Letter 200.2.

bus intersim. ne tu videris multo ante providisse quid im-
penderet tum cum hinc profugisti. quamquam haec etiam
auditu acerba sunt, tamen audire tolerabilius est quam videre. in campo certe non fuisti cum hora secunda comitiis
quaestori<i>s institutis sella Q. Maximi, quem illi consulem esse dicebant, posita esset;[1] quo mortuo nuntiato sella
sublata est. ille autem, qui comitiis tributis esset auspica-
tus, centuriata habuit, consulem hora septima renuntiavit,
qui usque ad Kal. Ian. esset quae erant futurae mane postridie. ita Caninio consule scito neminem prandisse. nihil
tamen eo consule mali factum est; fuit enim mirifica
2   vigilantia, qui suo toto consulatu somnum non viderit.
haec tibi ridicula videntur; non enim ades. quae si videres,
lacrimas non teneres. qui<d> si cetera scribam? sunt enim
innumerabilia generis eiusdem. quae quidem ego non
ferrem nisi me in philosophiae portum contulissem et nisi
haberem socium studiorum meorum Atticum nostrum.
cuius quoniam proprium te esse scribis mancipio et nexo,
meum autem usu et fructu, contentus isto sum. id enim est
cuiusque proprium quo quisque fruitur atque utitur. sed
haec alias pluribus.

3   Acilius, qui in Graeciam cum legionibus missus est,
maximo meo beneficio est (bis enim est a me iudicio capitis
rebus salvis defensus) et est homo non ingratus meque vehementer observat. ad eum de te diligentissime scripsi

---

[1] est *Man.*

---

[2] Caesar.

[3] For the election of a Consul. Quaestors were elected by the
Assembly of Tribes.

[4] C. Caninius Rebilus.

dishonour I feel at living in the Rome of today. Farsighted
indeed you turn out to have been when you fled this country. Although the happenings here are painful enough in
the report, yet it is more tolerable to hear of them than to
see them. At least you were not in the Campus when the
elections to the Quaestorship began at nine o'clock in the
morning. A chair of state had been placed for Q. Maximus,
whom these people used to call Consul. His death was an-
nounced, and the chair removed. Whereupon *he*,[2] having
taken auspices for an assembly of the Tribes, held an assembly of the Centuries,[3] and at one o'clock of the afternoon declared a Consul elected, to remain in office until
the Kalends of January, the next morning that was to be.
So in the Consulship of Caninius[4] you may take it that
nobody had breakfast! However, at any rate no crime was
committed during the same period—the Consul's vigi-
lance was extraordinary. Throughout his entire term of office he never closed an eye! You find such things laughable,
for you are not on the spot; if you were here to witness, you
would have to weep. What if I were to tell you the rest? In-
cidents of the same character are innumerable. I could not
bear them, if I had not brought my boat into the harbour of
philosophy, and if I did not have our dear Atticus to share
my pursuits. You say you belong to him by legal ownership,
but to me by use and enjoyment. I am quite satisfied with
that position. What a man uses and enjoys *is* what belongs
to him. But of this more anon.

Acilius, who has been sent to Greece with an army, is
under a great obligation to me, having been twice defended by me in better days on a capital charge. He is not
without a sense of gratitude, and pays me many attentions.
I have written to him on your behalf with all care and am

449

eamque epistulam cum hac epistula coniunxi. quam ille quo modo acceperit et quid tibi pollicitus sit velim ad me scribas.

266 (XIII.50)

Scr. Romae in. an. 44

CICERO S. D. ACILIO[1]

1   Sumpsi hoc mihi pro tua in me observantia, quam penitus perspexi quam diu Brundisi fuimus, ut ad te familiariter et quasi pro meo iure scriberem si quae res esset de qua valde laborarem.

2   M'. Curius, qui Patris negotiatur, ita mihi familiaris est ut nihil possit esse coniunctius. multa illius in me officia, multa in illum mea, quodque maximum est, summus inter nos amor et mutuus. quae cum ita sint, si ullam in amicitia mea spem habes, si ea quae in me officia et studia Brundisi contulisti vis mihi etiam gratiora efficere, quamquam sunt gratissima, si me a tuis omnibus amari vides, hoc mihi da atque largire, ut M'. Curium sartum et tectum, ut aiunt, ab omnique incommodo, detrimento, molestia sincerum integrumque conserves. et ipse spondeo et omnes hoc tibi tui pro me recipient, ex mea amicitia et ex tuo in me officio maximum te fructum summamque voluptatem esse capturum.

Vale.

1 aucto (*Lallemand*)

---

1 Probably Acilius Caninus.

enclosing my letter herewith. I should be glad if you would write and tell me how he receives it, and what promises he makes you.

266 (XIII.50)
CICERO TO ACILIUS

Rome, beginning of 44

From Cicero to Acilius[1] greetings.

In view of your habitual courtesy towards me, of which I had full experience throughout the time of my residence in Brundisium, I have made bold to write to you without ceremony and almost as of right on any matter which deeply concerns me.

Manius Curius, who is in business at Patrae, is on the closest and most familiar terms with me. I am indebted to him for many services, as he is to me. And, what is most important, there is a cordial and reciprocal affection between us. That being so, if you pin any hopes upon my friendship, if you wish to make me even more grateful for the services you so readily rendered me in Brundisium (though most grateful I am), and if you see that all those near to you hold me in affection, then of your favour grant me this request: Keep Manius Curius windtight and watertight, as the phrase goes, safe and sound and free of all embarrassment, loss, and trouble. I give you my personal guarantee (and all your people will undertake as much on my behalf) that my friendship and your good offices to me will yield you no small returns and no slight pleasure.

Good-bye.

267 (VII.31)

Scr. Romae m. Febr. an. 44

CICERO CURIO S. D.

1   Facile perspexi ex tuis litteris, quod semper studui, et me a te plurimi fieri et te intellegere quam mihi carus esses. quod quoniam uterque nostrum consecutus est, reliquum est ut officiis certemus inter nos; quibus aequo animo vel vincam te vel vincar abs te.

2   Acilio non fuisse necesse meas dari litteras facile patior. Sulpici tibi operam intellego ex tuis litteris non multum opus fuisse propter tuas res ita contractas ut, quem ad modum scribis, 'nec caput nec pedes.' equidem vellem uti pedes haberent ut aliquando redires. vides enim exaruisse iam veterem urbanitatem, ut Pomponius noster suo iure possit dicere

nisi nos pauci retineamus gloriam antiquam Atticam.

ergo is tibi, nos ei succedimus. veni igitur, quaeso, ne tamen semen urbanitatis una cum re publica intereat.

267 (VII.31)
CICERO TO MANIUS CURIUS

Rome, February 44

From Cicero to Curius greetings.

I readily perceive from your letter that you have a great regard for me, and that you are aware of my affection for yourself. It has always been my endeavour that this should be so. Having both achieved this result, we now have only to vie with one another in acts of friendship, a contest in which the victory of either will leave me equally content.

Just as well that you had no need to give my letter to Acilius. I understand from yours that you did not much require Sulpicius' help,[1] because your affairs have contracted to a point at which, as you say, 'there is neither head nor foot to them'[2]—for my part I wish they had *feet,* to bring you home at long last. You see how the sources of ancient wit have dried up. Our friend Pomponius can truly say 'Save that we few keep the ancient Attic glory living still.'[3] He is your successor, and I am his. Pray then come back, so that the seed of wit at least does not perish along with the commonwealth.

[1] Cf. Letter 283.
[2] I.e. they are worth nothing.
[3] Source unknown.

268 (XIII.43)

Scr. Romae hieme an. 47–46

M. CICERO Q.[1] GALLIO[2]

1   Etsi plurimis rebus spero fore ut perspiciam, quod tamen iam pridem perspicio, me a te amari, tamen ea causa tibi datur in qua facile declarare possis tuam erga me benevolentiam. L. Op‹p›ius M. f. Philomeli negotiatur, homo mihi familiaris. eum tibi unice commendo eoque magis quod cum ipsum diligo, tum quod negotia procurat L. Egnati Rufi, quo ego uno equite Romano familiarissime utor et qui cum[3] consuetudine cottidiana tum officiis plurimis maximisque mihi coniunctus est.

2   Oppium igitur praesentem ut diligas, Egnati absentis rem ut tueare aeque a te peto ac si mea negotia essent. velim memoriae tuae causa des litterarum aliquid quae tibi in provincia reddantur, sed ita conscribas ut tum cum eas leges facile recordari possis huius meae commendationis diligentiam. hoc te vehementer etiam atque etiam rogo.

---

[1] 1 Quintio
[2] Gallio DV: Gallo M: *om.* H
[3] et qui MV: et cum DH *(Man.)*

268 (XIII.43)
CICERO TO Q. GALLIUS[1]

Rome, winter of 47–46

From M. Cicero to Q. Gallius.

I hope your affection for me, which to be sure has long been apparent, will be shown in many contexts, but here you have a matter in which you can easily demonstrate your good will towards me. A friend of mine, L. Oppius, son of Marcus, is in business at Philomelium. I recommend him to you very specially, all the more so because, besides the regard I have for himself, he is managing the affairs of L. Egnatius Rufus. Now Egnatius is of all Roman Knights on the most familiar terms with me; daily intercourse and many important services rendered have created a close attachment.

So I am asking you to look kindly on Oppius, who is on the spot, and to protect Egnatius' interests in his absence just as though his affairs were mine. I should be grateful if, to aid your memory, you would write a few lines to be delivered to you in the province—but write in such terms that, when you read them, you can readily recall the urgency of this recommendation of mine. This I beg of you as a special favour.

---

[1] The manuscripts vary and the name of the addressee (also in Letter 270) may have been Q. (?) Quinctius Gallus, an unknown. In any case he was about to join Q. Marcius Philippus, governor of Cilicia, as Quaestor or Legate.

269 (XIII.74)

Scr. Romae hieme an. 47–46

M. CICERO Q. PHILIPPO PRO COS. S.

Etsi non dubito pro tua in me observantia proque nostra necessitudine quin commendationem meam memoria teneas, tamen etiam atque etiam eundem tibi L. Oppium, familiarem meum, praesentem et L. Egnati, familiarissimi mei, absentis negotia commendo. tanta mihi cum eo necessitudo est familiaritasque, ut, si mea res esset, non magis laborarem. quapropter gratissimum mihi feceris si curaris ut is intellegat me a te tantum amari quantum ipse existimo. hoc mihi gratius facere nihil potes, idque ut facias te vehementer rogo.

270 (XIII.44)

Scr. Romae, hieme an 47–46

CICERO GALLIO S.

Etsi ex tuis et ex L. Oppi, familiaris[1] mei, litteris cognovi te memorem commendationis meae fuisse idque pro tua summa erga me benevolentia proque nostra necessitudine minime sum admiratus, tamen etiam atque etiam tibi L. Oppium praesentem et L. Egnati, mei familiarissimi, absentis negotia commendo. tanta mihi cum eo necessitudo

[1] -rissimi *(Bengel)*

269 (XIII.74)
CICERO TO Q. PHILIPPUS

Rome, winter of 47–46

From M. Cicero to Q. Philippus, Proconsul, greetings.

Although, in view of your attentiveness to me and the friendship between us, I do not doubt that you are bearing my recommendation in mind, I would none the less recommend to you yet again my friend L. Oppius, who is on the spot, and the affairs of my very good friend L. Egnatius, who is not. My connection with the latter is so close and familiar that I should not be more concerned if my own money were at stake. So you will greatly oblige me if you make clear to him that your affection for me is as great as I myself believe it to be. You can do nothing to oblige me more, and I beg it of you earnestly.

270 (XIII.44)
CICERO TO Q. GALLIUS

Rome, winter of 47–46

From Cicero to Gallius greetings.

Letters from yourself and from my good friend L. Oppius have informed me that you have been mindful of my recommendation, which in view of your notable good will towards me and the attachment between us did not at all surprise me. However, I should like once again to recommend L. Oppius, who is on the spot, and the affairs of my very close friend L. Egnatius, who is not. My connection

est familiaritasque ut, si mea res esset, non magis laborarem. quapropter gratissimum mihi feceris si curaris ut is
intellegat me a te tantum amari quantum ipse existimo.
hoc mihi gratius facere nihil potes, idque ut facias vehementer te rogo.

271 (XIII.45)

Scr. Romae an. 47 vel 46, ut vid.
CICERO APPULEIO PRO Q.[1]

L. Egnatio uno equite Romano vel familiarissime utor.
eius Anchialum servum negotiaque quae habet in Asia tibi
commendo non minore studio quam si rem meam commendarem. sic enim existimes velim, mihi cum eo non
modo cottidianam consuetudinem summam intercedere
sed etiam officia magna et mutua nostra inter nos esse.
quam ob rem etiam atque etiam a te peto ut cures ut intellegat me ad te satis diligenter scripsisse; nam de tua erga
me voluntate non dubitabat. id ut facias te etiam atque
etiam rogo.
Vale.

[1] proqu(a)estori *(SB)*

with the latter is so close and familiar that I should not be more concerned if my own money were at stake. So you will very much oblige me if you make it clear to him that your affection for me is as great as I myself believe it to be. You can do nothing to oblige me more, and I beg it of you earnestly.

271 (XIII.45)
CICERO TO APPULEIUS

Rome, 47 or 46 (?)

From Cicero to Appuleius, Proquaestor.[1]

Of all Roman Knights L. Egnatius stands on the most familiar footing with me, and I recommend to you his slave Anchialus and his business affairs in Asia as warmly as if I were writing of my personal interests. I should like you to be aware that apart from a great deal of day-to-day contact we are indebted to one another for important services mutually rendered. So let me earnestly request you to let him understand that I have written to you in appropriately serious terms—for as to your friendly disposition towards me he is in no doubt. May I particularly beg this favour of you?

Good-bye.

---

[1] Evidently in the province of Asia. He cannot be securely identified with any of the contemporary Ap(p)uleii.

272 (XIII.46)

Scr. Romae an. 47 vel 46, ut vid.

CICERO APPULEIO S.

L. Nostius Zoilus est cohores meus, heres autem patroni sui. ea re utrumque scripsi ut et mihi cum illo causam amicitiae scires esse et hominem probum existimares, qui patroni iudicio ornatus esset. eum tibi igitur sic commendo ut unum ex nostra domo. valde mihi gratum erit si curaris ut intellegat hanc commendationem sibi apud te magno adiumento fuisse.

273 (XIII.73)

Scr. fort. in Tusculano aestate an. 46

M. CICERO Q. PHILIPPO PRO COS. S.

1   Gratulor tibi quod ex provincia salvum te ad tuos recepisti incolumi fama et re publica. quod si Romae fuissem, te vidissem coramque gratias egissem quod tibi L. Egnatius, familiarissimus meus, absens, L. Oppius praesens curae fuisset.

2   Cum Antipatro Derbete mihi non solum hospitium verum etiam summa familiaritas intercedit. ei te vehementer suscensuisse audivi et moleste tuli. de re nihil possum iudi-

---

[1] 'A local dynast in south Lycaonia, holding Derbe and Laranda, both places of some consequence' (R. Syme).

272 (XIII.46)
CICERO TO APPULEIUS

Rome, 47 or 46 (?)

From Cicero to Appuleius greetings.

L. Nostius Zoilus is my coheir and the estate is that of his former master. I mention these two particulars so you may know that I have cause to be his friend and may judge him a man of good character to be favoured by his ex-master with such a mark of esteem. So I recommend him to you as though he were one of my own domestic circle. It will be very agreeable to me if you will let him understand that this recommendation has done him great service with you.

273 (XIII.73)
CICERO TO Q. PHILIPPUS

Tusculum (?), summer of 46

From M. Cicero to Q. Philippus, Proconsul, greetings.

I congratulate you on your safe return from your province to the bosom of your family with your reputation and the public interest unimpaired. If I had been in Rome, I should have seen you, and thanked you in person for taking care of my very good friend L. Egnatius in his absence and of L. Oppius on the spot.

My relations with Antipater of Derbe[1] are not only of hospitality, but of the most familiar acquaintance. I heard that you have been very angry with him and was sorry for it. On the merits of the case I can make no judgement, apart from my persuasion that, being the man you are, you

461

care, nisi illud mihi persuadeo, te, talem virum, nihil temere fecisse. ⟨a⟩ te autem pro vetere nostra necessitudine
etiam atque etiam peto ut eius filios, qui in tua potestate
sunt, mihi potissimum condones, nisi quid existimas in ea
re violari existimationem tuam. quod ego si arbitrarer,
numquam te rogarem, mihique tua fama multo antiquior
esset quam illa necessitudo est. sed mihi ita persuadeo (potest fieri ut fallar) eam rem laudi tibi potius quam vitupera-
tioni fore. quid fieri possit et quid mea causa facere possis
(nam quin[1] velis non dubito) velim, si tibi grave non erit,
certiorem me facias.

274 (XIII.47)

Scr. fort. Romae in. m. Mai. an. 51
CICERO SILIO S.

Quid ego tibi commendem eum quem tu ipse diligis?
sed tamen ut scires eum a me non diligi solum verum
etiam amari, ob eam rem tibi haec scribo. omnium tuorum
officiorum, quae et multa et magna sunt, mihi gratissimum
fuerit si ita tractaris Egnatium ut sentiat et se a me et me a
te amari. hoc te vehementer etiam atque etiam rogo.

Illa nostra scilicet ceciderunt. utamur igitur vulgari
consolatione, 'quid si hoc melius?' sed haec coram. tu fac
quod facis, ut me ames teque amari a me scias.

[1] quid (ς)*

---

[1] Reference uncertain.

have done nothing without due consideration. But in virtue of our old friendship, I would urgently request you to spare his sons, who are in your hands, if only as a favour to me, unless you think your reputation would thereby be in any way compromised. If *I* thought that, I should not dream of asking you—your credit would be of much more consequence in my eyes than the connection I have mentioned. But I am persuaded (I may be wrong) that such action will bring you commendation rather than criticism. If it is not troubling you too much, I should be glad to learn from you what can be done, and what you can do for my sake—of your will I have no doubt.

274 (XIII.47)
CICERO TO P. SILIUS

Rome, ca. early May, 51 ?

From Cicero to Silius greetings.

Why should I recommend to you a person for whom you yourself have a regard? However, to let you know that I have not only a regard but an affection for him, I am writing you these lines. Of all your good offices, which are many and great, it will be to me the most agreeable if you will deal with Egnatius so as to make him feel that I am fond of him and that you are fond of me. I beg this of you as a special favour.

You may take it that those plans[1] of mine have fallen through. Well, let me apply the proverbial comfort—it may all be for the best. But of this when we meet. Be sure to keep your affection for me, and be satisfied of mine for you.

275 (XIII.78)

Scr. fort. Romae an. 62

M. CICERO ALLIENO S.

1   Democritus Sicyonius non solum hospes meus est sed etiam, quod non multis contigit, Graecis praesertim, valde familiaris. est enim in eo summa probitas, summa virtus, summa in hospites liberalitas et observantia, meque praeter ceteros et colit et observat et diligit. eum tu non modo suorum civium verum paene Achaiae principem cognos-
2   ces. huic ego tantum modo aditum ad tuam cognitionem patefacio et munio; cognitum per te ipsum, quae tua natura est, dignum tua amicitia atque hospitio iudicabis. peto igitur a te ut his litteris lectis recipias eum in tuam fidem, polliceare omnia te facturum mea causa. de reliquo, si, id quod confido fore, dignum eum tua amicitia hospitioque cognoveris, peto ut eum complectare, diligas, in tuis habeas. erit id mihi maiorem in modum gratum.

Vale.

275 (XIII.78)
CICERO TO A. ALLIENUS

Rome, 62 (?)

From M. Cicero to Allienus[1] greetings.

Democritus of Sicyon is not only a former host of mine, but a familiar friend, which not many (especially Greeks) can say. He is a most honest, worthy, and sedulously hospitable person, and pays me particular respect and attention and regard. You will find that he is the leading man, not only in his own town, but almost in Achaea as a whole. I would only open the door and pave his way into your acquaintance. Once you get to know him, your own disposition will do the rest: you will judge him worthy of your friendship and hospitality. So may I request you after reading this letter to take him under your wing, and promise to do all you can for him for my sake? As for what may follow, if, as I am confident will be the case, you find him deserving of your friendship and hospitality, I would ask you to make much of him and include him in your circle. I shall be greatly obliged.

Good-bye.

---

[1] The following letter (276) is addressed to Allienus as Proconsul, which he was in Sicily in 48–46. But the recommendation of a citizen of Sicyon suggests that this letter belongs to an earlier period in his career when he may have been serving in Greece. He was probably Quaestor ca. 62.

276 (XIII.79)

Scr. Romae an. 47 vel 46

M. CICERO S. D. ALLIENO PRO COS.

Et te scire arbitror quanti fecerim C. Avianium Flaccum et ego ex ipso audieram, optimo et gratissimo homine, quam a te liberaliter esset tractatus. eius filios dignissimos illo patre meosque necessarios, quos ego unice diligo, commendo tibi sic ut maiore studio nullos commendare possim. C. Avianius in Sicilia est, Marcus est nobiscum; ut illius dignitatem praesentis ornes, rem utriusque defendas te rogo. hoc mihi gratius in ista provincia facere nihil potes, idque ut facias te vehementer etiam atque etiam rogo.

277 (XIII.10)

Scr. Romae fort. in. an. 46

CICERO BRUTO S.

1   Cum ad te tuus quaestor, M. Varro, proficisceretur, commendatione egere eum non putabam; satis enim commendatum tibi eum arbitrabar ab ipso more maiorum, qui, ut te non fugit, hanc quaesturae coniunctionem liberorum necessitudini proximam voluit esse. sed cum sibi ita persuasisset ipse, meas de se accurate scriptas litteras maximum apud te pondus habituras, a meque contenderet ut quam diligentissime scriberem, malui facere quod meus

---

¹ M. Terentius Varro Gibba. Brutus was governor of Cisalpine Gaul.

276 (XIII.79)
CICERO TO A. ALLIENUS

Rome, 47 or 46

From M. Cicero to Allienus, Proconsul, greetings.

I think you know how high a regard I had for C. Avianius Flaccus, and I heard from his own lips (he was an excellent man, most appreciative of a kindness) how handsomely you treated him. His sons are thoroughly worthy of their father, and very dear friends of mine. May I recommend them to you as warmly as I possibly can? C. Avianius is in Sicily, Marcus is here with us. I beg you to enhance the standing of the former, who is on the spot, and to protect the interests of both. You can do nothing in your present province to oblige me more, and I do most particularly request it of you.

277 (XIII.10)
CICERO TO M. BRUTUS

Rome, beginning of 46 (?)

From Cicero to Brutus greetings.

When your Quaestor, M. Varro,[1] was setting off to join you I did not think he needed any recommendation. Traditional usage, I thought, was in itself sufficient to recommend him to you—which, as you are aware, has decreed that this relationship of Quaestor to superior should stand next to that of children to parents. But Varro himself is persuaded that a carefully drafted letter of mine concerning him will carry great weight with you, and urges me to write as fully as possible. So I have thought it better to comply

familiaris tanti sua interesse arbitraretur.

2   Ut igitur debere me facere hoc intellegas, cum primum
M. Terentius in forum venit, ad amicitiam se meam contulit; deinde, ut se corroboravit, duae causae accesserunt
quae meam in illum benevolentiam augerent: una, quod
versabatur in hoc studio nostro, quo etiam nunc maxime
delectamur, et cum ingenio, ut nosti, nec sine industria;
deinde, quod mature se contulit in societates publicorum;
quod quidem nollem, maximis enim damnis adfectus est.
sed tamen causa communis ordinis mihi commendatissi-
mi fecit amicitiam nostram firmiorem. deinde versatus in
utrisque subselliis optima et fide et fama iam ante hanc
commutationem rei publicae petitioni sese dedit hono-
3   remque honestissimum existimavit fructum laboris sui. his
autem temporibus a me Brundisio cum litteris et mandatis
profectus ad Caesarem est; qua in re et amorem eius in
suscipiendo negotio perspexi et in conficiendo ac renun-
tiando fidem.

Videor mihi, cum separatim de probitate eius et moribus dicturus fuissem si prius causam cur eum tanto opere
diligerem tibi exposuissem, in ipsa causa exponenda satis
etiam de probitate dixisse. sed tamen separatim promitto
in meque recipio fore eum tibi et voluptati et usui. nam et
modestum hominem cognosces et prudentem et a cupiditate omni remotissimum, praeterea magni laboris summaeque industriae.

---

2 Forensic oratory.
3 As prosecutor and defender.

with my friend's wish, since he attaches so much importance to it.

To show you then that in so doing I am fulfilling an obligation, let me mention that when M. Terentius first entered public life he sought my friendship. Then, when he had established himself in the world, two additional circumstances served to increase my good will towards him. One was that he was engaged in my own chosen avocation,[2] in which even today I take most pleasure, and showed natural ability, as you know, and considerable application; the other, that at an early age he involved himself in the companies managing public contracts—to my regret, for he lost a great deal of money. However, the common interest of a class which stands very high in my regard made our friendship the firmer. Then, after a record of highly conscientious and creditable activity on both benches,[3] he became a candidate for office (that was before this recent constitutional upheaval), and regarded the office as the most honourable reward of his hard work. I may add that latterly he travelled from Brundisium with a letter and oral message from myself to Caesar. I was impressed by his friendly spirit in undertaking this mission and the conscientiousness with which he discharged and reported it.

I had intended to deal specifically with his good character and personality after explaining the reason why I have so high a regard for him, but it seems to me that in doing the latter I have sufficiently covered the former. However, I do specifically promise and personally guarantee that he will make you a pleasant and useful associate. You will find him a man of modesty and good sense, a stranger to any form of self-seeking, hard-working and painstaking furthermore in the highest degree.

4   Neque ego haec polliceri debeo, quae tibi ipsi, cum
bene cognoris, iudicanda sunt. sed tamen in omnibus novis
coniunctionibus interest qualis primus aditus sit et qua
commendatione quasi amicitiae fores aperiantur. quod
ego his litteris efficere volui. etsi id ipsa per se necessitudo
quaesturae effecisse debet; sed tamen nihilo infirmius
illud hoc addito. cura igitur, si me tanti facis quanti et
Varro existimat et ipse sentio, ut quam primum intellegam
hanc meam commendationem tantum illi utilitatis attulisse quantum et ipse sperarit nec ego dubitarim.

278 (XIII.11)

Scr. Romae an. 46

CICERO BRUTO S.

1   Quia semper animadverti studiose te operam dare ut
ne quid meorum tibi esset ignotum, propterea non dubito
quin scias non solum cuius municipi sim sed etiam quam
diligenter soleam meos municipes Arpinatis tueri. quorum
quidem omnia commoda omnisque facultates, quibus et
sacra conficere et sarta tecta aedium sacrarum locorum-
que communium tueri possi‹n›t, consistunt in iis vecti-
galibus quae habent in provincia Gallia.[1] ad ea visenda
pecuniasque quae a colonis debentur exigendas totamque
rem et cognoscendam et administrandam legatos equites
Romanos misimus, Q. Fufidium Q. f., M. Faucium M. f.,
Q. Mamercium Q. f.

---

[1] Cisalpine.

I ought not to promise what you will have to judge for yourself when you come to know him well. Still, in all new associations something depends on the nature of the first approach, the sort of recommendation which opens as it were the door of friendship. That was my purpose in this letter. It should have been achieved, to be sure, by the official bond automatically; all the same, that bond will be none the frailer for this extra link. So if you think as much of me as Varro believes and I myself am conscious that you do, I trust you will make it your business to show me as soon as possible that this recommendation of mine has proved as advantageous to him as he expects (and I do not doubt) it will.

278 (XIII.11)
CICERO TO M. BRUTUS

Rome, 46

From Cicero to Brutus greetings.

I have always noticed the particular care you take to inform yourself of all that concerns me, so I do not doubt that you not only know which township I hail from but also know how attentively I look after the interests of my fellow townsmen of Arpinum. All their corporate income, including the means out of which they keep up religious worship and maintain their temples and public places in repair, consists in rents from property in Gaul.[1] We have dispatched the following gentlemen, Roman Knights, as our representatives to inspect the properties, collect sums due from the tenants, and take general cognizance and charge: Q. Fufidius, son of Quintus; M. Faucius, son of Marcus; Q. Mamercius, son of Quintus.

2   Peto a te in maiorem modum pro nostra necessitudine
ut tibi ea res curae sit operamque des ut per te quam commodissime negotium municipi administretur quam pri-
mumque conficiatur, ipsosque quorum nomina scripsi ut
quam honorificentissime pro tua natura et quam liberalis-
3 sime tractes. bonos viros ad tuam necessitudinem adiunxe-
ris municipiumque gratissimum beneficio tuo devinxeris,
mihi vero eo etiam gratius feceris quod cum semper tueri
municipes meos consuevi tum hic annus praecipue ad
meam curam officiumque pertinet. nam constituendi municipi causa hoc anno aedilem filium meum fieri volui et
fratris filium et M. Caesium, hominem mihi maxime ne-
cessarium. is enim magistratus in nostro municipio nec
alius ullus creari solet. quos cohonestaris in primisque me
si res publica municipi tuo studio[1] diligentia bene adminis-
trata erit. quod ut facias te vehementer etiam atque etiam
rogo.

279 (XIII.12)

Scr. eodem tempore quo ep. superior

CICERO BRUTO S.

1   Alia epistula communiter commendavi tibi legatos
Arpinatium ut potui diligentissime; hac separatim Q.
Fufidium, quocum mihi omnes necessitudines sunt, dili-

[1] studio ⟨et⟩ ⌐

May I particularly request of you in virtue of our friendship to give your attention to the matter, and to do your best to see that the business of the municipality goes through as smoothly and rapidly as possible with your assistance. As for the persons named, let me ask you to extend them, as you naturally would, all possible courtesy and consideration. You will attach some worthy gentlemen to your connection and your favour will bind a township which never forgets an obligation. As for myself, I shall be even more beholden than I should otherwise have been, because, while it is my constant habit to look after my fellow townsmen, I have a particular concern and responsibility towards them this year. It was my wish that my son, my nephew, and a very close friend of mine, M. Caesius, should be appointed Aediles this year to set the affairs of the municipality in order—in our town it is the custom to elect magistrates with that title and no other. You will have done honour to them, and above all to me, if the corporate property of the municipality is well managed thanks to your good will and attention. May I again ask you this favour most earnestly?

279 (XIII.12)
CICERO TO BRUTUS

Rome, same date as the preceding

From Cicero to Brutus greetings.

In a separate letter I have recommended the representatives of the people of Arpinum jointly to your favour as warmly as I was able. In this letter I am recommending Q. Fufidius, with whom I have all manner of friendly ties, in-

gentius commendo, non ut aliquid de illa commendatione deminuam sed ut ad ⟨illam⟩[1] hanc addam. nam et privignus est M. Caesi, mei maxime et familiaris et necessari, et fuit in Cilicia mecum tribunus militum; quo in munere ita se tractavit ut accepisse ab eo beneficium viderer, non dedisse. est praeterea, quod apud te valet plurimum, a nostris studiis non abhorrens. qua re velim eum quam liberalissime complectare operamque des ut in ea legatione quam suscepit contra suum commodum secutus auctoritatem meam quam maxime eius excellat industria. vult enim, id quod optimo cuique natura tributum est, quam maximam laudem cum a nobis, qui eum impulimus, tum a municipio consequi. quod ei continget si hac mea commendatione tuum erga se studium erit consecutus.

2

280 (XIII.13)

Scr. Romae an. 46

CICERO BRUTO S.

L. Castronius[1] Paetus, longe princeps municipi Lucensis, est honestus, gravis, plenus offici, bonus plane vir et cum virtutibus tum etiam fortuna, si quid hoc ad rem pertinet, ornatus. meus autem est familiarissimus, sic prorsus ut nostri ordinis observet neminem diligentius. qua re ut et

[1] *(Wes.)**
[1] *cf.* 78 *(VIII.2).2*

dividually and with special warmth; not in any way to detract from the force of my other recommendation, but to add this one to that. He is the stepson of my particular friend and connection M. Caesius, and served with me as Military Tribune in Cilicia. His conduct in that capacity was such as to make me feel that I had not conferred a favour but received one. Furthermore, a point to which you attach special importance, he is not without a leaning towards our favourite pursuits. So I hope you will give him the most generous of welcomes, and do your best to ensure that his activity in a mission which he undertook contrary to his own convenience in deference to my wishes may shine as conspicuously as possible. He is desirous (the natural instinct of a man of mould) to gain all the commendation he can from me, his instigator, and from the municipality. In that he will succeed, if through this recommendation of mine he enlists your good will.

280 (XIII.13)
CICERO TO M. BRUTUS

Rome, 46

From Cicero to Brutus greetings.

L. Castronius Paetus is without question the leading man in Luca, a gentleman of distinction and consequence, always ready to serve a friend—a thoroughly honourable man, whose virtues (if it be anything to the purpose) are set off by worldly fortune. He is also an intimate of mine; in fact there is no member of our order[1] whom he cultivates

[1] The senatorial.

meum amicum et tua dignum amicitia tibi commendo. cui quibuscumque rebus commodaveris, tibi profecto iucundum, mihi certe erit gratum.

Vale.

more assiduously. So I recommend him as my friend and worthy to be yours. Any service you render him will, I feel sure, tend to your own gratification, as it will certainly oblige me.

Good-bye.